THE CAMBRIDGE
COMPANION
THE SONNET

EDITED BY

A. D. COUSINS
Macquarie University

and

PETER HOWARTH
Queen Mary, University of London

CAMBRIDGE
UNIVERSITY PRESS

CAMBRIDGE UNIVERSITY PRESS
Cambridge, New York, Melbourne, Madrid, Cape Town, Singapore,
São Paulo, Delhi, Mexico City

Cambridge University Press
The Edinburgh Building, Cambridge CB2 8RU, UK

Published in the United States of America by Cambridge University Press, New York

www.cambridge.org
Information on this title: www.cambridge.org/9780521735537

First published 2011
Reprinted 2012

Printed in the United Kingdom at the University Press, Cambridge

A catalogue record for this publication is available from the British Library

Library of Congress Cataloguing in Publication data
The Cambridge companion to the sonnet / [edited by] A. D. Cousins, Peter Howarth.
p.   cm. – (Cambridge companions to literature)
Includes bibliographical references and index.
ISBN 978-0-521-51467-5 (hardback) – ISBN 978-0-521-73553-7 (paperback)
1. Sonnets, English–History and criticism.   2. Sonnets, American–History and
criticism.   3. Sonnet–History and criticism.   I. Cousins, A. D., 1950–   II. Howarth, Peter,
1973–   III. Title.   IV. Series.
PR509.S7C36 2011
821'.04209–dc22
2010040683

ISBN 978-0-521-51467-5 hardback
ISBN 978-0-521-73553-7 paperback

THE CAMBRIDGE COMPANION TO
THE SONNET

Beginning with the early masters of the sonnet form, Dante and Petrarch, this *Companion* examines the reinvention of the sonnet across times and cultures, from Europe to America. In doing so, it considers sonnets as diverse as those by William Shakespeare, William Wordsworth, George Herbert and E. E. Cummings. The chapters explore how we think of the sonnet as a 'lyric' and what is involved in actually trying to write one. The book includes a lively discussion between three distinguished contemporary poets – Paul Muldoon, Jeff Hilson, and Meg Tyler – on the experience of writing a sonnet, and a chapter which traces the sonnet's diffusion across manuscript, print, screen and the internet. A fresh and authoritative overview of this major poetic form, the *Companion* expertly guides the reader through the sonnet's history and development into the global multimedia phenomenon it is today.

A. D. COUSINS is Professor of English at Macquarie University.

PETER HOWARTH lectures in the Department of English, Queen Mary, University of London.

A complete list of books in the series is at the back of this book

For David and Matthew

CONTENTS

CONTENTS

CONTRIBUTORS

CATHERINE BATES University of Warwick

STEPHEN BURT Harvard University

MATTHEW CAMPBELL University of Sheffield

A. D. COUSINS Macquarie University

HEATHER DUBROW Fordham University

MARCELLE FREIMAN Macquarie University

DIANA E. HENDERSON Massachusetts Institute of Technology

JEFF HILSON Roehampton University

PETER HOWARTH Queen Mary, University of London

WILLIAM J. KENNEDY Cornell University

ARTHUR F. MAROTTI Wayne State University

PAUL MULDOON Princeton University

MICHAEL O'NEILL University of Durham

MEG TYLER Boston University

R. S. WHITE University of Western Australia

HELEN WILCOX University of Wales, Bangor

ACKNOWLEDGEMENTS

For advice and encouragement we should like to thank Stephen Burt, Helen and Neil Cadzow, Jim and Maureen Cahillane, Matthew Campbell, Robyn Cousins, Geoff Payne, Manfred Mackenzie, Marea Mitchell, Dani and Tony Napton, Mauro Di Nicola, Julie Sanders, Sarah Stanton of Cambridge University Press and colleagues at Queen Mary.

Copyright Acknowledgements

A. D. COUSINS AND PETER HOWARTH

Introduction

A lawyer invented the sonnet. Sometime in the mid 1230s, at the Sicilian court of Emperor Frederick II, Giacomo da Lentini created a lyric form that has now travelled a long way from its small, but cosmopolitan, place of origin. It has since been written in dozens of languages and dialects, on vellum, parchment, paper, screen and Valentine's card. It has circulated between lovers and would-be lovers, among coteries, as celebrity confession, religious meditation and appeal to the public conscience. It has been held up as poetry's epitome and poetry's enemy; it has been the language of lords and the reply for bondsmen, a foreign import and a cultural talisman, and has proved itself capable of joint ventures with everything from the novel to the haiku.[1] It has been fashionable, neglected, and fashionable again for reasons that would have been incomprehensible to the people who first made it fashionable. The sonnet has become the international and transcultural form it is today, in other words, not simply because it had the good fortune to hitch-hike round the world on the back of English imperial power a few hundred years later, but because that lawyer's invention was very good at being adapted, adopted, and talking back.

This capacity to flourish in dialogue and persuasion was endemic to the form from the very start. From its legal beginnings, the sonnet brought together music, desire and the arguing of a case, through the turn or *volta*, which allows the sonnet to state more than one point of view, change its mind or adapt an interlocutor's. Because da Lentini and his friends exchanged sonnets discussing the nature and experience of desire, it also brought together love and its public performance, making the sonnet a form at once expressive, imitative and performative. Moreover, by way of its early affinity with the *strambotto* it bears kinship to the epigram, and so unites the ideas of brevity and of saying much in little: of fashioning microcosms or miniature heterocosms. Sometime around the middle of the thirteenth century, a successor to da Lentini, named Guittone d'Arezzo, began to write sequences of sonnets. Thereafter the sonnet could either stand alone or be patterned into extended discourse. The main directions for the sonnet's development, that is to say, had been set within decades of its invention.

Its future success was not guaranteed, however, since every form depends on the historic and economic circumstances in which people want to use it. Unlike the ballad, the sonnet has done well from being a predominantly written form circulated among a globalizing cultural elite, whether Italian courtiers, English aristocrats or modern participants in higher education. It has always had aspirational connotations: hoping to woo a lover, to form inchoate feelings into something more resolved, to impress a courtly master, or to show the nation that your kind of people feel and think in just as sophisticated a way as the elite. For these reasons, the sonnet has had to bear the weight of tremendous cultural expectation or snobbery. But it also succeeded because it could encourage rejoinders. Its internal turns of thought involve anticipating and pre-empting a response – to oneself or by another – in a space whose smallness makes foreclosure inevitable. For this it has been much resented, but that 'fore-' is itself dramatic, and it invites a 'not so fast'.[2] By claiming closure so quickly, it opens the space for an alternative reply in a way that longer genres do not. The response may be a new sonnet dealing with the emotions suppressed by foreclosure, or it may be the series of surprises that changing circumstances bring to the *Rime sparse* of the sonnet sequence. Or it may come in the sonnet's later adoption by poets sensing an analogy between the way it conspicuously cuts and selects so much and their own foreclosed and artificially presented lives, as women, homosexuals or colonial subjects. The sonnet has survived so long and across so many different cultures and audiences because its internal checks and imbalances provide ready encouragement for anyone wanting to remake it in a manner more suitable to themselves.

For the same reason, it has survived tremendous changes of poetic culture – from mimetic to expressive, from coterie to public, from the authoritative to the informal – by provoking poets to adjust it precisely where it needles the priorities of an age. So the English form adopts the couplet when the display of individual wit as well as longing becomes a necessity for courtly advancement. The Romantics fret at the sonnet's shortness, and then write sonnets that override a set turn to shuttle unendingly between past and present or subject and object instead. The modernists hate the sonnet's decorum and invent the free-verse, unrhymed or natural-speech sonnet; more contemporary poets despair of the idea of form as destiny, and produce poems that revel in the chances created by bouncing apparently indifferent sentences off the sonnet's walls. Just as an individual sonnet may look finished, but is not, so the sonnet has many times looked finished as a genre, but has not been.

Critical responses to the sonnet have had their own lines of development. Down the centuries, commentary has been especially preoccupied with the sonnet's formal constraints and with the scope of its subject matter. Among the most vigorous writers on those concerns have been, as is hardly surprising, writers of sonnets about sonnets. In the mid eighteenth century, Anna Seward combatively praised the sonnet for its demanding design. She imagined Apollo, weary of anyone who can put 'trite ideas' in 'loose verse' calling himself a poet, thereupon creating 'The rigorous sonnet; to be framed alone / By duteous bards, or by just taste admired' ('On the Structure of the Sonnet', 2–3, 7–8). To master the sonnet's formal constraints is to be a true poet; to appreciate them is to be a true critic. Seward's better-known contemporary, William Wordsworth, wrote of finding artistic liberation in the sonnet's confines, of finding its small and private space a free zone of creativity ('Nuns fret not at their Convent's narrow room', 8–14). Elsewhere, unfolding an honour roll of famous sonneteers, he warned against undervaluing the sonnet because of its compactness, since the history of the form shows that it can serve valuable private ends, or even great social purposes ('Scorn not the sonnet; Critic, you have frowned'). And with that address to the critic, rather than the lady or the public, Wordsworth raises the self-consciousness about the form to a new level. Since in Romantic poetics imitating a model is no longer a good in itself, but only desirable insofar as it aids the poet's public self-expression, choosing a sonnet is a self-conscious restriction of other possibilities and invites technical criticism of the means. In the light of the free-verse revolution Wordsworth himself helped foster, every modern sonnet becomes partly a sonnet about sonnets, because its very use calls attention to the poet's explicit procedural choices, an effect amplified by the poets from non-white and non-English backgrounds making a statement about just what their language can do to the sonnet too.

There has also long been an anxiety about the sonnet's appropriate content. In 1610, George Herbert wrote a sonnet for his mother in which, however, he addresses God and asks: 'Doth poetry / Wear Venus' livery, only serve her turn? / Why are not sonnets made of thee, and lays / Upon thine altar burnt?' ('To His Mother', 3–6). The scope of the sonnet's subject matter, Herbert suggests, should be much larger than the carnally desirous self. About a decade later, Michael Drayton also complained about Poetry wearing the livery of Venus, but his complaint introduces an ironic sequence of love sonnets. Fashionably defining himself against use of the sonnet as a means for expressing unfulfilled sexual desire, he announces: 'Love from mine eye a tear shall never wring, / Nor in *Ah me's* my whining sonnets dressed' ('To the Reader of These Sonnets', 6–7, prefacing *Idea*). From Milton to Wordsworth to Owen to Berrigan, sonnet writers have had to fight the assumption that the sonnet is a genre with one proper subject and aim, like tragedy or elegy. But the sonnet's association with sexual desire is so strong that using the form often lends a passionate edge to non-sexual relations, a connotation that the best poets turn to their advantage. By writing a sonnet, Keats longs to be worthy of Homer's realms of gold with a yearning that does not pretend to be disinterested, because Keats's class makes that impossible for him. Claude McKay's rebellion against the 'America' that despises him for his race equally suggests how much she is the cruel mistress who can be fought but never escaped, as his later cat-and-mouse relation with the FBI perhaps shows.[3] Now that the sonnet is one of the few lyric forms still widely recognized, the weight of critical self-reflexiveness has increased to the degree that some see it as a curse on self-expression. Auden once warned that 'conventional forms like the sonnet are so associated with a particular tradition of thoughts and attitudes that the immature writer can do little with them'.[4] But that, as Auden knew, was as much a provocation as a warning, and the form's surprising reappearance among today's most experimental poets suggests how well the sonnet suits the avant-garde principle that art be an intervention in the discourse about art, rather than simply lyric self-expression. Indeed, 780 years of sonnets make it inevitable that writing a new one always involves some blocking, channelling and realignment of public and market expectation, rather than the autonomous stay against social pressure its modernist-traditionalist defenders have cultivated.

Today the sonnet is probably the most widely read, taught, practised and written-about of lyric forms. The aim of this book is in no small part to show how that happened and, by taking the long view, to ask why the sonnet continues to fascinate contemporary poets. Although it is the first book for many years to offer a survey of the sonnet from its inception to the present, it does not seek to offer an all-encompassing history of the sonnet's globalization or of its ups and downs in status, although these enter into discussions of particular poets. Nor is it concerned with discussing every great writer who wrote sonnets, since many magnificent poets are not at their best in the form. Rather, it focuses on inventive and landmark uses of the sonnet, and their interactions between tradition and experimentation, social and poetic form, vision and revision, emphasizing variation in the designs and uses of the sonnet just as much as continuity. Throughout, the contributors focus simultaneously on how a formal pattern shapes and suggests desires, and how the poems' historical situation recognizes and misrecognizes them. In this historicized attention to a form, they look for the ways in which the sonnet's internal music and its cultural resonance meet, blend or clash, including the alterations that the sonnet's transmission by way of manuscript, print and electronic media make to its meaning. Those are critical questions about how the academy should read poetry, of course, but they are also what every poet has to face when actually writing a sonnet: not just 'How can I accomplish this in fourteen lines?', but 'What will this form make my poetry become?' and 'What will other people find in it?'. With our poets' discussion, then, this is a companion both to reading and to making sonnets: a guide to appreciating past and current practices of the sonnet as a literary form, and also, we hope, a springboard for writing more of them.

Notes

1 Vikram Seth, *The Golden Gate* (New York: Vintage, 1991); *Renga: A Chain of Poems*, trans. Charles Tomlinson (London: Penguin, 1979).
2 Michael R. G. Spiller, *The Development of the Sonnet: An Introduction* (London: Routledge, 1992), p. 11.
3 James R. Keller, '"A Chafing Savage, Down the Decent Street": The Politics of Compromise in Claude McKay's Protest Sonnets', *African American Review* 28:3 (1994), 447–56; William J. Maxwell, 'F. B. Eyes: The Bureau Reads Claude McKay', in Bill V. Mullen and James Smethurst, eds., *Left of the Color Line: Race, Radicalism, and Twentieth-Century Literature of the United States* (Chapel Hill: University of North Carolina Press, 2003), pp. 39–65.
4 W. H. Auden, *The Complete Works of W. H. Auden: Prose*, ed. Edward Mendelson, 3 vols. (Princeton: Princeton University Press, 2002), Vol. II: *1939–1948*, p. 48.

I

PAUL MULDOON, MEG TYLER AND JEFF HILSON,
EDITED BY PETER HOWARTH

Contemporary poets and the sonnet: a trialogue

This conversation was initiated by poets' individual answers to the editor's questions, and then developed as they responded to each other's replies.

> Auden once said that the sonnet was a trap for new writers because it had too much history to it. How do you help aspiring sonnet writers manage the reverberating meanings and connotations of the form?

MT: Part of the pleasure of writing (and teaching) sonnets is that you have an instant sense of community. The sonnet relieves us of our loneliness; as soon as you settle into its parameters, the conversation begins. As Christopher Ricks says, 'the one thing allusion provides and calls upon is company (the society of dead poets being a living resource in its company)'.[1] I think about Heaney's 'Out of Shot' (from *District and Circle*), where he quietly calls upon several fellow poets (Petrarch for the rhyme scheme, Yeats for content). By using the words 'lost' and 'loosed' repeatedly, Heaney echoes the prophetic Yeats, 'Mere anarchy is loosed upon the world, / The blood-dimmed tide is loosed' from 'The Second Coming', which is not a sonnet but hints at the dimensions of one as the first stanza is eight lines long and the second is fourteen lines; this poem is definitely a sounding-board or springboard for Heaney's sonnet (of a donkey, he writes, 'Loosed from a cart that had loosed five mortar shells / ... / Lost to its owner, lost for its sunlit hills.'). Note how Heaney positions his rhyming partners at line's beginning and middle, not line's end.

Some ambitious young writers compose sonnets in order to act out against the tradition – I think of the younger Heaney, who when he sat down to compose the Glanmore Sonnets, composed them as a sequence that in essence talked back to the English sonnet. He purposefully used words like 'cuckoos' and 'corncrakes' to make them clash with the Latinate vocabulary.

I think recent sonnets need to revisit the great ones of the past – to learn from them. Enough of what Iris Murdoch calls 'the fat relentless ego'.[2] Does the first line of any recent sonnet quicken the heart and mind like Wyatt's 'Whoso list to hunt, I know where is a hind'?

Another way the aspiring writer can combat a worry about being trapped in a closed form is to take the advice of T. S. Eliot, who reminds us that 'a poet cannot help being influenced, therefore he should subject himself to as many influences as possible, in order to escape from any one influence'.[3]

JH: I would from the start want to distinguish two different kinds of history in sonnet form. One is the history of the form's development, which requires a painstaking account of its transformations over time. The other is the emergence of a sonnet canon, the 'construction' (by practitioners, literary historians and the editors of sonnet anthologies) of a received history of the form. In a way the problem with the sonnet is that there's not been *enough* history. One recent sonnet anthology claims to tell 'the full story' of the form, an impossibly totalizing assertion that on inspection, unsurprisingly, turns out to be wildly false. But it's a publication by a major press that will be bought (in both senses of the word) by an unsuspecting public. The history of the form that we've acquired often feels more like heritage than history – a neatly packaged (as well as sanitized and sentimentalized) version of the history of the form, which avoids many of the more unorthodox and challenging paths that poets have taken it down, especially when it comes to the twentieth century.

As a teacher I think the only thing to do with writers approaching the sonnet for the first time is to be honest with them about the historical record. Sure, show them Thomas Wyatt, show them Shakespeare, show them Milton and Wordsworth, show them Robert Lowell and Seamus Heaney, but also show them Edwin Denby and Ted Berrigan, Bernadette Mayer and Alice Notley, Tim Atkins and Sophie Robinson. I speak here as someone who has recently assembled an anthology of 'linguistically innovative' sonnets by poets most of whom have been disregarded by the available anthologies either through lack of knowledge of alternatives, or, more worryingly, for ideological reasons. The story of the sonnet *has* to be as inclusive as possible if new writers are going to write sonnets. They have to be made aware of how poets of all schools have extended the meanings and connotations of the form. Surely knowing the history of the form also means not getting trapped. Traps only work if you don't know the terrain.

I worry about the notion of 'aspiring' sonnet writers, as if the sonnet were a kind of 'ultimate' form that all poets should aim to write, which seems to me the wrong reason for writing them. In this case, the sonnet becomes little more than a trophy. I do think that too many poets write sonnets merely to show how clever they are in doing something 'new' with aspects of the form – with the traditional turn or *volta*, or with the couplet for instance. The form's connotative aspects then become little more than commodified parts, endlessly updatable or exchangeable, like the parts of a sewing machine or a car. Ezra Pound's injunction to 'make it new' can feed easily into more pernicious modes of production.[4]

MT: So much of the history of the sonnet remains untapped. In the early Sicilian sonnets rhyme was not used – repeated words were; some contemporary writers have consciously seized upon this old practice as a strategy but unfortunately very few. Frank Bidart is one poet who recognizes the form's earliest impulses. His fourteen-line poem, 'Song', relies upon repeated words and phrasing, the meaning of which changes with each utterance. (In his early writing life, Bidart worked closely with Lowell as he revised hundreds of sonnets. When turning to the form as a poet himself, he perhaps deliberately did not want to write the American sonnet; reaching further back in the past gave him a cleaner energy source.)

JH: One of the things a sequence should do is lay down various lexical patterns including the repetition of words. Repetition of this kind is even more imperative in open-form procedure, where closed-form staples of repetition – most obviously metre and rhyme – are absent (though of course it's also present in closed-form sequences). Lexical repetition becomes a vital structuring device. Ted Berrigan's *Sonnets* is a key work in this respect as he takes repetition a stage further by recycling his own words, phrases and even whole lines.

> Are the processes of writing a sonnet different from writing other forms? Can you give us an idea of the mental dialogue between your imaginative decisions and the direction it seems to want to push them in?

MT: The shapes come later for me. I usually end up writing something that has 'sonnet thought', a shift in direction, and the lines may be amenable to some re-shaping. I do not start out with a particular form in mind, but I do believe I am influenced (mostly subconsciously) by whatever it is I have been reading a lot of at the time.

Form can be a straitjacket. I am reminded of the sonnet-writing periods of some poets, like Robert Lowell, who wrote little else between 1967 and 1972; maybe doing it over and over means it gets a little easier: like remembering a dream.

This question makes me ask another one. Why do poets of stature turn to it (or not) at a certain age? American poets following in the wake of Lowell have strained similarly against and toward the sonnet. For example, Bidart has written only six fourteen-line poems, and yet each one consciously reckons with the sonnet tradition. His 'You Cannot Rest', a fourteen-line poem with a white space in between each couplet, turns in part on its relationship to Elizabeth Bishop's 'North Haven', the elegy (not a sonnet) for Robert Lowell (which ends, 'Sad friend, you cannot change'). 'You Cannot Rest', while it flamboyantly defies the traditional shape of the sonnet, adheres to its emotional proportions, offering shifts in thinking and a concluding couplet that reflects upon the whole. The sonnet is the ground against which the figure of Bidart's fourteen-line poems should be seen.

For me, the acoustics of the sonnet provide the most intriguing challenge. In such a small echo chamber, the correspondence between sounds in modern sonnets need not be as blatant as in, say, Renaissance sonnets (Sidney's 'might' and 'right'). While the ballad (for example 'Lord Randal') relies on repeated phrasing as a cohesive device (the story is erratic in nature, full of lacunae), the repetition is not all that you end up hearing or remembering. But if you repeat the same phrase over and over again in the smaller confines of the sonnet – I think of Frost's 'Acquainted with the Night' – it becomes not only the presiding sound but also the prevailing meaning of the poem. The phrase above all else stays with you.

I think of this as I work on sonnets here in my study while my infant son is crawling around the small confines of the room. Although day after day he accompanies me as I write, he never repeats the same pattern of movement exactly, and the sounds he makes, although similar, are not exactly the same either. But there is comfort, if not joy, I suspect, in knowing that the dimensions are familiar.

JH: Up until now, I have tended not to write using traditional closed forms such as haiku or villanelle; or rigid stanza forms such as the quatrain, the favoured stanza of such a lot of English poetry. I have tended to use forms that allow for more open-form procedures, forms that allow for aleatory development, discovering themselves as they go on. However, I am currently nearing the end of a sonnet sequence called 'In the Assarts', and in a way the sonnet seemed an inevitable next step. I was interested to see what happened when I tried working with a form that has, historically, acquired a self-imposed limit while using open-form procedures.

There is a significant body of writers who think of the sonnet form as something sacrosanct, a form that needs protecting against barbarians who are out to do it damage. But its properties have become habitual and familiar, actively preventing us from seeing the form clearly. What is needed is a defamiliarization of the form to make us see its potentialities anew. I find that the most useful approach to writing sonnets is to forget about the accumulated connotations in terms of both form and content. This might sound very dubious but I have found that because the conventions are so well known, overdetermined even, they feed unconsciously into the poems I have written, and often in unexpected and exhilarating ways. So I might find that in the middle of the poem a rhyming couplet will appear. It doesn't have to come at the end. Or I'll find myself using a *volta* where it's not supposed to be. However, rather than try to move it I'll leave it where it is. I'm entirely happy with these kinds of accidents (and I'd distinguish these from the 'showiness' I mentioned earlier). It's not unlike that old Godard quote where he says that his films do have beginnings, middles and endings but not necessarily in that order. It's the poet's responsibility to be irresponsible toward form. That's another way of ensuring that you don't become trapped by it.

PM: I love the observation of W. H. Auden that 'those who confine themselves to free verse because they imagine that strict forms must of necessity lead to dishonesty do not understand the nature of art, how little the conscious artist can do and what large and mysterious beauties are the gift of language, tradition, and pure accident'.[5] It's central to my own sense of things that the conscious artist is ill-equipped to meet a reality that is quite indifferent to her or his being conscious. All great art (like all great scientific revelations) is about the purely accidental, the intersection of the individual unconscious with what used to be called the collective unconscious. The very idea that one might be in the business of writing a sonnet at all should itself be accidental. One should realize only when one is part way into it (at line 8, maybe?) that a sonnet is indeed the received pattern into which the poem is falling. Some writers will be more predisposed than others to the capacities of the sonnet, particularly those who are familiar with the history of what's come into the world in that form. It's a form, finally, that is predisposed to us and, frankly, to the spectacular limitations of our consciousness. The sonnet, like most of us, can just about deal with one to two thoughts at a time. We have thought 1. In addition to thought 1 we have thought 2, or by contrast, we have thought 2. It's precisely because of what might be construed as its dullness that the sonnet has managed to be so durable.

MT: Lyric poetry implicitly wants us to forget that it is written – if it works right we do not wake up while sleep-walking. And yet, our endurance or our attention cannot be put to too great a test. In a long poem, for example, would we be able to attend closely to what Eliot calls the 'ethereal music' of sounds other than end-rhymes?[6]

The sonnet is one of the primary representatives of 'closed' form in an age that prides itself on openness. And yet it flourishes. Is this a cultural contradiction, or a problem with our ideas of what 'closed' and 'open' form mean?

JH: In spite of using them myself, I'm not sure how useful the terms 'open' and 'closed' are. The two constantly play off each other such that they invade each other's territory. Nothing can be truly closed or open (unless perhaps we are talking about the simplest digital circuits that are governed by binary 'open'/'closed' or 'and'/'or' gates, and yet even within such systems an 'and' can be turned into an 'or'). So-called 'open-form' poetry also requires closed operations within it for it to work and to be perceived *as* open. A truly 'open' poem could not exist. How could it! The same is true of so-called 'closed-form' verse.

This aside, there are various ways to avoid the restrictions of what is perceived to be 'closed' in a form such as the sonnet. One method is to disrupt those aspects of the poem that are perceived as closing it off, its signifiers if you like, such as structure, shape, rhyme scheme, metre, as well as content. The other way is simply to write more sonnets, indeed to write a sequence, to keep extending indefinitely what is perceived as finite. It comes as no surprise to find so many sonnet sequences in the form's history.

PM: There's some resistance to the idea that a poem, as it investigates the crime scene of itself, may follow its own leads. This is often described as some version of the tail wagging the dog. My own view is that it's sometimes only when a tail wags that we become aware that there's a dog attached to it, though it might also turn out to be an elephant, or a comet, or even a shirt. The serendipitous aspect of writing that Auden refers to as 'pure accident' may be no more accidental than play, and no less productive. As the biologist Paul Grobstein once put it in an entry in the *Encyclopedia of Human Behavior*, play 'is not purely entertainment or a luxury to be given up when things get serious. It is itself a highly adaptive mechanism for dealing with the reality that the context for behavior is always largely unknown.'[7] The ability of the sonnet to manage what I described earlier as 'meeting a reality' is astonishing in that regard, for it allows for flexibility rather than fixity, pliability rather than petrification.

In that respect, the description of the sonnet as a 'closed' form is itself a bit closed. It fails to take into account that the sonnet is no more closed than an arena is closed and that, for better or worse, the funeral games played there are played for fun and that, to borrow Frost's phrase, all games might have 'mortal stakes'.

MT: What makes a sonnet successful is that even though it must adhere to certain strict proportions, measures, it must contain a sense of opening; it opens up to a new direction, perhaps, a genuine insight; or the break in a predictable metre or rhyme scheme can make it feel open. The trick in writing one is finding the key to the garden, so to speak, to make it feel open. Wyatt found that key in his final line of 'Whoso list to hunt' when he writes (in the voice of the deer, the 'hind', of Anne Boleyn, and of the sonnet form itself) 'And wild for to hold, though I seem tame'. Because of its established size, the form may 'seem tame'. But the scope of this particular sonnet is vast, immeasurable (as are the contents of anyone's heart), and what it contains is more than 'wild'; you could say it's even life-threatening, treasonous material.

The good sonnet should carry within it a contradiction. I think again of Heaney's 'Out of Shot', where he recovers traces of his own thought association. What he sees on TV the night before has disturbed his sleep, returned to in mind the next day. (We don't find this out until the sestet). And this disturbance (which burbles up, as if muck from a clogged drain had come to the water's surface to dissipate) plays havoc with the Petrarchan rhyme scheme that he sets in place in the octave (*abba abba*). The *a* rhyme carries over to the first two lines of the sestet and that particular rhyme sound is k-k-k. That mortar fire as described in the poem is probably not a coincidence. Heaney finds a playful way to counter what Eliot had alluded to as the limitations of rhyme in 'Reflections on *Vers Libre*'.

Another way of thinking about what Heaney does in this sonnet is to remember that Francis Bacon would sometimes throw paint at the canvas – out of frustration, perhaps, or, I imagine, the limitations of the materials. Heaney makes certain gestures in sound that in their energy and aggression are like throwing paint at the canvas of the sonnet.

The closed – or enclosed? – form is an opportunity for coherence, intensity, tautness; a more open form risks dissipation of dramatic unity and integrity.

> For much of the twentieth century, detractors of the sonnet have complained about its cultural overtones; formally hoity-toity or prissily unreal. Does that background of opposition to the form affect your own creative processes at any level?

JH: I have been influenced by, and involved in, a writing culture that is broadly oppositional to prevailing – one might even say hegemonic – poetic modes, so for me coming to the sonnet I was already, as it were, armed. However, the sonnet was, and remains, broadly representational of the kind of poetry I was trying to avoid – it's virtually a synecdoche for the poetic tradition itself, its most venerable and enduring object. William Carlos Williams railed against what he saw as parlour-room sonneteers, those practitioners who merely demonstrated what he called 'apt use' of the form.[8] That phrase 'apt use' captures perfectly the legions of poets who trot out sonnet after sonnet following the accepted (and acceptable) procedures. Williams of course saw the form as quintessentially English and a barrier to the implementation of a more authentically vernacular, and specifically American, poetic idiom.

For me it's not so much writing out of opposition to the form itself as writing out of opposition to what's been done with it by others, as well as the claims made by these writers (and by their supporters) as to what they've actually achieved with it. The cultural overtones of which you speak have in a way been perpetuated by the refusal to question radically the form's conventions. One of the major barriers is iambic pentameter, which many poets continue to use in the writing of sonnets. I don't think there's anything more likely to create that sense of 'the prissily unreal' than a metre that is as removed from everyday speech as it is possible to get. The American modernists recognized that nearly a hundred years ago and it's hard to believe so many still adhere to the misguided notion that iambic pentameter is in some way the 'natural' rhythm of the English Language. Only poets who *use* iambic pentameter try to make you believe that.

The kinds of poets I'm interested in tend to avoid the overly refined cultural overtones the sonnet has gathered round itself. American poet Bernadette Mayer's sonnets are wonderfully 'real' in the sense that they don't hide their content behind traditional constraints. The repressed female voice is constantly bursting through her sonnets in often alarming and disconcerting ways, distorting and forcing them into new shapes that correspond to the constantly shifting boundaries of desire. She shows no particular reverence for a form that has traditionally 'enclosed' women, but clearly revels in inhabiting its structure. For Mayer the sonnet as a whole is more a psychopathology than a form, and her deviations from accepted practice are very appealing. I'm also with Ted Berrigan whose sonnets were, I think, written out of a recognition that the form was defunct, a kind of cultural impossibility that paradoxically compelled him to carry on writing them. They are some of the most inventive, necessary contributions to the tradition and he is in many ways responsible for the rise of the sonnet in the second half of the twentieth century after years of neglect. But there's no standing on ceremony: 'Dear Margie, hello. It is 5.15 a.m. / fucked til 7 now she's late to work and I'm / 18 so why are my hands shaking I should know better' ends the second of his sonnets.

MT: If a sonnet strikes one as 'hoity-toity' or 'prissily unreal', it has entrapped the writer; lesser poets (or lesser poems) adopt the sonnet as a style instead of living inside the form.

One response to its restrictions is to reject it altogether. William Carlos Williams wrote a sonnet a day for one year while he was a student in Pennsylvania. His brother-in-law remembers him calling the experience 'brainwash' or something worse. The new forms that Williams discovered were made possible by his rejection of the sonnet. But here we are, one hundred years later with a few poets writing remarkable sonnets. Why? Modern sonnet writers have gone prospecting in the new territory Eliot glimpses at the end of 'Reflections on *Vers Libre*'. Eliot anticipated that the 'rejection of rhyme' would impose:

> a much severer strain upon the language. When the comforting echo of rhyme is removed, success or failure in the choice of words, in the sentence structure, in the order, is at once more apparent. Rhyme removed, the poet is at once held up to the standards of prose. Rhyme removed, much ethereal music leaps up from the word, music which has hitherto chirped unnoticed in the expanse of prose.[9]

Eliot suspected that the sonnet – unlike the heroic couplet in the hands of a good satirist – might have lost its edge in the twentieth century. He mentions 'the decay of intricate formal patterns'. But since that time, the sonnet has staged a comeback. The challenge now is to make the 'ethereal music' leap 'up from the word'. I see this happen successfully in, say, Wallace Stevens's 'Autumn Refrain', or Alice Oswald's 'Wood Not Yet Out'. I also experience this when I read some of John Ashbery's fourteen-line poems, poems that embrace the uneasy relationship between a sense of improvisation and a sense of confident order.

While Ashbery may appear to eschew certain traditional patterns like rhyme scheme, he insists upon his place within the sonnet-writing tradition by opening *A Wave* with a fourteen-line poem, addressing the sonnet's history in the opening sestet (inverting the expected order of octave and sestet) in 'At North Farm':

> Somewhere someone is traveling furiously toward you,
> At incredible speed, traveling day and night,
> Through blizzards and desert heat, across torrents, through narrow passes.
> But will he know where to find you,
> Recognize you when he sees you,
> Give you the thing he has for you?

The poem begins with the indefinite longing for definition; 'somewhere' and 'someone' eventually find 'you', a word that is uttered six times in as many lines – (as in Shakespeare's Sonnet 15, which, as Helen Vendler points out, enacts the act of focusing, zooming in, repeating 'you' seven times in its sestet).

Ashbery ingrafts anew a 'you' (which we recognize as the addressee of all sonnets). Why this furious accumulation of 'you's? Is the secret hope of repetition to bring about presence? An urgency riddles both sestets, and the urgency is all about the need to give or bequeath something to the 'you' of the two poems. The comedy of Ashbery's – 'Through blizzards and desert heat' – does not dilute the sense of need. Time is the force both writers work against (and the element they essentially work in). Both must step outside the natural order of things to craft a monument to counter time's destructive power. Four of Ashbery's lines end with 'you', creating a sound pattern that is not mellifluous but is nevertheless forceful. Repetition is used as a method to command presence, to delay (momentarily) an end. He creates clusters of sound and these repeated sounds, simply as sounds, weave the lyric into a unit. The reader experiences the internal sound echoes (occult rhyme) not as rhyme but as something beautiful and coherent. This sound-play in a sonnet teaches us that order and beauty and even meaning remain present when not always obvious. In recent fourteen-line poems, Ashbery (and Bidart and Heaney, to name but a few poets) creates a pattern of cadences and sounds that perform the work of persuasion.

Geoffrey Hill uses this sound patterning in his fourteen-line poem 'September Song', almost imperceptibly:

> Undesirable you may have been, untouchable
> you were not. Not forgotten
> or passed over at the proper time.

In the poem's first line, 'un-' (which intimates both *not* and *one*, making emphatically singular the 'you') and '-able' are repeated twice. The twice-repeated 'you' appears once more, in the fourth line, and then disappears as 'the smoke of harmless fires drifts to my eyes', the 'you' drifting into the invisible but, when recollected, painful – the invisible that makes us wince:

> As estimated, you died. Things marched,
> sufficient, to that end.
> Just so much Zyklon and leather, patented
> terror, so many routine cries.
>
> (I have made
> an elegy for myself it
> is true)

His pleasure in what he makes is broken as in the enjambment,

> (I have made
> an elegy …

The poem ends:

> September fattens on vines. Roses
> flake from the wall. The smoke
> of harmless fires drifts to my eyes.
>
> This is plenty. This is more than enough.

Usually the construction 'this is ...' sounds languid, without force, like Lowell's weary 'it is so dull'. But its repetition here ('This is plenty. This is more than enough.') signals that there is a point when description no longer serves or suffices. In his movement away from the colourful or precise we see how the force of language has been neutralized, or neutered, by the terror of history. And how quietly the tense shifts from simple past to present perfect to present in the poem. What 'drifts' away from the obscenity of men's actions and the recurrence of suffering concerns Hill on another occasion in the sonnet-sequence 'Funeral Music', where he relates an encounter between armies:

> '... all that survived them was the stark ground
> Of this pain. I made no sound, but once
> I stiffened as though a remote cry
> Had heralded my name. It was nothing ...'
> Reddish ice tinged the reeds; dislodged, a few
> Feathers drifted across; carrion birds
> Strutted upon the armour of the dead.

The past participles accumulate here, amplifying the pastness of the past – survived, stiffened, heralded, tinged, dislodged, drifted, strutted – and the impossibility of return. And yet this is part of a sonnet sequence that is all about return, reassembling, attempting to resolve, to bury the dead.

> I believe in my
> Abandonment, since it is what I have.

The dignity of these lines is heightened by the absence of a rhyming pattern. Hill wants to risk nothing; any hint of the sing-songy would disturb the poem's perfect proportions. As he writes, 'I made no sound'. He is trying to remove from the sonnet its tendency to 'jingle' or to seduce with patterned sound (a seduction that, say, Stevens is in thrall to in 'Autumn Refrain'). Oddly, it is Ashbery's lack of artificiality (in 'At North Farm') that corresponds most closely to Hill's. Both desire a movement away from the entrancing power of song. Hill comes closest to patterned sound by the grouping of past participles and the use of some consonance. Guttural if visually discreet 'r's abound in the poem: 'survived', 'stark ground', 'remote', 'heralded', 'Reddish', 'reeds', 'Feathers drifted across; carrion birds', 'Strutted', and 'armour'. And fricatives hold together the enjambed

> a few
> Feathers drifted ...

The 'armour of the dead' relieves us of a sense of the dead's vulnerability; in Hill's estimation, they are beyond touch, beyond pain, beyond what Stevens would call 'desolate sound'.

In other sonnets, Hill uses end-rhyme as a device to quicken the pace of the poem. In 'An Apology for the Revival of Christian Architecture in England', the closing sestet of the 'Idylls of the King' section reads:

> 'O clap your hands' so that the dove takes flight,
> bursts through the leaves with an untidy sound,
> plunges its wings into the green twilight
>
> above this long-sought and forsaken ground,
> the half-built ruins of the new estate,
> warheads of mushrooms round the filter-pond.

Here the swiftness of flight is encouraged or complemented by the sonorous line sounds, not at all 'untidy'. The time of day ('green twilight') evoked here might at first glance offer a suggestion of peace, of respite won at the end of the day, but any such suggestion is complicated by the eruption of 'warheads of mushrooms' in the final line. And the pond is not an emblem of the pastoral but rather the artificial; it is a 'filter-pond', as we are not allowed to forget the artificiality of the sonnet form. Such juxtaposing – the fungal warheads (an image that lingers darkly if comically) and the 'filter-pond' – recalls Peter McDonald's observation about Hill's *Scenes from Comus*: 'Hill's style never rests: no phrase is allowed to settle back on itself without being upset by what succeeds it; no isolated effect, however brilliant, is allowed to remain unshadowed.'[10] Shadows that play against brilliance – the warheads that disturb the twilight – occur throughout Hill's poetry, as in 'Psalms of Assize' where

> holiness itself falls
> to unholy rejoicing

and the angel Gabriel descends

> and light
> sensitive darkness
> follows him down.

'[H]oliness' transmutes to 'unholy'. Each word is considered, borne forward and changed. Seamus Heaney comes at Hill through simile. He writes that 'Words in [Geoffrey Hill's] poetry fall slowly and singly, like molten solder, and accumulate to a dull glowing nub.'[11]

What the best sonnets do is find words that work as adhesives born of fire.

PM: It's true, of course, that there's a long tradition of sonneteering and sonnetizing that allows the casual observer to stigmatize the sonnet as the preserve of the fuddy-duddy and the fart, young and old. The real problem here has nothing to do with the sonnet per se but the widespread belief cherished by many poets, even quite well-known ones, that they actually know what they're doing. They're right, of course. They *do* know what they're doing, along with the rest of us and, as Warren Zevon would have said, it ain't that pretty at all. To go back to Auden, I like the idea that, if anything, the sonnet might 'lead to dishonesty'. It sounds a lot more interesting than wherever it is most poems lead us.

What sonnets should every aspiring sonnet writer know, and why?

MT: The first sonnet in Dante's *Vita nuova* sequence: it is a poem both to the self and to the public – interesting because it stands at one of the thresholds of the tradition – about the potency of dream, the way it invades our (daytime) thinking mind. (See Bidart's version, 'Love Incarnate'.)

Any sonnet by Wyatt, who best captures the opposing poles of Petrarch's feeling (burning and freezing), which Petrarch inherited from Catullus and before him, Sappho: Wyatt's sonnets teach us much about the reach of the lyric tradition.

Donne's Holy Sonnets: see 'At the round earth's imagined corners ...' for a beautifully crafted Shakespearean sonnet. The enjambment bespeaking the sonnet's great range, wants to explode its boundaries, this calling for the dead to awaken:

> blow
> Your trumpets, angels; and arise, arise
> From death, you numberless infinities
> Of souls.

Wallace Stevens's 'Autumn Refrain', which reminds us how endlessly varied is both the season and the form: Stevens takes unembarrassed joy in the sounds and structure of the language. There is only a faint shadow of a rhyme scheme in place and the end words paired by sound (gone/sun/moon in the first three lines, bird/sound in lines 12 and 14) tell a small story in themselves. Sun and moon are what we see; the bird (the nightingale) is something Stevens never sees *or* hears but only imagines. The sonnet moves from sight to hearing, which, as Dickinson noted in her poetry, is the last sense to leave us before dying. Here is the second half of 'Autumn Refrain':

The stillness of everything gone, and being still,
Being and sitting still, something resides,
Some skreaking and skrittering residuum,
And grates these evasions of the nightingale
Though I have never – shall never hear that bird.
And the stillness is in the key, all of it is,
The stillness is all in the key of that desolate sound.

By the final couplet of 'Autumn Refrain' we arrive at a suggested conclusion,

And the stillness is in the key[.]

The 'stillness' itself is key, the stillness and solidity of the sonnet form, which after centuries of tampering and re-tuning is something 'that resides'.

Sonnets by Alice Oswald: when she writes, Oswald listens for sound patterns to emerge. 'Ted Hughes taught people to approach their poems as if stalking an animal – utterly patient and focused and swift. My own practice is different – something I've developed over twenty years and now do automatically whenever I sit down to write. It's a primitive kind of echo-location, like they use on ships.'[12] In this interview with Janet Phillips, Oswald also explains why she frequents the sonnet form: 'It feels very perfect, like an in-breath and an out-breath', she explains:

> When I'm writing about the mind or the heart I use a Shakespearean or a Miltonian form, a more entangled version, because that's more how the mind feels to me. If I'm writing about the natural world, I like to use the form that John Clare discovered, where you've got a series of couplets, and closure between each pair, so it's not all entangled together. The natural world is made of differences and new beginnings, so in a way the sonnet is quite alien to that, but I think Clare discovered a way of using it.

In 'Wood Not Yet Out', she uses seven rhyming couplets where there is no syntactical closure. What prevents the rhyming couplets from feeling stagnant or too rote are the enjambed lines, the syntax that shifts its weight over eight lines and then six, forming two sentences (the second of which has no closing punctuation) strung across the architectural frame. What at first glance might be seen as sentimental patching in this sonnet:

the wood keeps lifting up its hope

– woods are dark and tangled and archetypically suggest something other than hope – becomes something else when we remember Clare's sonnet, 'The Instinct of Hope', where he writes of the way hope can be read in the landscape: ''Tis nature's prophecy that such will be'.

JH: It would be stupid not to start at the beginning with the likes of Petrarch, Dante and Wyatt and then move on to the Elizabethans and Shakespeare before going on to Milton and then the Romantics. Of pre-twentieth-century figures, however, I would single out John Clare, and especially his sonnet '[The Mouse's Nest]':

> I found a ball of grass among the hay
> & proged it as I passed & went away
> & when I looked I fancied somthing stirred
> & turned agen & hoped to catch the bird
> When out an old mouse bolted in the wheat
> With all her young ones hanging at her teats
> She looked so odd & so grotesque to me
> I ran & wondered what the thing could be
> & pushed the knapweed bunches where I stood
> When the mouse hurried from the crawling brood
> The young ones squeaked & when I went away
> She found her nest again among the hay
> The water oer the pebbles scarce could run
> & broad old cesspools glittered in the sun

There can't be a better model for writing sonnets than this: there's no reaching, no aspiration to write 'the perfect sonnet'. Nor is there any self-conscious straining for literariness to make what he's saying 'signify' in any way. Indeed, I find the casualness both in the narrator's actions and in the poem's execution utterly mesmerizing. In fact, there's an almost wilful disregard of what a sonnet is 'supposed' to do here. I love the way he mentions that he 'turned agen' in line 4, four lines before a Petrarchan sonnet's official turn at the end of line 8, though I don't suppose that Clare even thought about it. Neither is there any attempt to delineate an intricate argument: rather, the poem proceeds through parataxis with Clare repeating occasional words and phrases, like 'old' and 'went away', as if he's forgotten that he's already used them. The ampersands going down the right-hand margin in lines 2, 3 and 4 contribute to this sense of artless design. The couplet is perhaps the most interesting thing about the poem. If you really want a 'turn' in the poem then it happens here with Clare actually *turning away* from his ostensible subject matter – the mouse and its brood – to address a completely different set of criteria. Again, it's as if he's forgotten the poem he has been writing. There's almost an indifference to his finishing the sonnet.

The techniques that Clare employs here – and one hesitates to call them such because of the artlessness of the sonnet as a whole – seem remarkably modern. But the poem's disinterest in being important is what makes it significant. It succeeds through what it doesn't do as much as what it does. I would far rather see a poet, to paraphrase Louis Zukofsky, making visible the joins of language to good advantage and exhibiting admirable awkwardnesses, than smoothing it all out.

Clare's approach here is, it seems to me, shared by later figures I would also recommend such as the Americans Edwin Denby, the aforementioned Ted Berrigan and Bernadette Mayer, and Ron Padgett, all second generation New York School poets. However, Denby is the poet I return to again and again, not least because he wrote mainly using the sonnet form. Probably better known as a dance critic than a poet, his first poem in his 1948 book *In Public, In Private*, is called 'The Climate':

> I myself like the climate of New York
> I see it in the air up between the street
> You use a worn-down cafeteria fork
> But the climate you don't use stays fresh and neat.
> Even we people who walk about in it
> We have to submit to wear too, get muddy,
> Air keeps changing but the nose refuses to fit
> And sleekness is used up, and the end's shoddy.
> Monday, you're down; Tuesday, dying seems a fuss
> An adult looks new in the weather's motion
> The sky is in the streets with the trucks and us,
> Stands awhile, then lifts across land and ocean.
> We can take it for granted that here we're home
> In our record climate I look pleased or glum.

Ron Padgett points to this poem's stop-start rhythms and subtle shifts: for instance the use of the reflexive pronoun in line 1; the strangeness of 'seeing the climate' as if you were 'seeing' a cloud; and the use of singular 'street' in line 2, which jars because 'obviously nothing can be between one thing.'[13] This is, however, in many ways, a 'traditional' sonnet. But within this structure, the lines of the poem move about in ways that, like the nose in line 7, 'refuse to fit'. The eighth line for example – 'And sleekness is used up, and the end's shoddy' – looks forward to the untidinesses of death as well as addressing the sonnet itself. If you do look at the 'end' of the poem it is kind of shoddy precisely because it refuses to be 'sleek' or 'slick'. Rather than having a couplet that shows us the poem ending or that makes us comfortable by resolving the poem's themes as couplets in sonnets are supposed to, its second line wanders off from the first (not unlike Clare's) in a non sequitur that is also spectacularly flat in the options it offers. Yet what Denby does with the couplet is also very knowing. Line 13, 'We can take it for granted that here we're home', is clearly Denby referencing his beloved New

York. On the other hand he's also talking about the couplet itself, which we usually 'take for granted' as being where the sonnet begins to 'bring us home' – i.e. where the sonnet ends (and 'here we're home' is also about being comfortable and relaxed, as in 'being at home').

Like Clare's '[The Mouse's Nest]', Denby's 'The Climate' doesn't try too hard to impress. His ego never gets in the way of the poem. As a counter to Clare and Denby, the other poet I'd recommend is Stephen Rodefer, whose sonnet sequence *Mon Canard* is a bravura performance. It's essentially a list of as many different ways of addressing a lover as it's possible to imagine. Apart from the sheer inventiveness of the conceit (and that word is more double-edged than ever in these particular poems), it returns the sonnet to the potentialities of the form (as outlined by Michael Spiller in his informative book *The Development of the Sonnet*) before it became petrified into what we know it as today.[14]

Mon Canard ends with a visual sonnet, and I'd also like to draw attention to the visual sonnet as an underappreciated subgenre of the form. Dismissed by John Fuller in his influential 1972 book *The Sonnet*, visual sonnets emphasize aspects of the form that are usually missed in normative reading, such as the 'look' or 'gestalt' of the poem. All poetry signifies in this way – as Edwin Morgan stated in 1965, we are all essentially viewers before we are readers – and with the sonnet in particular we register its unique shape before anything else.[15] The visual sonnet, like all good visual poetry, has an immediate appeal that runs counter to the still-prevailing Aristotelean notions of persuading and convincing the reader through argument. Because of this, visual poetry continues to be treated as marginal, if not trivial, and the visual sonnet has been completely ignored by editors of all the available anthologies. As responses to their materiality, I find visual sonnets stimulating and witty additions to the form's history.

MT: I would like to add at the close that sonnets have gone from being little songs (*sonetti*) to little stages for acting out irreconcilable oppositions and making sense of them. The parallelism at play in, say, Stevens's 'Autumn Refrain' sings to the parallelism of earlier sonnets; all sonnets require a careful act of balancing. Part of this balance depends upon the layering of words and their sounds, ones that often transmute before our eyes: in Stevens, 'measureless' shifts toward 'measures', 'resides' at the end of line 9 becomes 'residuum' in the next, and 'still' ventures into 'stillness'. In each case the word shifts from an adjective, adverb or verb to a noun, a thing. If a poem is an act of becoming, by poem's end the thing has been made. It could be said that a sonnet without sound-patterning is no longer a little song; it's a bit like trying to half-sell a duck, which is, as we know, not to sell a duck at all. But then again, as Eliot says, 'much ethereal music leaps up' from language, even without the deliberate pattern of rhyme, music that may have otherwise 'chirped unnoticed' there.

Notes

1 Christopher Ricks, *Allusion to the Poets* (Oxford: Oxford University Press, 2002), p. 1.
2 Iris Murdoch, 'On "God" and "Good"', in *The Sovereignty of Good* (London: Routledge and Kegan Paul, 1970), p. 51.
3 T. S. Eliot, 'Tradition and the Practice of Poetry', in James Olney, ed., *T. S. Eliot: Essays from the* Southern Review (Oxford: Clarendon, 1988), p. 13.
4 Ezra Pound, *Make it New* (London: Faber and Faber, 1934).
5 W. H. Auden, 'A Literary Transference', in *The Complete Works of W. H. Auden: Prose*, ed. Edward Mendelson, 3 vols. (London: Faber and Faber, 1996–), Vol. II: *1939–1948* (2002), p. 48.
6 T. S. Eliot, 'Reflections on *Vers Libre*', in *Selected Prose of T. S. Eliot*, ed. Frank Kermode (London: Faber and Faber, 1975), p. 36.
7 Paul Grobstein, 'Variability in Brain Function and Behavior', in V. S. Ramachandran, ed., *Encyclopedia of Human Behavior*, 4 vols. (San Diego: Academic Press, 1994), Vol. IV, p. 458.
8 William Carlos Williams, *The Embodiment of Knowledge* (New York: New Directions, 1974), p. 17.
9 Eliot, 'Reflections', p. 36.
10 Peter McDonald, 'Truly Apart', *Times Literary Supplement* (1 April 2005), p. 13.
11 Seamus Heaney, 'Englands of the Mind', in *Finders Keepers* (London: Faber and Faber, 2003), p. 92.
12 Alice Oswald, interview with Janet Phillips for the Poetry Society, available online at www.poetrysociety.org.uk/content/publications/poetrynews/pn2005/asprofile/.
13 Ron Padgett, *The Straight Line: Writings on Poetry and Poets* (Ann Arbor: University of Michigan Press, 2000), pp. 81–2.
14 Michael R. G. Spiller, *The Development of the Sonnet: An Introduction* (London: Routledge, 1992).
15 Quoted in Bob Cobbing and Peter Mayer, eds., *Concerning Concrete Poetry* (London: Writers Forum, 1978), p. 20.

Sonnets discussed and suggested sources

Anon., 'Lord Randal', in *The English and Scottish Popular Ballads*, ed. Francis James Child (New York: Dover, 1993), no. 12.
Ashbery, John, 'At North Farm', in *A Wave* (New York: Viking, 1984).
Berrigan, Ted, *The Sonnets* (London: Penguin, 2000).
Bidart, Frank, 'Love Incarnate', in *Desire* (New York: Farrar, Straus and Giroux, 1997).
  'Song', in *Star Dust* (New York: Farrar, Straus and Giroux, 2005).
  'You Cannot Rest', in *Watching the Spring Festival* (New York: Farrar, Straus and Giroux, 2009).

Bishop, Elizabeth, 'North Haven', in *The Complete Poems, 1927–1979* (New York: Farrar, Straus and Giroux, 1983).
Clare, John, 'The Instinct of Hope', in *Poems of the Middle Period*, eds. Eric Robinson, David Powell and P. M. S. Dawson, 5 vols. (Oxford: Clarendon, 1996–2003), Vol. IV, p. 279.
 'The Mouse's Nest', in *Poems of the Middle Period*, Vol. V, p. 246.
Dante Alighieri, *La vita nuova*, trans. Barbara Reynolds (London: Penguin, 2004). [Or, to compare Italian and English, *Canzoniere*, ed. and trans. H. S. Vere-Hodge (Oxford: Clarendon, 1963).]
Denby, Edwin, 'The Climate', in *Complete Poems*, ed. Ron Padgett (New York: Random House, 1986).
Donne, John, *Complete English Poems*, ed. A. J. Smith (London: Penguin, 2001).
Frost, Robert, 'Acquainted with the Night', in *Collected Poems, Prose and Plays*, ed. Richard Poirier and Mark Richardson (New York: Library of America, 1995).
Heaney, Seamus, 'The Glanmore Sonnets', in *Opened Ground* (London: Faber and Faber, 1998).
 'Out of Shot', in *District and Circle* (London: Faber and Faber, 2008).
Hill, Geoffrey, 'September Song', 'Funeral Music', 'An Apology for the Revival of Christian Architecture in England', and 'Psalms of Assize', in *New and Collected Poems 1952–1992* (Boston: Houghton Mifflin, 1994).
Oswald, Alice, 'Wood Not Yet Out', in *Woods etc.* (London: Faber and Faber, 2005).
Rodefer, Stephen, *Mon Canard* (Great Barrington, MA: The Figures / London: Alfred David, 2000).
Sidney, Philip, 'I Might, Unhappy Word' [Sonnet 33 from *Astrophil and Stella*], in *Philip Sidney: The Major Works*, ed. Katharine Duncan-Jones (Oxford: Oxford University Press, 2008).
Stevens, Wallace, 'Autumn Refrain', in *Collected Poetry and Prose*, ed. Frank Kermode and Joan Richardson (New York: Library of America, 1997).
Wyatt, Thomas, 'Whoso list to hunt', in *Complete Poems*, ed. Robert Rebholz (London: Penguin, 1988).
Yeats, W. B., 'The Second Coming', in *W. B. Yeats: The Major Works*, ed. Edward Larrissy (Oxford: Oxford University Press, 2008).

2

HEATHER DUBROW

The sonnet and the lyric mode

'Let us inspect the lyre' (Keats): introduction

At first glance the relationship between the sonnet and lyric seems transparent: if one adopts the common definition of a mode as an overarching and transhistorical category encompassing many genres, surely the sonnet is not merely an instance but also a textbook example, even a prototype, of the lyric mode. Lyric is, for example, often defined in terms of its length, and, according to common though not unchallenged definitions, the sonnet weighs in at fourteen lines; lyric is frequently represented as the genre of internal and individualized emotions, and the principal subject traditionally associated with the sonnet is love; lyric is typically associated with song and music, as is the sonnet. To be sure, many critics have claimed that prototypical status for elegy, maintaining that its emphasis on death and loss renders it a prime example of the preoccupation with absence often attributed to lyric. But the candidacy of that genre for the status of prototype does not preclude and may even support another contender, since the sonnet too often dwells in and on loss, whether it be the death of the lady in the originary sonnets by the Italian poet Francesco Petrarca (Petrarch), her loss in poems by many of his followers, or the permutations on disappearance and absence in numerous later sonnets ('So help / me God to another dollop of death, / come on strong with the gravy and black-eyed peas', Rosanna Warren implores in her witty sonnet 'Necrophiliac', 2–4).[1]

Sonnets often incorporate a twist or turn, and one is due, even overdue, right now: the relationship between the sonnet and lyric is far more problematical than that brief and preliminary overview would suggest. My aim in opening on these connections is not, however, the creation of a straw man that can readily be ignited and reduced to ashes with sparks of critical scorn. It is essential to observe, as this chapter proceeds to do, that in many respects, in addition to the ones already sketched in, the form in question is indeed prototypical of lyric verse – and it is no less essential to proceed

25

to complicate their relationship by acknowledging such problems as the risks inherent in defining and describing each of the categories in question, as well as their variability and changeability. (That variability is of course intensified by the popularity of the sonnet in many languages and cultures. My chapter, like the rest of this volume, will necessarily focus primarily on Anglo-American traditions; but the sonnet is an international form, in fact a form in which English sonnets and their writers negotiate connections with other cultures and their poetry, and occasionally I will adduce those traditions as well.)

This chapter will demonstrate that the sonnet is clearly totally representative of lyric in certain respects and not representative at all in others, while the links between them are hard to evaluate in yet other instances. What emerges from that panoply of possibilities, however, is not a stalemate of repeated 'on the one hand/on the other hand' observations but rather insights about both the sonnet and lyric in general, many stemming precisely from the complexities of linking them. The challenges this chapter confronts are finally more instructive than destructive: their very existence helps us to understand how sonnets work, and most of them can be resolved in ways that do not preclude and indeed facilitate comparing that form to lyric.

'How shall I paint thee?' (Wordsworth): problems in comparing sonnet and lyric

A well-established glossary of literary terms declares that, 'In the most common use of the term, a *lyric* is any fairly short poem, consisting of the utterance by a single speaker, who expresses a state of mind or a process of perception, thought, and feeling' (emphasis in original).[2] Fair enough as an opening sally, but more fully to understand lyric and its connections to the sonnet we need to move above, behind and around encapsulations like that one. The first step in doing so is meeting the methodological problems arising from defining both sonnet and lyric, and from comparing them.

To begin with, each varies historically in significant ways. For example, many early Greek lyrics were public, communal poems, such as celebrations of heroism, while later eras often associate the mode with more personal and private subjects and with the meditative. Whereas lyric poetry and the sonnet are often connected through their association with music, that link operates differently in eras like the early modern one (a term used in this essay for the span between about 1500 and 1700, though other usages of 'early modern' are common in the academy as well), a time when sonnets, like other lyrics, might well be set to music and sung. And that same period witnessed anxieties about the suasive, indeed sexualized, power of music that affected the association in question, while in many later periods song was more likely to be seen as inconsequential (witness the expression 'for a song') than as threatening. Indeed, whereas connections with music in general and song in particular certainly have not disappeared from lyric in our own day (most obviously, many recent African American poets draw on blues or rap rhythms, as Gwendolyn Brooks famously does in 'We Real Cool'), the visual is more important than the auditory for many poets today. Sonnets also differ historically in terms of what Northrop Frye termed the 'radical of presentation': for instance, early modern versions were often circulated scribally, read aloud and sung; while many of their Romantic counterparts were published in newspapers. Distinctions like these bear on the relationship of the sonnet to expectations and assumptions about lyric poetry in general, involving not only the connections to music sketched above but also the common image of the lyric poet engaged in solitary meditation.

Yet another reason historical changes matter is that, as many students of literary form have observed, genres participate in conversations with a whole range of other genres, interchanges that often involve an emphasized and intensified antithesis: pastoral is not-epic, the buddy movie is not-romantic comedy, and so on. Hence, understanding how the relationship of the sonnet to lyric works in the late twentieth and the twenty-first centuries, unlike earlier periods, demands recognizing that many, though not all, sonnets announce themselves as not-free verse. In the Romantic period, sonnets are not-blank verse and hence, given the use of that medium in the period to represent everyday language, also not-conversational poetry; this is a significant gesture given the championing of quotidian, conversational discourse by Wordsworth in particular, though of course he composed sonnets as well. And to return to the early modern era, many sonnet writers then are very conscious of their form as an alternative to writing epic. Such comparisons are significant for the purposes of this article in part because they often register in changing approaches to characteristics of lyric; for instance, the contrast between sonnet and epic evokes the comparison of narrative and lyric poetry in general.

The normative connection between the sonnet and the two primary subjects in the Renaissance, love and politics, declines in later eras; but the twentieth and twenty-first centuries have witnessed many political sonnets, such as the work of Robert Lowell. Another, related historical shift is the diminution of the influence of Franceso Petrarch, the fourteenth-century Italian writer whose *Canzoniere* (also known as the *Rime sparse*) was the principal model for the sonnets written in England and on the continent in the sixteenth century. Diminution and deflection – not disappearance. The twentieth-century sonneteer John Berryman appends the parenthetical subtitle 'After Petrarch

and Wyatt' to one of his poems, thus at once suggesting historical distance
and poetic debt. And when our contemporary Marilyn Nelson writes a sonnet, 'Chosen', in which a slave, coerced into sex by her master, perceives
his face above her as a moon, arguably the poem is gesturing toward the
commonplace Petrarchan comparisons of the lady to the sun, thus gesturing
toward a connection even while emphasizing the vast differences between the
worlds and relationships being evoked. As all these instances demonstrate, it
is essential to negotiate historical changes – and equally essential not to oversimplify them in the interests of a neat argument.

Analyses of both lyric and sonnet are also complicated by how loosely
and variously the categories have been deployed. Both poets and critics have
provided grounds to justify Northrop Frye's complaint that 'there is a popular tendency to call anything in verse a lyric that is not actually divided into
twelve books'.[3] And who determines when something is a lyric or a sonnet?
The author? Some poets insert the word 'sonnet' into their titles to establish
links to the form; to winnow just a few examples, Robert Burns writes a
poem called 'A Sonnet upon Sonnets', Billy Collins entitles one of his poems
'American Sonnet' and Ron Wallace uses 'Bad Sonnet' to introduce a poem
that, like so many of its species, breaks the rules and in so doing calls attention to them. As the final instance suggests, discussions of what constitutes
a sonnet and how it relates to lyric are further complicated by the fact that
writers may use that first label playfully or polemically or just mischiev-
ously, a strategy to which this article will return. Does the critic determine
the category when compiling a collection of sonnets? Does the reader do so?
Even a preliminary glance at a poem that is roughly square in shape, or has
its two final lines positioned differently from the rest, may lead the reader
to try to decide if this is a sonnet. In this immediate, visualized triggering of
categorization, the sonnet differs from many other lyric forms, and, as we
will see, the reflexive process in question is not the least way these poems
qualify the immediacy they establish in other ways.

But the main reason analyses of the linkage between the sonnet and lyric
are so fraught is that both forms have become a locus of contested critical issues and of problematical professional investments: definitions and
descriptions are too often distorted by self-serving agendas. Although lyric
is often categorized with a formulation like the one on which this section
opened, and the sonnet simply defined as a fourteen-line text, such definitions are rendered problematical by dubious generalizations that facilitate
either celebrating or condemning the form in question. Thus lyric has been
represented as the site and even source of precisely the values – a celebration of private and universal experience, a denial of historical and political
determinants – that many critics reject. In particular, academics eager to

dismiss all lyric as the product of bourgeois individualism neglect its roots in communal poetry, as well as the instances of later lyric that do not focus on a solitary individual. (Indeed, the presence of multiple voices is a marker of many contemporary experimental poems with all the hallmarks of lyric save its putative isolated speaker.) This type of dismissive over-generalization occurs among practitioners as well as critics; thus in contrasting their work to earlier lyric, which they condemn on the political grounds I just specified as well as for many other reasons, the Language Poets often accept and support a definition of that lyric as inevitably focusing on sentimentalized personal experience. Conversely, when Helen Vendler insists in her brilliant but not unproblematical study of Shakespeare's Sonnets that lyric may *refer to* the social, but 'a social reading is better directed at a novel or a play; the abstraction desired by the writer of, and the willing reader of, normative lyric frustrates the mind that wants social fictions or biographical revelations', surely her statement is a polemical rebuttal of the emphasis on cultural studies that she elsewhere explicitly condemns.[4]

Definitions also suffer from the common tendency to make the texts that one studies oneself normative, whether out of ignorance of other writings or an agenda of establishing a special status for the texts and periods on which one works. Thus Jonathan Culler's repeated attempts to establish apostrophe as the signature of lyric, however brilliant they may be, neglect the fact that that figure is far less common in, say, medieval and early poetry than in its Romantic counterparts.[5] Otherwise acute readers of twentieth- and twenty-first-century texts have been known to suggest that the Renaissance sonnet was a flatly static form in its subject matter and structure, happily rescued from immobility and even inanity by the liberating experiments performed by the more contemporary poets the critic in question studies. Been there, done that, sixteenth-century sonneteers mutter in response while turning over in their graves. More broadly, treating a given period as normative occludes intriguing connections. For example, those who study the sonnets written in the sixteenth century sometimes neglect telling analogues from later centuries that would variously enrich and complicate their arguments about such subjects as the workings of linked sonnets and of sequences.

'What is thy substance, whereof art thou made?' (Shakespeare): comparing sonnet and lyric

Length

Despite all the problems noted above, certain characteristics widely, though not universally or consistently, associated with lyric in a range of periods can be winnowed from all the loose and varied discussions of it that I have summarized – characteristics that prepare us to locate the sonnet in relation to lyric. As I have already noted, shortness is central, though many critics have pointed out the problems of determining just how short a poem has to be to qualify. Other problems with emphasizing shortness arise from how frequently poems are linked together; even before turning to the example most relevant to this essay – the sonnet sequence or cycle in its several forms – one can note that other genres, such as hymns and pastorals, are also often grouped together. Blake's *Songs of Innocence and Experience* and the autobiographical sequence 'child of the enemy' in our contemporary poet Quan Barry's book *Asylum* are among a host of examples demonstrating that often apparently separable texts are visually and semantically so closely associated that they can be unyoked only by violence. Indeed, in some instances a seemingly separable text may function more like a stanza within the larger composite poem. In short, lyric can in general be characterized by brevity, but the slipperiness of that category permits, even encourages, ways of rethinking it – an invitation to which many sonnet writers eagerly respond.

For if a carefully specified, indeed dedicated, version of brevity is fundamental to commonplace definitions of the sonnet, challenges to our assumptions about its shortness are fundamental to redefinitions by poets and critics. To be sure, much as a sestina consists of six stanzas of six lines each, so the sonnet is normally conceived as a fourteen-line form. Normally, even normatively, but not universally. First of all, some subgenres of sonnet stretch out that line length (the so-called caudated or 'tailed' sonnet, for example, typically appends one or two units of three-foot lines at the end). But this sort of variation soon became an accepted option for the form, and in contrast sonneteers often delight in marking their distance from other sonnets by writing poems that position themselves within that genre yet are neither fourteen lines long nor a well-established variant on that pattern. Labelling his sequence *Modern Love* to distinguish it from the less cynical Petrarchan vision, the Victorian poet George Meredith also creates that distinction by writing sixteen-line poems. The twentieth-century writer Anthony Hecht writes what he terms a 'double sonnet', a technique also adopted by many other sonneteers. Two poems, both entitled 'Maple Syrup Sonnet', neither fourteen lines long, have been composed by the experimental poet Bernadette Mayer.

Such variations demonstrate that for the sonnet in particular, as for lyric in general, the criterion of length can be problematical; but experiments like these do not threaten the status of the poem as essentially short. More germane and unsettling is the undeniable fact that sonnets, like dogs, are pack animals. Indeed, sonnet and pastoral are arguably the two forms most likely to be written in series, a practice that in the former case many have traced to the model of Dante's *Vita nuova*, in which poems are linked by prose. To be sure, in the late twentieth and early twenty-first centuries many poets have written linked series of short poems other than sonnets, motivated in part by many publishers' preference for this type of connection; but the fact remains that the sonnet is distinctive, though not unique, in its propensity for clustering. (As a student of mine observed, 'OK, how many sequences of villanelles can we think of?')[6]

To other implications of this clustering we will return, but for now it's important to observe that a number of different ways of grouping together sonnets have become enshrined in poetic practice and theory. The corona or crown is a series of either seven or fourteen sonnets in which the last line of one becomes the first line of the next one, a poetic technique of repetition known as *concatenatio*; the whole group then ends on what had been the first line of the first poem. A series of religious poems by John Donne termed *Corona* is one of many examples of the form, and in our own day Sandra Gilbert wrote "Belongings", a corona on the decline and death of her mother. In England as on the continent, sonnets were often published in a so-called sequence or cycle; some versions, like Sidney's *Astrophil and Stella*, have enough plot to justify the term 'sequence' and intensify the question of to what extent we are looking at a single, short poem, while others are more loosely connected. Many scholars have asserted the presence of groupings within Donne's Holy Sonnets, and recent scholarship has demonstrated that they often circulated in groups. More problematically, some students of early modern literature have posited the so-called Delian structure, a strategy of connecting a group of sonnets, shorter lyrics that are not sonnets and a narrative poem, as Daniel does in his *Delia*. Cognate practices continued in later periods; Wordsworth, for example, composed a series about the river Duddon, and Seamus Heaney wrote series about subjects ranging from a home in Glanmore to an ancient corpse, found in the bogs of Scandinavia, whom he imagines as riding the London subways. In other words, paradoxically the sonnet variously resembles lyric in being short and also in having some predilection for linkages that complicate that classification. These linkages are, however, far more common than in most other species of lyric, thus signalling one of the ways these fourteen-line poems are not wholly typical, let alone prototypical, of their mode.

It would be tempting to finesse such complexities by asserting that in the instance of the sonnet, no less than lyric in general, the primary unit remains the individual sonnet, thus protecting the criterion of brevity. But considerable evidence suggests that in many instances poets and their printers neither see it this way nor encourage their readers to do so. For instance, in her manuscript of *Pamphilia to Amphilathus*, the sixteenth- and seventeenth-century poet Mary Wroth inscribes most of her sonnets on separate pages, but the ones that form a crown are written with a few lyrics per page and with so little space between them that only the inserted numbers make it clear where one poem ends and another begins. The sonnets within Heaney's *District and Circle*, the sequence about the revenant subway passenger to which I just referred, do not have separate titles or even numbers, and though each appears on its own page, a leaflike printer's symbol at the bottom of each further connects them.

Song and music

Descriptions of lyric as songlike are as thick on the ground as assertions that it is brief – but like other types of undergrowth, they are entangled enough to trip the unwary. Is it even true that lyric resembles song? The critic Northrop Frye asserts with his characteristic decisiveness that it is more connected to chant than song – but surely the latter affinity is significant as well and need not be discarded if we also look at ways lyric may resemble chant.[7] Figuring out in what senses it is songlike is more of a challenge, though, like so many other puzzles about both lyric and sonnet; what may at first seem like an impediment to understanding can be reconfigured as an avenue toward it. Some lyric poems clearly were written to be sung and are composed with characteristics, such as a refrain, that facilitate performance; settings survive for a number of early modern poems, and the work of African American poets such as Gwendolyn Brooks draws on – and arguably in turn influenced – blues songs. Yet even lyrics that were never sung, that in fact, are syntactically constructed in ways that would make it impossible to set them, often seem connected to song in other ways.

One such connection is the possibility of performance, indeed repeated performances, that complicates the idea of lyric as a spontaneous emotional outpouring and further complicates the already fraught concept of sincerity. Sometimes too the connection is realized in the ways lyric, like song, may invite its audience to identify with the speaker and as it were sing along, voicing its words as though they were one's own. Critics ranging in generation and field from Helen Vendler to the comparatist William Waters among many others posit this identificatory voicing as the normative pattern for lyric, though others, including myself, consider it only one of several ways lyric may relate to its readers.[8] After all, lyric, like song, often includes more than one positionality with which the reader can identify; a female reader will not necessarily identify with the male reader of an early modern sonnet.

I would suggest that a more consistent connection between lyric and song lies in the ways both reconfigure the discursive practices preceding and succeeding them. Both are typically ruptural, demanding a significantly different change in register. Both bestow a significant measure of authority on the writer or performer: interrupting a song by beginning to talk in the middle of it is a far more transgressive gesture than interrupting a conversation to interject another comment, and similarly, although scribal culture gave opportunities to add stanzas and so forth, in some important senses the poet as it were holds on to the mike. Ophelia's mad scene certainly testifies to the instability of her mind, arguably testifies to the powerlessness of her social status – but also bears witness to the powerfulness of her song.

How does the relationship between lyric in general and vocal music relate to the genre on which this chapter focuses? The very term *sonnetto*, or little song, suggests a particularly close link. And indeed certain sonnets were set to music; considerable evidence suggests that, like other early modern love poems, they were performed in courtly gatherings and functioned as part of courtship rituals. Nor was this musicality confined to the early modern period; Benjamin Britten's rendition of Donne's Holy Sonnets surely ranks among the most exciting examples. On the other hand, the early modern sequences that intersperse poems labelled 'song' with their sonnets – witness, for example, Sidney's *Astrophil and Stella* and the work of his niece Mary Wroth – insist on a distinction between the two. Often the song introduces a voice different from that of the speaker of the sonnets or evokes a dialogue, though this is a difference in degree, not kind, given the dialogic elements within sonnets that will be discussed below.

Temporality, immediacy, subjectivity

In addition to being considered short and songlike, lyric is often seen in terms of a moment of heightened personal experience – 'the simplest verbal vestige of an instant of emotion, a rhythmic cry', as James Joyce puts it in his *A Portrait of the Artist as a Young Man*.[9] Such views about the mode need to be unpacked in terms of its implications for temporality, immediacy and subjectivity, with critical debates about the concept of the individual especially important in that third arena. When critics approach that first category, temporality, lyric is generally associated with the present, and George T. Wright has persuasively developed the concept of the 'lyric present', a special version of that time period with characteristics often found in sonnets as well as many other poems – enchantment, intensification and the realization of fantasy.[10] If there is a distinctive type of present tense in lyric, other critics have insisted, it is special not least because of the ways it juxtaposes and conflates many temporal moments besides its own. In particular, meditation on an event in the past can make it present emotionally, intellectually and even tactilely. In the anonymous Anglo-Saxon lyric 'Dream of the Rood', for example, the cross at once addresses its contemporaneous readers as though it is present with them and yet relives and revives Calvary. Many lyrics evoke future potentialities in ways that suggest they are occurring in the present; witness 'The Apparition', Donne's fantasy of betrayal by a scornful mistress after his death.

As I have already noted, certain critics engaging with deconstruction, notably Jonathan Culler, have posited a distinctive relationship with the past as the signature gesture of lyric: it reaches out toward what is absent and dead, attempts to call it forth in a process initiated by the rhetorical figure apostrophe – a process doomed to failure and the replication of loss. In this model, then, the present engages with the past only to find that it is not-present. Thus Keats's 'Ode on a Grecian Urn' suggests that that object preserves a moment of unchanging youth and beauty from the past, a moment that is preserved and recreated as well by the poem – but many critics have maintained that this lyric then calls those assurances, not least the hope of recovering and preserving an ideal past, into question. Of course, all these analyses of time sequences are further complicated by the mating habits of lyric poetry that I detailed above: that is, the propensity of the mode to appear in groups of poems. The grouping may build in its own time sequence, as the sixteenth-century poet Edmund Spenser does when he associates each of the pastorals in his *Shepheardes Calender* with a month of the year, thus creating a linear movement and an anticipation of the future, as well as the cyclical movement created by opening and closing on winter. In short, lyric poetry also often teeters on the brink – or the abyss – between temporalities, just as it locates itself on so many other edges.

Turning from lyric in general to the sonnet in particular, the best introduction to the latter's potentials for temporality is David Wojahn's 'Mystery Train', an intriguing series of sonnets about contemporary music, appearing in a collection of poems with the same title. The primary referents of its title are a song Elvis Presley – the principal character in the sequence's long cast of characters – performed, and a film that, like this poetic sequence, involves separate plots and people; but, more to my purposes here, 'train' also suggests movement and hence time. In particular, suggesting the articulation of a group of wagons, the image of the train also alludes to the linkages among the poems in the series, and those linkages involve additional versions of temporality. Some poems on this train are a snapshot of an individual moment, demonstrating Wright's lyric present in their intensity; thus 'Photographer at Altamont: The Morning After, 1969' engagingly describes the scene after the concert, though at the same time its subtitle looks backward, as even or especially lyrics grounded in the present so often do. The next poem, 'Fragging: Armed Forces Radio, Credence on the Mekong, 1969', ironically plays, as it were, the music on the soldiers' radios against the horrors of the war; like so many lyrics, it stops and shivers on the brink of an anticipated future, in this case the death of a member of the company. Patterns of forward movement recur on several levels: the sequential dates in each title, the speaker's development from a young child in the opening poem to an adult who himself takes a young boy to Graceland, the stages in Presley's career.

Wojahn's temporal patterns and others as well recur in a range of sonnets from a range of periods. To begin with, sonnets are so often not only located in a present moment but locked within it: they involve obsessive meditations from which the speaker cannot escape. Petrarch himself models this type of temporality, and the sixteenth-century poet Thomas Wyatt's 'Whoso list to hunt' evokes a speaker who cannot stop desiring a woman despite recognizing the folly of doing so. And, like other lyrics, sonnets often involve meditations on the past or future that seem to be occurring within a present moment, thus conflating temporalities. Shakespeare's procreation sonnets, for example, brood on the alternatives for the future of the young man, and in 'The Soldier', Rupert Brooke's speaker famously anticipates his own death: 'If I should die, think only this of me; / That there's some corner of a foreign field / That is for ever England' (1–3).[11] The African American poet Claude McKay's 'If We Must Die' looks ahead both to death and the events that may precede it in terms so stirring that apparently it was read by prisoners during the Attica revolt. Poems of praise that attempt to immortalize reach toward the future in a different sense.

Like other lyric poetry and like Wojahn's work, sonnets often play several temporalities against each other. In particular, the preoccupation with unsatisfied or threatened or lost love in the work of Petrarch and his followers determines the temporality of many sonnets. As Roland Greene has observed, they are often grounded in the binary of then–now: then she was alive and now she's dead, then I saw her and now she has vanished.[12] The 'then' does some of the work Culler attributes to apostrophe even if it doesn't use the form – that is, it calls up a past only to demonstrate its inaccessibility. One might add that other versions of then–now occur in a common device in sonnets, the evocation of a dream that is played against the world into which the dreamer wakes. But this binary pattern is, I maintain, less common than the conflations of several temporalities that so often characterize sonnets. Some of these poems, for example, blur time sequences through what I have called the 'anticipatory amalgam': a strategy that melds present and future by focusing so intensively on the future that it becomes present in more senses than one.[13] Modelled on the French poet Pierre Ronsard's description of his lady's aging, sonnets by a range of English language poets, including Samuel Daniel, Michael Drayton and William Butler Yeats, evoke their lady's old age in this way. Moving between and among temporalities need not involve linearity, however; intriguing versions of such movements are found in poems that involve recurrent events. Thus through its repeated references to Elvis, Wojahn's poem also has affinities with how Petrarch's anniversary poems, a series marking the return of the day when he first saw Laura, establish a different type of time, at once linear and circular: Petrarch's lyrics emphasize the time that has passed since the first vision of this most visionary of ladies, they circle back to that day, and yet in their incessant brooding on that sight they also exemplify entrapment in a tense present and enchantment by the present tense defined by Wright.

Furthermore, again as in the introductory instance from Wojahn, joining the wagons of individual sonnets into the train of a sequence can produce additional temporal patterns. For example, critics have found the stages in a relationship chronicled in many sonnet cycles, though I believe often the evidence is more elusive, if not illusory, than is claimed; Spenser's *Amoretti* refers to the liturgical calendar, and a sequence to which I referred earlier, Sandra Gilbert's "Belongings", culminates on the death of her mother. Does this linearity simply expand the temporal range of lyric or transform the poems into narratives? To that question we'll return. But for now it is clear that the sonnet, like other genres, decisively rebuts, if more rebuttal is needed, an undue emphasis on the present-ness of lyric.

However one resolves these issues of temporality, seeing lyric as a special, heightened moment, Wright's 'lyric present', has encouraged many readers to associate it with presence in the sense of the immediate, the here and now. If the etymology of 'stanza' links the word and the genre associated with stanzas with a room, one might say that lyric lives in the very room its readers and writers inhabit, sharing the same space and breathing the same air, not in a past over one's shoulder nor in the cyberspace of virtual reality. The conundrums raised by this model, and above all the question of whether there is any reality unmediated by representation, have been extensively debated by both philosophers and critics, though those complexities are necessarily the subject of a different essay. But if we finesse those disagreements by talking about an impression of immediacy, its recurrence in lyric, often intensified by appeals to several senses, is beyond debate. To winnow one example from among the many possible ones, William Blake's 'Tyger, Tyger' illustrates the ways lyric may use apostrophe; an address either to an absent person or something non-human calls the beast forth from its 'forests of the night' to the world of the poem and its readers.

Yet many studies of lyric emphasize immediacy at the expense of recognizing the many ways it may be qualified, compromised or simply rejected. We have already observed that attempts to call back the missing are typically doomed to failure. On more formal levels, we may be distanced from the text by the title (an effect many poets today challenge by using the type of title that functions as the opening words of the poem). We may be distanced by other types of frame, notably references in the beginning or end that separate us from the situation or speaker, such as Milton's shift to 'Thus sang the uncouth Swain to th'Oaks and rills' at the end of 'Lycidas' (186), a line that effects that separation both by moving from first to third person and by redefining direction of address from the reader to the trees and streams of pastoral.[14] As that instance reminds us, we may be distanced as well by reflexive references, notably reminders that we are reading a poem, a representation of experience rather than the experience.

Sonnets are more prone than most other types of lyric to undermine the immediacy they apparently create, thus alerting us to the less obtrusive forms of that undermining in other lyric poetry and, indeed, urging us to think further about routine generalizations on the subject. To be sure, one student of the sonnet insists, 'The sonnet, because of its brevity, always gives an impression of immediacy, as if it proceeded directly and confessionally or conversationally from the speaker, and therefore from the creator of that speaker.'[15] And it is not hard to amass some evidence for claims like this. For example, the dreams that sonnets evoke typically have the Technicolor insistence of the hallucinatory, in part because of the depth of two subjects central to sonnets, love and loss. Witness the fantasy in a poem about both those subjects, Petrarch's 'Una candida cerva' ('A white deer', *Rime sparse*, 190), which creates a vision of the beloved that abruptly appears and just as abruptly disappears. Although Marilyn Hacker's sonnets differ from the Petrarchan models of which they are clearly conscious in their determinedly down-to-earth diction and their focus on same-sex love, they too can create an extraordinary impression of the here and now, in part through the use of sensual details and snippets of conversation or thought. Until its more reflective conclusion, Yeats's 'Leda and the Swan' evokes the impressions, especially the tactility, of Leda's rape by Jove in the guise of that bird.

But the undermining of immediacy is arguably more significant – and more distinctive – in the sonnet tradition than its creation. Yeats's reflective and highly controversial conclusion – 'Did she put on his knowledge with his power / Before the indifferent beak could let her drop?' (13–14) – draws attention to some ways sonnets typically qualify the immediacy they so often create: the couplet that so often ends them may retreat into summary or moral, and in many instances this sort of rhetorical change is emphasized visually by the placement of the couplet to the left or the right of the rest of the poem rather than flush with it.[16] And whereas the immediacy of all lyrics may be qualified by reminders of fictiveness and representation, because of the characteristic self-consciousness of the sonnet tradition those reminders are especially frequent and prominent. Early modern sonnet sequences, for example, often open on allusions to their own genre; at the first poem of Spenser's *Amoretti*, he envisions the poems as being held by the woman to whom they refer, thus reminding us that we are watching a representation of someone reading a representation – yet through the emphasis on the senses (the pages will be touched and seen) returning some of that sense of immediacy. Henri Cole shifts abruptly from an image of himself lying in bed with his mother to 'Little poem, / help me to say all I need to say, better' ('Chiffon Morning' 1.2–3).[17]

But, as is so often the case when juxtaposing lyric and sonnet, apparent contradictions need not usher in fogginess or stalemate. Because it packs so many degrees and types of immediacy and distance within its compact space, I would suggest that the sonnet even more than other forms invites us to reject the binary of immediacy and distance in favour of a model that traces various degrees of what we might term *here-ness*. Just as some languages, such as Turkish, have different words for 'right here', 'a little further away', 'still further' and so on, so the sonnet often includes degrees of our *here-ness*, and indeed often expresses meaning in part through the movement among them. In the Cole poem I just mentioned, the thematized preoccupation with presence and separation (his closeness to his mother in contrast to his father's distance, the current moment versus 'rehearsing death' (7)) is mirrored in many versions and degrees of both immediacy and its opposite, or apparent opposite. We have the tactile proximity to the mother, the body that is here yet hidden under a nightgown, the nearby flower – all of which culminates on a conclusion that sharply contrasts his mother's enfeebled condition with the fantasies of Hollywood: 'From the television screen, a beauty- / pageant queen waves serenely at me' (13–14). Thus rather than simply presenting the bedroom as an immediate world that is merely contrasted to the realm of the television, the ironic reference to the wave (notice 'at me' not 'to me') bridges the worlds, creating yet another type and degree of *here*: an unsettling of spatiality that is mirrored by the unsettled and unsettling sounds of internal and slant (that is, partial) rhymes: 'screen', 'queen', 'serenely'. Recognizing these degrees of *here-ness* in sonnets, one of the prime arenas for such patterns as I've maintained, invites us to look further at how both deictics like *here* and *this*, as well as the issues about immediacy they signal, operate in other lyrics. As Bonnie Costello has shown, ecphrastic poems, those that engage with a work of art, often play on these issues in especially intriguing ways.[18]

Address and audience

Closely related to questions of temporality and immediacy are the debates about whether lyric is an internalized meditation on individual experience that is nonetheless somehow shared by the reader or more social and inter-active. So complex is this issue and so varied are the controversies surround-ing it that any treatment here will necessarily be sketchy – but once again juxtaposing sonnet and the lyric mode can suggestively illuminate even when it cannot definitively resolve. Certainly many of the most familiar, even iconic lyrics in the language do fit that model of internalized medita-tion – the long list might include William Wordsworth's 'Lines Composed a Few Miles above Tintern Abbey' and Robert Frost's 'Stopping by the Woods on a Snowy Evening', to cite just a couple. But I earlier noted too the con-troversy surrounding such assertions. The classicist W. R. Johnson goes so far as to assert that lyrics involving communal experience are the norm for the genre from which many poems have unfortunately deviated.[19]And how about the roots of lyric in the praise of heroes and the branches of the mode that involve political events, such as Milton's poem on the massacre of beleaguered Christians at Piedmont? How about poems that have many other lyric qualities but include multiple voices, such as the framed lyrics noted above? Impelled by questions like these, many recent studies of lyric, especially modern and contemporary lyric, have focused on the presence of an audience.

The sonnet itself variously offers textbook examples of all these patterns, from apparently internalized meditation to what is indubitably interchange between two voices or even among several. In Shakespeare's Sonnets, for example, we encounter poems that, I maintain, are often internalized medi-tations, although some critics have attempted to establish them as dramatic. Reflecting on the nature of the sonnet in the poem that begins, 'Nuns fret not at their convent's narrow room', Wordsworth locates his own voice within the confines of this genre and his own mind. In addition to thus illustrating patterns of address found in many other lyrics, sonnets often exemplify dis-cursive possibilities that bridge the internal and address a single person, the beloved; for example, some critics have suggested the letter as a model for how many sonnets work, and George T. Wright in turn developed the model of what he terms 'silent speech'.[20] But on the other end of the spectrum from that internalized reflection, some sonnets, especially political ones, are clearly public address rather than private reflection. Such poems may in fact address more than one audience; thus Milton's poem 'On the Late Massacre in Piedmont' cries out to God, opening 'Avenge, O Lord, thy slaughter'd Saints', but at the same time it implicitly aims to rouse the indignation and anger of human readers. Indeed, charting the direction of address in sonnets we encounter many examples of prophetic outcries.

It would appear, then, that the sonnet simply offers impediments to resolving the question of to what extent, if at all, we should identify it, as well as lyric in general, with interior reflection. In other words, 'on the one hand/ on the other hand'. But I suggested earlier that such impasses can often be resolved in ways that illuminate rather than obfuscate. And in this instance our fourteen-line poems are a particularly potent though not unique avenue toward a resolution: recognizing forms of dialogism that bridge internalized reflection and social intercourse. Other lyrics may be dialogic as well, but because of their rhyme structure and their interactions with the ghosts of sonnets past, dialogism in this genre is especially frequent and revealing. Examples abound in the sonneteering of all periods, but so skilful are Philip Sidney's interpretations of the dialogic propensities of his genre that all my examples will be culled from his *Astrophil and Stella*. So often the very poems that we would confidently label internalized thought pursue that thought through a two-way conversation in which the speaker addresses another side of her- or himself, thus miming a conversation between two voices; Renaissance models of psychology that emphasize conflict between the faculties of reason and of will encourage seeing conflicts in terms of such interchanges. Sidney's *Astrophil and Stella*, Sonnet 47 famously ends on this description of the effects of seeing the beloved lady: 'O me, that eye / Doth make my heart give to my tongue the lie' (13–14).[21] We have observed the impact of a continuing awareness of Petrarchan traditions even on poets as separated from Petrarch in many ways as, say, Marilyn Hacker and Marilyn Taylor; we have observed as well that many sonnets engage in an implicit conversation with Petrarch. Thus *Astrophil and Stella*, Sonnet 71 piles up a series of statements about the superiority of asexual, Neoplatonic love, thus appearing merely to imitate one of Petrarch's poems on a similar subject. But in the dramatically intrusive final line – '"But ah", Desire still cries, "give me some food"' (14) – not only does Desire resist the idealizations in the earlier statements, but also that voice represents a view of love that rebuts the Petrarchan idealizations to which the poet apparently subscribed earlier.

In fact these are but two of several ways in which the genre on which this essay focuses is profoundly and pervasively dialogic. Most obviously, sonnets do sometimes include conversations with another voice, such as the friends who rebuke Sidney's Astrophil. The poems in a sequence may operate dialogically, as thesis and antithesis; witness Spenser's juxtaposition of poems that glorify his lady with ones that denigrate her. The segments of a sonnet may relate to each other dialogically; for one of the best examples in the language, we might return to the moment, cited above, when the stable Neoplatonic edifice that Sidney erects in Sonnet 71 is toppled by the final line, or adduce the same author's move from the series of questions in the first twelve lines of *Astrophil and Stella* ('When nature made her chiefe worke, *Stella's* eyes'; emphasis in original) to the answer in the couplet. More commonly, the relationship between octet and sestet, or among the quatrains, or between the opening of the poem and its couplet, can often be fruitfully described as dialogic.

Although the critic primarily identified with theories of dialogism, M. M. Bakhtin, at some points contrasts the dialogism of prose forms with the monody of lyric, in other essays, often though not conclusively attributed to him, he acknowledges dialogic elements in lyric as well; and later studies, notably the penetrating work of David Schalkwyk, have explored them further.[22] Such work encourages us to resolve debates about whether internalized reflection is the norm for the forms in question by adopting the controversial but sound position that the sonnet is typically dialogic and the lyric in general is frequently so.

Subject, status, tone

The examples cited above encourage a brief summary of yet another connection between sonnets and the broader category of lyric poetry: whereas other types of lyric verse, such as hymns and wedding poetry, represent only a fraction of the subject matter customarily explored in lyrics, the sonnet is the vehicle for most if not all of the subjects associated with its mode. We have repeatedly observed that both these forms often pivot on love, loss and the connections between them; if lyric sometimes celebrates fulfilment, more often it is a diary of unsatisfied longing. That maker of twisted and twisting myths and legends, the contemporary poet Mark Strand, suggests that the mythological figure Orpheus sings three songs, which culminate on one that 'came in a language / Untouched by pity, in lines, lavish and dark, / Where death is reborn and sent into the world as a gift' ('Orpheus Alone', 54–6)).[23] When poets show up at dinner parties, this is the gift they often bring in lieu of wine or chocolates.

At the same time, as many examples above indicate, sonnets have been written about a much wider range of material than readers and critics often admit. That very association with love and loss is surely why poets so defiantly kidnap the sonnet for very different subjects, thus gesturing toward its more customary topics precisely to stress its own alternatives. Like Petrarch and like writers of many other forms of lyric, the form often addresses political issues; it participates in traditions of poetry of praise, whether the figure celebrated is a major public figure or, in Robert Hayden's allusion to and adaptation of that tradition, a hardworking and loving father ('Those Winter Sundays'). Both the natural and the supernatural worlds have often been central to lyric, and both are central to the sonnet tradition as well. A convert from Anglicanism to Catholicism, the Jesuit priest Gerard Manley Hopkins dedicated himself as well to converting poetic practices, especially prosodic ones. His words about the 'grandeur of God' ('God's Grandeur', 1) aptly gloss the extraordinary energies of his own sonnets about both the physical world and the world of the spirit: his own language 'flame[s] out, like shining from shook foil' ('God's Grandeur', 2).[24] But this is a mere sampling: poets often at once allude to and rebel against earlier traditions of love poetry by including subject matter very different from that in more canonical sonnets – Emma Lazarus writes a sonnet about the Statue of Liberty; Gwendolyn Brooks writes a sonnet about parenthood; Ronald Wallace writes a sonnet about his socks.

As these instances suggest, the decorum of each of these forms (that is, the rules for what is appropriate to them) and ensuing issues of their social status intriguingly separates them. Lyric has generally been the arena for both the most elevated of poems (that is, 'high' in both their dignified subject matter and the elite audience with which they are associated) and far lower ones – hymns and drinking songs, spiritual and bawdy approaches to love. The sonnet has enjoyed, or endured, long periods where it was primarily associated with elevated subject matter and elite audiences – an association that not surprisingly bred reactions and rebellions. Although some of that variety was present in the Italian proto-sonnets that preceded Petrarch's, for most of the Renaissance the sonnet was a 'high' form in all these senses. During that era, the poems that rebelled against Petrarchan traditions, such as those that praise unattractive or lower-class women, acquire power precisely from their reversal of the usual decorum of sonnets. By and large the form remained associated with the more elite subjects, linguistic registers and social interchanges until our own era. One way poets demarcate their differences from earlier works in the genre is by introducing determinedly undignified tones and subjects. Intensely conscious of being a working-class poet adducing a form often associated with elite writers and cultures, the English poet Tony Harrison repeatedly plays lower diction against the norms of the sonnet and often does so in poems that allude to but do not exemplify the sonnet's typical structure and length, thus enacting formally his own fraught relationship to the English Establishment. He writes of and in 'a forged music on the frames of Art, / The looms of owned language smashed apart!' ('On Not Being Milton', 10–11), lines that, like the rest of the poem in which they appear, demand and repay the most intense close reading.[25]

'For was our traffic not in recognition?' (Heaney): conclusions

Comparing lyric and the sonnet in the ways this chapter has done supports many long-standing assumptions about both modes. However various they may be, connections with music remain significant. However significant alternative temporalities may be, both often focus on a moment. However complicated the issues of length may be, both frequently manifest a kind of intensity related to compression.

But the comparison also crystallizes problems in the conventional wisdom about both. Dialogic propensities need to be emphasized more than they sometimes are – and explored even more than they have been to date. We need, for example, to think further about both lyric and sonnet in terms of a series of units that can be attached in any number of ways and with any number of techniques, acknowledging that sometimes the most intellectually and aesthetically significant unit will be not a single poem but a group, that the connections between the line at the end of one sonnet in a crown and the opening line of its neighbour may be quite as significant as, say, the couplet or quatrain within a given poem.

Studying the relationship between lyric and sonnet also provides useful examples of dangers to avoid and opportunities to pursue in many other literary endeavours as well. The attraction to bold and broad generalizations should be qualified by recognizing exceptions, and we have repeatedly encountered the distortions that arise from self-serving approaches to the apparently objective study of literary types. Given the renewed interest in form, these temptations in our professional marketplaces deserve more attention. If one holds stock in a given genre or mode, it is too easy to define and describe it in a way that increases its value; if one holds stock in a particular historical period, it is too tempting to locate the most significant of changes within it. Students of Renaissance literature often see their period as far more central than any other in the development of the sonnet. Conversely, students of later literature oversimplify the Renaissance sonnet in order to locate the most significant changes in that form within their own periods. Similarly and no less destructively, lyric is often defined in ways that facilitate uncritical celebrations or condescending dismissals.

I opened with a reference to the apparent transparency of the interactions between the sonnet and lyric. We are now in a position to observe that if the relationship between lyric and sonnet can be termed transparent, it is so in the same senses a waterfall is: clarity is accompanied by cloudiness, and smoothly flowing ideas coexist with the foam of turbulently provocative problems and questions.

Notes

1 I cite Phillis Levin, ed., *The Penguin Book of the Sonnet: 500 Years of a Classic Tradition in English* (New York: Penguin, 2001).

2 M. H. Abrams, *A Glossary of Literary Terms*, 7th edn (Fort Worth: Harcourt Brace, 1999), p. 146.

3 Northrop Frye, 'Approaching the Lyric', in Chaviva Hošek and Patricia Parker, eds., *Lyric Poetry: Beyond New Criticism* (Ithaca, NY: Cornell University Press, 1985), p. 31.

4 Helen Vendler, *The Art of Shakespeare's Sonnets* (Cambridge, MA: Harvard University Press, 1997), pp. 1–2.

5 See, for example, Jonathan Culler, *The Pursuit of Signs: Semiotics, Literature, Deconstruction* (Ithaca, NY: Cornell University Press, 1981), Chapter 7.

6 I thank Jordan Windholz for this comment and am additionally grateful to him and other students in my spring 2009 graduate seminar on the sonnet for more insights than can be individually specified.

7 Northrop Frye, *Anatomy of Criticism: Four Essays* (Princeton: Princeton University Press, 1957), pp. 273–4. Connections between lyric and chant are also cogently discussed by Andrew Welsh in *Roots of Lyric: Primitive Poetry and Modern Poetics* (Princeton: Princeton University Press, 1978), Chapter 7.

8 Vendler makes this point frequently; see, for example, her assertion that 'lyric is intended to be voiceable by anyone reading it' (*Art*, p. 2); William Waters subtly discusses this and other auditory positions in *Poetry's Touch: On Lyric Address* (Ithaca, NY: Cornell University Press, 2003).

9 James Joyce, *A Portrait of the Artist as a Young Man*, ed. Jeri Johnson (Oxford: Oxford University Press, 2008).

10 George T. Wright, *Hearing the Measures: Shakespearean and Other Inflections* (Madison: University of Wisconsin Press, 2001), Chapter 2. An earlier version of this important essay appeared as 'The Lyric Present: Simple Present Verbs in English Poems', *PMLA* 89:3 (May 1974), 563–79.

11 I cite Levin, *The Penguin Book of the Sonnet*.

12 Roland Greene, *Post-Petrarchism: Origins and Innovations of the Western Lyric Sequence* (Princeton: Princeton University Press, 1991), esp. Chapter 1. I am indebted to his important work on lyric in general and the sonnet in particular throughout this essay.

13 On the anticipatory amalgam, see my essay 'The Interplay of Narrative and Lyric: Competition, Cooperation, and the Case of the Anticipatory Amalgam', *Narrative* 14 (2006), 254–71.

14 All citations from Milton are to John Milton, *Complete Poems and Major Prose*, ed. Merritt Y. Hughes (Indianapolis: Bobbs–Merrill, 1957).

15 Michael R. G. Spiller, *The Development of the Sonnet: An Introduction* (London: Routledge, 1992), p. 5.

16 The citation from Yeats is to W. B. Yeats, *The Collected Poems of W. B. Yeats*, 2nd edn (New York: Macmillan, 1950).

17 I cite Levin, *The Penguin Book of the Sonnet*.

18 Bonnie Costello, *Planets on Tables: Poetry, Still Life, and the Turning World* (Ithaca, NY: Cornell University Press, 2008).

19 W. R. Johnson, *The Idea of Lyric: Lyric Modes in Ancient and Modern Poetry* (Berkeley: University of California Press, 1982), esp. Chapter 1.

20 Wright, *Hearing the Measures*, Chapter 13.
21 Throughout this chapter I cite Philip Sidney, *The Poems of Sir Philip Sidney*, ed. William A. Ringler, Jr (Oxford: Oxford University Press, 1962).
22 David Schalkwyk, *Speech and Performance in Shakespeare's Sonnets and Plays* (Cambridge: Cambridge University Press, 2002).
23 Mark Strand, *New Selected Poems* (New York: Alfred A. Knopf, 2009).
24 Levin, *The Penguin Book of the Sonnet*.
25 *Ibid*.

3

DIANA E. HENDERSON

The sonnet, subjectivity and gender

The sonnet is a little poem with a big heart – and at its core lie subjectivity and gender. Both words are grammatically basic yet surprisingly slippery. Although people usually think they know what gender means, subjectivity is a more specialized term, a word that puns on the tensions it captures: whether or not one is familiar with the subject–object split (a basic philosophical problem associated with epistemology since Descartes), the essence of the matter is that the subject of a sentence is also 'subjected' to forces beyond itself. Moreover, the human grammatical subject, the self that is supposed to be 'one', also knows itself to be multiple and unruly – if 'one' is inclined to a modicum of introspection, as poets are wont to be. What does it mean poetically, then, to express one's own subjectivity, to speak (metaphorically) in one's own voice?

The sonnet form originated in an age when poets were also political 'subjects' to princes, when emotions were perceived as external forces pressuring internal spirits and when earthly experience was deemed subject to heavenly will; the sonnet allowed poets a fourteen-line space in which they could at least articulate, if not exert, their own wills. As Europeans in a hierarchical world that presumed male superiority even if exceptional virgins were subjects of veneration, writers of the first love sonnets expressed the cultural and social paradoxes their desires engendered, as well as their personal experiences of emotional contradiction. Out of this maelstrom arose the split personalities that would become models of great art, and the richly expressive vocabularies that would allow centuries of poetic followers – including women and non-Europeans – to make the sonnet their own, adapting it to capture vastly different perspectives, needs, values and definitions of selves.

A brief history of the subject

Whatever else it has become, the sonnet as a literary mode began as a means of staging the desiring self and its objects of erotic desire. When the fourteenth-century Italians Dante and Petrarch pursued their lady loves in sequences of exquisite sonnets, they launched a poetic movement that quickly came to signify modernity, including the artistic emergence of vernacular European languages rather than Latin, the self-consciousness of a lover aware of the gap between his actions and his wishes, and the paradox of fleshly sensibility confronting metaphysical yearning. Beatrice and Laura, their respective beloveds, were both real women and symbols invested with resonant names and allegorical fates. Dying young, they were useful to the poets as means to express the passionate struggle of life in the body and the attempted sublimation of carnal love into Christian spirituality, leading from the lady to the Lord. Across their sonnet sequences as a whole, if not within individual poems, a gendered hierarchy was ultimately restored.

During the sixteenth century, poets such as Ronsard, Marot and Louise Labé in France; Camões in Portugal; Lope de Vega and Cervantes in Spain; and Sir Thomas Wyatt and Henry Howard, earl of Surrey in England famously adapted Petrarch's model to different social, and especially courtly, contexts – an early modern example of cosmopolitan internationalism. At Henry VIII's post-divorce court, the political side of subjectivity understandably induced anxiety; a translation of Petrarch's 'Una candida cerva', which established the oft-used metaphor of love as a hunt, allowed Sir Thomas Wyatt to express the strain he must have felt as a former intimate of Anne Boleyn, before she became Henry's second wife. The sestet of Wyatt's beautifully wistful 'Whoso list to hunt' seems to reiterate the poet's initial despair of pursuing his 'deer' but then concludes with a disjunctive addition (signalled by the grammatically extra-logical 'And') both presuming an arresting new level of visual proximity and eventually introducing a third specified person:

> Who list her hunt, I put him out of doubt,
> As well as I, may spend his time in vain.
> And graven with diamonds in letters plain
> There is written, her fair neck round about,
> *Noli me tangere*, for Caesar's I am,
> And wild for to hold, though I seem tame.[1]

The hunter hovers close, the grammatical 'I' shifts from himself to the lady, but the lovers are not united. Flitting from the biblical Latin to imperial possession to the enduring wildness of the deer figuring the beloved lady, the couplet moves away from easy resolution or acceptance, while the poet's direct address to other would-be male lovers is itself aptly displaced by layered citation to more powerful men. Wyatt's biography encourages us to interpret the conclusion as referencing an earthly royal Caesar in Henry, rather than Petrarch's spiritual Lord who synthesizes Christian and classical allusions. The propriety of ownership becomes suspect, self-erasing rather than enabling for the poet-hunter, while the female figure remains paradoxically deceptive – only *seeming* tame – rather than elevating or edifying. We have come a long way from Dante's sublime Beatrice.

The uneasiness of this lordly displacement epitomizes a shift in English sonneteering from the Italian, where the 'ladder of love' logic that moved from women to God had been more consonant with religious ideology, and especially with the role of the Madonna. By the time of the great sonnet sequences written during the reign of Henry's daughter Elizabeth I, the difference of Protestantism, as well as a female ruler and an emergent national sensibility, led to new dramatic tensions within the sonnet, and new desires and aims for the poetic speaker. With a brash bluntness that dares the reader to challenge him, Sir Philip Sidney, darling of the international humanist intelligentsia but from the queen's perspective a Protestant hothead to be sidelined, writes repeatedly in his hundred-plus-sonnet sequence *Astrophil and Stella* of his frustration or indifference regarding courtly norms of behaviour. He recasts his 'star-loving' speaker's desires as very much an earthbound affair, for all his awareness of its philosophical impropriety:

> So while thy beauty draws the heart to love,
> As fast thy Virtue bends that love to good:
> 'But ah', Desire still cries, 'give me some food'.[2]

The conflict between reason and desire, between 'should' and 'want', would soon become a standard theme-for-variation among the many non-aristocratic poets who would follow in Sidney's footsteps, a theme capacious enough to embrace political, professional and philosophical as well as erotic desires.

Literally hundreds of poems show the influence of Sidney's aristocratic self-presentation and struggles with amorous subjugation, even as the sonnet moved from courtly manuscript circulation to the emergent world of print publication. Among the generally sceptical *Idea* poems by Michael Drayton, for example, is an exquisite poem that reverses the tonal shift within Sidney's structure in Sonnet 71 while drawing on many of his other techniques (as well as his sometimes jocular distress at male subordination to female power). Beginning with the colloquially pragmatic 'Since there's no help, come let us kiss and part; / Nay I have done, you get no more of me', and moving through an extended personification allegory at love's deathbed, the poem ends by using the English couplet to imagine desire overcoming 'rational' complaisance despite his initial assertion that 'so cleanly I myself can free':

> Now if thou wouldst, when all have given him [love] over
> From death to life thou mightst him yet recover.[3]

Drayton's lively dramatization and present-tense suspense shows how the sonnet could both build upon and depart from the kind of internally focused meditation often associated with lyric, be it Petrarchan or, later, Romantic.

It had been part of Sidney's remarkable achievement that he both excelled within the metrical boundaries and experimented with novel adaptations, such as composing his opening sonnet in alexandrines. Furthermore, he played artfully with the gaps and doubleness allowed by adopting a named persona, Astrophil, who is and is not identifiable with the poet Sidney. In so doing, Sidney (and his followers) helped make the sonnet a more overtly dramatic device: less wonder, then, that it became a resource for the remarkable playwright who would both mock the courtier-poet by staging sonneteers as forsworn amateurs in *Love's Labour's Lost* and pay him homage by extending the theatrical possibilities for such poems in the more enduringly popular story of star-crossed courtly lovers, *Romeo and Juliet*.

Edmund Spenser, by contrast, preferred directness in using metrical regularity, his biography and temporal logic as signs of his accord with a Protestant ordered cosmos in his *Amoretti*, pursuing subtler shades of personal distinction. Some would say his continued use of Petrarchan metaphors such as the hunt and devices such as the blazon (cataloguing the beloved's body parts and, arguably, thereby dispersing the threat of her powerful, independent wholeness) marks a male-dominant model of subjectivity; however, as in his epic *Faerie Queene*, Spenser also displays an ability to shift his 'subject position' to allow greater mutuality as well as mutability across gender. In Sonnet 75, 'One day I wrote her name upon the strand', he incorporates both nature's physical challenge to his writing and his beloved's vocal criticism of his 'vaine assay / A mortall thing so to immortalize', unusually (*pace* Wyatt's poem above) allowing the female access to language. In this case the woman's perspective occupies the entire second quatrain: while the poet will counter-argue in the sestet for the appropriateness of his praise as a means to 'eternize' her virtues (constructing a Protestant version of a ladder to the afterlife by projecting his writing itself into 'the hevens'), the effect of the dialogue is to allow the final assertion of 'Our love' a credibility and weight that stands in contrast to the projections and self-involvement of many a loving sonneteer.[4]

The Protestant spirituality that allows Spenser to find a rare happy conclusion to his love affair as well as his sonnet sequence, in sacramental marriage, would become a standard device in narrative forms. Most English poets, however, continued to exploit the sonnet's associations with the writing subject's internal contradictions, oxymora and erotic struggles. Fulke Greville's tortuous *Caelica* sonnets, and more famously Donne's Holy Sonnets such as 'Batter my heart, three-personed God' juxtaposed sensory immediacy and delusion with spiritual longing, without the satisfaction of a calm resolution. In Donne's case, the poet assumes a traditionally feminized position as the object of ravishment, and in desiring subjection to God calls attention to the paradox of willing submission inherent in Christianity. The all-male drama here stands in contrast to – or in reflective dialogue with – his 'profane' love poetry addressed to women. Tellingly, the unconventional Donne would rarely write in fourteen-line sonnet form to his earthly beloveds, nor would most seventeenth-century writers who followed. Perhaps with the print publication in 1609 of Shakespeare's sonnet sequence – successfully incorporating both an idealized male 'master mistress' and a tormenting 'dark' female beloved, and ringing the changes that time and desire could provoke – the worldly love sonnet was perceived by most to have run its course.

It had not, of course. Nourished by changes in the conception of loving behaviour and the circumstances surrounding it, as well as assumptions about what the subject might say and be, there were many generations of love sonnets still to be written. One direction was signalled by the man who would also initiate a whole new universe of possibilities through deployment of a public political voice in the sonnet form: John Milton. His lyrics, like his epic writing, serve both as a culmination of the Renaissance and a beacon of a new republican self, supremely confident of the right to voice its particular situation directly. 'Methought I saw my late espoused saint' builds on the more affectionate, wistful tonalities in Spenser and Shakespeare, using the sonnet form to memorialize his dead wife. Milton typically incorporates classical Greek mythology and Hebraic religious reference into his octave's Christian dream vision of her return, then breaks through with the stark simplicity of an entirely monosyllabic final line to mimic his harsh, heartbreaking awakening to both his physical blindness and love's loss: 'I waked, she fled, and day brought back my night'.

Two centuries later, American Henry Wadsworth Longfellow's sonnet 'The Cross of Snow' would similarly capture the poignance of a wife's early death, this time by fire, and her haunting 'white' soul in the night. However, the difference of his titular allusion to the natural landscape of a 'sun-defying' 'mountain in the distant West' captures both national difference and one of the most notable additions of the intervening Romantic movement: the first-person subject's explicit desire for correspondence with and through nature. To have such a desire, of course, presupposes the recognition of distance or lack – directly addressed in sonnets such as Keats's 'Bright Star' or Mary Locke's 'I hate the Spring in parti-colored vest'. Certainly earlier writers had recognized the poetic potential of disrupted similitude between the self and the elements (as in the earl of Surrey's 'The soote season', for example), and Shakespeare was hardly alone as a lover 'all in war with time' and thus the natural order of mortal being. But the new attention accorded to the natural landscape as itself an object of desire would inspire a wide range of sonnets, including some valuing mutability per se, as well as the capacity of sensory associations to evoke memories (see Wordsworth's *The River Duddon: A Series of Sonnets* or Coleridge's 'To the River Otter'); the aesthetics of the sublime, recognizing the power of time and nature to dwarf human values and achievements, would prompt new versions of paradox in compact masterpieces such as Percy Bysshe Shelley's 'Ozymandias' or Horace Smith's lesser-known poem of the same name. Like the love sonnet, the nature sonnet lives on, in verbally extravagant observations such as Amy Clampitt's 'The Cormorant in Its Element' and a goodly number of post-Romantic poems that simultaneously shame and inspire the writer by comparison, such as Richard Wilbur's 'Praise in Summer', or Robinson Jeffers's 'Love the Wild Swan'.

Romanticism's increased attention to the natural world accorded greater importance to sensory cultivation and types of sensibility at least theoretically accessible to all. While the print revolution had enlarged the circulation of texts, and seventeenth-century Britain's political upheavals catalyzed what were already increasing numbers of those who felt entitled to self-expression, the combination of democratic impulses with the sonnet form truly came of age in the wake of the French Revolution. Working-class poets such as John Clare and women struggling to make a living such as Charlotte Smith found a way to participate in what was now a substantial poetic tradition, but one that did not require a classical education or extensive allusiveness to arcane knowledge. At the same time, a gendered 'outsider' such as Anna Seward used the Petrarchan rather than English form to make a case for her own learnedness and metrical mastery (in her *Original Sonnets*, 1799).

Moreover, many sonnets followed in the alternative public rhetorical tradition of Milton's 'To the Lord General Cromwell, May 1652' and 'On the Late Massacre in Piedmont' to address contemporary outrages and praise martyrs of conscience, as would Wordsworth's 'To Toussaint L'Ouverture' (the imprisoned leader of the Haitian slave revolt) or Shelley's 'England in 1819'. The latter poem's righteous anger follows in the path of Wordsworth's direct address to Milton in 'London, 1802', even as Shelley and other younger Romantics felt betrayed by Wordsworth's retreat from progressive politics. In an era when individualized ode stanzas and 'organic' forms accorded with a Rousseauian desire to venerate natural man, the sonnet now might be seen as more constraining than in its paradoxical past, and yet that very formality could be turned to advantage as a public voice with some definitiveness. Shelley exploits the potential to build one grammatical sentence

across the sonnet's entire length to pile up a monstrous weight of apposi-
tives testifying to England's corruption from the top ('An old, mad, blind,
despised, and dying king') right through to 'A people starved and stabbed
in the untilled field' and back around to the government, only to pronounce
them 'graves' and conclude with the possibility of release through resurrec-
tion-as-revolution ('from which a glorious Phantom may / Burst, to illumine
our tempestuous day'.[5] *Vive la Révolution.*

In addition to the overt connections between many Romantic poets and
progressive, even revolutionary, thinking that embraced more rights for
women, the age-old gendering of Mother Nature suggested a symbolic feminine importance. However, as feminist critics such as Margaret Homans have
delineated, such associations of nature with the maternal implied a poetic
narrative in which the (male) poet finds his voice by distancing himself from
the mute, unlearned feminine. Even Wordsworth's beloved sister Dorothy is
positioned in his work as closer to unreflective nature, the sweet naïf whom
the poet subsumes and transcends precisely through his meditative artistry.
The most famous example of this dynamic occurs in 'Tintern Abbey', but it
appears in his sonnets as well. Furthermore, the sublime elements of nature
are often gendered male and associated with a traditional patriarchal deity,
distinct from the picturesque or beautiful feminized attributes. In 'It is a
beauteous evening, calm and free', for example, 'the mighty Being' is masculine, 'his eternal motion' making 'A sound like thunder – everlastingly',
whereas the divinity of Wordsworth's female addressee is unconscious:

> Dear Child! Dear Girl! That walkest with me here,
> If thou appear'st untouched by solemn thought,
> Thy nature is not therefore less divine;

concluding with the comfort of 'God being with thee when we know it not'.[6]
She may be no less divine, but she certainly lacks the kind of discursive
awareness that a verbal artist needs.

A gender gap of another sort becomes the stuff of sonneteering in George
Meredith's sequence 'Modern Love', its title announcing its ironic difference. Far from the saintly lost wives of Milton and Longfellow, here the
poet charts the unhappy dissolution of a bourgeois marriage using the
established tradition of paradox in a disturbingly fresh way. In Victorian
England, 'subjectivity' has become not only the perspective of the poet but
the prisonhouse from which he cannot escape, nor can his sophisticated perception of parallelisms between their mental states reanimate their domestic
bond as anything other than a spectral mockery.

The sequence opens with a sadly intimate bedroom scene described with a
novelist's third-person combination of detachment and direct knowledge:

> By this he knew she wept with waking eyes;
> That, at his hand's light quiver by her head,
> The strange low sobs that shook their common bed
> Were called into her with a sharp surprise,
> And strangled mute, like little gaping snakes,
> Dreadfully venomous to him.[7]

Gradually moving from the starkly descriptive to the figurative, Meredith also reveals this as a marriage horrifically soured – and his own. The traditional love sonneteer's conflicting internal emotions are now transformed to dramatize the tension between bourgeois propriety and private suffering, often shifting to a cold, sardonic key that is therefore all the more haunting:

> At dinner, she is hostess, I am host.
> Went the feast ever cheerfuller? She keeps
> The Topic over intellectual deeps
> In buoyancy afloat. They see no ghost.[8]

Finding a temporary bond of fellowship and admiration in their false performance of domestic bliss, he becomes part of a marital 'we' who 'waken envy of our happy lot' before cutting through in the final turn, the work of what is often formally called the sonnet's *volta*:

> Fast, sweet, and golden, shows the marriage-knot.
> Dear guests, you now have seen Love's corpse-light shine.
>
> (lines 13–14)

So much for the angel of the house, or domesticity as a refuge from the depersonalized alienation of the masculine Industrial Age workplace.

Be the arena domestic, societal, or cosmic, from the mid nineteenth century onward the sonnet became a form in which scepticism and fear increasingly contested modern notions of progress and certainty. Some poets of course continued to capture the confident, normative or idealized public subject in sonnet form: notable examples include Robert Browning's 'Why I Am a Liberal', Rupert Brooke's 'The Soldier' ('If I should die, think only this of me; / That there's some corner of a foreign field / That is for ever England') and Emma Lazarus's 'The New Colossus', which concludes with the oft-quoted lines now inscribed upon the pedestal of the Statue of Liberty in New York Harbor. In a related vein, the sprung rhythms of Gerard Manley Hopkins's radically experimental sonnets testify as much to his 'dare-gale' soaring faith ('how he rung upon the rein of a wimpling wing / In his ecstacy!') as to his bouts of soul-rending spiritual doubt ('cliffs of fall / Frightful, sheer, no-man-fathomed'). But from Edgar Allan Poe's 'To Science' to Thomas Hardy's 'We Are Getting to the End', the sense of a hostile modernity increasingly dwarfed the poetic subject. The voice of patriotism was as likely to be parodied (see, for example, E. E. Cummings's 'next to god america i') as it was to be upheld. By the time Robert Frost produced 'Design', the prospect of a metaphysical plan could 'appall' just as surely as does the sensation of emptiness enveloping the lonely wanderer in his hauntingly beautiful 'I have been one acquainted with the night'.

The preponderance of twentieth-century sonneteering faced the erosion of faith and the rejection of universals head on. Nowhere was this more shatteringly evident than in the poetry produced by First World War soldiers Siegfried Sassoon and, especially, Wilfred Owen – himself killed on the battlefield, with numbing irony, after the official declaration of the Armistice. Sonnets such as Sassoon's 'On Passing the New Menin Gate' typify their sense of betrayal and outrage. The Great War demonstrated to many the failure of Europe's claims to 'advanced civilization', as technological progress became a means of mass slaughter, the quintessentially perverse use of scientific knowledge being the military deployment of chemical gas. In his stunning double sonnet 'Dulce et Decorum Est', Owen vividly recaptures the horror of experiencing a gas attack as well as the unheroic desperation of war's routine that precedes it, using shifting perspectives and pronouns to construct a complex rhetorical argument. Beginning as part of the soldierly collective as 'we cursed through sludge', and 'All went lame; all blind', the poet's 'I' emerges through separation at precisely the moment (and in the fourteenth line) when he can do nothing but witness the 'someone' who, amidst an 'ecstasy of fumbling' does not get his mask on in time:

> Dim, through the misty panes and thick green light,
> As under green sea, I saw him drowning.
>
> In all my dreams, before my helpless sight,
> He plunges at me, guttering, choking, and drowning.

Building on the horrible irony of the subject's emergence through impotence and isolation, he then turns to address directly the 'you' who does not share his dreams and memories, one with whom he posits only a hypothetical bond that allows the climactic expression of an all-embracing political anger and the poem's titular irony:

> If you could hear, at every jolt, the blood
> Come gargling from the froth-corrupted lungs,
> Obscene as cancer, bitter as the cud
> Of vile, incurable sores on innocent tongues, –
> My friend, you would not tell with such high zest
> To children ardent for some desperate glory,

> The old Lie: Dulce et decorum est
> Pro patria mori.[9]

In recasting the Latin praise of dying for one's country as 'the old Lie', Owen addresses not only the 'friend' who is not his friend but also a masculine poetic tradition that does not capture his experience, for the classical line derives from Horace's Odes. Owen's 'Anthem for Doomed Youth' similarly evokes familiar sonnet techniques (the blazon become a litany of mourning) and echoes ('shrill, demented choirs of wailing shells' rather than Shakespeare's merely belated 'bare, ruined choirs where late the sweet birds sang') to capture the cost of war. He again mixes these literary gestures with a precisely observant eye for physical detail – as in the gentle sadness of the sonnet's and the day's conclusion, in the home of the dead soldier's loved ones: 'And each slow dusk a drawing-down of blinds'. For this male subject, the past – communal and poetic – is a lost world.

Although this brief history has focused primarily on the dominant Anglo-American tradition (and appropriately so, given the audience for this volume and the importance of reading poetry in the original language), the sonnet developed rich traditions in other tongues as well, producing such innovators and masters as Alexander Pushkin in Russian; Baudelaire and Mallarmé in French; Rainer Maria Rilke in German; and, later, Pablo Neruda in (Chilean) Spanish. By the twentieth century, the European internationalism of the sonnet's first centuries expanded to embrace the globe, with imperial traces and diasporic histories generating creative hybrids across political boundaries.

Among the more audacious examples of this new cosmopolitanism is Indian-born Vikram Seth's 'novel in verse' about California yuppies in the early 1980s, made up (entirely, including acknowledgements, dedication, contents and author's note) of tetrameter sonnets modelled on 'Pushkin's masterpiece / In Johnston's luminous translation: / *Eugene Onegin*'.[10] The nineteenth-century Russian's hybrid rhyme scheme (*ababccddeffegg*) allows it to function like either the Italian sonnet's 8–6 or the English 4–4–4–2 model, depending on where the poet chooses his pauses and turns; Vladimir Nabokov compared its movement to 'that of a painted ball: you see the pattern clearly at the beginning and at the end of its movement, but in mid-spin all you get is a colorful blur'.[11] This variety and unpredictability is well suited to lengthy narrative but also to the type of story Seth chooses to tell: of a modern world in which choices and random chance destabilize lyric's putative assertion of a stable subject.

Asserting the value of using the 'dusty bread molds of Onegin / In the brave bakery of Reagan', Seth mixes such flippant couplets with serious psychologizing, social satire, and musings both philosophical and aesthetic. The San Francisco Bay area and a Silicon Valley ex-workaholic named John provide the unlikely starting place for his epic-novel vision (complete with invocations of both the muse and Dear Reader): Seth gradually shifts and enlarges the perspective to embrace those with East Asian, African American and Midwestern backgrounds, with straight and gay and bisexual orientations. As to his line length, he declares his reason for distress at the degenerated fate of the four-foot line in English in a sestet (with a nod to Marvell's tetrameter masterpiece of *carpe diem* mannerism, 'To His Coy Mistress', not in sonnet form):

> But why take all this quite so badly?
> I would not, had I world and time
> To wait for reason, rhythm, rhyme
> To reassert themselves, but sadly
> The time is not remote when I
> Will not be here to wait. That's why.　　　(5:4, p. 102)

With mortality at his back, the poet returns to the work of his poetic fiction, reclaiming that which has been viewed by many as (artistically or socially) degenerate, trivial or out of fashion. In an America where, as in W. B. Yeats's iconic sonnet of modernist entropy 'The Second Coming', 'the centre cannot hold', Seth captures the double potential of the sonnet to dramatize subjective contradictions and to place those individual struggles within a long, allusive history that can either dwarf or enlarge them. Gesturing at everything from pop jingles and Arnold Schwarzenegger back to both Wyatt and Astrophil-like doggerel ('Thus the young yahoos coexist / With whoso list to list to Liszt' (13:32)), Seth provides a brave new world of possibilities, a cosmopolitan polyglot style that befits the variety of his characters' sexualities, desires and disappointments. The comic associations of the tetrameter couplet allow the admittedly quotidian nature of their emotional traumas, careerist and family priorities, and even a shattering premature death, to resonate without maudlin or disproportionate importance: he balances everyday losses as well as cosmic and political rudderlessness with a sense of formal order and artistic control.

In Seth's novel, the once courtly, putatively patriarchal sonnet has become the vehicle for an overtly democratic, non-sexist vision of the late twentieth century. Nor is he alone in finding the sonnet a capacious vehicle for progressive, experimental expression. Yet given the ironies briefly noted earlier regarding the place of the feminine in Romantic poetry, as well as the sonnet's deep involvement with culturally formative metaphors such as the hunt, the woman as animal or a collection of body parts, and models of masculinist sublimation ranging from Catholicism to Freud, this enduring love affair with the sonnet form may continue to surprise. To understand better how and why this happened requires looking back again, somewhat more selectively, at the form's history – this time, with a difference.

The difference of gender

The history of the sonnet provides an excellent entrée into the world of gender studies as a contemporary discipline, and conversely that field's methodology has transformed the history of the poetic form. From the start focusing on heterosexual desire as a destabilizing force within a world of gendered hierarchy, the early sonnet both attended to women and presumed identification with a male subject. What would happen if viewed with an eye to female subjectivity, or with different forms of desire in mind? The picture that emerges includes a set of complications and competing narratives that help explain both the form's endurance and the variety of approaches and priorities that have enriched the domain of gender analysis. Indeed, the effects of this reconsideration have now become so enmeshed in the literary field that even my attempt at a 'straight' history here bears traces of what feminist analysis has recently revealed. Nevertheless, if gender is made the central category of analysis, the voices absent above radically revise the story.

Virginia Woolf's *A Room of One's Own* (1929), among the most important foundational texts for feminist literary analysis, suggested many of the questions and approaches that would later be elaborated within academic discourse. At the same time, the fact that Woolf does not discuss the sonnet form in her wide-ranging essay indicates just how much our account of female authorship and poetics has been transformed by subsequent scholarship. Granting that she cited selectively to build an argument about the historical exclusion of women from access to privileges including self-expression and literacy, it is less her agenda than the normative literary history of her day that led her to imagine that the earliest notable female writers appeared only in the mid seventeenth century, after the first flourishing of English Renaissance sonneteering. We now think otherwise.

The first stage of analysis with the rise of academic feminist inquiry during the 1970s and 1980s involved looking for the 'missing women' who had fallen from, or never been included in, the canon of literary study, as well as bringing to consciousness the male biases of the seemingly 'universal' poetic speaker. Anthologies such as Betty Travitsky's *The Paradise of Women*, Katharina M. Wilson's *Women Writers of the Renaissance and Reformation* and Germaine Greer *et al.*'s *Kissing the Rod*, and archival efforts that culminated in online resources such as the Brown University Women Writers Project, revealed that there had been numerous female sonneteers, many of whom had written more than a few poems.[12] Consequent analysis of these poems uncovered instances both of equality (in craft and wit) and difference (in topics, emphases and modes of circulation).

Take a particularly striking example from the reign of King James I: Lady Mary Wroth, unnamed by Woolf, wrote an epic romance, closet drama – and a sonnet sequence to rival in length that of her uncle Sir Philip Sidney, while reversing his gendered address. Selections from *Pamphilia to Amphilanthus* are now a part of standard twenty-first-century poetry anthologies. Wroth had long appeared in such verse collections – not, however, as the subject but rather as the object of poetic address by Ben Jonson, and as a patron of the arts like Lucy, Countess of Bedford. Despite the rarity of a sonnet in Jonson's poetic corpus and of his explicit praise of her writing, the authorial dimension of his tribute was long dismissed as mere flattery, perhaps in part attributable to Jonson's light touch in using what are known as 'feminine rhymes' in the opening quatrains:

> I that have been a lover, and could shew it,
> Though not in these, in rithmes not wholly dumb,
> Since I exscribe your sonnets, am become
> A better lover, and much better poet.
> Nor is my Muse or I ashamed to owe it
> To those true numerous graces ...[13]

Yet Wroth's own poetry was far from light and gay, instead emphasizing the suffering and passivity in great measure demanded by her sex within a social order that privileged activity as masculine. Drawing on a common trope punning on leaves (of trees, of books), she presents herself as 'distressed' among 'leafless naked bodies' of trees with 'dead leaves', conflating in a sorrowful parody the conventional sonneteering catalogue of the female body and the inadequacy of literary imitation.[14] Calling attention to herself as a site of pity, darkness and limited agency, she dramatizes female subjectivity as the position of comparative powerlessness and passivity, awaiting her errant but sunny male beloved.[15] Tellingly, Wroth takes a particular interest in the oxymoronic juxtaposition of presence and absence, an opposition found as well in Sidney and Shakespeare and crucial to much postmodern (especially deconstructionist) reading – but her female subject usually remains in the shadows, aligned with darkness and pain.

Arguably Wroth is consciously illustrating the cultural situation of the female writer even in so privileged a family as the Sidneys, in which her father

Robert as well as her more famous uncle had composed sonnet sequences, and she had the gendered precedent of an aunt Mary who wrote psalms and translated plays. Natasha Distiller has recently reminded us that Wroth's gender conspires against seeing her (as she claims Christopher Warley and others have) as aligned simply with conservative class distinctions; Distiller returns our attention to Wroth's exceptional desire to publish, which prompted others (notably one Lord Denny) to view her as 'a hermaphrodite and a monster'. Denny, whose own ox had been gored by her allegorized topicality in the romance *Urania* (1621), to which her sonnet sequence was appended, no doubt had his allies in so judging Wroth. Nevertheless, Ben Jonson was not alone in indicating that some viewed her 'public speaking' more positively – including those who had nothing to gain from her patronage, such as Lord Herbert of Cherbury. In a poem that may attest as well to the surprising sexual latitude within some Jacobean circles, he playfully hails Wroth's maternity of two children out of wedlock (by her cousin William Herbert) alongside her poetic making: she 'can, as everybody knows, / Add to those feet fine dainty toes'.[16] Even if advantaged by her aristocratic birth, Wroth did defy conventions repeatedly in her life, and in her poetry she shows a consciousness of gendered assumptions that indicates serious scrutiny, if not explicit critique, of masculine norms and dichotomies.

To discuss Wroth's poetry in terms of the difference encouraged by her gendered subjectivity is to engage in what Elaine Showalter dubbed 'gynocritics', another fundamental approach within 1980s feminist criticism. The value of this technique has not faded any more than has the archival recovery of female writers, although the difficulties of attributing the cause for particular techniques or emphases to gender became obvious as more texts became available: the field soon recognized the varieties of female experiences, prompted by analysis of the intersections between gender and other categories such as class, race, period, sexuality and region. Moreover, more sophisticated application of linguistic, literary and social theory unsettled any easy attribution of 'voice' to poetic speaker, of verbal stance to biographical subject. To take a Victorian example: even if Robert Browning would call Elizabeth Barrett Browning 'his little Portuguese', her 'Sonnets from the Portuguese' were not in fact translations, nor could their rhetoric be translated back into a literal portrait of their marriage without denying layers of craft, convention and indeterminacy. Despite the understandable desire to recover the lost experiences of 'real' women (and other socially disadvantaged groups), then, such poets were no more easily equated with the lyric 'I' than had been Sidney with Astrophil – and, given cultural restraints on their public speaking and the habits of subterfuge thereby encouraged, often far less so.

Such scepticism about the relationships between authorial subjectivity and poetic voice accorded with practices of literary criticism in the late twentieth century, and also allowed the third formative strand of gender studies – critique of masculine normativity – to become more suggestive than just clichés about Dead White Men. Nuanced analyses of Renaissance sonnets by Nancy Vickers helped call attention to implicit sexism in what had previously seemed apolitical artistic devices (such as the blazon of female beauty or the hunt for love referenced earlier). Vickers showed how the myth of Actaeon and Diana, with its rending or *sparagmos* of the young man who unwittingly gazed upon a goddess, enacted a gendered role reversal that revealed the threat implicit within the quotidian cataloguing of female beauty (the eyes, the lips, the breasts) by the male poet. More recently, Judith Haber has argued that the involvement of lyric in the erotic narrative of *Romeo and Juliet*, leading to consummation as death, creates a master narrative that other dramatists interested in subjectivity had to twist and bend if they wished to create a productive rather than fatal space involving female desire. Whether this account fully credits the complexity of Shakespeare's love story or not, it does capture the trajectory of the sonnet form within Romeo's tragedy, as (following the fatalistic prologue sonnet) he moves from Petrarchan vacuity to witty exchange in the 'pilgrim sonnet' at Capulet's ball – but finally to the climactic blazon over Juliet's seemingly dead body before his suicide.

The three initial strands of feminist criticism described above have in combination provided a rich repertoire for use in analyzing the sonnet, and as a result the story of the sonnet has been altered. The first Elizabethan sonnet sequence used to be a given: Thomas Watson's *Hekatompathia*; now some say Anne Lok's holy sonnets of the 1560s should be the origin, moreover preceding John Donne in that religious subgenre – and they would also note the New World innovations of Sor Juana Inés de la Cruz in the later seventeenth century, in Mexico. Tracing the writing of Sor Juana's contemporary noblewomen in England led to similar complexity, in that 'progressive' gendered assertion seemed to cohabit with conservative royalist politics. One way to view this was, as Catherine Gallagher put it, to see the *roi absolu* providing a precedent for the *moi absolu*, the self as sovereign.[17] More recently, analyses of republican and commonwealth women writers have led to some questions about the very presumption that privileged classes led the way in constructing a female poetic canon. Notwithstanding these debates within the early modern field, the juxtaposition of class and sex clarified that literary history was neither exhausted nor definitive. Reviewing our narratives of artistic production through the lens of gender analysis radically altered assumptions, and perforce led to epistemological as well as historicist revisionism. This presented a thoroughgoing challenge to traditional critical practice, upending presumptions about what was known and valued in ways that made space for new voices, new conceptions of authorial success and new motivations to read poetry.

Virginia Woolf began her account of female writers with Margaret Cavendish as an oddity, among the first great ladies to express themselves however awkwardly. Now, by contrast, we may read Cavendish's sonnets on atoms as remarkable contributions at the beginning of the scientific revolution (from which the gendered protocols of her day attempted to exclude her, as Woolf had duly noted). Where we first saw the English Romantic poets as a great men's club of six, and then noted the objectification or symbolization of the female in nature, now Charlotte Smith, Anna Seward and Mary Robinson are all read alongside and in dialogue or alliance with the former masculine canon. And whereas *The Barretts of Wimpole Street* once provided a sentimental frame for reading the sonnets of Elizabeth Barrett Browning, now we can see that 'How do I love thee? Let me count the ways' is but one of the many remarkable voices of a 'Victorian Sappho': classicist, feminist epic romancer and formally adept sonneteer.[18]

The gendered change of perspective also prompted another look at poets once deemed odd, quaint or passé – a fate no doubt shared by many male poets, but befalling exceptional women writers at an alarming rate. Christina Rossetti, for instance: while it could hardly be denied that the author of 'After Death' and 'Dead before Death' has a morbid streak, the meditative beauty and craft of her haunting sonnets has only recently been recaptured. Revealing the many layers of reflection involved in portraiture (in this case, seemingly her brother Dante Gabriel's painting of his ill-fated wife, Elizabeth Siddal), she wonderfully triangulates the gaze as well as the subject 'In an Artist's Studio':

> One face looks out from all his canvasses,
> One selfsame figure sits or walks or leans:
> We found her hidden just behind those screens,
> That mirror gave back all her loveliness.[19]

His obsessive 'selfsame' mirroring contrasts with her 'hidden' self 'behind those screens', and the dynamic grows more disturbing as 'every canvas means / The same one meaning' (7–8). 'He feeds upon her face by day and night, / And she with true kind eyes looks back on him' (9–10) perceives the witnessing writer (who had also served as a model to Dante but here becomes the mediating 'third term', a positionality absent in earlier poetic meditations such as Marvell's 'The Gallery'). The sad cost of artistic objectification and time's passage comes to a climax in the final couplet, though with a delicacy and apparent pity for all involved that dwarfs judgemental conclusions:

> Not as she is, but was when hope shone bright;
> Not as she is, but as she fills his dream.

'Lizzie' died young, of a drug overdose, but the poem's poignancy is not reliant upon or confined to one biographical relationship. Formally, Rossetti's sonnet resembles Elizabeth Cobbold's *Sonnets of Laura* a half-century earlier, which reimagined the original Petrarchan beloved's perspective using third-person description, but the stark yearning here remains far more broadly resonant – almost anticipating Woolf's argument about women serving as looking-glasses reflecting men's idealized selves.

It would take a 'flapper' to turn the tables, and while Edna St Vincent Millay was far more than that, she did break through the conventions inhibiting female expressions of sexual desire with modernist bravado:

> I, being born a woman and distressed
> By all the needs and notions of my kind,
> Am urged by your propinquity to find
> Your person fair ...[20]

Not only would Millay take the position of the active desirer, she would also frankly decouple sex from love and sentimentality:

> ... let me make it plain:
> I find this frenzy insufficient reason
> For conversation when we meet again.   (12–14)

Ouch. Although more formally experimental modernists might disdain Millay's use of the sonnet (as well as her popularity), one must imagine that just as many male readers were startled if not put off by this unconventional frankness.

Millay would likewise refuse the 'one and only' romance of the Petrarchan idealist, admitting 'What lips my lips have kissed, and where, and why, / I have forgotten ...'.[21] Was this the beginning of what it truly meant to speak freely as a woman, as Natasha Distiller (working in a Lacanian feminist frame) asserts?[22] Certainly Millay addresses sexuality in a way rarely seen, with the possible exception of some of Aphra Behn's racier Restoration lyrics – though Millay also has her melancholy inheritances, resembling Lady Mary Wroth when she asserts 'Night is my sister' and waxes wistful for her fading youth. Millay's is a self-consciously gendered performance of self-assertion, full of memorable declarations such as 'I will put Chaos into fourteen lines / And keep him there', and 'I drink – and live – what has destroyed some men'.[23] What indubitably had changed between the seventeenth and twentieth centuries, however, was the size of a public audience willing and eager to hear this bold a female subject. Comparing herself to a cat in heat, Millay challenged and dared successfully, emerging as a best-selling poet and making the sonnet fit for a 'fast' era, a jazz generation.

But Millay did not confine her attention to the love sonnet alone: she also composed an elegiac sequence capturing an unhappy rural couple's estrangement (no doubt drawing on her own upbringing in Maine), and an apocalyptically inflected *Epitaph for the Race of Man*. She wrote a tribute 'To Inez Mulholland', her teacher and onetime beloved, and (along with Louise Bogan among others) enlarged the spectrum of female sexuality to embrace same-sex desire. In any number of ways, then, Millay played an important role in further 'queering' the sonnet, challenging its still-conventional masculine heterosexual subjectivity and thereby making it new – and making it the kind of flexible instrument that would later appeal to Vikram Seth and others wishing to give voice to a range of once-marginalized poetic subjects.

Most overtly, Millay provided a precedent for other women to use the sonnet sequence to capture new angles on female desire and on new forms of American experience. Julia Alvarez, for example, would choose the form to tell, in 33 and later in 44, what it felt like to be a bilingual Latina immigrant at those resonant ages.[24] These are sonnets by and for women, rather than the blossoming youths of *carpe diem* lyrics and suicide pacts. And, by the turn of the millennium, such voices could be heard as authoritative, even etched in stone. At the New York Public Library's poetry walk, the path quotes Alvarez's line-14 assertion: 'Who touches this poem touches a woman'. Of course, time is and is not a forward march, and the triumphalism of concluding with Alvarez's sonnet belies the mixed messages and doubts her poems express, especially for one caught within and between multiple cultural locations. But then, the subject of the sonnet has always been paradoxical.

Endless monuments

In the space of this chapter it has not been possible to do justice to the theorists as well as practitioners who helped describe, but also shape, new directions for the sonnet. From Roman Jakobson to Joel Fineman to Eve Kosofsky Sedgwick, the sonnet has provided a fruitful object for theorizing, and serious students of the form (and literary studies more generally) would do well to read their influential analyses.[25] Summary paraphrase cannot do justice to many of these readings. For example, Fineman's work melds awareness of the classical tradition with deep immersion in Lacanian psychoanalysis: he begins with the recognition that Renaissance love lyrics were categorized as 'epideictic' rhetoric focused on praise or blame in the present tense, and then considers how Shakespeare complicates both that motif and the congruence between the poet's gaze and poetic object in order to create a shiftily modern verbal subject of analysis. But this description does not capture the nuanced readings (nor the dense prose) that continue to make his criticism vital. Sedgwick's radical reconsideration of the sonnet as a form *Between Men* opened up new horizons of political interpretation and helped found queer studies, not as another form of identity politics but as an inclusive, critical, dynamic understanding of verbal and embodied relationships, a way of reading that led in unexpected directions and allowed the personal to become fluidly transformative without losing its bite.

The sonnet was, for these theorists as it has become for modern poets, a supremely social form, the litany of great sonneteers having constructed a tradition that straddles lyric, drama and narrative, and allows each generation to remake it in their own image, with their own versions of gender, their own subjectivities. Whereas other chapters in this volume will explore the particular sensibilities in greater depth within an age, an equally important way to think about the sonnet is across time, comparing and contrasting the possibilities of a particular poetic form, vocabulary and set of techniques as they redound across centuries. Be it Milton lauding Shakespeare, Wordsworth invoking Milton or John Berryman recalling Sidney, the conversation across generations now allows what began as a radically internalized form to create communities of sense and sensibility, to be both individualized and in dialogue, to tear down and reconstruct identities. From fourteen lines to infinity: the sonnet carries on.

Notes

1 Throughout I cite modern-spelling and standard anthologies as much as possible, for ease of access and pithiness of citation: here, see Eavan Boland and Edward Hirsch, eds., *The Making of a Sonnet: A Norton Anthology* (New York: Norton, 2008), p. 79. The reader should be aware, however, of the interpretive role of the editor and the effects of regularization on early modern writers' spelling, punctuation and metrics.
2 Sir Philip Sidney, *Astrophil and Stella*, 71:12–14, in Phillis Levin, ed., *The Penguin Book of the Sonnet: 500 Years of a Classic Tradition in English* (London: Penguin, 2001), p. 25.
3 Boland and Hirsch, *The Making of a Sonnet*, no. 91, lines 13–14.
4 *Ibid.*, no. 84. See also Spenser's remarkable use of syntactic self-subordination in no. 67.
5 'England in 1819', 13–14, in Levin, *The Penguin Book of the Sonnet*, p. 104.

6 *Ibid.*, p. 91, lines 10–12, 14.

7 *Ibid.*, p. 130, Sonnet 1:1–6.

8 *Ibid.*, Sonnet 17:1–4.

9 *Ibid.*, p. 192, lines 13–16, 21–8.

10 Vikram Seth, *The Golden Gate* (New York: Vintage Books, 1986), 5:5, p. 102.

11 *Ibid.*, p. 344.

12 Betty Travitsky, ed., *The Paradise of Women: Writings by Englishwomen in the Renaissance* (New York: Columbia University Press, 1989); Katharina M. Wilson, ed., *Women Writers of the Renaissance and Reformation* (Athens, GA: University of Georgia Press, 1987); Germaine Greer, Jeslyn Medoff, Melinda Sansone and Susan Hastings, eds., *Kissing the Rod: An Anthology of Seventeenth-Century Women's Verse* (New York: Farrar, Straus and Giroux, 1988).

13 Ben Jonson, 'A Sonnet to the Noble Lady, the Lady Mary Wroth', 1–6, in Levin, *The Penguin Book of the Sonnet*, p. 64.

14 Mary Wroth, *Pamphilia to Amphilanthus*, Sonnet 4:10; Sonnet 19:9–11. See Mary Wroth, *The Poems of Lady Mary Wroth*, ed. Josephine A. Roberts (Baton Rouge: Louisiana State University Press, 1983), pp. 87, 98.

15 See Diana E. Henderson, 'Female Power and the Devaluation of Renaissance Love Lyrics', in Yopie Prins and Maeera Shreiber, eds., *Dwelling in Possibility: Women Poets and Critics on Poetry* (Ithaca, NY: Cornell University Press, 1997), pp. 38–59.

16 Mary Wroth, 'A Merry Rime', lines 5–6, in *Poems*, p. 26.

17 Catherine Gallagher, 'Embracing the Absolute: The Politics of the Female Subject in Seventeenth-Century England', *Genders* 1 (1988), 24–9.

18 I borrow the phrase from Yopie Prins, *Victorian Sappho* (Princeton: Princeton University Press, 1999), a deeply learned study of nineteenth-century women poets.

19 Boland and Hirsch, *The Making of a Sonnet*, no. 167, lines 1–4.

20 *Ibid.*, no. 186, lines 1–4.

21 *Ibid.*, no. 43, 1–2.

22 Natasha Distiller, *Desire and Gender in the Sonnet Tradition* (Basingstoke: Palgrave, 2008).

23 Edna St Vincent Millay, *Fatal Interview*, 7:1; *Mine the Harvest*, lines 1–2 in Levin, *The Penguin Book of the Sonnet*, p. 123.

24 Julia Alvarez, *Homecoming*, rev. edn (New York: Plume, 1996).

25 Roman Jakobson, *Shakespeare's Verbal Art in th'Expence of Spirit* (The Hague: Mouton, 1970); Joel Fineman, *Shakespeare's Perjured Eye: The Invention of Poetic Subjectivity in the Sonnets* (Berkeley: University of California Press, 1986); Eve Kosofsky Sedgwick, *Between Men: English Literature and Male Homosocial Desire* (New York: Columbia University Press, 1985).

4

ARTHUR F. MAROTTI AND MARCELLE FREIMAN

The English sonnet in manuscript, print and mass media

As communication theorists have repeatedly observed, each medium meta-communicatively defines the nature of the messages being transmitted as well as the relationship between their senders and receivers. It matters whether one encounters texts in oral, handwritten, printed or electronic forms. It also matters whether the texts are spoken or sung; recorded by amateur or professional scribes, either in inelegant or presentationally artful forms; published in ephemeral pamphlets, newspapers or magazines; printed in paperback or hardback books; experienced on radio, television, film, tape, records, CDs or DVDs; or found in various forms of casual or institutionally mediated emails and websites. Finally, the cultural context is crucial: the oral or written (scripted and/or printed) or electronic and visual modalities dominant in the world in which texts are transmitted shape the different kinds of relationships their originators and receivers have to them. Marshall McLuhan's assertion that 'the medium is the message' was a provocative overstatement, but it is certainly true that messages are inseparable from the media through which they are transmitted, and the mediated message in its material, rather than ideal, form is the one that is experienced in particular ways. And so there is no culturally faithful history of a literary form such as the sonnet without considering the communicative channels through which such poetry flowed through the late medieval, early modern, modern and postmodern eras. This is true of the general history of the form as well as of that of the sonnet in the anglophone world.

Colin Burrow calls the early modern sonnet 'a form which was located at the intersection between private papers and printed record'.[1] Poetry was only gradually being thought worth preserving through print, and sonnets bore the marks of privacy and audience-restriction, especially the love sonnets by Sidney and Shakespeare, or the religious sonnets by William Alabaster and John Donne. Printed lyric poetry, as its publishers emphasized, gave many readers access both to the social worlds from which they might have been excluded and to the private emotional worlds of its authors. As more and more writers conceived of a print readership as their first and preferred audience, the situation then changed.

Like so many other literary forms in the late medieval and early modern periods, the sonnet was an import to England from continental Europe. Fabricated as a subgenre of the lyric in the late medieval period in Sicily and Provence, given prestigious treatment by the *Stilnovisti* poets of Italy, most notably Dante, the sonnet reached an apex of literary and cultural prestige in the work of Francesco Petrarca (Petrarch), whose *Rime sparse*, written and revised over a period of twenty-five years, set the model for an ambitious sonnet collection or sequence (including *canzoni* or substantial 'songs' in the contents). Petrarch's example influenced scores of poets in Renaissance Italy, Spain, France and other European countries – including Pietro Bembo, Pierre Ronsard, Joachim DuBellay and Garcilaso de la Vega – to write sonnets and sonnet sequences. In a pre-Gutenberg world, though, these sonnets could only circulate in a manuscript medium; after the invention of movable type, sonnet collections such as those of Dante, Petrarch and Ronsard reached a wide readership through print.

The early Tudor poet Sir Thomas Wyatt tried his hand at 'Englishing' Petrarch, but his psychological make-up, his stylistic proclivities and the English language itself altered both the sound and sense of the sonnets he translated, converting the polite, self-effacing, mellifluous and delicate language of Petrarch into a more masculine, assertive and plain-speaking idiom. For example, he turned Petrarch's Sonnet 140 ('Amor che nel penser mio vive et regna'), which is an apology for erotic blushing by a speaker who romantically asserts he will die for love, into a linguistically aggressive poem ultimately about martial male bonding ('The longe love, that in my thought doeth harbar'). Wyatt circulated his verse in manuscript within a social elite at the court of Henry VIII, the volatile and dangerous master in whose government he served. Not just Wyatt's temperament, then, but the social and political world to which the poet restricted the circulation of his verse conditioned the poetry and its subject matter. His translation of Petrarch's Sonnet 269 ('Rotta è l'alta colonna e 'l verde lauro'), the Italian poet's lament for the loss of his patron, Francesco Colonna, became a poem referring to Wyatt's own loss of his protector, Thomas Cromwell. Although the most textually reliable collection of Wyatt's verse is found in the British Library (Egerton MS 2711) with authorially inserted corrections, we can better discern the social milieu in which the verse circulated through the Devonshire manuscript (BL Add. MS 17492). This collection of poems was associated with a group of men and women who recorded verse circulating at court and who entered some of their own compositions in the album: such a social circle was able to perceive the immediate relevance of some of the poems whose meanings the author veiled.[2]

Wyatt's future elegist, Thomas Howard, earl of Surrey, also turned occasionally to the sonnet form. Responding more to the duplicity and social posturing of contemporary courtly life, his translation of Petrarch's Sonnet 140 ('Love that doth raine and live within my thought') emphasized the mutual deceitful game-playing between men and women in amorous situations. Surrey and Wyatt's poems both continued to circulate in manuscript, being collected, for example, in the large album kept by their contemporary Sir John Harington of Stepney (and later continued by his more famous son, Sir John Harington of Exton), the Arundel Harington manuscript.[3] The elder Harington may have been responsible for passing on to the printer Richard Tottel a collection of those poets' verse that became the main contents of the landmark poetical anthology known in literary history as *Tottel's Miscellany*, but published originally under a title that highlighted Surrey's aristocratic status: *Songes and Sonnettes, written by the right honorable Lorde Henry Haward late Earle of Surrey, and other* (1557). Much reprinted through the Elizabethan era, this collection contains 97 of Wyatt's poems, 40 of Surrey's and, in its first edition, another 128 poems by other early and mid Tudor writers. The vast majority of the pieces, however, were not sonnets, the fashion for which had not yet taken hold in England. In print, the verse took on more general, less topical meanings, as the author and/or editor gave generic titles to originally untitled pieces, typically making them the utterances of the conventional 'lover'. Following Tottel, printed poetical miscellanies became a familiar medium for the transmission of lyric poetry, including some sonnets.

The English sonnet sequence

Prior to the 1580s, the sonnet form was occasionally employed for dedicatory, epitaphic, didactic, encomiastic, religious and epistolary verse, for set-pieces in dramas or romances, and for songs designed for musical accompaniment. But it was not in frequent use, for English sonnet sequences or collections did not circulate in either manuscript or print until relatively late in the Renaissance. There were occasional longer forays into the sonnet – for example, in the 1573 edition of *A Hundreth Sundrie Flowres*, in 'A Discourse of the Adventures Passed by Master F. J.', where George Gascoigne embedded a *terza sequenza* of three sonnets, or the 'Seven Sonets in sequence' on the theme of courtly disillusionment in his collected poems. Only in the 1580s did poets take up the challenge of imitating European sonnet sequences. The rhetorical clumsiness of Thomas Watson's *Hecatompathia or Passionate*

Centurie of Love (1582) and John Soowthern's *Pandora* (1584) prevented their making much impact. But as they went to press Sir Philip Sidney was at work on his sonnet sequence, *Astrophil and Stella*, an autographically inflected narrative written in an accessible style that marked it as writing as different from contemporary verse as is the Pyrrhus speech in *Hamlet* from the sophisticated language of the rest of that drama.

Sidney did not publish his writing, however, so a miscellaneous set of 'Certaine sonnets' and the 108 sonnets and 11 songs of *Astrophil and Stella* were only initially available in manuscript form to a small circle of readers. After his death in 1586, however, any writing by Sidney in poetry or prose became highly valued because of his reputation as a military hero and champion of Protestantism, Sir Walter Raleigh calling him the 'Cipio, Cicero and Petrarke of owr tyme'.[4] In the wake of the 1590 publication of the first part of Sidney's incompletely revised prose romance, *The Arcadia*, the enterprising publisher Thomas Newman brought out a defective version of *Astrophil and Stella* in 1591, possibly with the help of Samuel Daniel or someone else in the Sidney circle. The poems were not elegantly printed, with sonnets spilling over from page to page, individual poems unnumbered, and an additional group of poems by other authors included to create an 'augmented' edition more appealing to book buyers. Nevertheless, the print publication of this sonnet sequence was a watershed event, running quickly to a second edition and a further one by another publisher in 1592, and spearheading the sonnet craze at the end of Queen Elizabeth I's reign, which included Barnabe Barnes's *Parthenophil and Parthenophe* (1593) and *A Divine Centurie* (1595), Thomas Lodge's *Phillis* (1593), Giles Fletcher's *Licia* (1593), Thomas Watson's *The Tears of Fancie* (1593), Henry Constable's *Diana* (1594), Michael Drayton's *Ideas Mirrour* (1594), Bartholomew Griffin's *Fidessa* (1596), Henry Lok's 'Sundrie Sonnets' and 'Affectionate Sonets' from *Ecclesiastes* (1597), Richard Barnfield's *Cynthia* (1597), Sir William Alexander's *Aurora* (1604), John Davies of Hereford's *Wittes Pilgrimage* (1605), William Shakespeare's *Sonnets* (1609) and Lady Mary Wroth's *Pamphilia to Amphilanthus* (1620). Still more stayed in manuscript, like the forty sonnets in *Caelica*, by Sidney's friend Fulke Greville, unpublished till 1633, or the collection by Philip Sidney's brother Robert, only published in 1984 (BL Add. MS 58435).[5]

Newman's unauthorized edition may bear witness to the residual 'stigma of print' feared by well-born and educated men of the period whose work was exposed to general readership.[6] Among the other sonnets in Newman's quarto, however, were twenty-eight by Samuel Daniel himself, who used this allegedly unauthorized publication to justify printing his whole sonnet collection, *Delia with the Complaynt of Rosamund*, in 1592. *Delia* exemplifies the double audience of much printed lyric verse in the period, aimed both at a patron or patroness and also more general readers. Dedicated to the Countess of Pembroke, the 1594, 1595 and 1598 editions contain a complimentary poem to her expressing his grateful clientage. However, the 1592 *Delia* is also a much more carefully presented publication than either the 1591 or 1592 editions of *Astrophil and Stella*, with only one poem per page, set above a fancy printer's ornament and numbered in roman numerals, an arrangement taken up in Drayton's *Ideas Mirrour* (1594). The complaint that follows the sonnets has a separate title page and the work's author is identified. When Sidney's full collection was published in the monumental 1598 folio, his sonnets would be numbered and artfully arranged as Daniel's had been. These new print designs show the growing confidence in the sonnet's public status, and by the end of the 1590s, thanks largely to Sidney's example, the printing of a respected gentleman's work was no longer a disgrace. Edmund Spenser's autobiographical sonnet sequence, *Amoretti* (1595), may have been the manuscript gift to his spouse the first poem claims they were, but it has survived only through its published versions. The new choice of print as a medium was quite deliberate for poets like Spenser, who had 'laureate' ambitions, and who had sought and won the patronage of the queen: it meant asserting literary as well as sociocultural authority.[7] Even King James VI of Scotland, Queen Elizabeth's successor as monarch in 1603, had published a series of twelve sonnets among his *Essayes of a Prentise and Poetical Exercises at Vacant Houres* (1584).

Shakespeare's Sonnets

William Shakespeare embedded some sonnets in such plays as *Love's Labour's Lost* and *Romeo and Juliet*, but his 154-sonnet collection represents his major achievement in the form. Although only a few of these poems show up in seventeenth-century manuscript compilations, they appear to have initially been written for private manuscript circulation.[8] In 1598 Frances Meres famously referred to Shakespeare's 'sugred Sonnets among his private friends' and the market-conscious publisher William Jaggard must have gotten his hands on copies of Sonnets 138 and 144 for the unauthorized volume he printed, *The Passionate Pilgrim by William Shakespeare* (1599 and 1612), a book pretending to collect the verse of this then-notorious playwright-poet. This indicates that at least some of the poems that appeared in the 1609 Quarto were known in the late 1590s, most probably the sonnets from the 'Dark Lady' or miscellaneous section of the collection (Sonnets 127–54). But if the sonnets addressed to the 'young man' portrayed as a friend, patron and lover were not among the circulating 'sugred Sonnets', the poems themselves indicate that they were sent, in manuscript, to their primary intended reader over a period of several years in which the poet relied upon his patronage and support.

We are indebted to the publisher Thomas Thorpe for his 1609 publication of *Shake-speares Sonnets*, a quarto whose title page notes that the poems were 'neuer before Imprinted'. This publication, however, is a strange one, in several ways. Firstly, the majority of the poems, addressed to a man, depart from the tradition of addressing an (inaccessible) woman – though homoerotic sonnets were also written by Michelangelo Buonarroti and the Elizabethan Richard Barnfield. Secondly, Thorpe's poetical pamphlet is a belated one in terms of the sonnet fashion, which tailed off after the spate of sonnet publication in the 1590s. Though the Scottish poet William Drummond of Hawthornden was attracted to the sonnet form and published seventy-one sonnets in his 1616 *Poems*, the fashion for love lyrics in the early Jacobean period had diminished, and love sonnets were not now pouring from the presses. Third, the *Sonnets* were printed in the form of a short quarto, one of the most perishable forms of publication since, like printed plays, they were sold unbound and were not, like prestigious large folios, expected to last in permanent library collections. Moreover, Thorpe's *Shake-speares Sonnets* contains an enigmatic dedication, not presented, as would be expected, by the author, but by the publisher: since authors whose books were printed were not paid by publishers (only given free copies) and they had to rely on dedications to patrons or patronesses for social and economic benefits, it is strange that the printer should have put himself in this position, and it may indicate that the text was intercepted or unauthorized. Whether or not Shakespeare deliberately chose to have his work put into print by Thorpe is a matter of debate – a controversy now affected by Brian Vickers's compelling argument that the long poem attached to the *Sonnets* in the 1609 Quarto, 'A Lover's Complaint', is almost certainly not by Shakespeare, but by John Davies of Hereford.[9]

No new edition of Thorpe's Quarto appeared: unlike Michael Drayton's sonnet collection, which went through many editions, *Shake-speares Sonnets* was a one-time publication, 'greeted largely in silence'.[10] In their next appearance in John Benson's *Poems Written by Wil. Shakespeare. Gent.* (1640), these sonnets lost their formal integrity as the editor not only gave titles to poems, but also fused many of the separate sonnets into larger units comprising between 2 and 5 quatorzains, the result being that 146 of the sonnets found in the Quarto were conflated into 72 poems in Benson's edition. Benson also changed male pronouns to female to make many of the young-man poems addressed to a female reader, copied both Shakespearean and non-Shakespearean poems from Jaggard's *Passionate*

Pilgrim, and added poems by other, mostly Caroline, authors in the last part of the book, immersing Shakespeare's verse in new political and aesthetic contexts.[11] The collection of 154 separate sonnets had to wait until Edmund Malone's 1780 edition to be republished in the arrangement of the original Quarto. Given the unabating popularity of Shakespearean drama, what is perhaps most strange is that there was not much of an audience for his sonnets beyond Shakespeare's own time. Seventeenth-century compilers of manuscript anthologies of poetry largely ignored them and, after Benson, publishers obviously did not believe them to be a saleable commodity.

The sonnet in private and public

Though the sonnet was now firmly a print genre, manuscripts from the first two-thirds of the seventeenth century do, however, contain some examples of the form. These documents do not record sonnet sequences, but usually individual poems, often not labelled with the designation 'sonnet' – a term that was used loosely at the time for many short love poems that do not follow the Petrarchan or Shakespearean forms. For example, the Wyatt papers (BL Add. MS 62135) have a poem apparently addressed to Margaret Wyatt, transcribed along with an introductory emblem of a rock in a stormy sea with a heavenly sun overhead shining a ray upon it, 'Neimoti immota' (immovable in the midst of motion):

> The Orient Peare which on firme Rocke doth grow
> Where Sea winds waves on it stil beating light
> Remaines yet safe within thin shel and light
> In movings thus unmoved ever so
>
> As it obtains therby more pleasing shew
> Through Heavens faire influence instilled right
> Where it lieth open to the cheirful light
> Glad to receive the beauties thence that flow
>
> You are this Pearle (sweet Lady) by faithe who
> Have stay on Christ your Rocke who shal you quit
> From this worlds stormes in your close sel below
>
> Open to hiest grace that skies bestowe
> Which like your noble name shal from dispight
> Stil hold you cleere stil their deere MARGARIT.
>   Fine   (fo. 277)

At the right of the poem is an image of a snail. In effect, what we have here is a sonnet, with two clearly demarcated quatrains and two tercets, presented along with visual material in what amounts to a seventeenth-century greetings card. Sonnets could be light, complimentary pieces speaking a language of affection.

But there was another, much more serious use of the sonnet form. There is a long-standing association of sonnets with religious and devotional expression, from the mixture of amorous and devotional material in Dante's *La vita nuova* to the sonnets of the last third of Petrarch's collection, written after the death of 'Laura'. So it is no surprise that both manuscript and printed remains from the early modern period contain religious sonnets. Poets such as William Alabaster and John Donne wrote emotionally charged holy sonnets, the first in connection to his conversion to Roman Catholicism, the second mainly in straitened personal and financial conditions in the first years after his marriage and loss of prospects for secular advancement. Alabaster's poems were not printed during his lifetime and are preserved in six manuscripts from which they were edited for a modern edition.[12] Donne's holy sonnets – both the mini-sequence, *La Corona*, and the larger group of sixteen poems usually referred to as Holy Sonnets – survive in very few manuscript copies, suggesting that they were kept quite close, though we know, for example, that he sent *La Corona* to the earl of Dorset and also showed it to Magdalen Herbert, Lady Danvers. The sequence enacts a set of private emotional and religious struggles that the poet was willing to share with close friends, but he was not willing to share them with the broad readership they would eventually reach through the posthumous publication of his work in 1633 and after.

The greatest religious poet of the seventeenth century was, however, a little more open to print. George Herbert composed religious sonnets in both Latin and English, and two manuscripts of Herbert's collection survive, the 'Williams manuscript' (Dr Williams's Library, London, MS Jones B 62) and the Bodleian manuscript (MS Tanner 307). But it was the printed edition of Herbert's masterpiece, *The Temple*, published after his death at the discretion of Nicholas Ferrar, which made him celebrated. Sonnets are not, of course, the main verse form found in this virtuoso display of prosodic variety (few verse forms are repeated in the collection), but there are sixteen in the work, including some of Herbert's best and most well-known poems: 'The Sinner', 'Redemption', 'H. Baptism I', 'Sinne I', 'Prayer I', 'Love I' (a double sonnet), 'Jordan I', 'The H. Scriptures I' (another double sonnet), 'Christmas', 'Jordan II', 'The Holdfast', 'Josephs Coat', 'The Sonne' and 'The Answer'. As part of his project of baptizing secular poetry, Herbert took a form mainly associated with amorous, adulterous desire and used it for his own religious and devotional ends. But by giving the collection to Nicholas Ferrar for possible publication, Herbert evidently foresaw that pieces originally made for his private devotions could, in print, be appropriated by a variety of readers for their own particular religious purposes. Noting the inclusion of two religious sonnets in a 1609 letter to his mother, Katherine Duncan-Jones suggests that '[p]ossibly the publication of *Shakespeare's Sonnets* was one of the factors that provoked George Herbert to embark on the programme of reclamation of secular poetic rhetoric that was to emerge as *The Temple*'.[13] When Herbert was writing, the immediate fashion for love sonnets had passed, and the time was right for a reinvention of the form. The 1633 edition of Herbert's poetry together with the first edition of Donne's poems both led to an outpouring of religious and secular verse in print.

The public sonnet

As well as using the sonnet for religious purposes, John Milton also used the form for 'academic' intellectual exchange, literary competition and passionate political utterance. Although the initial literary transmission of these pieces to particular individuals would have been in manuscript, they reached the print readership Milton sought for most of his works. Of his twenty-four sonnets (seven of them in Italian) the first ten were incorporated in the 1645 *Poems of Mr John Milton*, while the Restoration era edition, *Poems &c upon Several Occasions* (1673) printed an additional nine, omitting the fifteenth, sixteenth, seventeenth and twenty-second of the sonnets, which would have been unwise to publish in the new political environment. Milton's working literary papers (Trinity College, Cambridge, MS R.3.4), which contain some autograph versions of sonnets, can be used to supplement the printed record. But some sonnets were printed in other volumes, and in his own time and after, Milton was primarily a print author.

By the end of the seventeenth century, however, Milton's form seemed too small to be suitable for public matters. Samuel Johnson quipped that Milton 'was a genius that could cut a Colossus from a rock; but could not carve heads upon cherry-stones'.[14] Alexander Pope also mocked sonneteers in *An Essay on Criticism*, though he composed a 'curtal' 'Sonnet Written upon Occasion of the Plague, and found on a Glass-Window at Chalfont (In imitation of Milton)', which was published in the 1738 edition of Milton's works.[15] As the new culture of feeling of early Romanticism slowly returned the sonnet to literary fashion in the second part of the eighteenth century, however, the sonnet also reacquired an expanded public role thanks to increasing print publication, commercial newspapers and the gradual rise of a reading public. By the latter years of the eighteenth century, not only were volumes of sonnets being published and widely read, but sonnets were appearing in new places: novels, magazines and pamphlets. Ann Radcliffe, the best-selling English novelist of the 1790s, interspersed her Gothic tales with poetry, including several sonnet forms in her novel *The Mysteries of Udolpho, A Romance* (1794). Sonnets were also ideally suited for publication in the newspapers and magazines of these new print cultures. Its shortness enabled the sonnet to be a useful space-filler within the formatting styles and typesetting of the typical newspaper. But the revival in the sonnet's fortunes on both sides of the Atlantic was also helped by authors wanting to publish in print media that would reach greater audiences than ever before, and aware that these new media would decisively influence public taste.

The speed and impact of periodical publication certainly influenced the Romantic revival of the sonnet as a form for specific occasions. Brief and expressive, sonnets encouraged composition at specific times and occasions, as the diary-entry title of Wordsworth's 'Composed Upon Westminster Bridge, Sept. 3, 1803' suggests. When published in a newspaper, the occasional sonnet could then become a new kind of political commentary. In 1816 *The Advertiser* published Wordsworth's sonnet 'September 1815' followed by the poem's appearance in his local paper, the *Westmoreland Advertiser*, the same week.[16] Since this sonnet had first been published in 1816 by the magazine *Examiner*, its repeated re-publication in such a short time shows how quickly the political sonnet could now reach a broad and non-metropolitan audience.

This ability to spread poetry rapidly appealed to radicals like Leigh Hunt and his brother John, who in 1808 founded and edited the weekly *Examiner* as a venue of both verse and political commentary by members of their circle. John Keats's first published poem, a sonnet 'To Solitude', appeared in the *Examiner* in 1816, with most of his sonnets appearing between 1816 and 1817, including 'On First Looking into Chapman's Homer' in a consideration of promising new poets. The editors commended Keats, commenting that his experimentation was 'incorrect rhyme, which might easily be altered, but which shall serve in the mean time as a peace-offering to the rhyming critics'.[17] This rapid succession of public praise and criticism signifies a shift from the more intimate exchanges of sonnet composition and manuscript circulation amongst Hunt's circle. Sonnets were still exchanged as autographs in books and as drafts in letters, but their authors were now aiming toward print. Knowing they would be overheard, poets also wrote with a stronger sense of their public role, and the sonnet was developing into a convention of intimacy between the poem and its audience.

Coleridge had noticed this trend early on, when he followed his 1796 collection *Sonnets from Various Authors* by publishing three satirical poems, 'Sonnets, Attempted in the Manner of "Contemporary Writers"', in the *Monthly Magazine* in 1797, signing them 'Nehemiah Higginbottom'. He later described how his intention in this prank had been to expose 'three sins of poetry, one or the other of which is the most likely to beset a young writer', including a 'spirit of doleful egotism', 'low creeping language and thoughts, under the pretense of simplicity', and 'the indiscriminate use of elaborate and swelling language and imagery'.[18] Despite the ironic humour, these poems were serious creative-writing criticism for a form whose rapid increase in publication, Coleridge feared, was having a dubious effect on its authors' emotional sincerity.

Within the Hunt circle, however, publication spurred poets on to real heights. Private competitions between poets to write sonnets on a given subject became an opportunity for public votes on their skill, as when, in 1817, Hunt and Keats challenged each other to a sonnet writing contest on the subject 'the Grasshopper and Cricket', the poems appearing together in the *Examiner* in September 1817 (Hunt won by 612 to 201 votes). Shelley's sonnet 'Ozymandias', which appeared in the *Examiner* in 1818, was written in a competition with his friend Horace Smith after several visits to the British Museum to see ancient Egyptian exhibits, Smith's sonnet appearing a few weeks later. Both sonnets draw attention to Ozymandias' claim to immortality engraved on the statue's ruined pedestal. Shelley's sonnet presents Ozymandias' words as direct speech, 'Look on my works, ye Mighty, and despair!', followed with the comment 'Nothing beside remains ...', and the contrast in register lends an ironic tinge to the idea of the poem achieving immortality through print publication.

The editors' comments about Keats's 'incorrect' rhyme, however, also show how much the ideal of a correct sonnet form now involved displaced anxieties about politeness, class and nationhood, because the sonnets published in periodicals could be read and judged by so many. Keats expressed his concern with the form's potential in his sonnet, 'If by dull rhymes our English must be chained', enclosed within a letter written in May 1818 to George and Georgiana Keats. He prefaced it by remarking that 'I have been endeavouring to discover a better Sonnet Stanza than we have. The legitimate ... appears too elegiac – and the couplet at the end of it has seldom a pleasing effect – I do not pretend to have succeeded – It will explain itself –'.[19] New expression required new laws, even if this meant going beyond the rules of Petrarch or Shakespeare. Although this debate was ostensibly an aesthetic one, there had been an underlying sense of anxiety in England since the beginning of the sonnet revival about its suitability as a representative form for English poetry. Its Italian origin created much public criticism from conservatives interested in maintaining English decorum, to the point of attacking the form itself. The satirical essay 'Sonnettomania' in the *New Monthly Magazine* (1821) scathingly attacked the fashion for sonnet writing, criticism and competitions as a compulsion and a disease, a non-English 'contamination' of the nation: 'Wherever bred or born, we learn that the ravenous creature, in the early period of modern times, descended into the fertile plains of Italy, and, with a very fastidious taste, that has not been its subsequent characteristic, bit the choicest spirits of that enthusiastic land.'[20] Hunt's later 'Essay on the Cultivation, History and Varieties of the Species of Poem Called the Sonnet', on the other hand, declared that while the sonnet should retain the musicality and form of its Italian origins, it was flexible and detached enough to handle any mood: 'You can make love in a sonnet, you can laugh in a sonnet, you can lament in it, can narrate or describe, can rebuke, can admire, can pray.'[21]

That word 'cultivation' in Hunt's title acknowledges the new confidence about the home-grown sonnets of the Romantic sonnet revival, and it anticipates the civilizing mission the sonnet would increasingly assume. English literature and poetry were distributed throughout Britain and the imperial dominions, aided by the rise of literacy and education: the English curriculum began its development as part of imperial policy, with the passing of Lord Macaulay's memorandum on Indian education in 1835 recommending 'imparting to the native population a knowledge of English literature and science through the medium of English language'.[22] Educational democratization in Britain led to the establishment of Circulating Libraries, and the commercial publishing industry was bolstered by a growing world educational market: texts of the emerging literary canon, including Shakespeare's plays and poems, the poetry of Milton and that of the Romantic poets, led to the production of cheap, accessible books such as the 'shilling Shakespeare' produced in the 1860s. In a less consciously reformist way, sonnets also began to appear in the greetings cards and valentines that became enormously popular with the development of the penny post. As the sonnet became more a cultural model for poetry itself, enormous volumes of sonnets were produced by metropolitan publishing houses and distributed throughout the British Empire and America, anthologizing different sonnet writers and accompanying each one with an essay on the form. Shakespeare's Sonnets and those of Milton, Wordsworth and Shelley were constantly in print. While other forms of poetry were published, of course, the frequent appearance of English sonnet collections for readers and students throughout the British Empire with their focus on the sonnet as the epitome of English poetic form reflects a new confidence in the dominance of English national identity. William Sharp's introduction to *Sonnets of the Nineteenth Century* (1886) – published by the Walter Scott Publishing Company with offices in London, New York and Melbourne – asserts that 'Italy herself cannot present a finer body of pure poetry in the mould of this form than is to be found in the collective sonnets of these great English writers.' Their poems, he adds, reflect the 'noblest morality'.[23] The influence of Matthew Arnold's ideas on the role of English education for civic improvement is evident in this emphasis on the self-discipline required in the composition and reading of the sonnet. Sir Arthur Quiller-Couch's anthology *English Sonnets* (1897) argues that 'these English experimenters, while constant to the Petrarcan tradition ... allowed themselves a licence of innovation which gradually evolved a type so unlike the Petrarcan that some critics have believed it a plant of independent growth, indigenous to our island',[24] and hopes 'that a small volume containing specimens of the best English sonnet-writing of the past will provide the reader with a corrective and a touch-stone of taste'.[25]

The cultural overtones of the sonnet, however, were in turn affected by new developments in print media. As photographs began to appear in newspapers and magazines, so the sonnet began to play a role in contributing to the rapid construction of cultural memory. 'The Sonnet' (1873), an essay by William Davies in the British literary journal *Quarterly Review*, drew attention to the form's capacity to capture moments, incidents, thoughts and feelings with accuracy and brevity – a quality that links the sonnet, as it appeared on print pages of newspapers and magazines and the way it was received by the audience, to the photograph. The small, cheap book *Sonnets on the War* by Alexander Smith and Sydney Dobell, published in 1855, documents the contemporary events of the Crimea. Influenced by the swift publication in the *Examiner* of Tennyson's 'The Charge of the Light Brigade', these sonnets memorialized the war for readers, but their emphasis on individual participants and the 'snapshot' effect of brevity and voice gave private soldiers' feelings far more attention than Tennyson's painful but patriotic poem had done.[26]

Other sonnets became public proclamations, in keeping with the opening lines of Dante Gabriel Rossetti's 'Introductory Sonnet' to *The House of Life* (1870–81), which declare 'A Sonnet is a moment's monument, / Memorial from the Soul's eternity / To one dead, deathless hour ...'. 'The New Colossus' (1883) written originally for a fundraising literary auction by Emma Lazarus, a New Yorker of Portuguese Jewish descent who fought for refugee rights, was later engraved on a plaque at the base of the Statue of Liberty at the entrance to New York Harbor. Lazarus's poem echoes the direct speech of Shelley's 'Ozymandias' but here, in the context of the New World, Liberty's words rebuke the immortal power Ozymandias had claimed: '"Keep, ancient lands, your storied pomp!" cries she / With silent lips, "Give me your tired, your poor, / Your huddled masses yearning to breathe free"'.[27] Any tinge of irony in Shelley's sonnet is extinguished in this public statement of hopeful idealism. Sonnets could also gain a new public role through appealing to different audiences. The Jamaican Communist Claude McKay originally wrote 'If We Must Die' in response to race riots in Harlem and elsewhere during 1919 ('If we must die, let it not be like hogs / Hunted and penned in an inglorious spot'). But twenty years later, Churchill cited the poem to mobilize public sentiment to enter the Second World War.[28] His adaptation blended the racial defiance of McKay's protest with Rupert Brooke's patriotic 'The Soldier' (originally titled 'The Recruit'), from his sonnet sequence 1914, which had been read on 4 April 1915 by Dean Inge of St Paul's Cathedral as part of his Easter Sunday sermon, and published with the sermon in The Times the next day.

The sonnet on screen

Throughout the twentieth century and into the twenty-first century, public readership for print poetry has generally declined, although poetry continues to be published in literary periodicals, or the counter-public sphere of the modernist 'little magazines'. Yet sonnets continue to appear within film and television media, transforming the ways in which audiences understand them. The influence of poetry on the aesthetics of film was established with the Soviet director Sergei Eisenstein's interest in using effects of imagery and movement in Milton's Paradise Lost in his development of film's visual language, especially the use of montage and juxtaposition. It has been suggested that Milton's sonnet 'On the Late Massacre in Piedmont' (1655) could well have influenced Eisenstein's 1925 film Battleship Potemkin in the film's visual dramatization of the Odessa Steps massacre during the Russian Revolution of 1905.[29] In the film, the people of Odessa parallel Milton's 'slaughter'd saints' massacred by the Piedmontese, French and Irish forces on 24 April 1655. Scenes common to both the film and the text are found in the groans of the victims, rendered visually in the silent film, and in Milton's horrific image in the lines 'Slain by the bloody Piedmontese that roll'd / Mother with Infant down the Rocks', which are expanded in time and through repeated interpretive shots to achieve maximum impact. Eisenstein presents a long sequence of montages showing, firstly, a mother carrying her dead child and pleading for mercy and, secondly, a baby in its pram rolling very slowly down the steps, achieving through what Arthur Quiller-Couch termed this sonnet's 'noble impetuous Miltonic movement' a transliteration from the print medium into the medium of film.[30]

The verbal quotation of fragments of lyric poetry, including sonnets, in films has served to bring particular poems into public consciousness, and often publishers follow suit, bringing out publications of poems linked to film releases. Film makers use poetry within scripts for emotive effect, for characterization and to render historical accuracy. In Ang Lee's 1995 film adaptation of Jane Austen's *Sense and Sensibility*, readings of lines from Shakespeare's Sonnet 116 symbolize the characters' different understandings of love and underscore the novel's critique of early-nineteenth-century Romantic 'sensibility'. Shakespeare's sonnet becomes symbolic of Jane Austen's rendering of both 'sensibility' and 'sense' in its repeated appearances in the narrative: Marianne Dashwood (Kate Winslet) criticizes Edward Ferrars (Hugh Grant) for his clumsy reading of Cowper, which reflects his particular character, while Marianne and her suitor John Willoughby (Greg Wise) prefer Shakespeare's sonnet of love's constancy. But Marianne is also drawn to correct Willoughby's recitation of the poem, not for his awkwardness but for reciting an incorrect word. The Dashwoods value fine recitation and appreciate poetry, while Willoughby's emotional inattentiveness is signified by his inability to recognize the line's missing stress when he substitutes 'storms' for the correct 'tempests' in the poem. The irony is enhanced by Willoughby's proffered gift of a miniature pocket volume of Shakespeare's Sonnets to Marianne, the tiny size of which unwittingly predicts his affection's ultimately minor stature. When Marianne later discovers the less attractive but more reliable Colonel Brandon (Alan Rickman) in a scene close to the end of the film, the audience overhears him reading to her from the same sonnet, this time in a volume of regular size. Jane Austen did not refer to Shakespeare in her novel, yet the film accurately presents the context of the sonnet's distribution and popularity during the period through the additional inclusion in the scripted dialogue of the 1833 sonnet 'Is love a fancy, or a feeling?' written by Hartley Coleridge, son of Samuel Taylor Coleridge, ('Is love a fancy, or a feeling? No, / It is immortal as immaculate Truth'). Hartley Coleridge's sonnets were greatly admired in his lifetime (1796–1849), though Austen could not have read this sonnet, which was published after her death. For the film's modern audience, the sonnet's precision and formality, and the dexterity that a sincere performance requires, become an ideal symbol of Austen's culture, where marriage should be both pre-arranged and desired.

A quite different example of film media's use of Shakespeare's Sonnets to represent contemporary love is Derek Jarman's non-realistic film *The Angelic Conversation* (1985), made at the beginning of the urban homosexual AIDS crisis. The film is an exploration of homoerotic love, composed as a collage of fragmented images, music, sound and voice-over readings from

Shakespeare's Sonnets by Judi Dench. Its focus is on the ethics of homo-eroticism, signalled by the opening reading from 'Sonnet 151', 'Love is too young to know what conscience is'.[31] Jarman's film is experimental, aimed at a niche audience, and can queer *the* symbol of British cultural author-ity with relative confidence. When Shakespeare's Sonnets appear in popu-lar television series, however, their high-cultural status makes them more suspicious. One example is in *Star Trek: The Next Generation* (Season 5, Episode 21) titled 'The Perfect Mate', first broadcast in 1992. In this epi-sode, Shakespeare is referred to as a valuable book kept in a museum-quality glass case, and Shakespeare as an 'idea' is associated with the intelligent, well-read woman Kamala, who is a foreign influence on the masculine star-ship *Enterprise* and threatens their mission by attempting to 'bond' with the Captain. Paraphrasing Sonnet 127, Kamala ambiguously refers to herself as Shakespeare's 'Dark Lady', displacing her value as intelligent and sexu-ally attractive with a devalued 'dark' female power.[32] The introduction of Shakespeare's Sonnets to signify romantic love associated with a threatening feminine appears again in the episode of the third series of the revived *Doctor Who*, 'The Shakespeare Code', first broadcast on BBC 1 in April 2007, in which the Doctor (David Tennant) and Martha Jones (Freema Agyeman) travel to 1599 to meet William Shakespeare. *Doctor Who*'s brilliance is compared with Shakespeare's when the Doctor pronounces lines from the plays Shakespeare has not yet written, making him both Shakespeare's competitor and his muse. Sonnet 127 is again referenced: Shakespeare is attracted to Martha and writes a 'sonnet for my dark lady', yet the poem he recites is Sonnet 18 ('Shall I compare thee to a summer's day'), not one of the 'Dark Lady' sonnets (Sonnets 127–54) but likely to be one of Shakespeare's homoerotic poems. This elision of the homoerotic nature of the sonnets has the effect of evading any notion of sexual transgression in Shakespeare's Sonnets for a popular audience. Science fiction culture, while it respects Shakespeare as a reference, must always be shown to be more advanced and technologically more powerful than literary culture alone. Furthermore, the masculine dominance of the science fiction genre in these televisual medium examples seems to outweigh even the most attractive romantic love and, by implication, feminine power. In this context, the Shakespearean sonnet, as a popular emblem of romantic love, becomes a site of contestation between masculine power and feminine romance.

Visual media and film quotations of sonnets and poetry are one form of distribution. But the great recent change in poetry has been for poets to use technology to disseminate their work. CD-ROM technology allows inex-pensive or free audio dissemination of oral poetry, while digital e-poetry is created using combined visual images, sound, animation and hypertext links.

The Internet creates countless venues for the dissemination of contemporary writing, and blogs set up by poets both communicate and interlink their own work with others.[33] It also provides opportunities for collaborative composition reminiscent of Renaissance manuscript sharing: 'Intertidal: A Collaborative Crown of Sonnets' (2007) was written by seven poets over several months in an email correspondence and published as one work by all the poets in the print journal *Prairie Schooner*.[34] Rather than utterly changing the use of the sonnet form, or the way sonnets are read, the new media sometimes reanimate older cultural conditions. The surge in online poetry allowed by the Internet's accessibility also creates problems of quality, plagiarism and copyright not unlike those presented by the rise of print in Elizabethan times, or the late Romantic anxieties about 'sonnettomania'. While the period from the Renaissance to the twenty-first century is marked by astounding changes in the composition and distribution of poetry, the sonnet has proved extraordinarily resilient, and as the means of mass communication accelerate, it has always found new ways of speaking.

Notes

1 In William Shakespeare, *The Complete Sonnets and Poems*, ed. Colin Burrow (Oxford: Oxford University Press, 2002), p. 98.
2 See Elizabeth Heale, '"Desiring Women Writing": Female Voices and Courtly "Balets" in Some Early Tudor Manuscript Albums', in Victoria E. Burke and Jonathan Gibson, eds., *Early Modern Women's Manuscript Writing* (Aldershot: Ashgate, 2004), pp. 9–31.
3 See Ruth Hughey, ed., *The Arundel Harington Manuscript of Tudor Poetry*, 2 vols. (Columbus: Ohio State University Press, 1960).
4 *Ibid.*, Vol. I, p. 257.
5 See Robert Sidney, *The Poems of Robert Sidney*, ed. P. J. Croft (Oxford: Oxford University Press, 1984).
6 See J. W. Saunders, '"The Stigma of Print": A Note on the Social Bases of Tudor Poetry', *Essays in Criticism* 1 (1951), 139–64.
7 See Richard Helgerson, *Self-Crowned Laureates: Spenser, Jonson, Milton and the Literary System* (Berkeley: University of California Press, 1983).
8 See Arthur F. Marotti, 'Shakespeare's Sonnets and the Manuscript Circulation of Texts in Early Modern England', in Michael Schoenfeldt, ed., *A Companion to Shakespeare's Sonnets* (Oxford: Blackwell, 2007), pp. 185–203.
9 Brian Vickers, *Shakespeare, A Lover's Complaint, and John Davies of Hereford* (Cambridge: Cambridge University Press, 2007).
10 In William Shakespeare, *Shakespeare's Sonnets*, ed. Katherine Duncan-Jones (London: Arden Shakespeare, 2004), p. 69.
11 See Arthur F. Marotti, 'Shakespeare's Sonnets as Literary Property', in Elizabeth D. Harvey and Katharine Eisaman Maus *Soliciting Interpretation: Literary Theory and Seventeenth-Century English Poetry*, eds., (Chicago: University of Chicago Press, 1990), pp. 158–63.

12 William Alabaster, *The Sonnets of William Alabaster*, eds. Graham Story and Helen Gardner (Oxford: Clarendon Press, 1959).

13 Shakespeare, *Shakespeare's Sonnets*, pp. 70–1.

14 James Boswell, *Life of Johnson* (Oxford: Oxford University Press, 1965), p. 1301.

15 Alexander Pope, *The Poems of Alexander Pope*, ed. John Butt (New Haven: Yale University Press, 1963), pp. 826–7.

16 Duncan Wu, 'Wordworth and the *Westmoreland Advertiser*', *Notes and Queries* 43:4 (1996), 420–1.

17 *Examiner* (1 December 1816).

18 Samuel Taylor Coleridge, *Biographia Literaria* (1817), ed. George Watson (London: Dent, 1965), pp. 14–15.

19 John Keats, *The Letters of John Keats*, ed. Maurice B. Forman, 3rd edn (London: Oxford University Press, 1947), p. 342.

20 Anon., 'Sonnettomania', *The New Monthly Magazine and Literary Journal* 1 (1821), 644–8 (p. 644).

21 Martin Kallich, Jack Gray and Robert Rodney, eds., *A Book of the Sonnet: Poems and Criticism* (New York: Twayne, 1973), p. 137.

22 Janet Batsleer, ed., *Rewriting English: Cultural Politics of Gender and Class* (London: Methuen, 1985), p. 23.

23 William Sharp, ed., *Sonnets of the Nineteenth Century* (London and Felling: Walter Scott, 1886), pp. lxxii, lxxxii.

24 Arthur T. Quiller-Couch, ed., 'Introduction', in *English Sonnets* (London: Chapman and Hall, 1897), pp. x–xi.

25 *Ibid.*, p. xx.

26 See Natalie M. Houston, 'Reading the Victorian Souvenir: Sonnets and Photographs of the Crimean War', *Yale Journal of Criticism* 14 (2001), 353–83.

27 Phillis Levin, ed., *The Penguin Book of the Sonnet: 500 Years of a Classic Tradition in English* (New York: Penguin, 2001), p. lxvi.

28 James Giles, *Claude McKay* (Boston: Twayne, 1976), p. 41.

29 See Sidney Gottlieb, 'Milton's "On the Late Massacre in Piedmont" and Eisenstein's *Potemkin*', *Milton Quarterly* 19:2 (1985), 38–42.

30 Quiller-Couch, *English Sonnets*, p. xv.

31 Candace Vogler, 'Fourteen Sonnets for an Epidemic: Derek Jarman's *The Angelic Conversation*', *Public Culture* 18:1 (2006), 23–51.

32 Emily Hegarty, 'Some Suspect of III: Shakespeare's Sonnets and "The Perfect Mate"', *Extrapolation* 36:1 (1995), 55–64.

33 Craig Teicher, 'Poetry Off the Books', *Publishers Weekly* (10 April 2006), 22–5.

34 Judith Barrington, Annie Finch, Julie Kane *et al.*, 'Intertidal: A Collaborative Crown of Sonnets', *Prairie Schooner* 81:2 (2007), 116–20.

5

WILLIAM J. KENNEDY

European beginnings and transmissions: Dante, Petrarch and the sonnet sequence

Within the relatively short span of 100 years, southern Italian poets developed the enduring structural properties of sonnet form, northern Italian poets appropriated their invention and expanded its range, and two particular poets with vastly different outlooks and agendas – Dante and Petrarch – exploited its potentials with a lasting impact upon western literature. During these years, the conventional topics addressed by the sonnet form expanded from guileful entreaties of sexual seduction to more complex expressions of tangled erotic yearning, tumultuous sexual impulse and exalted amatory devotion, in associated ways laden with statements of religious conversion, philosophical conviction, political sentiment and even scientific insight. With so many possibilities at hand, the sonnet form carried within it seeds of experiment among poets old and young, male and female, amateur and professional. My chapter will explore the sonnet's early development from its invention in the thirteenth century to its dissemination throughout Europe in the sixteenth century. It will emphasize the sonnet's propensity for expressing self-awareness; for affirming local, communal and emergently national sentiment; and for enabling poets to chart a career path that intersects with public as well as private ambitions.

Sicilian origins (c. 1220–1250)

The sonnet form originated almost certainly at the Sicilian court of Emperor Frederick II (1194–1250), and its originator there was – again almost certainly – an administrative notary from Apulia named Giacomo da Lentini (fl. 1220–40).[1] Frederick, son of the Hohenstaufen Emperor Henry VI and Queen Constance of Sicily, became King of Sicily in 1198, King of Germany and Italy in 1212, and Holy Roman Emperor in 1220. His court at Palermo, attended by pre-eminent lawyers, jurists, counsellors, notaries and physicians, excelled as a centre of literary, artistic and scientific activity. Highplaced members of the imperial retinue (including the emperor himself and

84

his minister, private secretary and chief counsellor Pier delle Vigne) composed poetry in the Italo-Romance Sicilian dialect, drawing upon the metrical forms, rhetorical tropes and prevailing styles of troubadour love lyrics composed in Provence from the late eleventh century.[2] The troubadour *cansó* (an extended ode in five or more stanzas with an intricate and repeated rhyme scheme), *tensó* (a poetic debate between two interlocutors in alternating groups of stanzas) and *balada* (a dance song with refrains) became models for Sicilian – and later Tuscan – *canzone*, *tenzone* and *ballata*. The vocabulary of Provençal courtly love such as *joi* ('erotic fulfilment'), *cortezia* ('elevated courtliness') and *pretz* ('esteem') became Italianized as *gioia*, *cortesia* and *pregio*. Above all, the dominant concerns of love poetry mingled with those of moral, political and didactic verse.

By the time Giacomo emerged as a gifted poet, an eleven-syllable (*endecasillabo*) line had become the standard unit of Italian verse. In effect this line represents an historical process of fusion and dispersion, where seven-syllable (*settenario*) and five-syllable (*quinario*) lines of early Italian folk poetry join to form a single line of verse, losing a syllable through contraction or elision at its point of juncture. Giacomo's sonnets enact a similar process in terms of stanzaic combinations, where a unit of eight lines (the octave) joins with another stanzaic unit of six lines (the sestet), initiating a subtle change of tone, mood or attitude at its point of fusion. The sonnet beginning 'Per sofrenza si vince gran vettoria' ('A great victory is won through patience'), for example, plays on the double meaning of the word *sofrenza*: 'patience' and 'suffering'. The former meaning dominates the octave with the biblical example of Job. In the sestet, however, the speaker applies to his amatory woe the second meaning of 'suffering', now mixed with a *conforte grande* ('great comfort').

The bipartite structure crafted by Giacomo in turn generates two competing hypotheses about the invention of the sonnet.[3] One posits that an already familiar form – the *strambotto*, consisting of eight eleven-syllable lines with an alternating *ab* rhyme – was augmented by a contrasting but abbreviated second stanza consisting of six lines with a double *cde* rhyme. An extension of this hypothesis suggests that the asymmetrical relation of eight to six lines (further complicated by the sonnet's bipartite *ab cde* rhyme scheme, subdividing the poem into a relation of eight to six lines distributed as four alternating couplets to two symmetrical tercets) evinces mystical proportions of Pythagorean or Platonic musical number theory. But rather than suggesting any musical accompaniment, the word *sonetto* ('little sound') might instead imply a written or spoken presentation, emphasizing the form's propensity toward introspective, dialectical, meditative monologue. A different account posits that the sonnet originated as simply a single free-standing stanza from the Provençal-inspired *canzone* 'ode' form. The latter already supplied several internal divisions marked by rhyme and evolving argument, subdividing each stanza into an initial *fronte* ('beginning'), which consists of two *piedi* ('standing feet') and a shorter *sirima* ('wrap-up'), which consists of two *volte* ('turns'). An extension of this hypothesis suggests that several sonnets linked in a series or sequence might constitute an extended ode. In practice, however, most sonnets end with firm periods that obstruct connections with succeeding poems.

Consequently, the matter of a genuinely coherent sequence of sonnets is a more doubtful issue than it might seem, especially in poetic collections before Dante's *Vita nuova*. Many of Giacomo's sonnets are loosely related to one another in thematic terms (the beloved dominates the lover; she possesses beauty, virtue and perfection that are by turns angelic, rare and gem-like; she brings the lover both life-giving joy and mortal suffering). Three of these sonnets belong to two *tenzoni* ('debates') – the first with an unnamed 'Abbot of Tivoli', the second with Jacopo Mostacci and Pier delle Vigne – on the topic of defining Love. But in terms of a dramatic sequence, none of the extant Sicilian sonnets narrates or even suggests any sequential ordering. Still, the fourteen-line sonnet as produced at Frederick's Sicilian court represents a genuinely new and distinctively Italian form unprecedented in Provençal verse. As such, by mid century it emerges in central and northern Italy as well.

The sonnet form migrates north (1250–1290)

So strong was the prestige of troubadour models in northern Italy, that poets such as Sordello of Goito (*fl.* 1220–69) near Mantua and Lanfranco Cicala of Genoa (1234–69) had relinquished their local dialects to write poetry in the language of Provence. The importation of the Sicilian style to northern Italy brought with it Provençal-based neologisms coined at Frederick's court, along with some linguistic features native to Sicily, such as nouns ending in *-i* and *-u* rather than *-e* and *-o*, and verbs ending in *-io* and *-ia* rather than *-o* and *-e*. Occasionally used to expand possibilities of internal and end-line rhyme, these features generate a Siculo-Tuscan or Siculo-Bolognese poetic idiom. Its advent occurred largely in Guelf (rather than in opposing Ghibelline) municipalities such as Lucca, Arezzo, Florence and Bologna, where recent social divisions prompted merchant and banker magnates to emulate the cultural institutions of Frederick's southern kingdom.[4] The political alignments begotten of these divisions play significant roles in the development of the sonnet.

Credit for introducing the Sicilian mode into Tuscany goes to Bonagiunta Orbicciani, a judge and notary in Lucca (*fl.* 1242–67), who circulated some twenty sonnets and eleven *canzoni*, several in direct imitation of Giacomo and his contemporaries.[5] Bonagiunta writes of love as the 'candela che s'aprende senza foco' ('candle that is lit without a fire'), and he punctuates his verse with some sententious moral commentary in the Provençal manner, but he also finds fault with contemporary poets such as the Bolognese Guido Guinizelli (see below), who introduced *sottigliansa* ('intellectual subtleties') and *iscura parlatura* ('obscure discourse') into his verse. At the same time, Bonagiunta finds fault with poets such as the widely influential Guittone d'Arezzo (see below) for using facile puns, surface wit and intricate rhyme patterns. Bonagiunta's engagement with the serious representation of love, with questions of poetic form and with the sonnet in particular proved decisive for the new form among amateur poets within prosperous commercial classes.

The cultural environment in Florence that prompted Guido Cavalcanti and Dante Alighieri to produce their own sonnets was particularly varied. It runs a gamut from the prolific Chiaro Davanzati, who composed 61 *canzoni* and 122 sonnets, with a notable penchant for using animal imagery to represent the trials of love, to the anonymous 'Compiuta Donzella' ('Accomplished Young Woman'), who composed several on her father's cruelty in forcing her into an arranged marriage.[6] Women's voices, as it happens, emerge frequently in late-thirteenth-century Florentine poetry, but usually as ventriloquized by male poets to represent speakers betrayed by the masculinist rhetoric of courtly love. Often they accentuate poems composed in highly conventional *tenzoni* among poets from various political factions in the strife-torn Guelf-against-Ghibelline environment. Their ritualized exchange fosters a social bond, defusing their antagonisms and promoting their capacity for non-violent debate. Implicit in such an enactment, of course, is the risk of insincerity, cynical one-upmanship and outright hypocrisy. Monte Andrea, a Guelf banker who participated in many *tenzoni*, circulated 11 *canzoni* and 112 sonnets.[7] Monte's hyperbole, his frank treatment of love as hedonistic and his disturbingly materialistic emphasis on the pleasures of wealth constitute a challenge for Cavalcanti and Dante to represent a more elevated, nuanced and philosophical view of these themes.[8]

No less a challenge for Cavalcanti and Dante – again by contrast and antithesis – were the examples of two widely disseminated poets who wrote at least partly in turbulent Bologna. I have already mentioned Bonagiunta's criticism of Guido Guinizelli and Guittone d'Arezzo – both of them flourishing between 1260 and 1276 – for their opposing tendencies toward philosophical abstraction and superficial religiosity. Guinizelli, a native of Emilia-Romagna, and Guittone, a Guelf exile from Arezzo – and apparently unwelcome in Florence too – encountered each other in Bologna, where they came to represent divergent factions in that city's political struggles. Guinizelli, a university-educated member of the upwardly mobile notary profession, promoted the values of consensual republican government.[9] Guittone, an ideologue for the controlling magnates, promoted social and cultural interests of the aristocratic class. In 1265 he underwent a religious conversion and joined the lay order of Jovial Friars, which had been instrumental in repressing popular and progressive political movements.[10] For the subsequent bulk of his poetry, which moralizes upon his conversion in sententious tones, Guittone became the most influential poet in northern Italy before Dante.

Guinizelli, by contrast, refuses to define sacred and profane love as mutually exclusive. Appealing to a subtle Augustinian philosophical sense of love as a continuum from human to divine, he treats the amatory situation as an inward and high-mindedly ethical event, connected with the larger process of order and purpose in God's universe. His sonnet 'I' vo' del ver la mia donna laudare' ('I wish to praise my lady in all truth'), for example, concludes its list of the beloved's virtues with an observation that 'null'om pò mal pensar fin che la vede' ('no man can think evil from the time he has seen her'). Despite its brevity, Guinizelli's oeuvre of fifteen sonnets and five *canzoni* exercised an indelible effect on poets who followed him.

A few years older than Dante, Guido Cavalcanti (*fl.* 1275–85) enthusiastically embraced the philosophical seriousness of Guinizelli and carried it to highly pressured (and sometimes obscure) levels of meaning and expression.[11] His thirty-three sonnets, two *canzoni* and seventeen other lyric poems dramatize a diffuse, ever mobile range of erotic tones, moods and attitudes associated with the speaking voice of a distinctive person. Sonnet 28, with its playful repetition of *spirito* or its variants in each line, suggests at once a parody of Bonagiunta's and Guittone's rhetorical facility, as well as a self-parody of Cavalcanti's psycho-physiology and its Aristotelean-Thomistic framework. So the octave opens with a rarefied variant on the conventional Ovidian attack of love through the eyes:

> Pegli occhi fere un spirito sottile,
> che fa 'n la mente spirito destare,
> dal qual si move spirito d'amare,
> ch'ogn'altro spiritel face gentile.

> Through the eyes strikes a delicate spirit
> That awakens a spirit in the mind,
> From which stirs the spirit of loving
> That ennobles every other little spirit.

And so the sestet concludes with an animated effusion of spirit that affects both lover and beloved in their material senses:

> Lo quale spiritel spiriti piove,
> ché di ciascuno spirit' ha la chiave,
> per forza d'uno spirito che 'l vede.

> This little spirit rains spirits,
> For it has the key to each spirit
> By virtue of a spirit that sees.

Like his predecessors, Cavalcanti blends Latinisms, Gallicisms, Provençalisms and Sicilian turns of phrase, modulating them in registers of high, middle and low style as the dramatic situation warrants. But more than any of them, he brings to his verse a sense of intelligence, wit and urbane sophistication. It remained for Dante to transmute this variety into yet more complex lyric and philosophical sonnet forms.

Dante Alighieri (1265–1321)

About two years into his political exile, mandated by the Black faction of his own Guelf party, Dante began writing a treatise on language and vernacular eloquence, *De vulgari eloquentia* (1302–4). This treatise offers insights into its author's history and theory of the sonnet form less than a century after its debut. In 1:10 of his work, Dante judges the Italian vernacular capable of yielding poetry 'more sweetly and subtly' than other Romance languages, despite its geographical distribution into fourteen major dialects with countless local variants.[12] Its fragmentation reflects the social and political disarray of the Italian peninsula as well. Language is the chief instrument of philosophical and scientific knowledge, of moral and legal decision-making, and of history and politics. It is also an instrument of poetic discourse that can foster cultural values, social cohesion and public progress. A capacious version of the Italian vernacular that he calls 'illustrious, cardinal, courtly and curial' (p. 41) might capitalize upon the best features of many dialects and make them common to all. Its written version would be 'illustrious' in promoting clarity; 'cardinal' in affording direction; 'courtly' in echoing the ceremonial language of a royal court that had not existed since the days of Frederick II, but whose confederated principles could unite Italy; and 'curial' in evoking the well-balanced pronouncements of honest judges and administrators. It would stringently oppose the anarchic and self-serving 'municipal' dialects of cities, hotbeds of faction and frenzy, arrogance and divisiveness, chaos and ruination. As practitioners of these latter dialects, Dante names Bonagiunta da Lucca (1:13) and Guittone d'Arezzo (1:13,

2:6). As an example of a poet who traded his rough Apulian dialect for a smoother courtly idiom, he cites Giacomo da Lentini (1:12). As examples of all-round excellence, he repeatedly cites Guido Guinizelli (1:9, 1:15, 2:5, 2:6, 2:12) and his own 'best friend', Guido Cavalcanti (1:13, 2:6, 2:12).

De vulgari eloquentia projects a pattern of earlier Italian literary history in which the sonnet occupies a dominant space beside the *canzone*. By implication, its argument evokes a specifically Italian national sentiment. Within a few years, Dante would flesh out his literary history in various cantos of the *Divina commedia*, especially in *Purgatorio* 24:49–62, where the soul of Bonagiunta da Lucca sketches a development of lyric poetry that extends from Giacomo to Guittone and is supplanted by a *dolce stil nuovo* ('sweet new style'; line 57).[13] The latter term, which Dante implicitly attributes to an historical 'school' of poets that includes Guinizelli, Cavalcanti, Lapo Gianni, Cino da Pistoia and himself, receives further elaboration in his critique of *dolci e leggiadre* ('sweet and graceful') poems of love in *Purgatorio* 26:91–132. So convincing was Dante's explanation of this seemingly orderly historical progression from Giacomo's era to his own, that it has become a staple in the history of the sonnet amongst modern literary scholars. It nonetheless requires substantial modification to accommodate Dante's own career as a sonnet writer.

The chief product of this career is his *Vita nuova*. In 1292 or a little later, the poet compiled this self-described *libello* ('little book') by selecting twenty-five sonnets, five *canzoni* and one *ballata* from a larger corpus composed earlier (some perhaps as early as 1283) about his love for Beatrice and her death at a young age in 1290. The assemblage represents Dante's effort to assert authority over his youthful work, to delimit its range of possible interpretation, and to rank the vernacular lyric and especially the sonnet on a par with the lyric poetry of classical antiquity.[14] The question of control looms large, since the circulation of poetry in the manuscript culture of the late thirteenth century all but denied individual attribution to most poets. An extant scribal compilation of 50 *canzoni* and 250 sonnets by Guittone d'Arezzo (whether by the author or by an editor in the late thirteenth or early fourteenth century) represents one of the earliest efforts to secure vernacular poetry beyond oral transmission and rise above the fragmentation of late medieval manuscript anthologies.[15] Dante follows (or, depending on the still-undetermined date of Guittone's compilation, possibly leads) in this programme. By intervening in the circulation of his written work, he assigns to it a literary rather than oral status that bears his stamp of 'authorial publication', and so marks a decisive stage in the turn of poetry from oral performance to private reading. Further, by connecting his selected poems with prose that contextualizes them in a narrative and provides interpretative clues about their divisions of thought and meaning, Dante takes charge over the reader's understanding of his lyric innovations. Finally, by populating his 'little book' with sonnets and *canzoni* (and with five times the number of sonnets than *canzoni*), Dante accords these forms supreme status in his lyric canon.

That Dante should focus on the sonnet form proves crucial to his project. From a social perspective, he and his northern Italian contemporaries were emulating the achievements of Sicilian court poets and were trying to adapt them to the entrepreneurial society of their urban city-states. The Sicilian poets had brought a genuinely Italian innovation to the vernacular lyric when they invented the sonnet form. From an intellectual perspective, the sonnet in its earliest incarnations tended to celebrate sensual, erotic and often explicitly carnal love. Dante and his particular circle of poets aspired to more ambitious themes compatible with the newly evolved philosophical, theological and scientific teaching at universities in the north. From a critical perspective, the sonnet took shape against a background of Provençal and Sicilian conventions that encouraged dialogue, debate and verbal sparring in *tenzoni* matches. Dante and his associates engaged in similar self-reflexive exercises. The development of *Vita nuova* results from a convergence of these perspectives.

Its first poem is a sonnet that addresses a readership of lovers, 'A ciascun'alma presa e gentil core' ('To every captive soul and gentle heart'), who may respond to the poet, 'in ciò che mi rescrivan suo parvente' ('so that they in return may inscribe their views') and might haplessly distort the 'true meaning' of the experience depicted (3:10–15).[16] From the outset, then, the speaker insists upon prioritizing the meaning that he attributes to his sonnet, even though he acknowledges that others might construe its formal divisions rather differently. In consequence, one of his respondents emerges as 'first among my friends' (3:14), identified in the opening line of his reply as Guido Cavalcanti, and the pair initiate an on-and-off dialogue that occupies much of the ensuing prose narrative. At 8:1, a female companion of the beloved Beatrice dies, and the speaker honours her with a poetic lament, 'Piangete, amanti, poi che piange Amore' ('Weep, lovers, since Love weeps'; 8:4). This sonnet, couched in the same language, form and style as those about the beloved, raises a vexing question about candour and the truth-value of poetic discourse: if Beatrice is the speaker's only beloved, how and why does he write with equal conviction and emotion about another woman – even a dead one? Put another way, the question asks how readers might trust the sincerity of sonneteers who appear capable of valorizing any experience, good or bad.

By 13:1, the speaker acknowledges that 'many and diverse thoughts' assail him, so that his own verse generates paradoxes, ironies and competing claims:

Tutti li miei penser parlan d'Amore;
e hanno in lor sì gran varietate,
ch'altro mi fa voler sua potestate,
altro folle ragiona il suo valore.

All my thoughts speak of Love,
and they have in them such great diversity
that one makes me desire its power,
another argues its foolish worth.

The sonnet form, with its nested divisions into octaves and sestets, quatrains and tercets, manipulated in different and ever-changing directions by shifting rhyme schemes, becomes an appropriate vehicle to dramatize such *gran varietate*. Correspondingly, the poet's self-commentary on his verse becomes a way of opening up the reader's interpretation rather than closing it down to a single narrow application of meaning. 'Division is made only to open up the meaning of the thing divided' (14:13), proclaims Dante, and in so doing he empowers the reader to plumb his verse.

Despite allegiance to his 'best friend', who prompts him to express his turbulent emotions, the speaker in 20:1–4 acknowledges an entirely different poetic model:

Amore e 'l cor gentil sono una cosa,
sì come il saggio in suo dittare pone,
e così esser l'un sanza l'altro osa
com'alma razional sanza ragione.

Love and the gentle heart are one thing,
even as the sage affirms in his poem,
and so one can be without the other
as much as rational soul without reason.

This 'sage' is Guido Guinizelli, whose earlier sonnets of exalted love celebrate the experience within a physical and spiritual continuum that extends from human to divine. Dante henceforth gravitates toward Guinizelli's example. Leaving behind Cavalcanti's exasperation with love's suffering and contradictions, Dante substitutes for it an exploration of love's congruence with social, moral and spiritual ideals. In 25:1–10, he questions the conventions of rhetoric associated with love poetry among ancient classical authors, and in 26.5–7 – 'Tanto gentile e tanto onesta pare / la donna mia quand'ella altrui saluta' ('So gentle and so honest appears / my lady when she greets others') – he concludes that he might analyze his love only in a new style that accommodates 'un spirito soave pien d'amore' ('a spirit, soothing and full of love'). After affirming to Cavalcanti in 30:2 that he 'would write to him only in the vernacular', the speaker abandons the implied conversation with his 'best friend'.

Beatrice's death is announced in 28:1, and the poems that follow address her brother, a Compassionate Lady who might become a candidate for new love, some travelling pilgrims and two worthy gentle ladies, to whom he declares in his final sonnet (41:10–13) a transcendent attachment to the dead beloved:

> Oltre la spera che più larga gira
> passa 'l sospiro ch'esce del mio core:
> intelligenza nova, che l'Amore
> piangendo mette in lui, pur su lo tira.

> Beyond the sphere that circles widest
> penetrates the sigh that issues from my heart:
> a new intelligence, which Love,
> weeping, places in him, draws him ever upward.

The speaker's refusal of immediate gratification from the Compassionate Lady and his acceptance of a forever-unrequited devotion to Beatrice conclude the *Vita nuova*. As it happens, this conclusion conveys a sense of narrative form that subsequent sonnet sequences would reproduce. Petrarch in the mid fourteenth century adopts the beloved's death as an organizing principle for his *Rime sparse*, and so too do Lorenzo de' Medici in the later fifteenth century (when his mistress's passing leads him to focus his energies on civic virtue), and Vittoria Colonna and Veronica Gambara in the early sixteenth century (when their departed husbands leave them as virtuous widows). As it also happens, the great European Petrarchist collections of the mid-to-late sixteenth century project strong narrative outlines, too, though usually without the beloved's demise. But, with the partial exception of Michelangelo Buonarroti's sonnets (with echoes from the *Divina commedia* rather than from the *Vita nuova*), by the second quarter of the sixteenth century Dante's influence waned as Petrarch's grew dominant. Not until the nineteenth-century Romantic revival of Dante – even then a revival that focused on the *Divina commedia* instead of the lyric poems – would *La vita nuova* command serious attention.

Francesco Petrarca (1304–1374)

For all his independence, Dante belonged to a corporate medieval world, bound by literary, economic, political and class alliances to a circle of friends, associates and institutional bodies. Francesco Petrarca (Petrarch) worked largely outside such structures as neither a courtier like the Sicilian poets, nor a merchant-banker like most Florentine poets, nor a scholar-philosopher attached to a school or university, nor a quondam politician attached to a particular party like the pre-exilic Dante. Rather as a 'man-in-the-middle', he thought himself a professional writer adept in such genres as history, invective and epic verse, gravitating toward new divisions of labour in the worlds of scholarship, poetry, philosophy and ideas.[17] Trained for a career in law to serve at the papal court of Avignon, he abandoned that path in his early twenties in order to study Greek and especially Roman antiquity. He soon amplified this goal with a pursuit of poetry based on classical models, focused on composing *Africa*, a Latin epic in the Virgilian mode about Scipio Africanus and the Punic Wars. In his mid forties, he began compiling his *Epistolae familiares* ('Familiar Letters') in the Ciceronian mode, addressed to friends on diverse topics. Along the way he completed moral, historical and contemplative treatises, as well as a body of Latin poetry. He regarded his Italian poems – or at least professed to regard them – as trifles, comprising 6 allegorical *Trionfi* ('Triumphs') and 366 lyrics (among them 317 sonnets culled from a much larger corpus of sonnets) known alternately as *Rime sparse* ('Scattered Rhymes' – from the first line of Sonnet 1, 'Voi ch'ascoltate in rime sparse il suono' ('You who hear in scattered rhymes the sound')), or *Canzoniere* ('Song Book'), or *Rerum vulgarium fragmenta* ('Pieces Written in the Vernacular' –the Latin title of his manuscript).

Petrarch's course as an Italian poet evolved from a period before 1327 (when he claimed to have met his beloved Laura on Good Friday of that year) to the eve of his death in 1374. It encompasses countless developments in style and form, a great number of them preserved in working drafts as a record of his revisions from 1336 to 1368.[18] Not always charting a consistent direction, these drafts illuminate Petrarch as a poet of his own time, sometimes in thematic harmony with Dante and his contemporaries, sometimes in tension with them. They display, for example, standard conventions of personifying Love as a Cupid-like figure, of participating in *tenzoni* debates with his male friends, and of countenancing the trials of unrequited love with sublimated emotion. But they also document for the first time in European poetry a major author's own redactions, showing how Petrarch laboured over his craft to refine his verse, burnish its metrics, secure its syntax, sharpen its meaning. From this perspective, they foreground Petrarch's distinctive contributions to the history of the sonnet as it flourished under his later influence.

Sonnet 90, one of Petrarch's early poems, *c.* 1334–8, provides a good example of his fusion of Provençal and classical elements:

> Erano i capei d'oro a l'aura sparsi
> che 'n mille dolci nodi gli avolgea

e 'l vago lume oltra misura ardea
di quei begli occhi, ch' or ne son sì scarsi;
e 'l viso di pietosi color farsi
(non so se vero o falso) mi parea:
i' che l'esca amorosa al petto avea,
qual meraviglia se di subito arsi?

Non era l'andar suo cosa mortale
ma d'angelica forma, et le parole
sonavan altro che pur voce umana:
uno spirto celeste, un vivo sole
fu quel ch' i' vidi, et se non fosse or tale,
piaga per allentar d'arco non sana.

Her golden hair was loosed to the breeze, which was enfolding it in a thousand sweet knots, and the lovely light was burning without measure in her eyes, which are now so stingy of it; and it seemed to me (I know not whether truly or falsely) her face took on the color of pity: I, who had the tinder of love in my breast, what wonder is it if I suddenly caught fire.

Her walk was not that of a mortal thing but of some angelic form, and her words used to sound different from a merely human voice: a celestial spirit, a living sun was what I saw, and if she were not such now, a wound is not healed by the loosening of the bow.[19]

On the one hand, the poem records a memory of Laura's beauty as it once existed in the past, marking the present as a pale shadow of time gone by. On the other, it invites a response that the speaker cannot securely ground. The poem's most striking phonic effects reinforce this unsettling result with several irregular caesurae. In line 2, for example, the caesura occurs after the seventh syllable without a customary elision. The line plays on this irregularity by placing the noun *nodi* ('knots') at the point of fusion (the line's *nodo*, so to speak) uncoupling it from the verb *avolgea* ('was wrapping it up, enfolding it') as though to signal the anomaly. Several oral–aural equivocations reinforce it. For example, the vocable *or* occurs at the point of fusion in line 1 ('d'oro^a l'aura') as the first syllable of *oro* ('gold'), and again at the same point in line 4 as the adverb *or* ('now'): the beloved's young eyes have now (*or*) dimmed as has the lustre of her golden (*oro*) hair. The syllable returns in the fifth line as part of the noun *col-or* and two lines later as part of the adjective *am-or-osa*. In the poem's sestet, it resurfaces in the key word *m-or-tale* (sounding the motif of time's destructive force), in *f-or-ma* (accentuating the philosophical problem of matter and form implied in the argument) and, in the poem's penultimate line, in the adverb *or* ('now'), which reasserts the passage of time. The octave's rhyming *sparsi* (echoing the *rime sparse* of Sonnet 1), *scarsi* (signalling a diminution of the beloved's beauty), *farsi* and, in the eighth line, *arsi*, seal the poem's emphasis on the speaker's moral conflict as he burns in the flames of carnal desire.

In contrast, the sestet evokes Laura's *angelica forma* by directly summoning the spectral tone that Virgil produces when he describes Venus' appearance to Aeneas on the shores of Carthage in *Aeneid* 1:314–405. Significantly the Virgilian text dramatizes an interchange between divine illusion and human dis-illusionment as Aeneas misconstrues his mother's identity and the import of her prophecy. For Petrarch, this classical subtext heightens his speaker's uncertainty about Laura's redemptive role in his salvation, confounding her human exceptionality with the divine eminence of Virgil's Venus. Evanescent, elusive and profoundly haunting, the poem activates its verbal potency in a series of criss-crossing phonic, acoustic and rhetorical charges that accentuate its prosodic ingenuity, its figurative specificity, and the materiality of its form and style. In this respect, Petrarch recalls the technical brilliance of Cavalcanti and of the Provençal poets before him more than the relatively subdued style of Dante, and he overlays it with stylistic reminiscences drawn from classical Virgil. Associated with the sonnet form, this characteristically Petrarchan verbal dexterity would be imitated by countless poets until the seventeenth century.

A further example would be Sonnet 140 (dating from 1341–5), which dramatizes Laura's displeasure with the speaker for his boldness in approaching her. This sonnet begins by personifying Love not as a mischievous Ovidian boy-Cupid, but as a mature military commander who aggressively advertises his erotic intention:

> Amor, che nel penser mio vive et regna
> e 'l suo seggio maggior nel mio cor tene,
> talor armato ne la fronte vene;
> ivi si loca et ivi pon sua insegna.

Love, who lives and reigns in my thought and keeps his principal seat in my heart, sometimes comes forth all in armor into my forehead, and there sets up his banner.

The poem's linguistic markers impart a strangeness to the text that highlights its deliberate artifice. The contracted forms of *penser* (for *pensiero*), *cor* (for *cuore*), and *tene* and *vene* (for *tiene* and *viene*) derive from both Sicilian and archaic Tuscan dialects. The final noun *insegna* ('banner, insignia') generates an exact rhyme with the verb *'nsegna* ('teaches, instructs') assigned to the beloved in the next quatrain: 'Quella ch' amare et sofferir ne 'nsegna' ('She who teaches us to love and be patient'). Here the noun *insegna*, which refers to the lover's boldness, is undone by the verb *'nsegna*, which conveys Laura's opposition to it. As the quatrain proceeds to introduce other personifications, it blurs the action with obscure syntax: 'E vol che 'l gran desio, l'accesa spene / ragion, vergogna, et reverenza affrene' ('And she wishes that my great Desire, my kindled Hope, Reason, Shame, and Reverence might rein in'). Do Desire and Hope bridle Reason, Shame, and Reverence? Or, in a reverse construction that seems more likely, do the latter constrain the former? The verb offers no inflectional clue, as its third person singular form can refer to either compound subject. The Latinate -e marker of its subjunctive mood (rather than the grammatical -i marker of the Italian subjunctive) conveys a deliberately archaizing effect in a classical vein.

The poem's exaggerated Provençal, Sicilian and classical Latin echoes seem to parody its genre. In the first line of the sestet, Love reverts to the figure of the Ovidian boy-Cupid and absconds cowardly: 'Onde Amor paventose fugge al core' ('Wherefore Love flees terrified to my heart'). As though to mock the speaker, its last line evokes the *petite mort* ('little death') of sexual climax: 'Ché bel fin fa chi ben amando more' ('For he makes a good end who dies loving well'). Classically trained readers might associate this topos with Propertius' elegy 2:1, whose speaker praises those who 'die gloriously' as they enjoy the fruits of love. But Propertius' *bel fin* is a carnal conquest denied to Petrarch's speaker. The latter suffers sexual humiliation and, in a Christian scheme, moral defeat. So how does the sonnet conclude? Does it offer a witty riposte to sensualist love? Certainly many sixteenth-century poets would design entire sequences of sonnets to do just that.[20] Or does it instead propose a stern lesson about the delusional aftermath of love? Many commentators have claimed that it does. As a hinge between early modern and late medieval attitudes toward sexual relationships – perhaps better as a poem-in-the-middle between courtly and urbane values on the one hand and bookish and self-critical values on the other – the sonnet speaks to both sides, coercing the mutually opposed, forever competing structural divisions of its own form to express this ambivalence.

A final example illustrates Petrarch's evolving sense of imparting a structural order to his *Rime sparse*, his craftsmanship in revising the sequence to do that, and his willingness to experiment with an expansive new range of moods and tones. It is Sonnet 248, evidently composed after Laura's fatality in the Black Death of 1348 but now presaging it in the editorially re-assembled narrative. Here the speaker advises all who wish to see Laura that they should do so soon because in this world mortality vanquishes both beauty and virtue:

> Chi vuol veder quantunque po Natura
> e 'l Ciel tra noi, venga a mirar costei
> ch' è sola un sol, non pur a li occhi mei
> ma al mondo cieco che vertù non cura.

Whoever wishes to see all that Nature and Heaven can do among us, let him come gaze on her, for she alone is a sun, not merely for my eyes, but for the blind world, which does not care for virtue.

But such a bystander will quickly recognize that the poet's art proves insufficient to represent Laura's complete excellence in verse:

Allor dirà che mie rime son mute,
l'ingegno offeso dal soverchio lume.
Ma se più tarda, avrà da pianger sempre.

Then he will say that my rhymes are mute, my wit overcome by the excess of light. But if he delays too long, he shall have reason to weep forever.

The sonnet, as Petrarch inserted it into his eventual sequence around 1369, offers a sober reflection upon his moral intentions, his artistry and his paradoxical conferring of an ordered design upon his disordered *Rime sparse*. Over the next 250 years, Petrarch's poetry would attract extensive critical commentary and a great deal of poetic imitation. The rest of this chapter will cite prominent instances.

The transmission of Petrarch's sonnets in the early age of print (1471–1692)

With the advent of the first Italian printing presses in the late 1460s, Petrarch's *Rime sparse* and Dante's *Divina commedia* appeared in the new medium, the former in Venice in 1470 and the latter in Foligno in 1472.[21] Dante, it turns out, would increasingly run second to Petrarch in later years. Both authors had circulated widely in manuscript through the fifteenth century, and had attracted an impressive amount of learned commentary. Printed publication brought these commentaries into wide circulation. Slighted by the priority given to the *Rime sparse* and *Divina commedia*, the poetry of Dante's *Vita nuova* waited until 1527 to enter print. Cut loose from its author's own prose frame, its verse appeared in an anthology with poems by Guinizelli, Cavalcanti and Cino da Pistoia. Then, except for a reprint in 1576, it disappeared from view for nearly 200 years.

Meanwhile, Petrarch's fourteenth-century poetry emerged as the critical favourite. Accompanied by newer commentaries in ever-proliferating editions, the *Rime sparse* dominated the sixteenth-century Italian book market for poetry.[22] Its earliest annotated editions in print include one with glosses up to Sonnet 136 composed by the self-promoting humanist scholar Francesco Filelfo at the despotic court of Filippo Maria Visconti in Milan during the 1440s (published in Bologna in 1476); a rival edition with glosses composed before the 1440s by a Paduan judge named Antonio da Tempo (published in Venice, 1477); and a third with a continuation of Filelfo's glosses by the Veronese entrepreneur Hieronimo Squarzafico (printed in Venice, 1484). All three commentaries depict Petrarch as an expedient spokesperson for anti-papal, pro-imperial northern Italian *condottieri*, who supported him with patronage after his move from Avignon to Italy in 1353. In subsequent reprints, these commentaries were printed in tandem to project an ideological version of Petrarch congruent with early Renaissance ducal politics.

In 1501 Aldus Manutius produced in Venice an unusually careful edition of Petrarch's Italian poetry, for which he recruited the philological skills of the humanist scholar Pietro Bembo. The latter then proceeded to write a full-length critical defence of Petrarch in his *Prose della volgar lingua* ('Writing in the Vernacular'). Completed and published in 1525, this work authorizes Petrarch's composite style with its Sicilian turns of phrase and its Latin neologisms imposed upon its archaic Tuscan base as the supreme norm for poetic composition in the Italian vernacular. Bembo fortifies his argument with close analysis of the poems' syntax and semantics, juxtaposing their style against Dante's, whom he censures for his occasional descent into barbarism and vulgarity. To exemplify Petrarch's decorous *piacevolezza* ('charm') and his refined *gravità* ('seriousness'), Bembo cites the fifth verse of Sonnet 303, which evokes the sympathies of nature after Laura's death: 'Fior, frondi, erbe, ombre, antri, onde, aure soavi' ('Flowers, leaves, grass, shadows, caves, waves, gentle breezes'). In his view, this touchstone line offers a perfect clustering of 'masculine' consonants and 'feminine' vowels, with jagged sounds such as *fr*, *nd*, *rb*, *mb* and *nt* lending sharp definition to fluid diphthongs such as *io*, *au* and *oa*. Its strategic dissonance and prevailing harmony encompass an amazing range of effects accessible to Italian poets.

Later editions of the *Rime sparse* incorporate Bembo's evaluation while multiplying their views of Petrarch from different perspectives. Alessandro Vellutello, editor of the most widely circulated sixteenth-century volume of Petrarch's poems (Venice, 1525), situates the sonnets in a biographical context, and to this end he rearranges the sequence to recount a coherent narrative about the poet's life. From a humanist perspective, Giovanni Andrea Gesualdo and Sylvano da Venafro, both at Naples and producers of competing editions published in Venice in 1533, emphasize Petrarch's rhetorical attainments, and to that end they turn their attention to his deployment of literary and historical allusion, classical myth and poetic figuration. Pursuing a similar goal, Bernardino Daniello, a scholar and poet at Padua, corrects some of their assumptions by explicitly relating the *Rime sparse* to ancient Latin and Greek models (published in Venice, 1536). Meanwhile, in cities hospitable to currents of Lutheran reform, three very different commentators view Petrarch through the lens of reformist teaching. Fausto da Longiano (Modena, published in Venice, 1532) portrays Petrarch as a critic of the Avignon papacy. Antonio Brucioli (Ferrara, published in Venice, 1548) calls attention to Petrarch's quotations from scripture and St Augustine. Ludovico Castelvetro (Modena, published posthumously in Basel, 1582) identifies scriptural and doctrinal allusions in the *Rime sparse*, but also supplements them with attention to other literary echoes from classical and late medieval texts.

Taken together, these commentaries inscribe a wealth of ideas about the poet's astonishing erudition, his deeply evolved religious and political commitments, his single-minded pursuit of a literary career and his status as a model for continued emulation. The result is an accumulation of versions of Petrarch and hence of Petrarchism, multiple Petrarchs who appeal to readers and poetic imitators in different ways at different times and places. In Italy alone, the range of Petrarchan imitation is vast, from Bembo's own amatory sonnets for his several mistresses in an elegant style replete with classical allusions (published in 1530), to Ariosto's experimental and often satiric sonnets on topical issues (published posthumously in 1545), to Gaspara Stampa's sequence of sonnets narrating her doomed love for a wealthy nobleman in the salon society of the Venetian Republic (published posthumously in 1555).

Successive chapters in this book will trace specific developments of the sonnet form in Renaissance Petrarchism – and anti-Petrarchism – as well as in post-Petrarchan periods throughout Europe and the Americas.[23] This chapter will conclude with a synoptic overview of the sonnet's sixteenth-century diffusion outside Italy, to suggest tensions in the history of its composition by talented amateurs at courtly levels of society on the one hand, and by upwardly mobile writers who saw themselves as professional poets on the other. In Spain, for example, the prestige of the sonnet blossomed with the publication in Barcelona in 1542 of *Las obras* by Juan Boscán and his aristocratic friend Garcilaso de la Vega, whose imitations of Petrarch augured a new literary standard for King Charles V's Spanish Empire.[24] Designed in four volumes to celebrate the patriotic flowering of Castilian culture, their poems illustrate not only the appropriation of Italian forms abroad, but also and especially the talent of Spain's male nobility in their casual pursuit of letters to supplement their primary pursuit of arms. At the opposite end of this appropriation, the publication in Madrid in 1692 of poetry by Sor Juana Inés de la Cruz, a *criolla* nun at a Hieronymite convent in Mexico City, includes sixty-six sonnets on philosophical, mythological, religious and amatory themes elaborated in the Petrarchan mode. To fulfil her literary ambitions with a semblance of professional commitment, Sor Juana had left her youth at the viceregal court of New Spain for a cloistered life that allowed her to concentrate upon her writerly work. In the century-and-a-half between Boscán and Sor Juana, the contrast between amateur encounter and professional engagement could not be sharper.

In France, Joachim Du Bellay appropriates the Petrarchan style at the court of King Henry II in his sonnet collection *Olive* (1549), both to attract patronage from the king's Italian wife, Catherine de' Medici, and to exemplify literary tenets that he proposed in his accompanying *Defence and Illustration of the French Language* with the goal of advancing the cultural life of the emergent nation.[25] His later sonnet sequence *Les Regrets* (1558) deploys the Petrarchan mode in a satiric vein to express the poet's nostalgia for France during a period of his residence in Italy. While Du Bellay viewed himself as a public servant in employment to the crown, his friend Pierre de Ronsard saw himself as a professional poet advertising his literary craftsmanship and career-oriented ambitions in *Les Amours* (first edition in 1552). For the rest of his life, he continued to revise and amplify this sonnet collection about his love for Cassandre, to which he added sonnets for Marie, Sinope and other women as well. In 1578 he would boast of sustaining his virtuoso skills in his *Sonnets pour Hélène*. Honoured as the Prince of Poets and Poet of Princes, Ronsard upon his death in 1586 bequeathed the legacy of his career path to younger poets in France. Meanwhile, as early as 1555 in Lyon, Louise Labé had extended this same challenge to the women of her native city by publishing two-dozen amatory sonnets in her collection of poetic and prose *Oeuvres*.[26]

Petrarchism entered England in a precocious navigation from Italy to the court of King Henry VIII during the late 1520s with the amateur sonnets of the knightly adventurer Thomas Wyatt and his nobleman friend Henry Howard, earl of Surrey, both conveying the perils and spoils of gallant life under the Tudor monarch. Published posthumously in Richard Tottel's multi-authored miscellany of *Songs and Sonnets* (1557), their poems caught the imagination of a diverse London readership curious about the conduct of life among the upper ranks. Such conduct received its definitive courtly treatment in Philip Sidney's *Astrophil and Stella* (1582), which, although executed by a talented amateur, paradoxically inaugurated among aspiring professional writers a vogue for sonnet writing in England through the 1590s.[27] Late in his career, Spenser assembled a sonnet sequence about his marriage to Elizabeth Boyle, *Amoretti* (1594), ostensibly to honour his bride but also partly to assert his professional claims as England's foremost laureate poet in anticipation of publishing his expanded *Faerie Queene* (1596).[28] Even later, Shakespeare published his Sonnets (1609) to cement his claims as a professional poet and to complement his professional career as a successful dramatist. In 1621 Philip Sidney's niece, Mary Wroth, brought the English discourse of Petrarchan sonnet writing to an end with her sequence, *Pamphilia to Amphilanthus*, appended as an embellishment to her prose romance, *Urania*.[29] Following the model of earlier professional writers, the widowed Wroth reputedly turned to publication in order to repay crushing debt. In the context of England's turn to professional careerism, this strategy would make sense.

Through such routes, then, the sonnet form caught the attention of poets and readers across Europe and eventually the Americas. For these men and women, its development portended a passage: firstly, from oral poetry composed to be sung to written poetry designed to be read; then, from casual but beguiling entertainment to a vehicle for expressing elevated ideas about love, community, politics and society; and finally, from amateur exercise to professional authorial affirmation. The endlessly experimental possibilities of the sonnet, its close attachment to local or communal or emergently national sentiment, and its simultaneous propensity toward introspection, meditation and self-examination, make it early on an extraordinary form for poetic cultivation.

Notes

1 A comprehensive survey in English of the sonnet's Sicilian origins is Christopher Kleinhenz, *The Early Italian Sonnet: The First Century (1220–1321)* (Lecce: Milella, 1986), pp. 7–76.

2 Both Frederick and Pier figure in Dante's *Inferno*, the former among Epicurean heretics in 10:119 and the latter among suicides in 13:31–108. Their surviving works and those by other members of the Sicilian school appear in Roberto Antonelli, Costanzo Di Girolamo and Rosario Coluccia, eds., *I poeti della scuola siciliana: Edizione promossa dal Centro di studi filologici e linguistici siciliani*, 3 vols. (Milan: Mondadori, 2008), from whose text I quote in the following paragraphs. For Italian metrics and their early historical development, see A. Bartlett Giamatti, 'Italian', in William Wimsatt, ed., *Versification: The Major Types* (New York: Modern Language Association of America, 1972), pp. 148–64.

3 For the first hypothesis, see Ernest Hatch Wilkins, *The Invention of the Sonnet and Other Studies in Italian Literature* (Rome: Edizioni di Storia e Letteratura, 1959), pp. 11–39. For the second, see Kleinhenz, *The Early Italian Sonnet*, pp. 21–33. For the sonnet as a written or spoken presentation without musical accompaniment, see Paul Oppenheimer, *The Birth of the Modern Mind: Self, Consciousness, and the Invention of the Sonnet* (New York: Oxford University Press, 1989), pp. 1–29.

4 The terms Guelf (supportive of the papacy) and Ghibelline (supportive of the Holy Roman Emperor) prove highly fluid. For differences between the White Guelfs in pragmatic alignment with old Ghibelline families and the Black Guelfs composed of wealthy *popolo grasso*, see John M. Najemy, *A History of Florence, 1200–1575* (Oxford: Blackwell, 2006), pp. 72–95.

5 A comprehensive modern edition of Bonagiunta and his contemporaries is Gianfranco Contini, ed., *Poeti del duecento*, 2 vols. (Milan: Ricciardi, 1960). For translations, see the handy bilingual anthology, Frede Jensen, ed. and trans., *Tuscan Poetry of the Duecento* (New York: Garland, 1994), where poems by Bonagiunta appear on pp. 132–7, from which I quote below.

6 See the selections from each in Jensen, *Tuscan Poetry*, pp. 140–65.

7 Monte's sonnets are characterized by the addition of two extra lines in the octave; see the selection in *ibid.*, pp. 194–9.

8 See the analysis in Justin Steinberg, *Accounting for Dante: Urban Readers and Writers in Late Medieval Italy* (Notre Dame: University of Notre Dame Press, 2007), pp. 61–94, 145–69.

9 See Guido Guinizelli, *The Poetry of Guido Guinizelli*, ed. and trans. Robert Edwards (New York: Garland, 1987), from whose text I quote in the following paragraph. For his contrast with Guittone, see Steinberg, *Accounting for Dante*, pp. 27–48.

10 See Olivia Holmes, *Assembling the Lyric Self: Authorship from Troubadour Song to Italian Poetry Book* (Minneapolis: University of Minnesota Press, 2000), pp. 47–69. In *Inferno* 23, Dante punishes two Jovial Friars for the sin of hypocrisy, by extension an indictment of Guittone. See Guittone d'Arezzo, *Canzoniere: I sonetti d'amore del codice Laurenziano*, ed. L. Leonardi (Turin: Einaudi, 1994).

11 See Guido Cavalcanti, *The Poetry of Guido Cavalcanti*, ed. and trans. Lowry Nelson, Jr (New York: Garland, 1986), pp. xiii–lxiii, from whose text I quote below. See also Lowry Nelson, Jr, *Poetic Configurations: Essays in Literary History and Criticism* (University Park: Pennsylvania State University Press, 1992), pp. 93–114.

12 Quotations from Dante Alighieri, *De vulgari eloquentia*, trans. Steven Botterill (Cambridge: Cambridge University Press, 1996), p. 23.

13 For depictions of Bonagiunta, Guittone, Guinizelli and Cavalcanti in the *Commedia*, see Teodolinda Barolini, *Dante's Poets: Textuality and Truth in the Comedy* (New York: Columbia University Press, 1984), pp. 40–57, 85–153.

14 For Dante's precocious sense of authorship, see Albert Russell Ascoli, *Dante and the Making of a Modern Author* (Cambridge: Cambridge University Press, 2008), with attention to *Vita nuova* on pp. 178–200.

15 See Holmes, *Assembling the Lyric Self*, pp. 120–44.

16 Quotations from Dante Alighieri, *Vita nuova*, Italian text with facing English translation by Dino S. Cervigni and Edward Vasta (Notre Dame: University of Notre Dame Press, 1995). For critical commentary, see Robert Pogue Harrison, *The Body of Beatrice* (Baltimore: Johns Hopkins University Press, 1988), pp. 47–90; and Sherry Roush, *Hermes' Lyre: Italian Poetic Self-Commentary from Dante to Tommaso Campanella* (Toronto: University of Toronto Press, 2002), pp. 25–51.

17 For a critical account of Petrarch's individual works by various scholars, see Victoria Kirkham and Armando Maggi, eds., *Petrarch: A Critical Guide* (Chicago: University of Chicago Press, 2009). For the relationships of these works to Petrarch's Italian poetry, see Giuseppe Mazzotta, *The Worlds of Petrarch* (Durham, NC: Duke University Press, 1992).

18 This manuscript, housed in the Vatican Library as MS Vat. Lat. 3196, accompanies a second manuscript (MS Vat. Lat. 3195), which transcribes from 1366 to 1374 (partly in Petrarch's hand) the poet's final revisions and standing order of

his *Rime sparse*; for detailed studies of these manuscripts by various scholars, see Teodolinda Barolini and H. Wayne Storey, eds., *Petrarch and the Textual Origins of Interpretation* (Leiden: Brill, 2007).

19 All quotations and translations are from *Petrarch's Lyric Poems*, trans. and ed. Robert M. Durling (Cambridge, MA: Harvard University Press, 1976). Here and elsewhere I draw upon arguments for dating in the superbly annotated critical edition of Francesco Petrarca, *Canzoniere*, ed. Marco Santagata, 3rd edn (Milan: Mondadori, 2008).

20 See Thomas P. Roche Jr, *Petrarch and the English Sonnet Sequences* (New York: AMS, 1989).

21 See Brian Richardson, *Printing, Writers, and Readers in Renaissance Italy* (Cambridge: Cambridge University Press, 1999), pp. 3–46.

22 For an account of the major commentaries, including Bembo's *Prose della volgar lingua*, see William J. Kennedy, *Authorizing Petrarch* (Ithaca, NY: Cornell University Press, 1994), pp. 25–113. Bembo acquired a measure of fame as an eloquent (if distracted) spokesman for Platonic love in Baldassare Castiglione's *Book of the Courtier* (1529).

23 See Roland Greene, *Post-Petrarchism: Origins and Innovations of the Western Lyric Sequence* (Princeton: Princeton University Press, 1991); and *Unrequited Conquests* (Chicago: University of Chicago Press, 1999).

24 For the codes of style that they initiated in Spanish poetry, see Ignacio Navarrete, *Orphans of Petrarch: Poetry and Theory in the Spanish Renaissance* (Berkeley: University of California Press, 1994).

25 For patriotic, literary and social factors in the poetry of Du Bellay and Ronsard, see William J. Kennedy, *The Site of Petrarchism: Early Modern National Sentiment in Italy, France, and England* (Baltimore: Johns Hopkins University Press, 2003), pp. 77–159. Both poets offer several imitations of Petrarch's Sonnet 248. For Du Bellay's national sentiment, see Timothy Hampton, *Literature and Nation in the Sixteenth Century: Inventing Renaissance France* (Ithaca, NY: Cornell University Press, 2001), pp. 159–94.

26 See Kennedy, *Authorizing Petrarch*, pp. 160–94. Sonnet 15 of Labé's *Oeuvres*, 'Pour le retour du Soleil honorer', imitates Petrarch's Sonnet 310, 'Zephiro ritorna, e 'l bel tempo rimena'.

27 For Sidney's debts to Wyatt and Howard in advancing a self-critical national sentiment, see Kennedy, *Site*, pp. 163–233. Sonnet 71 of *Astrophil and Stella*, 'Who will in fairest booke of Nature know', imitates Petrarch's Sonnet 248.

28 See Kennedy, *Authorizing Petrarch*, pp. 195–280.

29 See Kennedy, *Site*, pp. 215–50. For emerging careerism, see Christopher Warley, *Sonnet Sequences and Social Distinction* (Cambridge: Cambridge University Press, 2005).

6

CATHERINE BATES

Desire, discontent, parody: the love sonnet in early modern England

If English Renaissance sonnet sequences are about anything they are about desire, but in order to appreciate the import of that word it might be worth, for a moment, transmuting it into a baser metal: to convert 'desire', that is, into the older and more native word, 'want'. 'Want' derives from the Old Norse *vant*, which entered the language via the Viking invasions of the Dark Ages and, from the beginning, signified a lack or deficiency, the state of missing or not having something, as in – to cite the *Oxford English Dictionary*'s example – *var vant kýr*, 'a cow was missing' ('to wane' – to reduce or diminish in size – derives, incidentally, from the same source). It was not until the eighteenth century, some thousand years later, that the verb 'to want' first came to develop the positive sense of yearning or longing for the missed object, while the noun never did, retaining its original negative sense to this day (as in 'a want of delicacy', 'the war on want', and so forth). When English Renaissance sonneteers use 'want', then, it is invariably to indicate a state of lack, as when Sidney's Astrophil complains, for example, that, since his beloved Stella is absent, 'I, alas, do want her sight'.[1] If they wished to indicate a positive craving or wish, the sonneteers did, of course, have the word 'desire' available to them. It had entered the language from the French in the later Middle Ages, and, when translating Petrarch's sonnets into English in the 1520s and 1530s, Wyatt and Surrey had no difficulty in rendering the Italian poet's *desire* and its cognates as 'desire'. Etymologically, of course, 'desire' also contains the sense of lacking or missing something, since its Latin root *dēsīderāre* also originally indicated the negative sense, but this had largely been lost by the time the word came to be naturalized in English. Although turning 'desire' back into 'want', therefore, momentarily reverses the direction that Wyatt and Surrey had been praised for taking – namely, for polishing 'our rude & homely maner of vulgar Poesie', as George Puttenham put it, and for bringing their native idiom up to the more polite standards of continental diction – it nevertheless serves a purpose.[2] For it drives home the fact that the positive state of desiring something always begins with a negative state – with the condition, that is, of wanting or of *not* having it.

This negative condition is what lies at the heart of every sonnet sequence, a gaping hole that opens up in the middle of both the lyric utterance and the persona or speaking voice that utters it. This lack can be figured in several ways. Sometimes, for example, it is figured as an anticipatory or pregnant space, waiting to be filled by an object that has been promised or is deserved but that has not, for some reason, yet been granted. In these cases, lack is often featured as an existential emptiness or physical starvation – as a gnawing hunger for 'my soules long lacked foode', as Spenser puts it.[3] Such complaints are frequently accompanied with expressions of injustice (the object is being undeservedly withheld) or impatience (for the long-awaited moment when the object will be delivered). At other times, lack is figured as a state of privation or loss – as a reified absence or emptiness, the vacated field left behind by an object that was once possessed but has since been lost. In these cases, lack is often featured as the apprehension of an evacuated space, as if the object that was there a moment ago has suddenly departed, leaving only its trace as a footprint on the grass, a still echoing chamber or a whiff of perfume on the air. Such complaints are frequently accompanied with expressions of betrayal (as the speaking voice rails against the object's heartless abandonment or neglect) or ineptitude (as the speaking voice curses itself for having lost what it once had). Lack also finds itself figured, classically, as a physical wound, as if the 'I' were once whole but now finds itself in bits, broken into pieces, with a pierced or broken heart, or with maimed or limping limbs. In these cases the lack that opens up within the subject is featured as a literal amputation, injury or cut, and such complaints are accompanied, predictably enough, with expressions of surprise and pain. In some cases, these various ways of figuring lack might all appear together in a single poem. Thus Astrophil, for example, complains of the cruelly emptied space – now 'this Orphane place' – in which he had fully expected to find Stella but which she has since deserted, leaving him only with a palpable sense of her all-too-vanished presence: 'O absent presence *Stella* is not here'. He goes on to present this loss as insatiable hunger of an unfed infant – 'where is that dainty cheere / Thou toldst mine eyes should help their famisht case?' – and concludes by describing himself as 'new maim'd', comparing his loss to that of a wounded soldier or amputee.[4]

In whatever way the speaking voice chooses to particularize its condition, however, its basic situation is the same: it lacks, it wants. To be sure, it wants or lacks *something*. As the last example suggests, what the 'I' misses takes on a distinct shape or form, most commonly (following Petrarch) that of a beloved female – 'the deare She'[5] or 'cruell Faire'[6] of worn sonnet convention. If lack, want or desire are to be thought of as transitive verbs then it is she who takes up position as their direct object: as if to say, 'the speaking voice lacks/wants/desires *her*'. Nevertheless, however much the 'I' might fill the frame with details of the mistress's beauty, fame or virtue, it is not she who is the prime concern and not she, when all is said and done, whom the sonnet sequence is really about. Ultimately, the focus of interest is not the desired object but the desiring subject. Indeed, the first is little more than a pretext or precondition for the second. Thus, however passionately the speaking voice might insist that he aches for his beloved – however urgently he might call on her name, however devoutly he might wish for or earnestly beseech her – the one thing he does *not* want, or not yet, is for her actually to materialize, to come down from her pedestal, or to acquiesce in his demands. So long as she is held off at a discreet distance – as an addressee to be importuned, a 'You' to be apostrophized and invoked – she creates a situation in which there is necessarily an addressing, importuning, apostrophizing 'I'. And so long as she continues to deny her lover what he says he wants, the identity of that 'I' remains affirmed as that of a subject, a subject who desires. This is why the sonnet mistress is usually held at a strategic distance – why Henry Constable's 'praises of his Mistress in certaine sweete Sonnets', for example, are addressed 'To his absent Diana'[7] – and throughout the Renaissance sonnet tradition poets came up with a number of tactical manoeuvres to ensure that the beloved object remained absent or at some remove. Thus, she might be unrelentingly chaste and/or married to someone else, she might be dead and as such be translated firmly from the earthly to the spiritual sphere, she might be so far her lover's moral and/ or social superior as to be similarly unreachable – the equivalent of some heavenly body, a sun or star, that her earthbound lover can only gaze at and admire from afar 'like him that both / Lookes to the skies, and in a ditch doth fall';[8] 'So doth the Plow-man gaze the wand'ring Starre'.[9] In many cases she is all or a combination of the above. 'She' might even be so etherealized as to be little more than a cipher or metaphor for something entirely abstract, such as the Platonic 'Idea' (for Michael Drayton) or 'his mistresse Philosophie' (for George Chapman).[10] In the prefatory letter to his sonnet sequence *Licia*, Giles Fletcher equivocates as to 'What my LICIA is' – some beloved woman, perhaps, or 'Learnings Image', or even 'Some Colledge' – and in the end leaves it up to the reader to decide.[11] The point is that the 'Lady' of sonnet tradition is not so much a being, however idealized, as an element within a structure, a position, a 'You' to which the 'I' can orient itself and relate. Her job is quite functional. She is there purely to create a relational field and, in so doing, to enable subjectivity. This is the reason why sonnet sequences are relatively receptive to a change of object, for within a relational field there is some room for flexibility. So long as an object position is set up, the 'Lady' can easily be replaced by something else without appreciably altering the basic dynamic of the sonnet sequence. Thus there are sonnet sequences in which that object is a man (as in the first 126 of Shakespeare's Sonnets, for example, or the sonnets addressed by the female character, Pamphilia, to her beloved Amphilanthus in Lady Mary Wroth's romance, the *Urania*), or others in which it is God (as in the religious sonnets of Anne Lok, George Herbert or John Donne). Whatever their local differences in subject matter or tone, these sonnet sequences all preserve the basic structure in which an object that is absent or elsewhere creates a subject that wants or desires.

It might be best, then, to think of the desire that runs through the early modern sonnet sequence as being of the *in*transitive variety: as if to say, 'the speaker desires', period, rather than 'the speaker desires *x* or *y*'. Looking at it this way has the advantage of explaining certain aspects of the sonnet tradition that even the most cursory survey will show to be wholly characteristic. The first of these is oxymoron. For the position of the subject who desires is necessarily a paradoxical one. The 'I' experiences both the negative state of not having something and the positive state of yearning for that thing at one and the same time: the two senses that the modern English usage of the word 'want' conveniently holds side by side. The experience that results is indeed a 'straunge desire', as the speaker of one of George Gascoigne's sonnets puts it, since it paradoxically both does and does not seek satisfaction.[12] This is the situation that Petrarch turned to the language of oxymoron to represent, so when Sidney's Astrophil claims, in an entirely typical move, to reject the language 'Of living deaths, deare wounds, faire stormes and freesing fires'[13] as a now stale, 200-year-old literary convention, he cannot do without it – not simply because he frequently resorts to just such statements of oxymoron in his complaints to Stella, but because the Petrarchan language of paradox encapsulates the basic situation of the desiring subject in the most economical way. It has often been noted, for example, that for all their familiarity with Petrarch as the founder of the sonnet tradition, English poets actually refer to only a tiny number of his poems. Of the 366 sonnets and other lyrics that go to make up the *Rime sparse*, a bare ten or twelve turn up as regular objects of imitation or variation, and of these the most popular by far are 'S'amor non è' and 'Pace non trovo'[14] in which the images of living death, delightful pain, fearful hope, icy fire and so on are catalogued with particular density (between them, these two sonnets inspired imitations by Chaucer, Wyatt, Gascoigne, Watson, Sidney, Daniel, Lodge, Spenser and a host of less well-known or anonymous poets). This is not because English poets were lazy or unadventurous but rather because they grasped the fact that the Petrarchan language of oxymoron got straight to the point and expressed the essence of the situation as economically as possible: it pared down to the most minute of metaphorical units the one thing that, at root, all amorous sonnet sequences are about, namely the thoroughly paradoxical nature of desire. It was enough simply to gesture in the direction of this language, as Astrophil did, in order to refer at a stroke to an entire psychological system and to the literary tradition devoted to exploring it. Michael Drayton's speaker is doing something similar when, in one of the closing sonnets of *Idea*, he sums up the situation he has been in for the preceding sequence: 'I have, I want; Despaire, and yet Desire, / Burn'd in a Sea of yce, and drown'd amidst a fire' (62.14–15).

As this example also suggests, furthermore, the 'I' is ultimately more occupied with its own experience of desire than it is with any object. The speaker remains piqued, enthralled – in a word, fascinated – by all aspects of this experience, paradox included, and, however tormenting, he generally chooses to prolong this state for as long as possible and, in most cases, to postpone any resolution or satisfaction indefinitely. This goes on, then, to explain a second feature that is wholly typical of the sonnet tradition: the ubiquitous presence of a figure that appears, variously, as Love, Amor, Cupid, Eros or Desire. For the latter is nothing less than the speaker's own desire in personified form. And, as such, it allows the speaker to stage – in conspiracies, conversations, struggles – encounters with what is basically its own experience: to engage with its own desire, as it were, face to face. Indeed, for a tradition that is supposedly about a love relation between two – an 'I' and a 'You' – it is striking how often the sonnet sequence's relational field makes room for this third figure, the (usually male) personification of Desire. Petrarch's 'I', for example, routinely addresses itself to 'o Amore o Madonna'[15] or to 'love or my lady' in Wyatt's translation,[16] and it is no exaggeration to say that there is not a single amorous sonnet sequence in the English Renaissance (and precious few individual sonnets either) in which this threesome does not, in some form or another, appear. The love relation in sonnets is thus, in practice, a triangulated one. The speaker relates to Love quite as much as he does to the Lady, if not more. A whole history – of previous vows, rows, triumphs and failures – opens up between the speaker and Love, as the former describes himself as the latter's creature, slave, victim, soldier, friend, companion, partner, pupil, apprentice, guest, host and so on (this is particularly true, for example, of Fulke Greville's sequence, *Caelica*, or at least of the first eighty-four poems that precede the speaker's final farewell to Love). But, if what really concerns the speaker is the whole complicated business of desiring (rather than the object as such), then this makes perfect sense. He is naturally going to dwell on the experience of loving – as dramatized in endless conversations with this personification – if that, rather than the Lady, is his prime concern. It is thus quite logical that, on looking at his Lady's face, for example, the speaker should find Love sitting there: Love perches on the Lady's face, uses her eyebrows as his bow, her eyes as the arrows with which he shoots at the lover's heart, and so forth. Indeed, the Lady's whole body can be requisitioned to Love's use, 'her lips is heralds arre: / Her breasts his tents, legs his triumphall carre: / Her flesh his food, her skin his armour brave'.[17] In cases such as this – and there are many – the Lady is simply a screen for the more important figure. She might be the ostensible object of (transitive) desire, but the speaker is finally more interested in (intransitive) Desire. It is because the Lady has effectively merged with the latter here that the speaker can claim with some justification that '*Love* gave the wound, which while I breathe will bleed' (Sidney, 2), that '*Love* on me doth all his quiver spend' (14; emphasis in original), that the 'murthring boy … pierc'd my heart' (Sidney, 20), and so on. The speaker, in other words, is in love with love – he desires desire, he wants to want – and images such as these are only a particularly graphic way of literalizing the situation.

Such images, furthermore, amply demonstrate the self-reflecting, self-mirroring and ultimately narcissistic nature of this desire and, in that respect, go a long way toward explaining why sonnet sequences can often seem to be so compulsively repetitive, to go round in circles and never to get anywhere. For circularity – like paradox – is built into the system. In the penultimate poem of Sidney's *Certain Sonnets*, for example, the speaker curses Cupid as 'Thou blind man's marke'.[18] The blind speaker, that is, has shot at the blind Cupid – made him his target for shooting practice – because the latter shot at him and made him blind. The speaker wants to be shot of desire altogether (so to speak), to be rid of it once and for all, and he ends the poem 'Desiring nought but how to kill desire'. But, although this sonnet is generally taken to be a conventional renunciation of desire (sometimes, for example, appended to the end of *Astrophil and Stella* by way of rounding off the latter), the circularity betrays the hopelessness of the situation and naturally pre-empts any conclusion: at the end the speaker is, after all, still 'Desiring' something. This situation neatly dramatizes the impossible, paradoxical, unappeasable state of desire: intransitive desire at its most intransigent.

Thinking about desire in this way, moreover, goes on to explain a third aspect typical of the sonnet tradition: namely, its characteristic treatment of time. For sonnet sequences generally present time as operating in two modes – along a horizontal and a vertical axis, as it were – onto which the different figurations of desire I have been describing might plausibly be mapped. The first, horizontal axis is that which tells the 'story' – the broadly linear, chronological narrative that starts at some beginning (the point, for example, before the speaker fell in love, when he was still 'whole', and so forth) and moves toward some end (the point at which the object will finally be possessed, or, failing that, at which desire is renounced and given up for good) – and sets out to chronicle the history of what happens in between. Since this horizontal axis is geared toward a final end or object-ive, it might be seen to correspond to what I have been calling transitive desire. This chronological narrative will often be structured by calendrical or numerological devices that record the passing of time – such as specific dates or anniversaries (as in Petrarch's *Rime sparse* or Spenser's *Amoretti*, for example), or the signs of the zodiac (as in Barnabe Barnes's *Parthenophil and Parthenophe*) – and this essentially historical sense of time – as a medium that relentlessly passes, never to be recalled – gives rise, naturally enough, to those oft-expressed fears of mutability and decay that find their classic articulation in commands to 'seize the day', in frequent invocations to Time, and in well-known meditations on the tragedy of an irreducibly time-bound human existence.

Intersecting with this historical or horizontal movement of time, how-ever, is the second, or vertical, axis, which is primarily concerned with the present moment – the speaker's current, immediate, existing and ongoing situation. Since this vertical axis is geared more toward the speaker's sub-jective experience of love, it might be seen to correspond to what I have been calling intransitive desire. For the final end of ending desire (by gain-ing the object) is, in most cases, indefinitely deferred beyond the end of the sequence, and, if the speaker seeks to end desire by renouncing it, well, as we have seen from the example of Sidney's *Certain Sonnets*, that end is no more obviously achievable either. Since the vertical axis situates the speaker in the present moment, it takes precedence over the horizontal axis, for the immediate 'now' of writing is the point around which everything else is oriented and from which both the past and the future are viewed. The dis-tant past and hoped-for future of the chronological 'story', after all, are not narrated within the sequence as such ('novelistically', as it were) but are pre-sented rather as memories and fantasies as seen from the vantage point of the tormented, love-crazed (and thus none too reliable) speaker. Besides, the 'events' of the chronological narrative, such as they are, turn out to be little more than a few key episodes (for the most part vague and generic) such as a kiss or a blush, a meeting or parting, an illness or some event at court, and are presented as detached and discontinuous – as snapshots of once present moments now frozen in time – rather than as events that might unfold any-thing resembling a plot. From this perspective, the numbers and calendars that recorded the passing of historical time can find themselves permanently arrested in the eternal moment of the present, as when one sonnet speaker, for example, finds 'My passion's Calender' in his beloved's beautiful face, her frowns eternal working days, her smiles eternal Sundays.[19] The present moment can even overtake the process of writing itself. Set against the actual act of writing right 'now', a finished, polished poem can already look dated, like the end-product of an ongoing process that has already moved on to the next poem. Thus 'Those lines that I before have writ do lie'[20] because the speaker's written expressions are always playing catch-up with a love that never stands still but is ever living, changing and growing. Sidney's Astrophil, of course, famously contrives to capture the process of writing poetry in his poetry itself, frequently presenting his sonnets not as completed outcomes but rather as the rough drafts, preliminary jottings and sketchy works-in-progress that will, at some unspecified point in the future, result in such finished productions: 'I sought fit words ... But words came halting forth',[21] 'Thus write I while I doubt to write' (Sidney, 34), 'As good to write as for to lie and grone' (Sidney, 40). By prioritizing the present moment in these ways – by foregrounding the immediate instant as it is lived in the here and now, or experienced in the present continuous, and by extending this moment as far as they can, if at all possible indefinitely – sonnet sequences thus enact the experience of pure duration: of living without growing, of chasing without catching, of running without moving forward (paradox and circularity again). They detail, in other words, the sheer state of lacking, of wanting, with no end or object realistically in sight, and they thus open up a unique space for the rehearsal of intransitive desire.

The speaker who desires in this way, however, is not prevented from desiring to *do* something: even if it is not attached to a direct object, that is, the verb can nevertheless be attached to an infinitive, as if to say 'the speaker desires *to do x* or *y*', rather than 'the speaker desires *x* or *y*' (this is still consistent with intransitive desire). It might be suggested, for example, that what the sonnet speaker really desires to do is *to persuade*. He does, after all, strain every muscle to bring the beloved round to his point of view, and pleads, argues, bargains, flatters, sues; even threatens, blackmails and bribes in order to convince her of the rightness of his position and the justice of his cause. From its very inception the sonnet form had been conceived as a forensic instrument, and indeed is often literalized as such in individual poems that present the metaphor of an actual courtroom in which the speaker is called to plead his case: 'How have my Sonnets (faithfull counsellors) / Thee without ceasing mov'd for day of hearing? ... How have I stood at barre of thine own conscience, / When in requesting court my suite I brought?'[22] Such forensic oratory is clearly designed to be instrumental. It has a distinct aim in view – to change the addressee's mind – much as, in the opening sonnet of *Astrophil and Stella*, for example, Astrophil sets out the series of logical steps by which Stella will read his poems, know of his suffering, pity him on that account and so grant him her 'grace'.[23] As Lorna Hutson has suggested, such 'plots of courtship' – insofar as they are discourses geared specifically to the persuasion of women – became in the sixteenth century a new arena for the exercise of masculine power since, in comparison with increasingly dated-looking military skills, they demonstrated that the rhetorical skills gained by a humanist education were considerably more efficient in getting one's way.[24]

Against this, however, we have to reckon with the fact that such attempts to persuade the other party for the most part spectacularly fail. In virtually every case, the sonnet speaker's words – however finely honed or convincingly presented – fall on deaf ears, as the beloved is absent, distant or at the very least not open to persuasion. Daniel's speaker, for instance, to cite only one example, disarmingly claims that his own forensic oratory is quite useless (not that that stops him):

> And you my verse, the Aduocates of loue,
> Haue followed hard the processe of my case:
> And vrg'd that title which dooth plainely proue,
> My faith should win, if iustice might haue place.
>
> Yet though I see, that nought we doe can moue her,
> Tis not disdaine must make me leaue to loue her
>
> (Daniel, *Delia*, Sonnet 8).

The speaker gains nothing and moves no further forward in pressing his suit – for neither the case nor the Lady are to be won – but he carries on regardless, in what can only be, as a result, a depressing replay of his own words' failure to change anything. The sonnet mistress, for her part, is no more persuasive either. On the rare occasions when she speaks – generally to say 'No', as Drayton's Lady does,[25] or 'No, No' or 'No, no, no, no', like the particularly emphatic Stella[26] – she is nevertheless no more effective in getting her lover to desist than he is in getting her to desire. Between these two voices – each one as ineffective as the other – the sonnet sequence stages a scene of almost total rhetorical redundancy: language is shown to be anything but instrumental and speech as utterly lacking in executive power.

If the sonnet speaker does not exactly desire to persuade – or not in any straightforward way – then perhaps we should say that what he really desires to do is *to write great poetry*, and here we are on much stronger ground. Petrarch, for example, famously turned his love for Laura into a mechanism for producing stunning verse, punning on her name so as to turn her into the *lauro* or laurel: the signifier of poetic fame and success that he could win for himself, even if he could not realistically hope to win her. Identifying with Apollo – the sun god and patron of poetry who pursued Daphne only to be left with the laurel or bay tree into which she was metamorphosed – Petrarch presents himself not only as a crowned, 'laureate' poet, but also as the implicitly godlike producer of golden or aureate verse (he also punned Laura into *l'auro*, gold). For Petrarch the idea was less to persuade the Lady than to praise her – his poetry, that is to say, was less forensic than epideictic – but much of that praise was, in practice, self-praise designed to reflect back flatteringly on the poet himself. The more wondrous his descriptions of the Lady and the more ingenious his metaphors, the more he was able to display his poetic skill and virtuosity, so that the Lady (as idealized object) eventually came to mirror the sonnet speaker as an equally idealized subject. The latter might claim that his love is a constant source of pain and torment, but, as William Kerrigan and Gordon Braden put it, the 'one thing the Petrarchan poet has, in compensation for his anguish, is poems'.[27] He is left, that is to say, with a very great deal to show for it. When (transitive) desire for the Lady thus turns into the (intransitive) desire to write, what had essentially been an unproductive relation suddenly becomes an extremely productive one: a fertile field – indeed, a constantly self-replenishing site – for the generation of poetry. This transmutation thus inspired generations of poets after Petrarch to follow suit, which is why one of the most common tropes of the sonnet tradition is the statement to the effect that, while love, the lover and beloved may all succumb to the passing of time, the writing will endure for ever. The sonnet sequence will become a permanent record, a substantial body of work, in which the fame of all parties is guaranteed: 'Ensuing Ages yet my Rimes shall cherish';[28] 'my verse your vertues rare shall eternize';[29] 'Your monument shall be my gentle verse'.[30]

Against this, however, we have to reckon with the fact that such claims – universal as they are – may not be as substantial as they first appear. And here I draw on recent re-evaluations of Petrarch that have come to see his poetry less as the product of a master poet – a dazzling monument, finished and achieved – and more as the product of a self-divided and self-alienated subject, of a self internally split and so eternally in crisis.[31] In place of a solid corpus, these critics see a collection of fragments, a radical dismemberment. Indeed, Petrarch's sonnets present themselves from the opening poem as *rime sparse*, 'scattered rhymes', and not only that, but as scattered rhymes that express nothing more substantial than 'il suono / di quei sospiri' ('the sound of those sighs').[32] This opening sonnet, as well as all those that follow it, ultimately present themselves as nothing more than recordings of this sound – from which, after all, they take their name (in Italian, *sonnetto*, a 'little sound', comes from *suono*, sound, or *sonare*, to sound. Dante – who was the first to use *sonnetto* as a literary term – derived the word, disparagingly, it seems, from the Latin *sonitus*, which meant a murmur, or merely empty sound, simple noise).[33] The masterly, golden verse of the laureate, aureate poet thus turns out to be based on something disconcertingly fragile and fleeting – a mere insubstantial breath of air – as Petrarch suggests when, in yet another pun on his beloved's name, he tropes Laura into *l'aura*, the breeze. What had appeared so solid and enduring – the golden monument the poet claims to bequeath for future generations to admire – thus seems to vaporize before our eyes, as we are left not with a written record but with a record of speech, and indeed not always with a record of words but of inarticulate sounds, mere out-breaths. If all that poetic inspiration leads, in the end, only to a poetic exhalation, then perhaps the sonneteer does not have quite so much to show for his anguish after all. Yet this apparent erasure of writing – its collapse or vanishing into sound – is something poets after Petrarch enthusiastically imitate, generations of them offering up to their mistresses 'These sorrowing sighes',[34] 'sighs, deere sighs',[35] 'sighes, which …Will never cease',[36] not to mention other inarticulate sounds such as moans, groans, sobs, cries, stammerings, stutterings, echoes, repetitions or endless reiterations of a single word such as the beloved's name. In this context, grandiose claims that the sonneteer is producing a brilliant sequence of polished poems intricately crafted with jewel-like precision in order to redound to his eternal fame begin to sound distinctly hollow, or at the very least as pathetically over-confident. Toward the beginning of his sequence, for example, Daniel's speaker sends forth his 'wailing verse, the infants of my loue' to 'Sigh out a story of her cruell deedes' in order to produce 'A Monument that whosoeuer reedes, / May iustly praise'.[37] But, if this is a monument, it is a very airy one indeed. Shakespeare's speaker, likewise, reassures his beloved that 'Your monument shall be my gentle verse', but in the end that monument turns out to be wherever 'breath most breathes'[38] – to be contingent, that is, on nothing more secure than readers at some distant point in the future reading that verse out loud.

The sonnet speaker cannot really be said to persuade, then. He certainly *wishes* to do so – and expresses an unambiguous desire to impress the object and to win them round – but what he actually does is create an arena for the endless staging of his words' failure, finally, to effect very much at all. In the same way, the sonnet speaker cannot really be said to leave behind a solid monument to his literary fame. Again, he clearly *wishes* to do so and expresses a repeated desire to erect a lasting testament – 'These are the Arkes the Tropheis I erect'[39] – that will redound to his immortal glory and endure for all time, but what he actually does is create a scenario in which his words disconcertingly escape him, melt away and evaporate before his eyes. We find ourselves back, therefore, with the very negativity we started out with – with the lack that is to be found at the heart of every sonnet sequence and of every sonnet speaker who utters it. We might well say, for example, that, insofar as he tries to persuade, the speaker *wants* (lacks/desires) conviction, or that, insofar as he seeks literary fame, he *wants* (lacks/desires) success. Shifting from transitive to intransitive desire – from the expressed aim of winning the object to the alternative aims of winning the argument and glory for himself – has not got around the problem at all, for failure, lack and negativity are just as much in evidence here as there. Moreover, the fact that this lack appears not only in the original object but also in its substitutes (success, fame and so forth) tells us, in turn, something crucial about the kind of subjectivity that early modern sonnet sequences are devoted to exploring. For it anticipates by several centuries the way in which that subjectivity would later come to be described by modern linguistic and psychoanalytic theory. When Petrarch's speaker shifts his attachment from Laura to the *lauro* or to *l'auro*, for example, these shift again to what those words in turn signify: the laurel leaf, poetic fame; gold, the aureate, Apollonian verse that is worthy of that fame. This is Petrarch's way, in other words, of showing what a later literary theorist might describe as the way signifiers relate in the first instance only to other signifiers. Meaning does not inhere within words as such but rather between them. Meaning emerges from absence and difference and is endlessly displaced from one word to the next in an endless chain of signifiers (*Laura–lauro–l'auro*). The result is that any final meaning or signified is infinitely deferred, and any hope of achieving such a thing effectively disappears in a puff of air (*l'aura*), leaving no one in control of their meaning or with mastery over words, least of all the writer. Petrarch presents the sonnet speaker, furthermore, as a subject who is, axiomatically, in love: as someone who is, by definition, driven by an overpowering, unappeasable and insatiable desire. This, in other words, is the poet's way of showing what a later psychoanalytic critic might describe as the way human beings – to the extent that they are born into and have their being only within language – are necessarily desiring subjects. If language is structured by absence and difference, and if meaning emerges from what and where it is not, then the compulsion to fill the gap, to chase from signifier to signifier in an interminable quest for meaning is nothing other than the human condition. According to this theoretical model, the human being is by definition a speaking, desiring subject, forever compelled to search for meaning but destined never to arrive at it, and, as a consequence, never at rest. And it is this subject that, anticipating literary and psychoanalytic theory by many hundreds of years, the Petrarchan sonnet sequence gives us in perhaps its purest form.

This is why discontent is so endemic in the Petrarchan sonnet sequence: why, indeed, discontent could be said to be its very content. For, if the sonnet tradition can be defined as a discourse of desire, and if desire is, by definition, the experience of lack or want, then it stands to reason that the sonnet speaker is going to be eternally unhappy and to complain about it all the time: for he is never going to have what he desires: 'what griefe it is againe / To live and lacke the thing should ridde my paine', as Surrey puts it.[10] This applies, moreover, to *all* the things he desires, not one of which he is destined to achieve. Thus, the experience of not having the Lady is essentially the same as the experience of not persuading or of not writing great poetry. The speaker's humiliation at finding that his words cannot move, persuade or effect anything at all, or his disappointment at finding that he cannot in the end bequeath a lasting monument to his literary fame are of the same order as his not having the Lady, even if the latter is expressed in more physical or emotional terms (as pain, hunger, torment, torture, suffering, distress, misery, despair, frustration, madness and so on). By the same token, being happy, healthy, whole, contented and in possession of the beloved object are no more achievable than being a master of meaning who is able to use words effectively and to be praised for doing so. All are equally unattainable, all held off and indefinitely deferred. Or, if they are achieved, then it is only as temporary stopping-off points or provisional moments when desire pauses all too briefly before it is off again on its hopeless, endless quest. That is why one comes away from the Renaissance sonnet with the impression of an eternally weeping and inconsolable lover, for such is the nature of desire. Not winning the Lady, not winning the argument, not winning the bays … it's all one. These are simply different expressions of and variant figurations for what is basically the same thing – the foundational lack or negativity, the original state of want or of not having – that structures human desire and human subjectivity alike.

I emphasize the point because this same negativity comes to afflict one further thing that the sonnet speaker says he desires, which is *to be different from Petrarch*. Petrarch's position at the head of the sonnet tradition is so important – his poetry an inspiration to so many hundreds of imitators across Europe throughout the sixteenth century – that it is no exaggeration to say that Renaissance lyric is always 'Petrarchan' to some degree or other. Petrarch was the great literary forebear and his followers necessarily stand in some relation to him, whether they humbly recognize his pre-eminence or seek to surpass him. Often, for example, this relation finds itself expressed in modest (if disingenuous) disclaimers: 'Though thou a *Laura* hast no *Petrarch* founde', Daniel's speaker tells his beloved, yet 'I loue as well, though he could better shew it';[41] 'Nor so ambitious am I', declares Sidney's Astrophil, 'as to frame / A nest for my yong praise in Lawrell tree'.[42] Sometimes poets would praise others as being better than Petrarch, as in a commendatory sonnet to *The Faerie Queene* where Sir Walter Raleigh compliments Spenser: 'Me thought I saw the graue, where *Laura* lay', the speaker opens, but there 'the soule of *Petrarke* wept' because Spenser's creation is so superior.[43] Perhaps the figure of Petrarch casts too long a shadow, however, for lyric poets in the Renaissance to be able in the end to differentiate from him completely. In which case it might be more accurate to say that what the sonnet speaker really desires is *to be different from other poets who imitate Petrarch*. Such a desire, indeed, would correspond to what Heather Dubrow has styled 'diacritical desire' insofar as it is, essentially, a desire to make one's mark, to stand out from the crowd and to emerge as the winner from an intensely competitive field.[44] Except that this desire, of course, is no more achievable than any of the others. The desire to be different is no less destined to be disappointed than the desire to win the Lady, or the argument, or the bays. Thus Sidney's Astrophil, for example, seeks to distance himself from other poets – 'You that poore *Petrarch*'s long deceased woes ... do sing'[45] – so as to differentiate his own sparky utterances from what he casually dismisses as the plodding and slavish imitations of Petrarch then being produced by poets on the Continent. But, as we saw earlier with his similar gesture of rejecting the Petrarchan language of paradox, this action of negating ultimately only negates itself. For Astrophil no more rejects Petrarchan paradox than he rejects Petrarchan 'woes', and any claim that he does so is necessarily contradicted by being situated within a sonnet sequence that is utterly beholden to the Petrarchan ethos. The desire to differentiate, that is, fails like all the other desires because – this being the nature of desire – it always leads the speaker back to the same place: negativity. 'Diacritical desire', therefore, is going to be yet another desire that remains unmet, another desire that will ultimately be found wanting. The sonneteer cannot 'not' be Petrarchan, whether he likes it or not, because that 'not' – that negativity – is the very essence of Petrarchan desire. There is nothing more Petrarchan, one could say, than not wanting to be so.

Astrophil and Stella was first published in 1591 (albeit in a pirated edition that was not authorized by the Sidney family) and it immediately sparked off the great English sonnet craze of the 1590s when poet after poet seems suddenly to have been impelled to follow suit, and during which time the bulk of English sonnet sequences were written. There was a particularly concentrated period between 1592 and 1597 when no fewer than seventeen amorous sonnet sequences were published, while many others are likely to have been written or composed at that time that were either left unpublished or published at a later date. In this climate, with the swell of Petrarchan imitations increasing exponentially, the desire to stand out from the throng naturally became stronger than ever. But it was no less destined to fail. Both Sir John Davies and Michael Drayton, for example, preface their collections of sonnets with dedicatory poems that make every effort to distance their authors from the Petrarchan crowd, yet the sonnets that follow effectively put them both right back there. Thus Davies prefaces his group of nine *Gullinge Sonnets* – a series ostensibly mocking the excesses of the sonnet craze – by indicating a desire for change, a heartfelt wish to move on from what had become a tired, stale and repetitive convention:

> Here my Camelion Muse her selfe doth chaunge
> To divers shapes of gross absurdities,
> And like an Antick mocks with fashion straunge
> The fond admirers of lewde gulleries.[46]

Yet, while the sonnets that follow are, he declares, going to distinguish themselves from the scorned productions of other poets – 'The bastard Sonnetts of these Rymers bace' – in fact they do so only by using tropes and devices that are immediately recognizable as Petrarchan: hyperbole, paradox, standard imagery and so on. Parody, that is, ends up being the sincerest form of flattery, for the parodist can only mock the tradition by doing more of the same, thereby adding to the pile rather than decreasing or obliterating it. Likewise, from 1599 Drayton prefaces *Idea* with a dedicatory sonnet 'To the reader of these sonnets', in which he resolutely asserts the difference between his own poems and those of the mediocre majority, which he casually sweeps aside in a single gesture of contempt:

> No farre-fetch'd Sigh shall ever wound my Brest,
> Love from mine Eye a Teare shall never wring,
> Nor in Ah-mees my whyning Sonnets drest.[47]

Yet the sequence that follows is full of little else. And the key as to why is contained within this same prefatory poem, for there Drayton (like Davies) expresses his desire for change: 'My Verse is the true image of my Mind, / Ever in motion, still desiring change' (lines 9–10). Like Davies, that is (and, one might add, like the speaker of Sidney's *Certain Sonnets* who ended 'Desiring' to kill desire) Drayton continues to remain subject to and a subject of desire, and for that reason he is no more going to achieve his end or get his way than they are.

This, then, accounts for why the early modern sonnet tradition bears such a curious relation to parody: why, for example, it often proves so difficult to say whether a particular group of poems (or an individual poem or a part of a poem) is 'Petrarchan' or 'anti-Petrarchan' (or 'pseudo-' or 'post-' or 'counter-' Petrarchan – the variability of critical terminology registers the same uncertainty). For if the sonnet tradition is a discourse of desire, and if desire is the experience of want, then, as I have been arguing, negativity will of necessity be central to its concerns. But if this is so, then it also follows that the sonnet tradition already contains its own negative – its own opposite, contrary or antithesis – within itself. Parody, that is to say, is built in. As noted above, any attempt not to follow the sonnet tradition is destined to end up in the same place. For a poet to parody some aspect of the tradition – as it were to say 'no' to it – is only to perpetuate the tradition. Indeed, we could say that the sonnet tradition is a self-parodying genre and that, as such, it gives a particularly pure example of the nature of parody itself, since the prefix *para* (from the Greek *paroida*) indicates similarity as well as difference, nearness to as well as distance from the text that is imitated.[48] The true parodist, that is, will be as attached to the tradition as he says he wants to be detached from it. He can go up to the very circumference of the tradition – to the outermost edge of what the sonnet tradition could, at a stretch, be said to allow for – but he will always be able to measure his distance from a central point and will thus always be connected to its most central concerns. To that extent he must remain within the circuit of desire. The sonnet tradition is thus a particularly intriguing form, for the more poets try to parody it the more they repeat its inbuilt negativity and so the more they end up perpetuating it. Parody, in other words, is no less self-defeating than everything else the sonneteer attempts, and we thus find we are back in a familiar position – going round in circles.

If, for example, we take the following as typical of the Petrarchan tradition – that the speaker loves a beautiful, chaste lady without end – then English Renaissance sonneteers would experiment with each of these features in turn – creating objects who are not beautiful, who are far from chaste, who are not even female, and speakers who do not love without end – but, in each case, any desire to break free from the tradition's discourse of desire is thwarted. When it comes to praising an object who is not beautiful, for instance, Sidney writes a sonnet in praise of the foul servant Mopsa (not, admittedly, in a sonnet sequence but in the *Arcadia*), but, although he might seem here to turn the sonnet tradition on its head, he nevertheless draws directly from its repertory: 'Her forhead jacinth like, her cheekes of opall hue, / Her twinkling eies bedeckt with pearle, her lips of Saphir blew'.[49] Moreover, in this as in other such 'ugly beauty' poems, the poet also has the sonnet tradition's all too conventional account of the mistress as cruel, stony hearted, tigerish, witch-like and so forth, on which to draw, not to mention warning descriptions of the withered skin, crows feet, baldness and toothlessness that are likely to afflict the Lady if she does not promptly 'seize the day'. From this perspective the odious Mopsa is not so different from the Cruel Fair – or the ancient crone she is destined to become – or, if she is, then she is different in degree but not in kind.

By the same token, when it comes to loving an object who is far from chaste, George Gascoigne in *The Adventures of Master F. J.* parodies one of the most sublime of Petrarch's sonnets by converting it into a poem that salaciously celebrates the speaker's sexual conquest of a wholly whorish mistress: 'That blessed hower, that blist and happie daye ... my Lady of her wonted grace, / First lent her lippes to me (as for a kisse:) / And after that hir body to embrace ... What followed next, gesse you that knowe the trade'.[50] Again, he appears to turn the sonnet tradition upside down, and yet he too nevertheless remains true to the tradition's central theme: desire. In *Rime sparse* 61 (as, indeed, in other poems) Petrarch's speaker had commemorated his first sight of Laura one Good Friday (actually, the anniversary of Christ's crucifixion) and from this inaugural event had dated the entire course of his decades-long, and finally unachieved love. Gascoigne sacrilegiously converts this into F. J.'s 'Frydayes feast' – a sordid consummation enjoyed on Venus' day – thereby bringing the most sublime down to the sexual, the spiritual down to the most crude and base. Yet, sexual desire is still an aspect, a manifestation of desire, and is still on the same spectrum, albeit at the opposite end of a desire that has been sublimated to the degree that Petrarch's had. Sexual desire thus still legitimately falls within the sonnet tradition's remit, much as it does in *Astrophil and Stella*, where Astrophil's interest is largely on Stella's body rather than her mind, and even in *Parthenophil and Parthenophe* where the speaker's desire actually culminates in rape. When it comes to the sonnet speaker not addressing a woman, Shakespeare, in the first 126 of his Sonnets, addresses his speaker to a male object of desire – 'my lovely boy', 'the master-mistress of my passion'.[51] But, while he, too, might be seen to be taking the sonnet tradition in a quite new direction, he can also be seen to be literalizing – simply taking to its logical conclusion – the Petrarchan model of praise in which an idealized object, 'Fair, kind, and true' (Sonnet 105), reflects back to the speaking subject an idealized image of itself. Insofar as this traditional model of praise puts two beings before one another who are, in this respect, the same – both equally ideal – Shakespeare is simply drawing out what one critic calls 'the homosexual truth subtending the poetics of admiration' that had characterized the Petrarchan mode from the beginning.[52] And when it comes, finally, to a lover who does not desire without end, Spenser in the *Amoretti* signals what could be taken as perhaps the greatest deviation from the sonnet tradition as we know it by having the speaker finally arrive at his long-deferred destination and actually win his lady – 'Most happy he that can at last atchyve / the joyous safety of so sweet a rest'[53] – all her gainsaying giving way (after sixty-two of the eighty-nine sonnets) to a resounding yes as she promises to return his love and commits to becoming his bride. Here again, however, any departure from the sonnet tradition turns out not to be as great as might at first appear, as we still remain within the more traditional scope of desire after all ('imaginatively', write Kerrigan and Braden, 'we are still on the frustration side of the barrier').[54] For the triumphal ending that Spenser's speaker looks forward to in the remaining *Amoretti* poems and then celebrates in the great wedding poem or *Epithalamion* that follows them might seem uniquely to parody the norm of perpetual disappointment that we find everywhere else in the sonnet tradition. But, as I have argued elsewhere, this great ending turns out to be more like the endings of *The Faerie Queene* – provisional, ambivalent, open-ended – for there are separations, failures, erasures, irresolutions and sorrows still to come.[55] For Spenser, as indeed for all the sonneteers I have been discussing here, the speaker essentially remains what he always was – subject to and of desire – and the poet's desire for a conclusive ending is necessarily suspended and held off to some distant and unrealizable point in the future.

Notes

1 Philip Sidney, *Astrophil and Stella* (composed 1581–2, first published 1591), Sonnet 56, in *The Poems of Sir Philip Sidney*, ed. W. A. Ringler, Jr (Oxford: Clarendon Press, 1962). Subsequent reference is to this edition.

2 George Puttenham, *The Arte of English Poesie* (1589), ed. G. D. Willcock and Alice Walker (Cambridge: Cambridge University Press, 1936), p. 60.

3 Edmund Spenser, *Amoretti* (1595), Sonnet 1, in *The Yale Edition of the Shorter Poems of Edmund Spenser*, ed. William A. Oram, Einar Bjorvand and Ronald Bond (New Haven: Yale University Press, 1989). Subsequent reference is to this edition.

4 Sidney, *Astrophil and Stella*, Sonnet 106.

5 *Ibid.*, Sonnet 1.

6 Samuel Daniel, *Delia* (1592), Sonnet 27, in *Poems and A Defence of Ryme*, ed. Arthur Colby Sprague (Chicago: University of Chicago Press, 1930). Subsequent reference is to this edition.

7 Henry Constable, *Diana* (1592), in Maurice Evans, ed., *Elizabethan Sonnets* (London: Dent, 1977).

8 Sidney, *Astrophil and Stella*, Sonnet 19.

9 Second quotation from Michael Drayton, *Idea*, Sonnet 43. First published in 1594 as *Ideas Mirrour*, Drayton's sequence was subject to numerous revisions and later editions. I quote here from the latest (1619) edition, in *The Works of Michael Drayton*, ed. J. W. Hebel, Kathleen Tillotson and Bernard Newdigate, 5 vols. (Oxford: Blackwell, 1931–41). Subsequent reference is to this edition.

10 George Chapman, *Ouids Banquet of Sence: A Coronet for His Mistresse Philosophie* (1595), containing ten sonnets.

11 From Giles Fletcher, the Elder, *Licia* (1593), in *The English Works of Giles Fletcher the Elder*, ed. Lloyd E. Berry (Madison: University of Wisconsin Press, 1964), pp. 79, 80. Subsequent reference is to this edition.
12 George Gascoigne, 'The Adventures of Master F. J.', in *A Hundreth Sundrie Flowres* (1573), ed. G. W. Pigman III (Oxford: Clarendon Press, 2000), p. 155.
13 Sidney, *Astrophil and Stella*, Sonnet 6.
14 Petrarch, *Rime sparse*, Sonnets 132, 134, in *Petrarch's Lyric Poems*, trans. and ed. Robert M. Durling (Cambridge, MA: Harvard University Press, 1976). Subsequent reference is to this edition.
15 *Ibid.*, Sonnet 57.
16 From poem 30 in Thomas Wyatt, *Collected Poems of Sir Thomas Wyatt*, ed. Kenneth Muir and Patricia Thomson (Liverpool: Liverpool University Press, 1969).
17 Sidney, *Astrophil and Stella*, Sonnet 29.
18 From Sidney, *Poems*, p. 161.
19 Barnabe Barnes, *Parthenophil and Parthenophe* (1593), Sonnet 84, in *Parthenophil and Parthenophe: A Critical Edition*, ed. Victor A. Doyno (Carbondale: Southern Illinois University Press, 1971).
20 Shakespeare, *Sonnets* (1609), Sonnet 115, from *The Sonnets and A Lover's Complaint*, ed. John Kerrigan (Harmondsworth: Penguin, 1986).
21 Sidney, *Astrophil and Stella*, Sonnet 1.
22 Anon., *Zepheria* (1594), Sonnet 20, in Sidney Lee, ed., *Elizabethan Sonnets*, 2 vols. (London: A. Constable and Co., 1904).
23 Sidney, *Astrophil and Stella*, Sonnet 1.
24 Lorna Hutson, *The Usurer's Daughter: Male Friendship and Fictions of Women in Sixteenth-Century England* (London: Routledge, 1994), pp. 98–9.
25 Drayton, *Idea*, Sonnet 5.
26 Sidney, *Astrophil and Stella*, Sonnet 4, 63.
27 William Kerrigan and Gordon Braden, *The Idea of the Renaissance* (Baltimore: Johns Hopkins University Press, 1989), p. 172.
28 Drayton, *Idea*, Sonnet 44.
29 Spenser, *Amoretti*, Sonnet 75.
30 Last quotation from Shakespeare, *Sonnets* (1609), Sonnet 81, from *The Sonnets and A Lover's Complaint*, ed. John Kerrigan (Harmondsworth: Penguin, 1986). Further reference is to this edition.
31 See in particular Marguerite Waller, *Petrarch's Poetics and Literary History* (Amherst: University of Massachusetts Press, 1980); Giuseppe Mazzotta, *The Worlds of Petrarch* (Durham, NC: Duke University Press, 1992); and Lynn Enterline, *The Rhetoric of the Body from Ovid to Shakespeare* (Cambridge: Cambridge University Press, 2000).
32 Petrarch, *Rime sparse*, Sonnet 1.
33 See Paul Oppenheimer, 'The Origin of the Sonnet', *Comparative Literature* 34 (1982), 289–304.
34 Daniel, *Delia*, Sonnet 21.
35 Sidney, *Astrophil and Stella*, Sonnet 95.
36 Fletcher, *Licia*, Sonnet 17.
37 Daniel, *Delia*, Sonnet 2.
38 Shakespeare, Sonnet 81.

39 Daniel, *Delia*, Sonnet 46.
40 From poem 7, in Henry Howard, earl of Surrey, *Poems*, ed. Emrys Jones (Oxford: Clarendon Press, 1964).
41 Daniel, *Delia*, Sonnet 35.
42 Sidney, *Astrophil and Stella*, Sonnet 90.
43 Raleigh's sonnet is reproduced in Edmund Spenser, *The Faerie Queene*, ed. A. C. Hamilton (London: Longman, 1977), p. 739.
44 Heather Dubrow, *Echoes of Desire: English Petrarchism and Its Counterdiscourses* (Ithaca, NY: Cornell University Press, 1995), pp. 11–12.
45 Sidney, *Astrophil and Stella*, Sonnet 15.
46 Probably composed in the 1590s, Davies's *Gullinge Sonnets* were not published until the nineteenth century. See John Davies, *The Poems of Sir John Davies*, ed. Robert Krueger (Oxford: Clarendon Press, 1975).
47 Drayton, *Idea*, 'To the reader of these sonnets', lines 5–7.
48 See Margaret A. Rose, *Parody: Ancient, Modern, and Post-Modern* (Cambridge: Cambridge University Press, 1993), pp. 48–51.
49 Sidney, *Poems*, p.12.
50 Gascoigne, *A Hundreth Sundrie Flowres*, p. 175.
51 Shakespeare, Sonnets 126, 20.
52 Joel Fineman, *Shakespeare's Perjured Eye: The Invention of Poetic Subjectivity in the Sonnets* (Berkeley: University of California Press), p. 17.
53 Spenser, *Amoretti*, Sonnet 63.
54 Kerrigan and Braden, *The Idea of the Renaissance*, p. 173.
55 See Catherine Bates, *The Rhetoric of Courtship in Elizabethan Language and Literature* (Cambridge: Cambridge University Press, 1992), pp. 138–51.

7

A. D. COUSINS

Shakespeare's Sonnets

Shakespeare's Sonnets, the most famous sonnets in the English language, are surrounded by uncertainties.[1] Almost all of them were probably written in the 1590s, at the height of the Elizabethan fashion for writing sonnets; but they were published in 1609 well after the fashion had passed, and we do not know whether Shakespeare authorized their appearance in print.[2] Consequently we don't know whether the order of the poems is that intended by Shakespeare. In the order as we have it, Sonnets 1–126 are closely concerned with a young man; from Sonnet 127 until 152, the so-called Dark Lady becomes a focus of attention. The sonnets ending the collection, 153 and 154, are playfully mythological poems associating love with disease and portraying desire as unquenchable. Yet many of the sonnets do not identify the gender of the person they address or discuss, so if we don't know whether the published order of the Sonnets is actually Shakespeare's, we cannot always be sure which sonnets refer to the young man and which to the Dark Lady.[3] Other things are also unclear, among them being the following. Was the young man a real person – and, if so, who? Was the Dark Lady real? If so, who was she? And who was the Mr W. H. to whom the publisher of the collection dedicated it? Are he and the young man the same person – assuming, of course, that the latter actually existed? How integrated with the Sonnets is *A Lover's Complaint*, which Shakespeare perhaps also wrote and which was printed with them? Those questions are important and some have virtually taken on lives of their own, within or beyond the wide domain of Shakespeare studies. Scholarly inquiry into the identity of Mr W. H. is ongoing (the two favourite candidates for the role are still Henry Wriothesley, earl of Southampton and William Herbert, third earl of Pembroke).[4] So too is the scholarly search for the name of the Dark Lady; and she has been featured prominently in novels.

Having more information about the Sonnets could, then, in many ways affect how we read them. Suppose for instance that the young man (and thus presumably Mr W. H.) was William Herbert, a member of the literary

Sidney family. We would therefore recognize the reference in Sonnet 5 to the *New Arcadia* of Sir Philip Sidney, Herbert's uncle, as a gracefully personalized allusion. Lines 9–11 of the fifth poem are, 'Then were not summer's distillation left / A liquid prisoner pent in walls of glass, / Beauty's effect with beauty were bereft', alluding to a speech in the *New Arcadia* where 'crystalline marriage' is likened to 'a pure rose-water kept in a crystal glass'.[5] In Sidney's prose romance the analogy is voiced by Cecropia who, having imprisoned her niece, seeks to persuade the young woman into marrying her son. In Sonnet 5, Shakespeare's speaker refashions that portion of Cecropia's self-interested advice. He offers it to the young man as part of an exhortation to escape from entrapment in self-love and marry for his own and his family's good.[6] If the young man were William Herbert, Shakespeare's speaker would thus be wittily recreating words penned by the earl's legendary uncle. He would be evoking their familial authority to reinforce elegant counsel that Herbert perpetuate himself through a son and thereby help perpetuate the Sidney dynasty.[7] We would be witnesses to a moment of deft and ingenious clientage.

Therefore, as the illustration above suggests, if such uncertainties make us wary readers of the Sonnets they by no means thwart our efforts to read them. In fact the primary challenge to our understanding the Sonnets is also of course that which draws us to them and inspires our fascination with them, namely their extraordinary intricacy of language. Stephen Booth makes this general observation about the poems' rich elusiveness of meaning: 'One great problem for both editors and readers of the [S]onnets is that words, lines, and clauses often give a multitude of meanings – of which none fits a single "basic" statement to which the others can be called auxiliary.'[8] With reference, however, to the order of the Sonnets as originally published, Colin Burrow ventures this:

> [T]here remain so many unanswered questions about the publication of the Sonnets in 1609 that it is impossible to be entirely sure that Shakespeare wished them to appear in exactly the form in which they were printed and at exactly that time, and whether he saw them as the culmination of his career as a poet. The passionate rationality of the poems can only have been the product of considered work, and ... it is very likely that Shakespeare at least provisionally put the sonnets into the order in which they appear in the 1609 Quarto.[9]

Burrow's hypothesis indicates a useful way forward – a mix of acceptance with caution. We can acknowledge the hints of narrative in the Sonnets but need not assume that the poems gesture toward a finally intended or fully coherent story. Nor of course need we believe that what looks like an implicit story should determine our understanding of the poems. We can acknowledge that Sonnets 1–126 seem recurrently addressed to or concerned with the young man, and that 127–52 likewise appear spoken to or preoccupied with the Dark Lady, but we must be circumspect in deciding what follows from either acknowledgement. Working 'provisionally' with the Sonnets in their published order, then, and exploring their complexity of language, we may begin to seek what makes them so powerful and distinctive a presence among the sonnets of Shakespeare's contemporaries.

A way to start is by considering how Shakespeare engaged with basic principles of sonnet design. According to George Gascoigne in his *Certain Notes of Instruction Concerning the Making of Verse or Rhyme in English* (1575):

> Some think that all poems (being short) may be called sonnets, as indeed it is a diminutive word derived of 'suonare', but yet I can best allow to call those Sonnets which are of fourteen lines, every line containing ten syllables. The first twelve do rhyme in staves of four lines by cross metre, and the last two, rhyming together, do conclude the whole.[10]

There Gascoigne describes what has become known as the sonnet's 'English' form. It was invented by Henry Howard, earl of Surrey, during the reign of Henry VIII and was subsequently used by Shakespeare throughout his Sonnets.[11] As Gascoigne's description indicates, the 'English' sonnet has three quatrains and a final couplet, rhyming *abab cdcd efef gg*. The individuation of its quatrains and couplet, in conjunction with its scheme of alternating rhymes, encourages parallelism and antithesis. Sonnets 12:1–8, 33:1–8, 53:1–12 and 64:1–10 are configured as elaborate and diverse patterns of equivalence, balance and contradiction. The separateness of the quatrains also offers scope for sequencing and accumulation of quite different kinds. Thus, in Sonnet 73, each quatrain is dominated by an image of natural decline and those images diminish as the quatrains succeed each other. Shakespeare's speaker portrays himself through lessening images of fading warmth and light: late autumn, twilight, a dying fire express his consciousness of having grown old. Through that sequence, as a result, the speaker both situates old age across the economy of nature and acts out its relentless process of decay. In Sonnet 66, on the other hand, the quatrains merge in a litany of the world's wrongs, whereas the quatrains of 129 elide in an insistent, veering, comprehensive denunciation of lust's qualities and consequences. Sonnet 91, by way of contrast, develops a syllogistic argument as quatrain follows quatrain – and, in doing so, divides into octave and sestet (the two sections of an 'Italian' sonnet). Sonnet 62 similarly unfolds, although in technique the poems are otherwise unlike. Shakespeare's interplaying of the quatrains in his Sonnets suggests the unique inventiveness and diversity with which he fashioned the 'English' sonnet form.

So too does his use of the final, epigrammatic couplet, although not everyone would agree. There has famously been comment that Shakespeare's final couplets can blandly or lamely conclude their preceding quatrains.[12] Sometimes they certainly do, as in Sonnet 111: 'Pity me then, dear friend, and I assure ye, / Even that your pity is enough to cure me.' It is not dissimilar to Shakespeare's sometimes laboured way of getting characters offstage. For all that, the inventiveness with which Shakespeare interplays the quatrains in his Sonnets means that their final couplets function more diversely than might be anticipated. They may, for example, bring a sequence to a climax (135), or bring judgement to bear on accumulated detail (130), or axiomatically conclude an elaborate pattern of parallelism and antithesis (94). They may also resolve a narrative in elaborate metaphors (69), question and subvert a precarious argument (92), or suddenly add new significance to a sequence of analogies (73). If they can be blandly or lamely conclusive, they can often be decisive, unexpected or unsettling in relation to what has preceded them.[13]

To illustrate more closely what contributes to the power and distinctiveness of the Sonnets, I want to focus initially on Sonnet 73, then on Sonnets 5 and 144. The first of those, as has been indicated above, exemplifies Shakespeare's virtuosity with quatrain and epigram in the 'English' sonnet form. I want to look further at how it does so – and at why. The other poems show different ways in which Shakespeare could charge the sonnet form with the energy of his theatrical skills (I have already glanced at how, in the fifth sonnet, Shakespeare uses allusion). Sonnets 73 and 5 are of particular interest for an additional reason, moreover, since each belongs to a suite of poems within the Sonnets as a whole. Earlier in this chapter, it was mentioned that we cannot know whether the published order of the Sonnets is actually Shakespeare's. However, from their lexical and rhetorical as well as their thematic ties, we can know that he intended some of the poems to constitute groupings within the larger collection. Sonnets 71–4, for instance, are linked meditations by the speaker on his proximity to death, on his physical decay and on what the young man's responses to his death should be.[14] Confronting the aristocratic young man with the inevitability of his own decline and death, Sonnets 1–17 join in urging him to marry and father a son who will perpetuate both his beauty and the dynasty to which he belongs. Sonnets 73 and 5 therefore have double functions within the Sonnets, contributing to defined suites of poems and at the same time to the textures of the sequence as we have it.

In Sonnet 73, Shakespeare's speaker portrays himself as on the edge of nothingness:

> That time of year thou mayst in me behold
> When yellow leaves, or none, or few, do hang
> Upon those boughs which shake against the cold,
> Bare ruined choirs, where late the sweet birds sang.
> In me thou seest the twilight of such day
> As after sunset fadeth in the west,
> Which by and by black night doth take away,
> Death's second self, that seals up all in rest.
> In me thou seest the glowing of such fire
> That on the ashes of his youth doth lie,
> As the death-bed whereon it must expire,
> Consumed with that which it was nourished by.
>   This thou perceiv'st, which makes thy love more strong,
>   To love that well which thou must leave ere long.

Earlier the point was made that, as the quatrains of this sonnet follow one another, Shakespeare's speaker voices perception of his old age chiefly through lessening images of fading warmth and light (late autumn, twilight, a dying fire) – and that in doing so he both situates old age across the economy of nature and mimes its unrelenting process of decay. Although those remarks help illustrate Shakespeare's inventiveness with the 'English' form of the sonnet, they do not by themselves suggest what makes Sonnet 73 so powerful and distinctive a use of the form to articulate consciousness of physical decline. To appreciate that, one must look more inquiringly at the poem's successive images and final couplet.

What makes those images compelling – what, in other words, contributes to much of the sonnet's power and distinctiveness in expressing the experience of age – is primarily their inverting and personalizing of conventional descriptive modes. Shakespeare reconceives rather than merely enlivens literary convention. Set-piece description of a time was an established technique among medieval and early modern writers. The technique was called *cronographia* and Puttenham observed: '[I]f we describe the time or season of the year, as winter, summer, harvest, day midnight, noon, evening, or such like: we call such description the counterfeit time. *Cronographia* examples are every where to be found.'[15] Chaucer's *The Canterbury Tales* opens with a description of spring. Skelton's *The Bowge of Courte* begins with a description of autumn; and so does Shakespeare's Sonnet 73 – but with an innovative difference.[16] Instead of placing himself within autumn, Shakespeare's speaker locates autumn within himself. He presents himself as an incarnation of the season, as a microcosm of decay in the natural cycle and yet, of course, as without hope of natural renewal. Winter is close; spring impossible. That description of 'the time or season of the year' then turns suddenly into a description of place, or *topographia*, as barren boughs metamorphose into broken chancel (line 4).[17] Shakespeare gives the sonnet's initial quatrain a stylistic energy and imaginative scope that make the speaker's portrayal of his physical decline an unexpected convergence of nature and art, time and history.

The inverting and personalizing of descriptive convention in the sonnet becomes more sombre when Shakespeare subsequently diminishes the image of autumn into that of twilight and, thereafter, the image of twilight into that of a dying fire. In the second quatrain, another *cronographia* turned inwards ('In me thou seest the twilight of such day / As after sunset fadeth in the west') is linked quickly with description of a time ('black night') both pictured as external to the speaker and half brought to life. The speaker presents himself not merely as incarnating a natural phenomenon but, consequently, as about to be caught up in a natural process where the predominant force seems almost to have a sinister life of its own. Then from the half-personified night, closing the quatrain just as it closes the light of day, he proceeds in the final quatrain to what is least among the images of fading warmth and light. Yet in those lines he formally describes not so much the 'glowing' of a nearly extinct fire as its process of self-consumption. Through internalizing description of that process he portrays himself as embodying an inexorable self-depletion – in fact, as embodying an entirely natural process that suggests the course of life to be, ultimately, self-defeat. Moreover, Shakespeare's final play with descriptive convention has his speaker turn inwards and personalize the description of an action (*pragmatographia*) that evokes the phrase 'ashes to ashes' from the Elizabethan service for the Burial of the Dead; except, here, the actual image of 'ashes' carries no spiritual significance.[18] This quatrain, like its predecessors, erases the idea of renewal. The speaker implies that his life is an autumn facing winter but without hope of spring, a twilight facing night but without expectation of dawn, a fire on the verge of extinction in ashes.

A solely material view on the experience of old age is developed throughout the quatrains and, at the sonnet's end, the speaker emphasizes how physically different he and the young man are. When he says to the young man, 'This thou perceiv'st ...' (line 13), he means of course that the young man is well aware of the physical decline suggested in the quatrains above. However, the speaker also means that the young man understands him just the way he understands himself. He alleges a oneness of mind between them that transcends their physical difference, so creating a fiction of their sameness.[19] That fiction is then made the basis of another. Their oneness of understanding, the speaker claims, intensifies the young man's love for him.[20] Thus the epigrammatic conclusion to the sonnet indicates why the speaker has been constructing his elaborate and materialist self-portrayal: it enables the ambitious insistence that he and the young man share an intense unity of spirit.

What the speaker maintains he and the young man share recalls Aristotle's observation, much quoted in Shakespeare's time, that a friend is 'A single soul dwelling in two bodies'.[21] However, in Sonnet 74 he develops a variant of that idea. There the speaker says, referring to the Sonnets (or, at least, some of them):

> My life hath in this line some interest,
> Which for memorial still with thee shall stay.
> When thou reviewest this, thou dost review
> The very part was consecrate to thee:
> The earth can have but earth, which is his due;
> My spirit is thine, the better part of me. (3–8)

Not one soul in two bodies, then, but souls united across a body and a body of verse – verse that often claims to immortalize the body and soul of the young man and that now is said also to be the monument containing the speaker's soul. The young man is depicted as being literally able to hold that monument ('memorial'), and therefore the speaker's soul, in his hands.[22] The suite of sonnets (71–4) began with the speaker disingenuously protesting that the young man should forget him and his verse:

> Nay, if you read this line, remember not
> The hand that writ it, for I love you so
> That I in your sweet thoughts would be forgot,
> If thinking on me then should make you woe. (71:5–8)

It ends with his radically inventive insistence upon their collective inseparability.

Considering what makes Sonnet 73 powerful and distinctive lets us see something of what makes the Sonnets as a whole stand out from the sequences by Shakespeare's contemporaries. So does similar consideration of Sonnets 5 and 144. In those poems, as I have suggested above, Shakespeare charges the sonnet form with the energy of his theatrical skills – and in interestingly different ways. The first presents the young man's life as participation in a spectacle, a courtly pageant at once personal and universal, immediate and yet perennial. The second presents the speaker's experience of divided desire as an im-morality play, a confused and contaminated conflict between better and worse impulses for dominance of his life. The poem by one of Shakespeare's contemporaries that comes closest to his achievement in Sonnet 5 is arguably Sir Walter Raleigh's sonnet, 'Methought I saw the grave where Laura lay'.[23] There, Raleigh unfolds a miniature, courtly pageant fabling Elizabethan England's rise to both cultural and political dominance in Europe. The most interesting analogue to Sonnet 144 may well be Christopher Marlowe's *Doctor Faustus*, itself a rewriting of the morality play. Shakespeare's speaker could be seen as an eroticized Faustus, making *his* choices in a personal universe that is compelled and riven by sexual desire, a universe that is material and ambiguous.[24]

Sonnet 5 is addressed to an aristocratic young man who, like many of the women addressed in other sonnet sequences, is alleged to be narcissistically preoccupied with his own good looks. In this sonnet, Shakespeare's speaker tries to make the young man look beyond himself, view a representation of his place in the economy of nature, and therefore accept as an imperative the idea that he must procreate in order to ensure his beauty's and his dynasty's survival.[25] By way of making the young man understand where he truly is in the scheme of things – beyond his beauty and his social status – the speaker images the young man's participation in the natural cycle as a brilliant but of course temporary role in a recurring courtly pageant:

> Those hours that with gentle work did frame
> The lovely gaze where every eye doth dwell
> Will play the tyrants to the very same,
> And that unfair which fairly doth excel;
> For never-resting time leads summer on
> To hideous winter and confounds him there,
> Sap checked with frost and lusty leaves quite gone,
> Beauty o'ersnowed and bareness every where ...   (1–8)

The stylized drama of the quatrains presents the young man as both the favourite and the victim of time (the 'hours'), linking his particular story with time's ritual destruction of summer: with the universal fate of beauty in the economy of nature. The ceremonial drama of the sonnet's opening, that is to say, emphasizes the young man's uniquely privileged place in the scheme of things but also confronts him with the fact that the natural forces that have especially favoured him will ultimately treat him just as they do everyone and everything else. Later in the suite of poems to which Sonnet 5 belongs, however, we discover that the young man is unreceptive to the truth set dramatically before him. Shakespeare's speaker begins overtly to contrast his creative power with the personal uncreativeness of the beautiful, socially powerful young man, announcing that he will immortalize in his verse the narcissistic youth who makes no move towards self-perpetuation (see, for example, 15:13–14 and 16:1–4, along with 17:9–14).

As has been indicated above, in Sonnet 144 the speaker dramatizes his experience of divided desire by parodying the format of a morality play and virtually turning himself into a Faustus whose concerns are wholly erotic:

> Two loves I have, of comfort and despair,
> Which like two spirits do suggest me still:
> The better angel is a man right fair;
> The worser spirit a woman coloured ill.
> To win me soon to hell my female evil
> Tempteth my better angel from my side,
> And would corrupt my saint to be a devil,
> Wooing his purity with her foul pride.
> And whether that my angel be turned fiend
> Suspect I may, yet not directly tell,
> But being both from me, both to each friend,
> I guess one angel in another's hell.
>   Yet this shall I ne'er know, but live in doubt,
>   Till my bad angel fire my good one out.

The speaker's sexual use of religious language – in fact, his sexual appropriating of morality-play convention – emphasizes how very worldly the Sonnets are. No less important is the duplicity of the speaker in fashioning his drama. The young man is said to be not merely 'a man right fair' (3) but the speaker's 'better angel' and his 'saint' (3, 7). The Dark Lady is not merely said to be 'a woman coloured ill' but the speaker's 'worser spirit' and 'female evil': implicitly, 'a devil' or 'fiend' (4–5, 7, 9). The speaker crudely demonizes the Dark Lady and disingenuously idealizes the young man. She is extravagantly transformed into a grotesque. He is declared to be an angelic or saintly friend, even though the speaker's hyperboles imply the implausibility of such a characterization.[26] Concluding this brief, embittered drama of wilful misrepresentation and uncertainty, the final couplet confirms our awareness that, if the speaker resembles Marlowe's Doctor Faustus, he is a Faustus likely to be betrayed by both of those closest to him but certainly by his determination to caricature them and their relationships to him.

The inventiveness variously to be seen in Sonnets 73, 5 and 144 is part, as I have indicated, of a more comprehensive originality that distinguishes the Sonnets as a whole from the sequences of love sonnets by Shakespeare's contemporaries. It distinguishes the Sonnets, in fact, especially from the ways in which those sequences make use of Petrarchan convention. A challenge confronting Elizabethan writers of sonnet sequences about love was how to make their work distinctive within the established practice of imitating

Petrarch's *Rime sparse*, long agreed to be the iconic sequence of love sonnets in Europe. (Thus that challenge didn't involve trying to repudiate the Petrarchan inheritance but, rather, seeking to make it one's own.[27]) They were evidently fascinated, for example, by Petrarch's speaker in the *Rime*: by his tortuous self-scrutiny, by his anxieties over the nature and status of his desire, by the emotionally intense and paradoxical rhetoric through which he expressed his longing and his self-doubt. But how could they reinvent him so that he would become theirs, staging their desires and concerns in their circumstances?

Shakespeare's originality among those heirs to the Petrarchan inheritance lies in his fashioning a speaker who, while profoundly un-Petrarchan in more than one respect, is in others truly Petrarchan. That is to say, in his Sonnets Shakespeare adapts the Petrarchan speaker to un-Petrarchan circumstances: he fashions a speaker whose experiences of desire acknowledge but also turn away from the Petrarchan model of what desire is. Some of that acknowledging yet turning away is immediately striking. The object of desire in Petrarchan love verse is female and usually, on the precedent of Petrarch's Laura, golden-haired. From the beginning of the 1609 Quarto, Shakespeare's speaker identifies a fair-haired young man, not a blonde woman, as the focus of his concern – thereafter, ambiguously, of his desire (see 1:9–14 with 10:13, thence 13:13 and 15:13). Furthermore, the speakers of Petrarch and, say, Sidney or Spenser accuse their ladies of being narcissistic: Shakespeare's speaker reproves the young man for narcissism.[28] He is reproached in Sonnet 1 for being 'contracted' – bound as if by a marriage contract – 'to [his] own bright eyes' (line 5). His fascination with his own eyes recalls that of Narcissus when he stared lovingly at his reflection in the water. Ovid wrote: '[I]t doth him [Narcissus] good to see / His ardant eyes which like two starres full bright and shyning bee'.[29] However, Shakespeare's speaker is at once more deeply un-Petrarchan and more truly Petrarchan than those illustrations imply.

He is not an original presence within Elizabethan sonnet sequences merely because he voices desire for a young man. After all, the speaker of Richard Barnfield's *Cynthia* (1595) does so with an overtly erotic intensity. The more profoundly un-Petrarchan aspects of Shakespeare's speaker, and hence in broad terms of the Sonnets, lie beyond that. He voices desire for a fair-haired young man whom he depicts as androgynous in beauty and as unstable or flawed in personality. He also voices desire for a woman whose dark colouring he connects with a darkness of personality that he alleges is hers as well. Petrarch's *Rime sparse* concentrates all its sexual longing on one person, Laura, and she is of course female, blonde, perfect. As it was in the *Rime*, so it would predominantly be in the Elizabethan sonnet sequences about love. A few celebrate several mistresses; none tells of desire focused on a man and a woman – much less a man and woman like the youth and the Dark Lady in the Sonnets. None tells of desire for a man and a woman who are in turn involved with one another. And the Shakespearean speaker's experience of desire is emphatically of this world – perhaps, it might be better said, of this world as imagined rather by Ovid than by Petrarch. Yet in his deeply un-Petrarchan experiencing of desire Shakespeare's speaker still reveals himself as truly Petrarchan. Divided in his responses to the young man, divided in his responses to the Dark Lady, and divided between each of them, he is a heightened embodiment of that self-division that characterizes Petrarch's speaker in the *Rime*. In the case of Shakespeare's speaker as of Petrarch's, it engenders or informs intricate self-analysis, anxiety or uncertainty over the meanings and value of desire, a passionate, troubled rhetoric of contradiction and paradox. An interesting consequence is that Shakespeare's speaker, like Petrarch's, comes to acknowledge that the myth of Narcissus has relevance to him as well as to the object of his desire (that is, one of the two objects – the young man).

That fashioning of Shakespeare's speaker appears strikingly in the 1609 Quarto soon after the so-called 'procreation sonnets' (1–17). Sonnet 20 opens with his identifying the young man as an androgyne, as desired because he transcends the boundaries of gender:

> A woman's face with Nature's own hand painted
> Hast thou, the master-mistress of my passion;
> A woman's gentle heart, but not acquainted
> With shifting change, as is false women's fashion;
> An eye more bright than theirs, less false in rolling,
> Gilding the object whereupon it gazeth;
> A man in hue, all hues in his controlling,
> Which steals men's eyes and women's souls amazeth.   (1–8)

The speaker's oxymoronic image of the young man as his 'master-mistress' (2) implies however that the youth does not seamlessly integrate male with female. It implies that in him the genders coexist rather than merge, and that the speaker's response to the young man is divided. So the sestet of the sonnet affirms, for the speaker concedes that, even if the young man is in some respects more genuinely female than are actual women, he is nevertheless biologically male: 'Nature', the speaker says in the little mock-fable of lines 9–12, 'by addition me of thee defeated, / By adding one thing to my purpose nothing'. The young man is thus a divergent rather than a transcendent object of desire; and, in the final couplet of the sonnet, we see that the speaker's analysis of his desire for the young man is itself ambiguous. He

says: 'But since she [Nature] pricked thee out for women's pleasure, / Mine
be thy love, and thy love's use their treasure'. The words in which he claims
to have no sexual interest in the young man contain two genitally focused
puns: 'pricked' and 'treasure', alluding respectively to male and female genitalia. '[N]othing', in line 12, is also a pun on genitalia – and can refer to male
or female genitals. The speaker's denial of sexual desire for the youth is, as
a result, intimately and insistently and uncertainly erotic.

Shakespeare is thus not fashioning a new kind of individual consciousness
in the Sonnets, but one that is innovative because, amidst an experiencing
of desire un-Petrarchan in its scope and its worldliness, it reveals itself as
nevertheless Petrarchan. He is not repudiating a now-exhausted 'poetry of
praise' as remade by Petrarch in his own image.[30] Shakespeare is making
the refracted Petrarchan idiom idiosyncratically his own. Just as that could
be seen in Sonnet 20, so too it can be seen in Sonnet 53. And that poem,
like its predecessor in the 1609 Quarto, indicates the difficulty with which
Shakespeare's speaker imposes idealizing fictions on the young man. As if in
a bewildered, epiphanic moment – and thereby in accord with a technique
from the *Rime* – he muses:

> What is your substance, whereof are you made,
> That millions of strange shadows on you tend,
> Since every one hath, every one, one shade,
> And you, but one, can every shadow lend?
> Describe Adonis, and the counterfeit
> Is poorly imitated after you;
> On Helen's cheek all art of beauty set,
> And you in Grecian tires are painted new;
> Speak of the spring and foison of the year:
> The one doth shadow of your beauty show,
> The other as your bounty doth appear,
> And you in every blessed shape we know.
>   In all external grace you have some part,
>   But you like none, none you, for constant heart.

According to the speaker's elaborate fiction, the young man defies ordinary
understanding as though he were a god: he is said to transcend not merely
the boundaries of gender but even those of space and time. His androgyny
is perfect, for he is both the archetype of Adonis and the exact counterpart to Helen of Troy if imagined at her best. He reconciles not merely
the opposites of gender in his person but, also, opposites within the natural cycle – although spring and autumn offer only analogues to his beauty
and generosity. In fact, every manifestation of beauty in the world points
toward him (much as the theology of Shakespeare's time stated that all the

world's beauty points toward the God who created it). Yet the speaker's deifying image of the young man is discordant amidst its assertions of concord. When he links the young man with Adonis, we remember Shakespeare's mixed characterization of Adonis in his *Venus and Adonis*, which was written around the time that the Sonnets were probably begun. There Adonis is androgynously beautiful, comic, knowingly self-ignorant, a figure of pathos and, ultimately, a victim. When the speaker links the young man with Helen of Troy, we remember that in early modern texts – including Shakespeare's *Lucrece*, written straight after *Venus and Adonis* – she is connected with flawless female beauty but also with treachery and destruction. The mythic allusions asserting the young man's perfect androgyny imply that he, if not it, is imperfect and unstable. So too does the syntax of the sonnet's final couplet. Momentarily, in line 14, 'like' reads as a verb: the speaker seems almost at the same time to deny and to proclaim the young man's constancy. Idealizing fictions crucial to the speaker's portrayal of the young man – namely, those of his androgyny and his spiritual oneness with the speaker – suggest the instability or uncertainty of them both.

The ambiguities attributed to the young man and evident in the speaker's responses to him recur throughout Sonnets 1–126 as we have them in the Quarto. In Sonnet 33, for example, the speaker indicates that the young man is the sun of his life (lines 9–12) but unavoidably flawed even if resplendent. However, although the speaker emphasizes that the young man is in some unidentified way imperfect, he more emphatically excuses his being so: 'Yet him for this my love no whit disdaineth: / Suns of the world may stain, when heaven's sun staineth' (lines 13–14). The Petrarchan image of the beloved as sun-like in possessing a unique and splendid beauty is reinvented to suggest the contaminated, worldly splendour of the young man and the self-division in the speaker's reaction to him. The young man is similarly associated with the sun, as well as with other things, in 35:1–4; nevertheless, the speaker's self-division is registered at greater length in the poem and more sharply. At its close the speaker says of his excusing the young man's offence against him: 'Such civil war is in my love and hate / That I an accessory needs must be / To that sweet thief which sourly robs from me' (lines 12–14). The lines show the speaker's contrary impulses engendering self-analysis that is – like so much of the self-scrutiny voiced in Petrarch's *Rime* – elaborate, disillusioned and powerless.

If by implication the young man surpasses Laura because of his androgynous beauty yet, unlike her, is personally flawed, the Dark Lady seems both his and Laura's dark parody. The speaker's imaging of her is not invariably negative; often, however, his responses to her are more violently at war with one another than are his divided reactions to the young man. He creates his most positive portrayal of the Dark Lady in Sonnet 130, where he begins with an unworried concession, 'My mistress' eyes are nothing like the sun'. He continues: 'If hairs be wires, black wires grow on her head' (line 4). And near the poem's end, he adds: 'I grant I never saw a goddess go – / My mistress when she walks treads on the ground' (lines 11–12). His mistress is, then, un-Petrarchan in her everyday humanity: she is benignly antithetic to the young man and to Laura. But in celebrating her, Shakespeare's speaker is not necessarily repudiating the Petrarchan ideal of beauty. Joking about that was a familiar practice within Petrarchan discourse itself.[31] More important, at the poem's close the speaker raises the issue of misrepresentation: 'And yet, by heaven, I think my love as rare / As any she belied with false compare'. In 130 he chooses to represent his mistress as a realistically attractive woman who doesn't need to be misrepresented by the use of Petrarchan cliché. In most of the other Dark Lady sonnets – as we have seen already in connection with 144 – he chooses to denigrate or to demonize her: to caricature her and, sometimes, in the process, himself.

That fashioning of caricature occurs with different emphases in Sonnets 147 and 148. Sonnet 147 begins with the speaker suggesting that his desire and his reason are violently in opposition, for his desire is diseased and seeks what is fatal to his wellbeing:

> My love is as a fever, longing still
> For that which longer nurseth the disease,
> Feeding on that which doth preserve the ill,
> Th'uncertain sickly appetite to please.
> My reason, the physician to my love,
> Angry that his prescriptions are not kept,
> Hath left me, and I desperate now approve
> Desire is death, which physic did except. (1–8)

His self-division drives an anxious, powerless scrutiny of a desire that is and, it seems, can solely be, carnal. The images of bodily illness and appetite imply that desire for the Dark Lady – unlike desire for the young man – can be concupiscent and nothing more. Consequently we see that here the speaker is Petrarchan in his response to an object of desire who is profoundly un-Petrarchan; in fact, we see that the portrayal of his response to the Dark Lady appears so intense as to verge on caricature of the way Petrarch's speaker voices lament and outrage. In the sestet, Shakespeare's speaker exclaims:

> Past cure I am, now reason is past care,
> And, frantic mad with evermore unrest,

> My thoughts and my discourse as madmen's are,
> At random from the truth vainly expressed:
>   For I have sworn thee fair, and thought thee bright,
>   Who art as black as hell, as dark as night.   (9–14)

If the speaker comes close to being a parody of Petrarch's speaker in the *Rime*, he certainly caricatures his mistress as a dark counterpart to the young man and ultimately to Laura. Lines 9–12 recall the experience of lust as described in Sonnet 129:6–9, thus stressing the carnality of the desire roused by the Dark Lady, and the final couplet's generic hyperboles turn her into a shadowy type of the monstrous. Reflecting that in the past he misrepresented his mistress as 'fair' and 'bright', Shakespeare's speaker concludes with what is a merely antithetic misrepresentation – no less a caricature than his idealizing of her. Sonnet 147 reveals that the speaker, his desire and its object are all flawed.

In Sonnet 148 the speaker implicitly denigrates the Dark Lady, keeping his portrayal of her in the domain of caricature, but overtly and distinctly caricatures himself. Pondering how confused his understanding of her has been, he asks:

> O how can love's eye be true,
> That is so vexed with watching and with tears?
> No marvel then though I mistake my view:
> The sun itself sees not till heaven clears.
>   O cunning love, with tears thou keep'st me blind,
>   Lest eyes, well seeing, thy foul faults should find.   (9–14)

His allusion to the sun contrasts with his uses of sun imagery in Sonnets 18, 33 and 34. There, images of the sun indicate either the perfection of the young man (18) or his finally excusable imperfection (33–4). Here, the speaker's image of the sun is used in self-excuse: it is natural, under the circumstances, that he has wrongly perceived his mistress. In the final couplet, however, he excuses his mistakenness through wry and witty self-caricature. '[L]ove' has remade him in its own image – into a type of Blind Cupid – and so he cannot see what he intuits as the error of desiring the Dark Lady. At the poem's conclusion, caricature expresses both loss of self and understanding of that loss – but understanding that leads nowhere.

The self-division that links the speaker of the Sonnets with his counterpart in Petrarch's *Rime* subtly extends beyond his having contrary responses to the young man or the Dark Lady. When, for example, Shakespeare's speaker magnificently promises the young man immortality in his verse (cf. the discussion of Sonnet 5, above), he cunningly evades his promise's fulfilment. In

Sonnet 18 he promises that the young man's perfect beauty will flourish forever in his 'eternal lines' (line 12). Yet because the speaker has already denied that anything in the natural order at its best could be used to signify the youth's beauty (lines 1–8), the poem offers no description of him.[32] Having made the young man a flatteringly absent presence in the poem, the speaker goes on to offer an insistent celebration of his own creative power (lines 9–14). In Sonnet 55, the speaker begins by fashioning a heroic assertion of his art's ability to conquer time, promising as he does so to eternize the young man (lines 1–8); but he ends with a triumphalist narrative, focused on them both, where the young man is a featureless actor whose immortalization still lies in a promise. In such poems the speaker's artistic power implicitly complements, or displaces, the social power of the young man.

The speaker indicates clearly throughout the Sonnets that his self-division cannot be resolved while desire lasts – and no less clearly he signals that, in one form or another, his desire is incessant. At one point he identifies himself as being, like the speaker in the *Rime*, permeated by self-love. 'Sin of self-love possesseth all mine eye, / And all my soul, and all my every part', he says (62:1–2). Yet he proceeds to image himself as a Narcissus whose gazing at his own likeness turns him from self-love to love for another, the other self who is the young man:

> But when my glass shows me myself indeed,
> Beated and chopped with tanned antiquity,
> Mine own self-love quite contrary I read;
> Self so self-loving were iniquity.
>   'Tis thee (my self) that for myself I praise,
>   Painting my age with beauty of thy days.   (62:9–14)

He can rewrite the story of Narcissus, whereas the young man can merely re-enact it. So the 'procreation sonnets' suggest about the young man, and they are not alone. Among the 'rival poet' sonnets, for instance, Sonnet 84 concludes with this remark to the youth: 'You to your beauteous blessings add a curse, / Being fond on praise, which makes your praises worse.' However, the last of the poems in the 1609 Quarto, Sonnets 153–4, are not about self-love; they do not allude to Narcissus. They evoke Cupid, Venus and Diana in order to imply that although the power of sexual desire can be displaced it cannot be conquered. In Sonnet 154, a nymph who has 'vowed chaste life to keep' (3) takes the 'heart-inflaming brand' (2) of Cupid and then immerses it in

>   a cool well by,
> Which from Love's fire took heat perpetual,
> Growing a bath and healthful remedy

> For men diseased; but I, my mistress' thrall,
> Came there for cure, and this by that I prove:
> Love's fire heats water, water cools not love.   (154:9–14)

For venereal disease there can be a cure, the speaker says, but for sexual desire, none. The Sonnets, in the form we have them, do not end with renunciation of physical desire (which occurs in Petrarch's *Rime*) or its sanctified fulfilment in marriage (anticipated in Spenser's *Amoretti*). Like Sidney's *Astrophil and Stella*, they end with elegantly expressed resignation to the persistence of sexual desire and its conflicts. Shakespeare's speaker tells throughout the Sonnets, nevertheless, of a desire differing in its human scope and its worldliness from that voiced by the speakers of Sidney, or Spenser, or Petrarch.

Notes

1 Reference to Shakespeare's Sonnets is from William Shakespeare, *The Sonnets*, ed. G. Blakemore Evans and introd. Anthony Hecht (Cambridge: Cambridge University Press, 1996). I am grateful to Catherine Bates and Helen Wilcox for their helpful comments on the initial version of this chapter.
2 With regard to problems of dating, authorization, order and so on, see especially: *ibid.*, pp. 110–15; William Shakespeare, *Shakespeare's Sonnets*, ed. Katherine Duncan-Jones (London: Thomas Nelson, 1998), pp. 1–69; William Shakespeare, *The Complete Sonnets and Poems*, ed. Colin Burrow (Oxford: Oxford University Press, 2002), pp. 91–111; James Schiffer, 'Reading New Life into Shakespeare's Sonnets: A Survey of Criticism', in James Schiffer, ed., *Shakespeare's Sonnets: Critical Essays* (New York: Garland, 2000), pp. 3–71; Heather Dubrow, '"Incertainties now crown themselves assur'd": The Politics of Plotting Shakespeare's Sonnets', in Schiffer, *Shakespeare's Sonnets*, pp. 113–33; and her '"Dressing old words new"? Re-evaluating the "Delian Structure"', in Michael Schoenfeldt, ed., *A Companion to Shakespeare's Sonnets* (Oxford: Blackwell, 2007), pp. 90–103.
3 See especially here Dubrow's 'Incertainties now crown themselves assur'd', in Schiffer, *Shakespeare's Sonnets*, pp. 123–8.
4 Discussion of the cases for and against each of them can be found in the commentaries by Evans (Shakespeare, *The Sonnets*, p. 15); Duncan-Jones (Shakespeare, *Shakespeare's Sonnets*, pp. 33, 52–69); and Schiffer (*Shakespeare's Sonnets*, pp. 24–31 – cf. p. 32).
5 That allusion to Sidney's *New Arcadia* has been often noted. Apparently the first to do so was H. C. Beeching in his *The Sonnets of Shakespeare* (London: Athenaeum Press, 1904), p. 83. See Philip Sidney, *The Countess of Pembroke's Arcadia (The New Arcadia)*, ed. Victor Skretkowicz (Oxford: Oxford University Press, 1987), p. 333.
6 On the youth's entrapment in self-love, as identified in the preceding sonnets, see: 1:5–12; 2:7–8; 3:7–8; 4:5–12.
7 For a general account of how the Sonnets interact with Sidney's *Astrophil and Stella*, see Anne Ferry, *The 'Inward' Language: Sonnets of Wyatt, Sidney, Shakespeare, Donne* (Chicago: University of Chicago Press, 1983), pp. 170–214.

8 See William Shakespeare, *Shakespeare's Sonnets*, ed. Stephen Booth (New Haven: Yale University Press, 1977), p. xii.

9 Shakespeare, *The Complete Sonnets*, ed. Burrow, p. 91. Cf. pp. 94–5, and Heather Dubrow's response in her *The Challenges of Orpheus: Lyric Poetry and Early Modern England* (Baltimore: Johns Hopkins University Press, 2008), p. 180.

10 George Gascoigne, *Certain Notes of Instruction Concerning the Making of Verse or Rhyme in English*, in Gavin Alexander, ed., *Sidney's* The Defence of Poesy *and Selected Renaissance Literary Criticism* (London: Penguin, 2004), pp. 237–47 (p. 245).

11 Three poems in Shakespeare's Sonnets aren't in fact sonnets (99, 126, 145). Moreover, the sonnet's 'English' form was of course used by other poets, such as Samuel Daniel in his *Delia*. Daniel's sequence appeared in 1592, at much the time when Shakespeare was probably beginning his. See also Thomas Watson's *The Teares of Fancie; or, Loue Disdained* (London, 1593), which makes use of the 'English' sonnet.

12 For discussion of such views see the second chapter of Rosalie L. Colie's *Shakespeare's Living Art* (Princeton: Princeton University Press, 1974), pp. 68–134 (pp. 68–79). The chapter as a whole offers a landmark account of the Sonnets in relation to Renaissance sonnet theory.

13 Shakespeare understood, as did Donne, 'that in all Metricall compositions … the force of the whole piece, is for the most part left to the shutting up; the whole frame of the Poem is a beating out of a piece of gold, but the last clause is as the impression of the stamp, and that is it that makes it currant'. See P. G. Stanwood and Heather Ross Asals, eds., *John Donne and the Theology of Language* (Columbia: University of Missouri Press, 1986), p. 68.

14 Perhaps we cannot be certain as to whether the young man or the Dark Lady (or even someone else) is the addressee here; nevertheless, it seems far more likely than otherwise to be the young man – on internal grounds and also because of the marked affinities between Sonnets 71–4 and poems such as 26 and 32.

15 George Puttenham, *The Arte of English Poesie*, ed. Gladys Doidge Willcock and Alice Walker (Cambridge: Cambridge University Press, 1936), p. 239. Puttenham's book first appeared in 1589. In *The Garden of Eloquence*, printed twelve years previously, Henry Peacham had written of 'Cronographia, when we do plainly describe any time for delectation's sake, as the Morning, the evening … the spring time, Summer, Autumn …'. See Henry Peacham, *The Garden of Eloquence* (London, 1577), fos. P1–P2. In both quotations, as below, I have modernized spelling but not punctuation.

16 See General Prologue, lines 1–18, in Geoffrey Chaucer, *The Riverside Chaucer*, ed. Larry D. Benson, 3rd edn (Boston: Houghton Mifflin, 1987); and John Skelton, *The Bowge of Courte*, lines 1–7, in *John Skelton: The Complete English Poems*, ed. John Scattergood (Harmondsworth: Penguin, 1983).

17 Puttenham wrote 'And if this description be of any true place, city, castle, hill, valley or sea, and such like: we call it the counterfeit place *Topographia*, or if ye feign places untrue …' (Puttenham, *The Arte*, p. 23; cf. Peacham, *The Garden*, fo. P1). Cf. Evans's note on line 4 (Shakespeare, *The Sonnets*, p. 179), and the note by Duncan-Jones, in Shakespeare, *Shakespeare's Sonnets* (p. 256). See, further: William Empson, *Seven Types of Ambiguity: A Study of Its Effects in English Verse*, 3rd edn (London: Chatto and Windus, 1963), pp. 2–3; William

Shakespeare, *Shakespeare's Sonnets*, ed. W. G. Ingram and Theodore Redpath (London: University of London Press, 1964), p. 168; William Shakespeare, *The Sonnets and* A Lover's Complaint, ed. John Kerrigan (Harmondsworth: Penguin, 1986), pp. 265–6; and Shakespeare, *The Complete Sonnets*, ed. Burrow, p. 526.

18 In *The Garden*, Peacham writes of *pragmatographia* as 'a description of things, whereby we do as plainly describe any thing by gathering together all the circumstances belonging to it, as if it were most lively painted out in colours, and set forth to be seen' (fo. O4r). Cf. Puttenham, *The Arte*, pp. 239–40. For 'ashes to ashes', see John E. Booty, ed., *The Book of Common Prayer 1559: The Elizabethan Prayer Book* (Charlottesville: University Press of Virginia, 1976), p. 310. The immediate context of the phrase is, '[W]e therefore commit his body to the ground, earth to earth, ashes to ashes, dust to dust, in sure and certain hope of resurrection to eternal life, through our Lord Jesus Christ ...'. Duncan-Jones sees an allusion to 'earth to earth' from that passage in 74:7 (Shakespeare, *Shakespeare's Sonnets*, ed. Duncan-Jones, p. 258).

19 Cf. 116:1–2.

20 He may additionally mean that the young man's understanding of him serves to increase the young man's appreciation of his own, fleeting youth. The last six lines of the sonnet obliquely offer a warning to the young man; thus, they link the poem to Sonnets 1–17 with their warnings to the young man that he recognize his being embedded in the economy of nature. The first eight lines link the sonnet with poems as diverse as 32, 60 and 62.

21 See Diogenes Laertius, *Lives of Eminent Philosophers*, ed. and trans. R. D. Hicks, 2 vols. (Cambridge, MA: Harvard University Press, 1972), 5. 20.

22 Cf. Spenser's *Amoretti*, Sonnet 1:1–3.

23 See Walter Raleigh, *The Poems of Sir Walter Ralegh: A Historical Edition*, ed. Michael Rudick (Tempe: Arizona Center for Medieval and Renaissance Studies, 1999), p. 2.

24 Cf. Evans's note on lines 2–3 (Shakespeare, *The Sonnets*, p. 262) and, in addition: Shakespeare, *The Sonnets*, ed. Kerrigan, p. 375; Shakespeare, *Shakespeare's Sonnets*, ed. Duncan-Jones, p. 402; Helen Vendler, *The Art of Shakespeare's Sonnets* (Cambridge, MA: Harvard University Press, 1997), pp. 605–6; Patrick Cheney, *Shakespeare, National Poet-Playwright* (Cambridge: Cambridge University Press, 2004), pp. 229–31 (cf. pp. 207–16); John Blades, *Shakespeare: The Sonnets* (Basingstoke: Palgrave Macmillan, 2007), pp. 166–75.

25 My discussions of Sonnets 5 and 144 are developed from the accounts of those poems in my *Shakespeare's Sonnets and Narrative Poems* (Harlow: Longman, 2000), respectively at pp. 130–2 and pp. 199–201. By 'the economy of nature', I mean what was conventionally identified in Shakespeare's time as the natural order directing the world, which expressed 'the classical notion that the world as a whole functions in diverse patterns of birth, growth, decline and renewal, of need and fulfilment, of forfeit and compensation' (*ibid.*, p. 129).

26 And much said of the young man elsewhere undermines it, of course.

27 On this topic, see generally Heather Dubrow, *Echoes of Desire: English Petrarchism and Its Counterdiscourses* (Ithaca, NY: Cornell University Press, 1995).

28 For example, *Rime* 45, 168, 361 (cf. 23 and 70); *Astrophil and Stella* 18, 27, 34, 90, 94; and *Amoretti* 35, 45.

29 See Ovid, *Ovid's* Metamorphoses: *The Arthur Golding Translation (1567)*, ed. John Frederick Nims (New York: Collier-Macmillan, 1965), 3:525–6.

30 The idea that Shakespeare created a new kind of western subjectivity in the Sonnets was asserted by Joel Fineman in 'Shakespeare's "Perjur'd Eye"', reprinted in his *The Subjectivity Effect in Western Literary Tradition: Essays Toward the Release of Shakespeare's Will* (Cambridge, MA: MIT, 1991), pp. 91–119. For an extended critique of Fineman's thesis see Gordon Braden, 'Shakespeare's Petrarchism', in Schiffer, *Shakespeare's Sonnets*, pp. 163–83. His identification of what is Petrarchan in the Sonnets has points of contact with my argument here. See also Dubrow, *Echoes of Desire*, pp. 119–21.

31 Cf. Cousins, *Shakespeare's Sonnets and Narrative Poems*, pp. 195, 189–91.

32 The opening lines of Sonnet 18, like the last lines of Sonnet 130, point to misrepresentation as one of the speaker's recurrent concerns.

8

HELEN WILCOX

Sacred desire, forms of belief: the religious sonnet in early modern Britain

Introduction

In 1560, a new poetic voice was heard in London with the publication of *A Meditation of a Penitent Sinner*, appended to *Sermons of John Calvin, upon the Songe that Ezechias made*. This *Meditation* introduced the religious sonneteer into English-speaking culture, presenting a strong persona with a paradoxically 'febled sprite', 'daseld' by the 'lothesome filthe' of a sinful life lived under the threat of God's 'mighty wrath'.[1] The opening poem announces the tone of the sequence as passionate and insistent, with a manner modelled on the penitential Psalms but crafted into the form of an English sonnet:

> Have mercy, God, for thy great mercies sake.
> O God: my God, unto my shame I say,
> Beynge fled from thee, so as I dred to take
> Thy name in wretched mouth, and feare to pray
> Or aske the mercy that I have abusde.
> But, God of mercy, let me come to thee:
> Not for justice, that justly am accusde:
> Which selfe word Justice so amaseth me,
> That scarce I dare thy mercy sound againe,
> But mercie, Lord, yet suffer me to crave.
> Mercie is thine: Let me not crye in vaine,
> Thy great mercie for my great fault to have.
> Have mercie, God, pitie my penitence
> With greater mercie than my great offence.[2]

These pleading lines, based on Psalm 51:1, encapsulate the mood of much early modern devotional verse: the desperate desire for forgiveness (highlighted in the repeated use of the word 'mercy'), the urge to address God while simultaneously feeling unworthy to take his name into a sinner's 'wretched mouth', the consequent paralyzing mixture of hope and dread, the perpetual circling of justice and mercy at odds with one another, and finally the 'greater' mercy required to redeem the speaker's 'great offence'. The tensions inherent in this situation are perfectly matched by the sonnet form, with its capacity to contain the twists and turns of the human spirit – the 'buts' and 'yets' of the lines above – within the confines of fourteen lines, the formal equivalent of the parameters of faith, love and judgement. A speaker's changes of mood and perspective can also be vividly expressed in the contrasts between individual sonnets within a sequence, and this sonnet is the first of twenty-one exploring the experience of 'feble faith with heavy lode opprest' (Sonnet 12, fo. Aa6r), preceded by a mini-sequence of five prefatory sonnets offering a spiritual self-portrait of the 'passioned minde of the penitent sinner' (fo. Aa2r). A Meditation, together with its 'preface', thus gives expression to personality and emotion while exploring widely shared dilemmas of desire and despair in a sequence of sonnets working both individually and collectively.

The description offered in that last sentence is almost a generic account of the early modern sonnet sequence: it could be applied quite accurately to Sidney's *Astrophil and Stella*, published posthumously in 1591, or Shakespeare's Sonnets of 1609. However, it can *first* be said of *A Meditation*, which dates from 1560 and is thus the earliest known sonnet sequence in English, preceding the outburst of secular sequences by at least twenty years. This is an important corrective to some commonly held misconceptions about the Elizabethan sonnet sequence – namely, that worldly sonneteers only turned away from physical to spiritual desires after exhausting their narratives of earthly longings, or that the sequence is a poetic form predominantly used as a means of declaring and exploring the desires of perplexed Petrarchan lovers. *A Meditation* was in fact the first of several religious sequences written during the heyday of the sonnet in England: other poets who wrote sets of spiritual sonnets, in many cases the poet's exclusive sonnet-writing focus, include Henry Constable, Henry Lok, Barnabe Barnes, William Alabaster, Nicholas Breton and John Donne. However, there is another important way in which the existence of *A Meditation* corrects and expands our sense of the early modern sonnet in English, and that is in its authorship. Though the sonnets are formally anonymous, they follow four sermons by Calvin known to have been translated by Anne Lok, and the general consensus is that the sonnets are also by her. Thus not only do these pioneering poems represent the beginnings of the sonnet sequence in English, and take as their subject sacred rather than secular experience, but they are also the work of a woman poet. Just as Mary Wroth undid the exclusively male perspective of the secular sonnet sequence with her *Pamphilia to Amphilanthus* in 1621, so Anne Lok found in the meditative sonnet a suitable medium for a woman's understanding of spiritual experience in 1560. In dedicating her work to a fellow religious exile in Geneva – Katharine, duchess of Suffolk – Lok places her work in a specifically Protestant and female tradition not usually associated with the sonnet.[3]

The history of the early modern religious sonnet in English, therefore, contains significant surprises and some challenges to long-held ideas about this great era of sonnet writing. The religious sonnets are interesting in their own right and for the questions they raise concerning the emergence of the sonnet sequence in English, the use and appropriateness of the genre in the service of sacred argument, and the gendering of authors and their personae. After ranging widely over these issues as well as considering the form and contexts of religious sonnets, including religious allegiance and the cultural significance of poetic traditions, this study will conclude by focusing on selected individual sonnets by Anne Lok, Henry Constable, William Alabaster, John Donne and George Herbert.

Addressees and readers

Since the sonnet is a social form of lyric verse, functioning as a dialogue and defined by the relationship of speaker to addressee, this discussion of early modern religious sonnets must begin with the question of for whom they were written and to whom they were addressed. As Anne Lok's first sonnet has already demonstrated, the primary recipient and audience of these sonnets is God himself, who fulfils the function of both beloved and judge in the same way as mistresses such as Stella, Diana or Delia do in male secular sequences (though perhaps with rather longer-lasting consequences for the speaker). In the opening sonnet of his sequence *The Soules Harmony* (1602), Nicholas Breton greets his God in rapturous tones linked closely to the language of the love sonnet: 'My soules loves life, & lifes loves soules delight'.[4] Henry Constable begins his sequence of *Spirituall Sonnettes* with separate poems 'To God the Father' (the pure divine 'essence'), 'To God the Sonne' (the 'Greate Prynce of heaven') and 'To God the Holy-ghost', the 'Aeternall spryght' vividly described as 'the Love / with which God, and his sonne ech other kysse'.[5] Like Breton, Constable draws on worldly and sensual vocabulary in addressing God, even while staying firmly within the doctrine of the Holy Trinity: one God in three persons who each receive distinct conversations in verse. Many poets do not distinguish between the Father and the Son when they write sonnets to their 'Lord', and indeed Donne speaks to the entire Trinity at once as he commands, 'Batter my heart, three person'd God'.[6] Here Donne demands direct and dramatic intervention by God, and no less than a full 'three person'd' response will do. Other poets are gentler in their approach, addressing God in terms of a predominant divine characteristic, just as a human mistress might become beauty, virtue or (more often) disdain personified. Herbert directs his words to 'Immortall Love, authour of this great frame' in the first of two devotional sonnets simply entitled 'Love', and laments the fact that, in their fallen state, human beings have 'parcel'd out thy glorious name' and given all the 'title' to 'mortall love'.[7] Despite the fact that religious sonnets took root in English before their worldly equivalent, the language and assumptions of the secular sonnet (as established earlier in Italian) shadow the sacred, and earthly love is never far from the imagination of those who write of things immortal.

Many religious sonneteers from the Elizabethan and Jacobean periods, especially the Catholic poets, bridge the gap between earth and heaven by holding their verse conversations with God's human proxies. Whether the addressee is the Blessed Virgin Mary, John the Baptist, Mary Magdalen or St Katharine, the saints are seen as inspirational examples of spiritual achievement in spite of their inherent human weakness: 'Teache me', as Constable says to St Margaret, 'how thou dydd'st prevayle'.[8] Donne, on the other hand, is more adversarial in his Holy Sonnets and often prefers to address figures whom he sees as the enemy: 'Death, be not proud', he pugnaciously declares; or 'Spit in my face you Jewes', he taunts in his shockingly provocative reconstruction of the crucifixion scene.[9] Whether in dramatic or in meditative mode, religious sonnets approach the divine by means of subjects that often reveal the doctrinal sympathies of the poet. The Anglican Herbert, for instance, writes two sonnets in honour of 'The H. Scriptures', that book of 'infinite sweetnesse' which leads 'to eternall blisse',[10] thereby praising the word of God, which plays so prominent a part in Protestant spiritual practice. The Catholic Alabaster, on the other hand, meditates in three sonnets 'Upon the Crucifix', embracing 'this standard' of the sacrifice of Christ, which is at the heart of Catholic doctrine of the Mass.[11] By the end of his sonnet, however, Alabaster has moved from the emblem of Christ's suffering to Christ himself. Indeed, what is fascinating about most of the religious sonnets that do not begin by addressing God is that they often shift toward an apostrophe to him before they finish. It is quite common for speakers to turn the spotlight on themselves in the opening lines – as in Donne's account of himself as 'a little world made cunningly' – before turning to God for help in the end: 'burne me, O Lord, with a fiery zeale / Of thee and thy house'.[12] In this dialectical pattern of introspection and vulnerability, meditation and openness, the religious sonnet resembles both a human conversation and the rhetoric of prayer.

For the most part, early modern religious sonnets appear to be instigated by the speaker's need for spiritual comfort and reassurance, or the desire to praise God. However, it would be wrong to suggest that they are unmotivated by a concern for the reader, the indirect recipient of these poems of conversation and argument. Izaak Walton claims that Herbert's purpose was to 'turn' his devotional poetry 'to the advantage of any dejected poor Soul',[13] and when Constable refers to his sonnets as 'comfortable meditations', he does not exclude the possibility that his poems might comfort others as well as himself.[14] Barnabe Barnes, publishing his *Divine Centurie of Spirituall Sonnets* in 1595, announces in his epistle 'To the favourable and Christian Reader' that his aim in doing so is 'movingly' to 'perswade and stirre up your Spirite to Divine contemplation of your Ghostly comfort'.[15] A small number of religious sonnets from the period anticipate specific individuals as readers; this is the case with Alabaster's sonnet entitled simply 'To His Sad Friend'[16] and with the Scottish aristocrat Elizabeth Melville, who wrote a sonnet to Mr John Welsch when he was imprisoned in 1605 for his loyalty to the Presbyterian cause: 'My dear Brother, with courage bear the crosse / Joy shall be joyned with all thy sorrou here'.[17] In addition to these individual sonnets envisaging a specific Christian brother or sister as their first readers, longer sonnet sequences, particularly those appearing in print, are invariably graced by named dedicatees. Henry Lok, aiming high, dedicates his *Sundry Christian Passions* (1593) to 'the right renowned Vertuous Virgin Elizabeth, Worthy Queene of happie England',[18] while Donne intended his sequence on the life of Christ, *La Corona*, for the spiritual benefit of Magdalen Herbert.[19] Some sonneteers, while not specifying particular readers, evidently assume and include an audience through their choice of rhetorical techniques. George Herbert (Magdalen's son) implies that his sonnets have listeners as he articulates the parable-like narrative of 'Redemption' or explains in the course of 'The Holdfast' that he 'heard a friend express, / That all things were more ours by being [God's]'.[20] Though the 'friend' here is probably Christ, the almost gossipy manner of Herbert's story-telling reminds us that the religious sonnet is an exchange between speaker, listener, reader and God. Indeed, the sonnet bears some resemblance, with its combination of enclosing form and interactive function, to an early modern closet, a small private chamber in which conversation, reading and prayer could take place in quiet yet sociable seclusion.

Addressees and readers frame the beginning and the end of a sonnet, in textual and social terms – but so, too, do the rhetorical skills with which the form of the poem is managed and manipulated. In a short poem, an arresting opening and strong ending are crucial, and in the intervening lines a tightly structured discourse maintains the sonnet's closely wrought tension. The interlocking rhymes of the Italian sonnet form (used by, for example, the Scottish lyric poet William Drummond of Hawthornden, as well as Constable, Barnes, Alabaster and Donne) create the effect of holding the words firmly in place, as does the resounding repetition in lines such as those with which Donne's 'Annunciation' sonnet begins: '*Salvation to all that will is nigh*: / That All, which alwayes is All every where, / Which cannot sinne, and yet all sinnes must beare / ... / ... yeelds himselfe'.[21] The pleasure taken here in the apparent impossibility of the redemption, as Donne celebrates the paradoxes of grace with the repetition and overlapping of words and sounds, reminds us of how the metaphysical subject matter of the religious sonnet can be made to work hand in hand with its compressed form. Perhaps more significantly for the spiritual sonnet, the prominent final couplet, found particularly in the Elizabethan form of the 'Quatorzaine', as Barnes terms the sonnet,[22] makes it a particularly end-focused lyric mode, and thus ideally suited emotionally and doctrinally to the eschatological emphasis of early modern Christianity. There are so many powerful conclusions to early modern religious sonnets that a representative few will have to suffice here. Among the most frequently admired are the ending of Donne's sonnet to Death – 'death, thou shalt die'[23] – and the dramatic response when the speaker arrives at the scene of the crucifixion at the close of Herbert's 'Redemption': 'there I him espied, / Who straight, *Your suit is granted*, said, & died'.[24] A haunting conclusion that is perhaps less widely known is that of William Drummond's sonnet 'For the Baptiste':

> There burst hee foorth: All yee, whose Hopes relye
> On God, with mee amidst these Desarts mourne,
> Repent, repent, and from olde errours turne.
> Who listned to his voyce, obey'd his crye?
>   Onelie the Ecchoes which hee made relent,
>   Rung from their Marble Caves, repent, repent.[25]

This magnificent climax plays to the strengths of the sonnet's final couplet with its echoing rhyme of 'relent' and 'repent, repent' ringing out evocatively in the ears of the listener or reader after the poem has ended. The sonnet's brevity poignantly calls attention to the fact that, despite John the Baptist's prophetic cries in the wilderness, no one 'listned to his voyce' or 'obey'd his crye' – except, perhaps, the reader moved by the closing words of Drummond's sonnet.

Contexts

When we study sonnet sequences in uniform twenty-first-century printed editions, or extracted into anthologies, it is possible to lose sight of the variety of settings in which the poems were first encountered by their early readers. These contexts are not only of historical interest, but can also yield important critical insights into the original roles and effects of the sonnets. Some began life in the most private of manuscript notebooks and remained there for reasons of safety, as is the case with Alabaster's sonnets written at the time of his 1597 conversion to Roman Catholicism (an act of treason in Elizabethan England). This would suggest that the primary function of his writing was to confirm his new-found faith and take personal delight in it. Other sonneteers, including Donne, seem to have allowed their devotional verse to circulate among friends in manuscript form only – possibly, in Donne's case, to serve as an aid to spiritual meditation on death and its consequences – while a further group of poets, including Henry Lok and Barnabe Barnes, saw their sonnets published in printed form, possibly for more mundane reasons such as financial gain or enhanced reputation, as well as for the spiritual benefit of the devout reader. It is revealing that the longest sequences found their way into print: Henry Lok (the son of Anne, with whose sonnet this chapter began) published *Sundry Christian Passions*, containing 200 religious sonnets, in 1593, and added another 120 in his *Ecclesiastes* four years later. In the meantime, Barnes had brought out *A Divine Centurie of Spirituall Sonnets* in 1595, establishing the religious sonnet sequence in the market of printed books.

The ambitious scale of these 'centuries' of poems certainly rivals the secular sequences that became popular in the 1590s; indeed, Thomas P. Roche Jr points out that Henry Lok's output represents 'the second most extensive collection [after Wordsworth] of sonnets in English'.[26] However, in poetic terms it is often the smaller clusters of sonnets that function more effectively. The seventeen sonnets of Breton's *Soules Harmony* (1602) were hugely popular, reaching a ninth edition by 1635. Donne's *La Corona* sequence comprises just seven sonnets with interlocking last and first lines, creating the spiritual intensity of a chain of prayers such as the Rosary, while some of his other divine sonnets explore, with systematic intensity, small groups of the so-called 'Last Things' such as death and judgement. Alabaster and Constable, too, construct what we might call mini-sequences or manageable sets of sonnets on the Passion of Christ and the biblical saints. Indeed, one of the paradoxes of the sonnet, making it so appealing to poets, is the fixedness of its own form in combination with the flexibility of its potential poetic contexts. While the sonnet can be cumulatively effective in sequence, establishing a narrative in clusters or over the course of hundreds of individual poems in the same form, it can also flourish in isolation or in the context of a variety of other poetic forms. Some early modern religious sonneteers chose to highlight the strengths of the form by contrast: Drummond, for instance, intersperses his sonnets with brief madrigals and more expansive hymns in *Flowres of Sion* (1623), while Herbert includes fifteen sonnets among the array of devotional lyrics in *The Temple* (1633), turning to this established mode at moments when its conciseness of form is most appropriate to his subject matter. Among the most innovative of Herbert's sonnets is 'Prayer' (I), a poem that struggles to find the ideal way of describing the nature of prayer itself, piling one epithet upon another until abandoning the attempt in the second half of the fourteenth line, ending with the understated yet all-encompassing phrase, 'something understood'. The single sonnet frame, tested to the extreme in the effort to understand the process of conversing with God, both suggests and (temporarily) limits the ultimately limitless 'milkie way' of prayer.[27]

Although there are religious sonnets from the early modern period written about subjects as shared and generic as prayer, and although it is quite possible to write sonnets for the education and inspiration of others, in most cases there is an overriding sense of the investment of personal experience in spiritual sonnets. This may well be an extreme case of the rhetoric of genuineness, a phenomenon associated with much lyric verse, but the fictionalizing of private emotion comes under severe scrutiny when sonnets are addressed to God, from whose sight 'nothing is conceald'.[28] A recurring concern of the sonneteers is the extent to which their own skills are stretched in their impossible desire to speak of and to God. As Drummond writes in his sonnet entitled 'Amazement at the Incarnation of God', the idea that God himself should 'Come meanelie in mortalitie to bide' is a 'wonder' that is 'so farre above our wit' that even angels are speechless when they 'muse on it'.[29] The sonneteers, being lower than the angels, are conscious of their own shortcomings in a way that can bring the conventional topos of humility closer to actual sincerity. In some cases, the context in which a sonnet is written can sharpen and clarify the sense of personal commitment to the religious subject matter. Mary Stuart (Mary, Queen of Scots) writes sonnets of both earthly and heavenly love, and those on patience and repentance composed in prison have an immediacy and honesty that intensify as a result of the reader's knowledge of her situation. When she states in a sonnet written just before her execution in 1587 that 'if, O great king, it should please thee still / I shall defend thee while I still draw air',[30] the context has the power to turn this biblical echo into a private commitment of urgent and poignant significance.

While the poetic and personal contexts of the early modern religious sonnet were hugely varied – in manuscript and print; set in sequences, clusters or pairs; alongside other lyric forms or in relative isolation; and inspired by private experiences ranging from conversion to impending execution – the cultural associations of the form were rather less flexible. Despite the fact that the earliest English sonnet sequence, Anne Lok's *Meditation*, was sacred rather than secular, the worldly love sonnet came to dominate the field in the late Elizabethan period. The religious sonnet, therefore, frequently assumes an oppositional cultural stance, defined by its difference from the prevailing fashion. Philip Sidney, author of the trend-setting secular sequence *Astrophil and Stella*, seems to have ended his writing of sonnets by turning his back on the very process he had begun, offering a moving sonnet of renunciation: 'Leave me, O love which reachest but to dust'.[31] Two decades later, Herbert began his work as a poet with a pair of sonnets addressing God and asking, 'Doth Poetry / Wear *Venus* Livery? only serve her turn? / Why are not *Sonnets* made of thee?'[32] Whether embraced at the beginning or the end of a poet's career, the religious sonnet is marked by an aesthetic of contrast. This is true not only of the general opposition of secular and sacred subject matter, but also in terms of the place of the sonnet within early modern devotional poetry. The dominant modes of spiritual verse in post-Reformation England were inspired by the Psalms: versified translations of the Psalms, particularly the metrical Psalms suitable for singing communally, were highly favoured in the Protestant tradition of biblical and personal spirituality.[33] Set against the expansiveness of these forms, the sonnet can appear constrained and inflexible, and it is no coincidence that a significant number of religious sonneteers of the early modern period are Catholic or have a background in Catholicism: Mary Stuart, Henry Constable, William Alabaster, John Donne. It has also been argued that the sonnet with its formal containment is well suited to the rigorous Catholic tradition of meditation on visualized scenes from the life of Christ as encouraged by the founder of the Jesuits, Ignatius Loyola.[34] This is undoubtedly true of the sonnets of Donne, in which there is an intensity of imaginative empathy creatively kept in check by the intricate patterns of the sonnet form; however, meditative features of this kind are frequently found in spiritual sonnets by non-Catholic poets such as Herbert, too. As James Turner has rightly observed, 'specific verse forms become welded to particular attitudes'[35] (though not necessarily particular parties or denominations), and the sonnet is no exception.

Despite the temptation, therefore, to associate the secular sonnet only with the male courtly tradition, and to link the religious sonnet primarily with the sensual yet ordered world of Catholic devotion as opposed to the expansive biblical poetics of the Protestants, there are really no satisfactory generalizations to be made. The first religious sonnet sequence in English is the work of a woman who was in fact closely connected to the leading Protestant John Foxe, and her poems are appended to her translation of Calvin's sermons, the epitome of Protestant theology in England. Anne Lok's sonnets function as personal glosses on a biblical text, thus setting the sequence firmly in the Protestant practice of private devotion through

Bible reading, even though the commentary comes in the form of sonnets. In the sonnets of early modern Catholic poets, the Bible is more important as a direct source of inspiration than might have been expected, given the stereotypical post-Reformation contrasts. Alabaster, for example, writes a sonnet 'Upon Christ's Saying to Mary "Why Weepest Thou?"',[36] linking his own experience of sorrow and joy at the Resurrection with that of Mary Magdalen by the tomb of Jesus (John 20:11–17). Taking the saint as subject is a particularly Catholic choice, but the centrality of the biblical text brings the sonnet closer to those of Protestant poets than may be apparent on first reading. The sonnet form has such cultural and poetic prominence in the early modern period, working as a mould in which to shape and express spiritual experience, that it seems to have appealed to poets across the spectrum of doctrinal, social and gender groupings.

Indeed, the boundaries of the early modern religious sonnet are so difficult to pin down that it is not only inappropriate to ally the form exclusively with any particular ecclesiastical allegiance but also virtually impossible to define the borderline of secular and religious sonnets. Edmund Spenser's sequence of love sonnets, dedicated to his wife and published in 1595 as *Amoretti*, follows the calendar of their courtship: when Easter Day is reached, the sonnet 'Most glorious Lord of lyfe' is clearly a holy sonnet addressed to Christ and inserted quite comfortably in a courtship narrative,[37] just as faith and daily life are inextricable in reality. Anne de Vere's sonnets on the death of her young son in 1583 hover between personal elegy and spiritual anguish:

> The heavens, death, and life have conjured my ill,
> For death has take away the breath of my son,
> Th'heavens receive and consent that he has done,
> And my life does keep me here against my will.[38]

The poem does not evolve into a prayer as many religious sonnets do, yet it explores the agony of loss and raises the same metaphysical questions as those that feature in devotional writing. Similarly on the borderline of the religious sonnet is a poem by the Catholic exile Toby Mathew, who does not write specifically about issues of faith but expresses the grief of exclusion from his own land because of his beliefs:

> Better it were for me to have been blind,
> Than with sad eyes to gaze upon the shore
> Of my dear country, but now mine no more,
> Which thrusts me thus, both of sight and mind.[39]

The context of this sonnet is geographically specific – it is entitled 'Upon the Sight of Dover Cliffs from Calais' – and its subject matter is intensely personal but apparently secular, though its implicit spiritual allegiance is confirmed by the author's being thrust out into exile in France during the Jacobean period. Again, the border of spiritual and worldly experience is blurred, just as devotional sonnets to the Virgin Mary share the language of secular love sonnets, which is also the rhetoric of courtly and political adulation of Elizabeth I. Early modern religious sonnet writing cannot and should not be disentangled from its worldly contexts: these are a vital part of its energy, whether in borrowing or renunciation, and integral to the fascination of the mode in all its range and depth. The spiritual sonnet in English in the early modern period both precedes and outlasts the wave of secular sonneteering but is always bound up with it in the negotiation of private and shared desires.

'These spirituall Poemes'

When Barnabe Barnes describes his *Divine Centurie of Spirituall Sonnets* (1595) as having been written 'in lively touche, motion, and feeling-anguishe of spirite, voyde of all colourable varnishe, and hypocrisie',[40] he sums up the qualities assumed to be appropriate for a religious sonnet: moving and expressive of emotion, dealing with doubt and despair as well as the more joyful experience of redemption, and free from the kind of poetic excess that might suggest falseness instead of sincerity. This claim is something of a customary pose, but its essentials ring true in the best of the early modern religious sonnets. In this section we will look more closely at examples of 'these spirituall Poemes' (fo. A2r) by five different authors, in order to perceive their 'lively touche' and 'feeling-anguishe' at work in parallel yet distinctive ways.

The eleventh sonnet from Anne Lok's pioneering sequence, *A Meditation of A Penitent Sinner* (published in 1560), is her intense and individual reworking of the ninth verse of the Psalm, 'Turn away thy face from my sinnes, and do away all my misdedes.' In defiance of the biblical original, Lok begins instead by asking for God's full attention:

> Loke on me, Lord: though trembling I beknowe,
> That sight of sinne so sore offendeth thee,
> That seing sinne, how it doth overflowe
> My whelmed soule, thou canst not loke on me,
> But with disdaine, with horror and despite.
> Loke on me, Lord: but loke not on my sinne.
> Not that I hope to hyde it from thy sight,
> Which seest me all without and eke within.
> But to remove it from thy wrathfull eye,
> And from the justice of thyne angry face,

That thou impute it not. Looke not how I
Am foule by sinne: but make me by thy grace
Pure in thy mercies sight, and, Lord, I pray,
That hatest sinne, wipe all my sinnes away.⁴¹

This complex sonnet of an anxious and 'whelmed soule' sounds the dreaded word 'sinne' six times in fourteen lines and struggles with the distressing idea that, in order for God to see her plight and 'wipe all [her] sinnes away', she must ask God to look on the very thing he despises. The trick is to separate the sinner from the sin: 'Loke on me, Lord: but loke not on my sinne.' As this line reminds us, it is not only the word 'sinne' that is frequently repeated in the sonnet, but also the command 'Looke' or 'Loke'. In the same way as Philip Sidney puns on 'Rich', the surname of the woman behind the fictional Stella, in *Astrophil and Stella* (24, 35 and 37 sonnets), and just as Donne knowingly informs God that 'When thou hast done, thou hast not done',⁴² so Lok – several decades earlier – also plays wittily on her own surname, even as she trembles at what God sees when he 'lokes' at Lok both 'without and eke within'.

Despite this rhetoric of repetition, which continues throughout the poem, the sonnet manages to present a clear poetic structure and a progressive spiritual and emotional argument. The first two quatrains focus on God's action in looking, despite the fact that this is painful to the speaker and a presumed source of 'horror' to the addressee. The third quatrain and concluding couplet, by contrast, make use of the convention of the *volta* by moving away from wrath and justice toward the saving mercy of grace. The redemptive disruption to regular patterns of thought and expression that this divine intervention represents is suggested by the daring structure of the final sentence, which breaks through the established restraint of quatrains, conventional metre and end-stopped lines. The poem's conclusion begins boldly with 'Looke not how I', unexpectedly breaking in halfway through the eleventh line, and proceeds to use enjambment to great effect at the end of that and the subsequent line. The vulnerable self ('I / Am foule') is transformed by the healing power of 'grace', whose influence is felt even before the poem is completed ('grace / Pure'). Lok's introduction of this positive adjective in such a prominent position, daringly breaking the metrical pattern as 'Pure' takes the first strong stress of the final couplet, suggests the confidence of the prayer with which the poem concludes: 'wipe all my sinnes away'.

In contrast to Anne Lok's sonnets, structured in three quatrains and a couplet as later popularized by Shakespeare, Henry Constable's seventeen *Spirituall Sonnettes, to the honour of God: and hys saintes* (written at the time of his conversion to Catholicism in the late 1590s) make use of a version of the Italian sonnet form. Unlike his secular sonnets, these religious poems remained in manuscript during Constable's own lifetime; as he knew to his cost – spending several months in the Tower of London in 1604 – it was a risky business to suggest that Catholicism and loyalty to the English throne could be compatible. The following sonnet, 'To our blessed Lady', takes as its subject a key aspect of Catholic devotion and is a fine example of what Constable's modern editor Joan Grundy refers to as his fusion of 'scholasticism and affective piety':[43]

> In that (O Queene of queens) thy byrth was free
>   from guylt, which others doth of grace bereave
>   when in theyr mothers wombe they lyfe receave:
>   God as his sole-borne daughter loved thee.
> To matche thee lyke thy byrthes nobillitye,
>   he thee hys spyryt for thy spouse ddyd leave:
>   of whome thou dydd'st his onely sonne conceave,
>   and so was lynk'd to all the trinitye.
> Cease then, O Queenes who earthly crownes do weare
>   to glory in the pompe of worldly thynges:
>   if men such hyghe respect unto yow beare
> Which daughters, wyves, & mothers ar of kynges;
>   What honour should unto that Queene be donne
>   Who had your God, for father, spowse, & sonne.   (p. 185)

This sonnet in praise of the Blessed Virgin Mary is as tightly structured as a legal argument: it begins with a premise ('In that') concerning Mary's sinless nature, and proceeds to a logical outcome ('Cease then') asserting her unique status in contrast to worldly queens. As a result, there are two distinct addressees to whom the poem is written – Mary herself, 'O Queene of queens', and the assembled multitude of other 'Queenes who earthly crownes do weare'. This is a sonnet built firmly on the contrast between its octet and sestet, and the pattern of its rhyme-changes highlights the difference between Mary's spiritual 'nobillitye' on the one hand and the empty 'pompe of worldly thynges' on the other. Writing in the last full decade of Elizabeth's reign, Constable's assertion of the inferiority of any queen other than the Blessed Virgin would necessitate a very private context for his spiritual sonnets. The poem again demonstrates the oppositional aesthetic on which religious sonnets are frequently constructed, not only setting spiritual values against those of the world (a recurring feature of any devotional verse) but also favouring heavenly over conventional earthly dedicatees and, in particular in this case, Catholic confidence over Protestant angst.

The basis of Constable's argument is the doctrine of the Immaculate
Conception, asserting that the Virgin Mary was born 'free / from guylt'
unlike all other human beings, who are considered to enter the world with
the burden of the Original Sin of Adam and Eve. Given this unique status,
Constable argues, Mary is appropriately 'lynk'd to all the trinitye', being
the 'sole-borne daughter' of God the Father, the 'spouse' of the Holy Spirit
and the mother of God the Son. Constable's claim that there is a female
connection to all three persons of the Trinity is not only a clever device to
fend off those who would diminish the role of the Virgin Mary in salvation;
it is also a radical feminizing of the divine image. Though women – even
when queens – are still limited to the roles of 'daughters, wyves, & moth-
ers' of men, the presence of one woman in intimate relationship with God
is boldly glorified in this sonnet that passionately challenges the hierarchies
of temporal above spiritual authority, and male above female sanctity. The
basic outline of the poem is rational, but its impact is emotive, partly on
account of its argument and partly because of incidental phrases such as the
unborn child being 'bereave[d]' of grace, or the powerful personalizing of
'your God' in the closing line of the poem. As Grundy observed, this writing
is not in itself sensuous or baroque in manner, yet 'the spiritual is expressed
through the sensuous, because the writer experiences it that way' (p. 57).

If, as Ceri Sullivan suggests, Constable took the artistic call-to-arms of the
Catholic Counter-Reformation to heart and 'initiated a Tridentine aesthetic
in his "Spirituall sonnettes"',[44] then an English poet who followed in his
footsteps in exploring the expression of Catholic spirituality in sonnet form
was the priest and poet, William Alabaster. Though he had returned to the
Church of England by 1614, Alabaster underwent a conversion to Roman
Catholicism in 1597 and it is probably during that time that he wrote his
nearly eighty religious sonnets. G. M. Story suggests that the key qualities
of his sonnets are 'close thought', 'conciseness' and 'tough texture', epitomized in the 'vigorous questioning note'[45] with which several of his sonnets,
including the following, begin:

> Lo here I am, Lord, whither wilt thou send me?
> To which part of my soul, which region?
> Whether the palace of my whole dominion,
> My mind? which doth not rightly apprehend thee,
> And needs more light of knowledge to amend me;
> Or to the parliamental session,
> My will? that doth design all action,
> And doth not as it ought attend thee,
> But suffers sin and pleasures, which offend thee,
> Within thy kingdom to continue faction;

Or to my heart's great lordship shall I bend me,
Where love, the steward of affection,
On vain and barren pleasures doth dispend me?
Lord I am here, O give me thy commission.   (p. 22)

The opening line (with which Alabaster's preceding poem ends) is an echo of several biblical expressions of response to God, including Samuel's answer, 'Here am I; for thou didst call me' (1 Samuel 3:8) and Isaiah's affirmation, 'Here am I; send me' (Isaiah 6:8). Alabaster's sonnet, however, is driven by a question: 'whither wilt thou send me?' There is a sense of urgency here: it seems as if the new convert is ready for action but still requires, as the last line complains, a 'commission', a task to be carried out and a clear idea of where to do so. The interlocking pattern of this Petrarchan sonnet, sustained with only two recurring rhymes throughout the fourteen lines, intensifies the poem's impression of impatience as 'send me' metamorphoses into 'amend me', 'bend me' and 'dispend me' before returning to the realization that the choice is not his to make but God's to impose.

The possible locations for the speaker's service of God are not actual but metaphysical, expressed in an extended metaphor of his soul as a 'dominion' with 'regions', a 'palace', a 'parliamentary session' and a 'great lordship'. The psychological state vividly depicted here is a kind of civil war, in which the ruling faculties of 'mind', 'will' and 'heart' are not only at odds with each other but are all disregarding divine authority through ignorance, misrule or indulgence. The poem has an intense and uneasy drama arising from its persistent uncertainty and inquiry – 'whither ... Whether ... Or ... Or?' – in combination with an underlying desire to be getting on now that the speaker is 'here' and ready to be deployed. The fact that eleven of the fourteen lines form just one extended sentence is an important part of the sonnet's effect; so too is its fluency and the expressive placing of phrases across line breaks, as in 'the palace of my whole dominion, / My mind' with its dramatic delaying of the main subject, a rhetorical device that recurs three lines later. After such a long sentence with repeated deferrals of subjects and answers, the brevity of the final line is all the more striking. There is no concluding couplet but a single line that returns to the poem's opening plea with even greater urgency. The speaker's desire to serve God is reiterated, but there is – within the poem – no sign of guidance in return.

It is important to recognize that John Donne, the most famous and inspired early modern religious sonneteer in English, was preceded and no doubt influenced by poets such as Lok, Constable, Alabaster and their contemporaries. The tormented anxiety of sinfulness, the analytical meditation on metaphysical issues, and the probing interrogation of God and the soul, as seen in the three preceding examples, are all to be found in Donne's twenty-six extant Holy Sonnets. These aspects are intensified by the voice of a strong persona suffering from overwhelming doubts yet fortified by ironic wit:

> Oh, to vex me, contraryes meet in one:
> Inconstancy unnaturally hath begott
> A constant habit; that when I would not
> I change in vowes, and in devotione.
> As humorous is my contritione
> As is my prophane Love, and as soone forgott:
> As ridlingly distemperd, cold and hott,
> As praying, as mute; as infinite, as none.
> I durst not view heaven yesterday; and to day
> In prayers, and flattering speaches I court God:
> To morrow I quake with true feare of his rod.
> So my devout fitts come and go away
> Like a fantastique Ague: save that here
> Those are my best dayes, when I shake with feare.[46]

Donne, born into a Catholic family but later a prominent Anglican preacher and Dean of St Paul's Cathedral, took delight in testing the truth of apparent contradictions and was at home with the wit of paradox throughout his writing. This sonnet explores a very familiar yet seemingly impossible experience: the speaker's spiritual 'Inconstancy' has become a 'constant' habit. This unchanging changeability is only the first of several 'contraryes' that 'meet' within the poem; it is swiftly followed by that chief alchemy of Donne's verse, the mingling of sacred desire and 'prophane Love'. Like any worldly passion, the speaker's love of God veers from one extreme to another, so that the 'contraryes' of speech and silence, infinity and nothingness, are all encompassed within the bounds of this relationship, just as these enormous and challenging ideas are themselves held within the frame of the sonnet's octet. As the sestet begins, the poem's language of courtship moves into the rhetoric of political relationships, and 'flattering speaches' and fear of the 'rod' proceed to combine the worlds of earthly power and heavenly judgement in another of the sonnet's 'contraryes'. This array of interconnected oppositions – constancy and inconstancy, sacred and profane desire, temporal and divine authority – is held together by the prevailing metaphor of devotion as an illness, governed by the bodily humours and thus 'humorous'. This is a rather startling idea for a religious sonnet, not because love for God is shown to be beyond the control of the individual believer (a recognized spiritual paradox), but because the desired state of devotion is feverous, 'like a fantastique Ague'. The 'best dayes' in

the speaker's relationship with God are, perversely, those when the metaphorical fever is at its height and he 'shake[s] with feare' of God's punishment – a condition presumably conducive to penitence. Paradoxical to the
end, the sonnet therefore asserts that, 'here' on earth at least, illness is true
health; in concluding it thus, Donne has brought the poem to echo the 'contrary' biblical teaching that weakness is strength and the last shall be first (1
Corinthians 1:27, Matthew 19:30).

The last of the five poems chosen here to illustrate the strength and
variety of the early modern English religious sonnet was indeed also a
first: George Herbert was the first English poet consistently to supply titles
for individual devotional lyrics, including the fifteen sonnets in his collection *The Temple* (posthumously published in 1633). The following is entitled 'Josephs coat':

> Wounded I sing, tormented I indite,
> Thrown down I fall into a bed, and rest:
> Sorrow hath chang'd its note: such is his will,
> Who changeth all things, as him pleaseth best.
>   For well he knows, if but one grief and smart,
> Among my many had his full career,
> Sure it would carrie with it ev'n my heart,
> And both would runne untill they found a biere
>   To fetch the bodie; both being due to grief.
> But he hath spoil'd the race; and giv'n to anguish
> One of Joyes coats, ticing it with relief
> To linger in me, and together languish.
>   I live to shew his power, who once did bring
>   My *joyes* to *weep*, and now my *griefs* to *sing*.[47]

Like Donne's 'Oh, to vex me', Herbert's sonnet 'Josephs coat' is not directly addressed to God but takes the form of self-analysis, again based on
the paradoxical experiences of '*joyes*' and '*griefs*' inherent in spiritual life.
Unlike Donne's sonnet of frustration, however, Herbert's lyrical poem establishes a characteristically perplexed narrative voice, puzzled by another of
the surprises in store for those who attempt to love God. The speaker does
not quite know whether to complain or rejoice (typified in the word 'indite',
meaning to write a song but also implying 'indict'): he has been 'Thrown
down' by the sorrows that were about to overwhelm him, yet has not landed
in the grave but on a comfortable bed for some much needed 'rest'. The
changeability experienced here is not that of humans (as in Donne's sonnet)
but of God, who 'changeth all things, as him pleaseth best'. Even the rhyme
pattern of the sonnet's first quatrain is overthrown by this unexpected divine reprieve – the first and third lines remain unrhymed as a reminder that

'Sorrow hath chang'd its note' – and, with similar irony of form, the *volta* comes a line later than anticipated, spoiling the pattern as the speaker grumbles that God has 'spoil'd the race' by his kindness.

Why, then, is this sonnet called 'Josephs coat'? There is a passing reference to the title in the eleventh line, where God is said to have relieved the speaker's 'anguish' with the gift of 'One of Joyes coats'; but in fact the idea of Joseph's 'coat of many colours' (Genesis 37:3) hovers over the whole poem. The multicoloured robe suggests the contrasting moods and experiences indicated from the first line onwards, making up the medley of human life; as a gift from Jacob to his favourite son, Joseph's coat represents the loving kindness of the Father who knows 'well' when to give 'relief' to his child's suffering, and throughout the poem there is the implied knowledge that this garment is an emblem of Christ's taking the coat of human flesh in the incarnation, leading to the joy of the redemption. The implicit presence of the title metaphor in all its richness, underlying the entire poem, is typical of the understated wit of this sonnet. So, too, is its lightness of touch as the 'Wounded' speaker rises above 'grief', 'anguish' and mortality's 'biere', and triumphantly ends the poem where it began, with singing – the poet's own vocation.

Conclusion

This chapter has sought to demonstrate the often underestimated variety and originality of the spiritual sonnets from a rich period of poetic invention and religious self-expression in English. In sonnets of Italian, Elizabethan and mixed forms, between them using the full range of structural devices including octets and sestets, interlocking rhymes, quatrains, *voltas* and final couplets, men and women from both sides of the Reformation schism and from as far apart as Scotland and Switzerland may be seen exploring doctrines, doubts, praises and hopes in single sonnets, themed clusters or extended sequences of poems. Each sonneteer achieves an element of individuality through form, voice, gender, subject matter, wit and devotional attitudes. Anne Lok, for example, is inspired by her chosen penitential Psalm to assume the role of a sorrowing sinner, while Donne creates a unique rhetoric of fear mingled with the bravado of argumentative defiance. It is possible to identify some respects in which sonneteers of a specific doctrinal allegiance are drawn to a shared aesthetic mode: Catholic poets, for example, tend to place a greater emphasis on sensuality, as in the 'poetry of tears',[48] and dramatize their dilemmas by addressing biblical figures and saints, particularly the Virgin Mary. It is also evident that ecclesiastical loyalties had an enormous impact on possible modes of publication. However, what is most noticeable is the common ground of spiritual experience underlying these sonnets, and it is the recurring traits among poets right across the doctrinal spectrum that are especially striking – traits such as questioning and debate, meditative analysis and prayer. The contrasts between male and female poets are also less marked than might be expected, perhaps because the soul (*anima*) is perceived as female regardless of the body it inhabits, and the speaker in many religious sonnets therefore adopts the role of a woman in relation to God. As Constable writes in his sonnet 'To St Mary Magdalen', 'lyke a woman spowse my sowle shalbee', and as he pleads in 'To St Margarett', 'let my soule mayd chaste, passe for a Mayde'.[49] In dialogue with God, the soul is always in the position of the 'weaker' sex.

Pioneered by a woman, and appealing to poets across the divisions of gender, geography, social status and religious doctrine, the early modern holy sonnet in English is a fine meeting-place of structural ingenuity and devotional exploration, matching sacred desire to formal constraints within which intensity of belief and experience can be expressed. These sonnets, in isolation and in sequence, are worthy of fuller exploration and deserve a high reputation – which, fortunately, among many readers and writers they already have. To take just one instance of this continuing popularity, in a recent George Herbert Poetry Competition (for which entrants had to submit poems written in the style of Herbert), despite all the varied lyric verse forms found in *The Temple* on which the contestants could choose to model their new poems, the winning entry was – yes – a sonnet.[50]

Notes

1 Anne Lok, Sonnet 1, 'The preface, expressing the passioned minde of the penitent sinner', in *A Meditation of A Penitent Sinner, upon the 51. Psalme*, appended to John Calvin, *Sermons of John Calvin, upon the Songe that Ezechias made* (London: John Day, 1560), fo. Aa2r. Subsequent reference is to this edition.

2 Lok, *A Meditation*, fo. Aa3v.

3 See John Ottenhoff, 'Mediating Anne Locke's *Meditation* Sonnets', in Helen Ostovich, Mary V. Silcox and Graham Roebuck, eds., *Other Voices, Other Views: Expanding the Canon in English Renaissance Studies* (Newark: University of Delaware Press, 1999), p. 295.

4 Nicholas Breton, *The Soules Harmony* (London: Randoll Bearkes, 1602), fo. A4v.

5 Henry Constable, *Spirituall Sonnettes, to the honour of God: and hys saintes*, BL Harl. MS 7553, fos. 32–40 (fos. 32–33r); see also Henry Constable, *Poems*, ed. Joan Grundy (Liverpool: Liverpool University Press, 1960). Subsequent reference is to this edition.

6 John Donne, 'Batter my heart, three person'd God', Holy Sonnet 14, in *The Complete English Poems of John Donne*, ed. C. A. Patrides (London: Dent, 1985), p. 443. Subsequent reference is to this edition.

7 George Herbert, 'Love I', in *The English Poems of George Herbert*, ed. Helen Wilcox (Cambridge: Cambridge University Press, 2007), p. 189. Subsequent reference is to this edition.
8 Constable, *Poems*, p. 189.
9 Donne, *English Poems*, pp. 440, 441.
10 Herbert, *English Poems*, pp. 208, 210.
11 William Alabaster, *The Sonnets of William Alabaster*, ed. G. M. Story and Helen Gardner (Oxford: Oxford University Press, 1959), p. 18. Subsequent reference is to this edition.
12 Donne, *English Poems*, p. 437.
13 Izaak Walton, *The Life of Mr George Herbert* (London: Richard Marriott, 1670), p. 74.
14 Constable, *Poems*, p. 182.
15 Barnabe Barnes, *A Divine Centurie of Spirituall Sonnets* (London: John Windet, 1595), fo. A3r. Subsequent reference is to this edition.
16 Alabaster, *Sonnets*, p. 28.
17 Elizabeth Melville, 'A Sonnet sent to Blackness [Castle] to Mr John Welsch, by the Lady Culross', in Jane Stevenson and Peter Davidson, eds., *Early Modern Women Poets: An Anthology* (New York: Oxford University Press, 2001), p. 118.
18 Henry Lok, *Sundry Christian Passions Contained in two hundred Sonnets* (London: Richard Field, 1593), fo. Aiiir. Subsequent reference is to this editon.
19 Donne, *English Poems*, pp. 429, 317.
20 Herbert, *English Poems*, pp. 132, 499.
21 Donne, *English Poems*, p. 430.
22 Barnes, *Divine Centurie*, fo. A3r.
23 Donne, *English Poems*, p. 441.
24 Herbert, *English Poems*, p. 132.
25 William Drummond of Hawthornden, Sonnet 11, in *Flowres of Sion or Spirituall Poemes, Poems and Prose*, ed. Robert H. Macdonald (Edinburgh: Scottish Academic Press, 1976), p. 94. Subsequent reference is to this edition.
26 Thomas P. Roche, Jr, *Petrarch and the English Sonnet Sequences* (New York: AMS Press, 1989), p. 157.
27 Herbert, *English Poems*, p. 178.
28 Lok, *Sundry Christian Passions*, fo. A1r.
29 Drummond, *Poems and Prose*, p. 93.
30 Mary Stuart, 'O Lord My God, Receive my Prayer', in *Bittersweet Within My Heart: The Collected Poems of Mary, Queen of Scots*, trans. and ed. Robin Bell (London: Pavilion Books, 1995), p. 99. The sonnet was originally written in French.
31 Philip Sidney, 'The Farewell to Desire', in *Selected Poems*, ed. Katherine Duncan-Jones (Oxford: Clarendon Press, 1973), p. 114. Subsequent reference is to this edition.
32 Herbert, *English Poems*, p. 4.
33 See Barbara Lewalski, *Protestant Poetics and the Seventeenth-Century Religious Lyric* (Princeton: Princeton University Press, 1979).
34 This case was first made by Louis L. Martz in *The Poetry of Meditation* (New Haven: Yale University Press, 1954).

35 James Turner, in David Loewenstein and Janel Mueller, eds., *The Cambridge History of Early Modern English Literature* (Cambridge: Cambridge University Press, 2002), p. 822.
36 Alabaster, *Sonnets*, p. 11.
37 Edmund Spenser, *Amoretti*, Sonnet 68, in *The Shorter Poems of Edmund Spenser*, ed. William A. Oram, Einar Bjorvand and Ronald Bond (New Haven: Yale, 1989), p. 641. Subsequent reference is to this edition.
38 Anne de Vere, opening lines of the third of 'Four Epitaphs made by the Countess of Oxford after the death of her young son, the Lord Bullock', in Marion Wynne-Davies, ed., *Women Poets of the Renaissance* (London: Dent, 1998), p. 17. All four epitaphs are written in sonnet form.
39 Toby Mathew, 'Upon the Sight of Dover Cliffs from Calais', in Robert S. Miola, ed., *Early Modern Catholicism: An Anthology of Primary Sources* (New York: Oxford University Press, 2007), p. 216.
40 Barnes, *Divine Centurie*, fo. A2v.
41 Lok, *A Meditation*, fos. Aa5v–Aa6r.
42 Donne, *English Poems*, p. 490.
43 Constable, *Poems*, p. 81.
44 Ceri Sullivan, 'Constable, Henry (1562–1613)', in *The Oxford Dictionary of National Biography* (Oxford: Oxford University Press, 2004), available online at www.oxforddnb.com/view/article/6103?docPos=2.
45 Story, in Alabaster, *Sonnets*, pp. xxxii–xxxiii.
46 Donne, *English Poems*, p. 447.
47 Herbert, *English Poems*, p. 546.
48 See Alison Shell, *Catholicism, Controversy and the English Literary Imagination, 1558–1660* (Cambridge: Cambridge University Press, 1999), p. 57.
49 Constable, *Poems*, pp. 192, 189.
50 'Joseph of Arimathea', by Tony Lucas, based on Herbert's 'Redemption'. For further details, see 'George Herbert Poetry Competition, 2008', *George Herbert Journal* 31:1–2 (Autumn 2007–Spring 2008), 20–32.

9

R. S. WHITE

Survival and change: the sonnet from Milton to the Romantics

Received wisdom tells us that from the time of Donne's Holy Sonnets in the early 1600s, through to Wordsworth in the early 1800s, the sonnet had been eclipsed, and that here as in other fields we may speak of a Romantic *revival*. The relatively low esteem granted to Shakespeare's Sonnets until Coleridge's *Biographia Literaria* seems to confirm the generalization that 'the sonnet in English had languished as a neglected and decidedly unfashionable form', and that between Milton and the Romantics, the form 'appeared to be dead, a defunct and antiquated genre'.[1] However, this chapter will suggest that such generalizations, stemming from the acceptance of some trenchantly expressed literary propaganda perpetrated by Samuel Johnson, are only half true. Neglected and unfashionable, yes, but not dead, defunct or antiquated. In quantity at least, if not always quality, sonnets survived, and by dispensing with the need for a sequence, writers opened up a new opportunity for the 'occasional' sonnet. As an indirect consequence, love and fame, the subjects that had dominated the form since Petrarch, were no longer taken for granted. Politics, scenery, moods, special occasions and other topics could act as starting-points and justifications for sonnets. Hence we can trace a steady expansion of the form's resources away from expressions of praise and unrequited love, and toward the Romantic use of it to express a spectrum of moods: from solitude to sociability, from politics to visions of nature that mirror human states of emotion or 'inner weather'.

John Milton, the last of the great Renaissance writers, generally used ancient poetic forms such as epic, elegy and ode, but he also contributed to the more 'modern' Italian form of the sonnet. In doing so he showed his supreme mastery of imitation by writing some in the Italian language itself, as he tried to emulate Petrarch and Michelangelo in lyrical beauty and depth of feelings. In his English sonnets, Milton initially respected the Petrarchan preference for love and praise, but later used the form in more experimental ways to explore different subjects: pre-eminently topical, political occasions of his own day, or subjects personal to his circumstances. His technical mentor was Giovanni Della Casa, who 'emancipated the Italian sonnet from a framework that had become too rigid' by using the flexibilities of enjambment instead of breaking the thought up into the Petrarchan divisions of two quatrains (the octave) and two tercets (the sestet).[2] In subject matter, his influence was Tasso, whose division of his own work into love sonnets, historical sonnets, and sacred and moral sonnets Milton adopted in his own, much smaller collection. Modern critics like William McCarthy also divide the sonnets into three parts: 'poems of youth', where the author 'dedicates himself to love and poetry'; 'poems of maturity', where 'the poet exerts his powers on public and private themes'; and a third group, which 'gives us the poet in retirement' calmly facing old age.[3] Milton's most striking innovation was in some sonnets to comment on state policy and the personal adversities he faced in serving Cromwell's Commonwealth.[4] These sonnets (IX, X and XIII in particular) have been likened to 'the prayer hymn of classical antiquity', in which Milton takes on 'the persona of the enraptured poet-priest'.[5]

Milton wrote only thirty-three sonnets over perhaps twenty years, publishing them as one group in 1645 (Sonnets I to X) and another in 1673 (all except XV, XVI, XVII and XXII, which were dedicated to political figures identified with pre-Restoration politics, and which survive in manuscript). Attempts have been made to interpret Milton's sonnets as a 'sequence' but not in the fictional or autobiographical sense of Petrarch, Spenser, Sidney or Drayton. Rather, they are seen at most as having a continuity based on chronology, lightly referring back to previous sonnets and to contemporary events. Seen like this, they record a series of *occasions* in the poet's life, and it is the occasional nature of their composition that seems the main point about them. Each comments on the limited nature of an event or circumstance, significant for its importance either to the poet personally or to his view of history. Sonnet I declares the young (1629) poet's joint discovery of poetry and love, on hearing the song of a nightingale, a classical and medieval trope:

> Whether the Muse, or Love call thee his mate,
> Both them I serve, and of their train am I.   (13–14)

Sonnet II is written in Italian, a language and culture experienced at first hand by Milton that also harks back to the sonnet's origins. It addresses a *Donna leggiadra* ('charming lady')[6]. Sonnet III connects back to it syntactically – '*As* on some rugged mountain ...' (emphasis mine; 'Qual in colle aspro') – by saying that the previous sonnet is 'like' the kind that would be written for a youthful shepherdess sitting by the River Arno for which writing in 'the new flower of a foreign language' Milton claims to exchange London's Thames. The following poem (named a *Canzone* because it is not strictly a 'little song' or *sonnetto*, having fifteen lines) allows amorous youths and maidens to gather around the speaking poet, asking 'why, O why do you write your love poems in an alien and unknown language?'[7] The lady answers for him that his poem is in the language of love. The Petrarchan mini-sequence continues on in Italian through to Sonnet VI, though there are sometimes hinted anticipations that 'There are other rivers and shores and other waters' for the poet to turn to (*Canzone*), in order to escape the 'incurable sting' of love (Sonnet VI).

Accordingly, he turns away from the subject of love, to address more serious and public themes. Sonnet VII, 'How soon hath Time the suttle theef of youth ...' returns to English and starts a new train of thought on the end of the poet's twenty-third year. Time is the theme, and the poet's initiation into manhood and the inception of his religious vocation. In VIII and the sonnets that follow, Milton not only broaches the political allegiances that would put his life in danger in the impending civil war, but also marks a new function for the sonnet. In these, he declares that the sonnet, previously associated mainly with courtly love and praise of famous people, can be a vehicle for polemical, political statements. As a Puritan supporter of the parliamentary, republican forces, and an implacable opponent of monarchical rule, he makes sonnets into poetic weapons of persuasion and intervention in contemporary events. Few had done this before so explicitly, and in their context the poems demonstrate the courage in adversity that was increasingly to mark Milton's embattled stance. The sonnets were to be both personal stepping-stones and historical milestones in the turbulent public events of the mid seventeenth century, as civil war ushered in the Commonwealth, only to be returned to monarchy at the Restoration.

Milton uses a traditional function of sonnets to praise men such as his friend, the musician Henry Lawes, and leaders of the revolution he supported, but in his uncompromising way he simultaneously implies his own reservations based on truth as he saw it. Sonnet XV was written for Sir Thomas Fairfax, who led forces against royalists in the north of England, won several famous battles, and was appointed commander-in-chief of the New Model Army, though he was also a soldier who, in Milton's view, was too inclined to negotiate with the king. When Charles I was ceremonially executed, Fairfax retired from public life, which would not have entirely pleased the dedicated Milton. He had already reproved Fairfax for his tendency to compromise, but in the sonnet gives credit to his military prowess. Rather than criticizing him directly, however, Milton turns his sonnet into a more general condemnation of war, and expresses universal attitudes that Fairfax could perhaps share by the end of his career:

> For what can Warr, but endless warr still breed,
> Till Truth, and Right from Violence be freed,
> And Public Faith cleard from the shamefull brand
> Of Public Fraud. In vain doth Valour bleed
> While Avarice, and Rapine, share the land. (10–14)

David Norbrook in *Writing the English Republic: Poetry, Rhetoric and Politics 1627–1660* notes that this Horatian poem was the first of Milton's to deserve the title 'heroic sonnet' in its concentration on a public theme. Its purpose is to reorientate attention away from the civil war, which had reached a point of 'uneasy peace', to the civic duties required to consolidate peace.[8] Milton addresses Fairfax as one whose name reigns through Europe for martial victories, stirring praise from republicans but jealousy and 'amaze' from monarchs daunted by his reputation. He is warned that he must pre-empt inevitable hostility by remaining vigilant in the face of coming threats from 'Public Fraud', 'Avarice' and 'Rapine', which will emerge to 'share the land'. Yet as Milton makes clear in his ringing condemnation of war in general terms and the way violence taints 'Truth and Right', he realizes that it cannot be a lasting solution to the civic uprisings that will follow victory. Sonnet XVI is for and about Cromwell, 'our chief of men', once again praising military prowess, but hinting that the Protector does not share all the poet's own values. High among these were religious tolerance and freedom of publication espoused in Milton's pamphlet *Areopagitica*, one of the most eloquent defences of freedom of the press ever written. But Cromwell, a Presbyterian, was intolerant of other religions and favoured censorship. In Milton's carefully chosen language, Cromwell also emerges as a man who has perhaps gone too far in shedding blood to achieve his ends, however admirable those ends might have been. The ideological plea comes tactfully as a request rather than recrimination:

> Helpe us to save free Conscience from the paw
> Of hireling wolves whose Gospell is their maw. (13–14)

Sonnet XVIII, 'Avenge O Lord thy slaughter'd Saints …', is not written for an individual, though it is equally political and public. Milton angrily denounces the persecution and massacre of Protestants in the European Alps, evoking the scene with visual power as the dying groan on the cold mountain-side and others die, 'Slayn by the bloody *Piemontese* that roll'd / Mother with infant down the Rocks'. The dramatic enjambment, teetering as it does on clumsiness, vocally imitates the sense of 'rolling', and the lines as they continue follow a similarly poetic dislocation: 'Their moans / The Vales redoubl'd to the Hills, and they / To Heav'n ...', enhancing the sense of shock and moral outrage. The sonnet takes on the purposes of a partisan press in times of war, offering both powerful reportage, political commentary and the construction of an historical pattern dwelling on 'martyr'd blood' created by tyranny. In his group of overtly political sonnets, Milton may begin with topical events but he generalizes them to illustrate some wider theme.

Two sonnets are more personal to Milton, and they still have a strong emotional resonance. Sonnet XIX, 'When I consider how my light is spent', broods on the poet's realization that he is going, or has already gone, blind: a painful process that began to afflict him around 1652. It shows in a different and more personally threatening context Milton's honesty to his own feelings and religious beliefs, which sometimes were in conflict with each other, and led to his great poems based on temptation, *Paradise Lost*, *Paradise Regained* and *Samson Agonistes*. One impulse is to despair and to accept that he has been made useless in his vocation 'To serve therewith my Maker', visualizing with even a hint of personal resentment a chiding God reprimanding him for his lack of activity without allowing him the daylight to work in. However, 'patience to prevent that murmur, soon replies' that God accepts different ways of service according to men's means and gifts, no matter what 'milde yoak' each may carry. The sonnet concludes with a memorably quietist acceptance that recalls George Herbert and is perhaps unexpected and hard-won from Milton: 'They also serve who only stand and wait.' Sonnet XXIII, 'Methought I saw my late espoused Saint', is an immensely moving poem of grief and loss, recounting a dream in which the poet meets once again his dead wife. We do not know which of Milton's two dead wives is meant – Mary Powell who died in 1652, or Katherine Woodcock who died in 1656 – since we do not know for certain when the sonnet was written:

> And such, as yet once more I trust to have
> Full sight of her in Heaven without restraint,
> Came vested all in white, pure as her mind:
> Her face was vail'd, yet to my fancied sight,
> Love, sweetness, goodness, in her person shin'd
> So clear, as in no face with more delight. (7–12)

His dismay on awakening abruptly lends the poem its grief-stricken closure, the pathos enhanced by understated brevity and passing reference to his blindness, which intensifies his emotional darkness:

But O as to embrace me she enclin'd
I wak'd, she fled, and day brought back my night.   (13–14)

The run-on lines can be expressive, sometimes suggesting not the emotional fluidity one would expect but, especially in these two most anguished sonnets, XIX and XXIII, suspended disappointment and aggrieved reluctance to clinch the thought until the last possible moment. As in all he wrote, Milton's sonnets celebrate 'the sanctity and inviolability of the individual human conscience',[9] while the technical contribution he made through enjambment was to make the sonnet into a single statement rather than a series of transitions made up of quatrains, octaves and couplets: 'For Milton was already writing sonnets that, if not ignoring the *volta* entirely, rushed through that point to the end of the poem.'[10] Milton also loosened the sonnet from its place in a fictional sequence, paving the way for treating it as a personal meditation on a significant occasion rather than advancing a narrative. His contested presence in literary tradition became a pivotal issue in the politics of eighteenth-century English literature and the formation of rival canons, and while the reputation of even Shakespeare's Sonnets remained low, Milton's example was praised by various writers who managed to keep the stream of sonnets flowing.[11]

Perhaps the oddest sonnets to be penned in Milton's generation were by his insignificant contemporary, Charles Cotton, in a group named *Resolution in Four Sonnets, of a Poetical Question Put to me by a Friend, Concerning Four Rural Sisters*. Cotton was a rather seedy fop known to many writers of the day, recalled in a memoir as a man who 'gave his best friends cause to have wished that he had not lived so long'.[12] Milton would have found him distasteful, not least because he was a confirmed royalist and detested Cromwell's Commonwealth under which his father was persecuted. Cotton wrote a 'Second Part' of Izaak Walton's *The Compleat Angler*, but his own output consists mainly of 'scatalogical burlesque' of classical works, slanderous verse epistles and 'mildly pornographic fantasy'.[13] His *Four Sonnets*, defying all literary traditions of sonneteering in England or Italy, are at least mock-bucolic (his 'Angler' background), slandering 'Four Rural Sisters' whose marriage prospects are assessed with lubricious speculation:

> She finds virginity a kind of ware,
> That's very very troublesome to bear,
> And being gone, she thinks will ne'er be mist.[14]

Probably 'satire' would be the most charitable category to apply, like the openly pornographic efforts of Cotton's younger, Restoration contemporary,

John Wilmot, earl of Rochester. But using the sonnet as a comic vehicle did expand the form's range.

Assumptions about the demise of the sonnet after Milton are based mainly on the fact that major authors such as Pope, Dryden and Johnson used the sonnet only sparingly, if at all, choosing rather to write satire and moral essays in verse. At least the first two of these poets had no strong prejudice against the form, however. Pope began his writing career by publishing sonnets 'in imitation of Waller' at the tender age of thirteen, while Dryden, translator of Boileau's *L'Art poétique*, noticed that while English is more suited to epic poetry, French language fits it for 'lighter' effects such as those in sonnets: 'The French have set up purity for the standard of their language; and a masculine vigour is that of ours. Like their tongue is the genius of their poets, light and trifling in comparison of the English – more proper for sonnets, madrigals, and elegies than heroic poetry. The turn on thoughts and words is their chief talent.'[15] There may be an element of damning with faint praise betrayed in 'trifling', but at least Dryden sees a poetic place for sonnets. However, Johnson in his life of Milton, after giving niggardly praise to the sonnets ('of the best it can only be said, that they are not bad'), more trenchantly restates the idea that sonnets are 'foreign': 'The fabrick of a sonnet, however adapted to the Italian language, has never succeeded in ours, which, having greater variety of termination, requires the rhymes to be often changed. Those little pieces may be dispatched without much anxiety ...'[16] – a scathing reference to the aristocratic facility that Johnson believed lay behind the Elizabethan sonnet sequences. In the spirit of a self-fulfilling prophecy he initiated the general view of the period that now prevails, by adding to his definition of 'sonnet' in his *Dictionary* (1755), 'It is not very suitable to the English language, and has not been used by any man of eminence since Milton.'

It is true that sonnets were not considered so voguish as they had been in the Renaissance by 'any man of eminence' in the eighteenth century, and it fell to less celebrated writers to keep the form alive in England until that country's second great flowering of sonnets in the hands of Romantic poets. However, their interest in the actual sonnet form itself testifies to a continuing enthusiasm for Petrarch's poetry, since until Thomas Warton in 1750, the sonnets written were generally translations or close imitations.[17] The period's Petrarchan interest was later confirmed in a five-volume publication by Capel Lofft in 1813–14 entitled *Laura; or, An Anthology of Sonnets*, and comprehensive publication in 1859 of the collection known as *Bohn's Illustrated Library: The Sonnets, Triumphs and other Poems of Petrarch, Now First Completely Translated into English Verse by Various Hands*. Lofft and Bohn's collections brought back into public circulation writers and their works that would otherwise have been forgotten, such as Philip Ayres, Dryden's friend and a translator from Greek, Spanish, German, French and Italian. His book, *Lyrick Poems* (1687), consisting almost entirely of translations, was evidently very popular in the Restoration, since five English editions were published over the thirty years from its publication. Ayres intended his sonnets to be sung, in the original spirit of Petrarch's *canzoniere*, so they are straightforward in syntax and language, focused as Petrarch's originals are on the ambivalencies of love, and the mingling of sweet and sharp tones reminiscent of Shakespeare's 'mingled yarn':

> Which way in this distraction shall I turn,
> That freeze in Summer, and in Winter burn? [18]

Perhaps surprisingly, given the tradition's manifestly carnal content, eighteenth-century translators of Petrarch's sonnets included clergymen such as Basil Kennet, John Langhorne and the Reverend William Collier, who is still of some passing interest for his Shakespearean scholarship.[19] There were also aristocrats who translated Petrarch as a hobby, like the hereditary Irish peer James Caulfield, earl of Charlemont, a libertine in his youth and later the author of posthumously published *Select Sonnets of Petrarch* (1822), and Alexander Fraser Tytler, Lord Woodhouselee, originally a lawyer who took an interest in pastoral poetry and history. His essay on Petrarch (1782) was reprinted several times, and included seven of the poet's sonnets translated from the Italian. Given the Romantic priority on originality rather than imitation and translation, it is not surprising that all these and others have been completely forgotten. But their very existence running from the Restoration through the eighteenth century is evidence that at least the Petrarchan sonnet did not disappear.

Furthermore, this continuity of the line did lead to some poets whose work genuinely deserves to be better known. They are now neglected largely because their language looks consciously archaic and 'poetic' beside Wordsworth's aim to provide 'a selection of language really used by men',[20] but the actual content of their poems was more innovative. They paved the way for the Romantic revolution by using the sonnet to discuss a whole new range of subject matter: 'disappointed love, radical politics, the natural world, friendship, art and aesthetics, historical and political figures, religion and spirituality'.[21] Thomas Edwards (d. 1757) devoted his sonnets to an array of topics including one written 'On a Family-Picture', whose image reminds him how 'insatiate Death' has robbed him of many of his family members. Another mocks the Shakespearean critic and editor William Warburton as a 'Tongue-doughty pedant', advising him to 'cease from Shakespeare thy unhallowed rage':

Know, who would comment well his godlike page,
Critic, must have a heart as well as head.[22]

Some years later, the *Sixteen Sonnets* (1778) of the colourfully named John
Codrington Bampfylde, who spent most of his mature years in a lunatic asylum, were considered 'some of the most original in our language' by Robert
Southey. Amongst his titles are 'Written at a Farm', 'On a Frightful Dream'
and 'On Christmas'.[23] Now completely forgotten, Thomas Russell's posthumously published sonnets, such as 'Oxford, since late I left thy peaceful
shore', were highly rated by Wordsworth.[24]

When Coleridge, however, specified Charlotte Smith and William Bowles
as the poets 'who first made the Sonnet popular among the present English',
he contrasted these writers of original sonnets with translators of Petrarch,
and Petrarch himself:

> In a Sonnet ... we require a development of some lonely feeling, by whatever
> cause it may have been excited, but those Sonnets appear to me the most
> exquisite, in which moral Sentiments, Affections, or Feelings, are deduced
> from, and associated with, the scenery of Nature. Such compositions generate
> a habit of thought highly favourable to delicacy of character. They create a
> sweet and indissoluble union between the intellectual and material world. [25]

But there was another writer, predating both Bowles and Smith, who had
more claim to have begun using the sonnet as 'a development of some lonely
feeling' creating 'a sweet and indissoluble union between the intellectual
and material world': Thomas Warton the Younger. Robert Southey later
acknowledged his influence over the Romantics, remarking in 1825, 'If any
man may be called the father of the present race, it is Thomas Warton.'
The new approach to the sonnet was his particular legacy. Warton was first
and foremost an Oxford academic with claims to be among the first academic literary historians. Being elected Professor of Poetry at Oxford for
ten years, and later appointed England's Poet Laureate, he published not
only his own poetry but also a study of Spenser's *Faerie Queene* (1754), a
History of English Poetry (published 1774–81), an edition of Milton (1789,
revised 1791) and contributions to editions of Shakespeare. It may even
have been Warton that Johnson had specifically in mind when he dispar-
aged the sonnet in England; although they were friends, Warton severely
criticized Johnson's *Dictionary* and also Johnson's general mockery of
Warton's own poetry and its preference for Spenser and Milton. Warton
seems to have been a corpulent and genial character who also wrote satires
and was reprimanded because 'he might occasionally have drunk ale with
inferiour persons'. His sonnets were related to the sensibilities revealed
in a form growing in contemporary popularity, 'graveyard poems' such

as Edward Young's *Night Thoughts* and Thomas Gray's *Elegy Written in a Country Churchyard*, which linked serious meditations on emotional states with particular scenery. (They were first published in *A Collection of Poems by Several Hands* (1748–58) assembled by Dodsley, a book-seller and publisher at the centre of a wide literary group that also included Johnson, Young and Gray.) In Warton's sonnets we find few vestiges of the anguished solipsism of a Petrarchan lover, or the public statements of Tasso, or even the comments on political figures that we find in Milton. Instead, the poem becomes a brief meditation on the poet's emotional state as reflected in a particular scene observed at first hand rather than, as in some of Shakespeare's Sonnets (such as 46 and 50) in a more generalized, imagined sense. This innovation would be of paramount importance to Charlotte Smith, Wordsworth and Coleridge. Secondly, Warton uses the sonnet as a vehicle for expressing friendship with a close, poetic acquaintance, not so much in the vein of praise or blame but rather in the tones of a familiar verse-letter, an innovation important for John Keats. More generally, Warton set the sonnet on its path toward modernity as a short 'thought adventure' where even the writer seems not to know where the ideas are going until the poem finds its own natural resolution. The first sonnet in his collection, 'Winslade, thy beech-capt hills, with waving grain Mantled ...' ends in nostalgia for lost days that the scenery stirs in the poet:

> In this alone they please, howe'er forlorn,
> That still they can recal those happier days.[26]

Stonehenge stirs thoughts of ancient British kings (Sonnet IV), as does contemplation of 'King Arthur's Round Table at Winchester' (Sonnet VIII), while Wilton House brings to Warton's mind the skills of architects and landscape gardeners in taming 'landskip' into art and creating by contrast 'the dungeon's solitary gloom' (Sonnet V). Most often, the scenes lead the poet into a melancholy, retrospective appreciation of his own youth viewed from resigned maturity, as in 'While summer-suns o'er the gay prospect played', anticipating Wordsworth's more illustrious 'Tintern Abbey' and other poems exhibiting a distinctive kind of Romantic alienation. Sights of the onset of autumn reinforce the poet's sense of having wasted summer, 'Which late in careless indolence I passed', and intensify his sense of transience and loss, as the new season, chiming with his current mood, makes his 'past delight' all the more irretrievable:

> And Autumn all around those hues had cast
> Where past delight my recent grief might trace.
> Sad change, that Nature a congenial gloom
> Should wear, when most, my cheerless mood to chase,
> I wish'd her green attire, and wonted bloom! (Sonnet VII)

One of Warton's sonnets that still finds its way into anthologies is 'To the River Lodon'. Beginning 'Ah! what a weary race my feet have run', the poet finds himself in the place where his 'muse to lisp her notes begun!' The 'pensive memory' triggered by being back beside the 'sweet native stream' compresses a whole lifetime of consciousness into the allotted fourteen lines, evoking the regret that the same sun does not shine as it did in his youth. The soothingly lugubrious scenes that stimulate Warton's thoughts are initially similar to those of his friends associated with the 'graveyard' school of poetry, Young and Gray. Warton wrote a 'familiar sonnet-letter' to the latter, according him bardic status:

> My rustic Muse her votive chaplet brings;
> Unseen, unheard, O Gray, to thee she sings! –
> While slowly-pacing thro' the churchyard dew,
> At curfew-time, beneath the dark-green yew,
> Thy pensive genius strikes the moral strings. (Sonnet VI)

Gray himself wrote a sonnet expressing grief at the death of another mutual friend, the artist Richard West, and this too finds its way into anthologies. To an even greater extent than Warton in his sonnets, Gray uses the form to reflect the interplay between external landscape and the internal landscape of the mind in its changing moods, which was to become a preoccupation of Romantic poets:

> In vain to me the smiling mornings shine,
> And reddening Phoebus lifts his golden fire:
> The birds in vain their amorous descant join,
> Or cheerful fields resume their green attire:
> These ears, alas! for other notes repine,
> A different object do these eyes require.
> My lonely anguish melts no heart but mine;
> And in my breast the imperfect joys expire.
> Yet morning smiles the busy race to cheer,
> And new-born pleasure brings to happier men:
> The fields to all their wonted tribute bear;
> To warm their little loves the birds complain.
> I fruitless mourn to him that cannot hear,
> And weep the more because I weep in vain.[27]

Gray's use of plain language (apart from 'reddening Phoebus') contrasts with Warton's poeticisms and vocabulary borrowed from art criticism, moving the sonnet further toward the Romantics. The fact renders rather curious Wordsworth's criticism of this sonnet in particular for what he sees as its overly poetic diction.[28] Technically Gray follows the structure of Shakespeare's sonnets in using three quatrains to mark shifts of perspective between nature and feelings, ending with two lines (though not a couplet) asserting the disjunction between outer and inner; but the rhyme scheme is more interlaced, carrying throughout a thread of essentially two dominant rhymes ('shine'/'fire') repeated in minor keys with half-rhymes ('join'/'complain' and 'bear'/'hear') in an intricate musical stitching.

Apart from Johnson's rejection, the other reason for the apparent eclipse of the eighteenth-century sonnet is the way that until quite recently the contribution of women to poetic history has been neglected and even denied. Anna Seward was one who helped to 'Romanticize' the sonnet, and she did so by remaining true to the line of Milton in explicit opposition to Johnson. She was reading Milton, Pope and Shakespeare by the age of three, and by nine she could recite the first three books of *Paradise Lost*. A spirited woman known as 'The Swan of Lichfield' alongside Samuel Johnson, the 'son of Lichfield', she promoted the cause of independent women while suffering from patriarchal assumptions herself. Erasmus Darwin had guilelessly told her father that the poetry written when she was fifteen was better than her father's, whereupon the latter forbade her to write poetry. Fortunately she overcame this, but later engaged in an acrimonious public battle with Johnson, whom she had known all her life since he had been taught by her grandfather, and whose recent literary lionization had aroused her disgust. Johnson, however, blackmailed her into silence by hinting that he could reveal unsavoury details about her past. They were reconciled on his deathbed, but later the vitriol spilled over toward Boswell, whom Seward regarded as a sycophant to the overrated Johnson. In her sonnets, written between the 1770s and 1799, and collected in *Original Sonnets on Various Subjects: and Others Paraphrased from Horace* (1799), Seward expressed her fury that Johnson should use his authoritative position in a hypocritical and arrogant way to denigrate poets such as Milton, Gray and Chatterton, while celebrating others who were on the line from Dryden. 'On the Posthumous Fame of Doctor Johnson' castigates his 'ruthless hand', claims he was 'goaded by jealous rage' and thinks him entirely undeserving of Britain's 'high claims' for him:

> A radiant course did JOHNSON'S Glory run,
> But large the spots that darken'd on its sun.[29]

In 'On Doctor Johnson's Unjust Criticisms in His Lives of the Poets' Seward is even more critical, accusing him of 'spleen' and malice, and of lacking a 'poetic ear' in elevating the 'mean' while laying low the mighty poets:

> ... [He] proves that each sneer,
> Subtle and fatal to poetic Sense,

> Did from insidious Envy meanly flow,
> Illumed with dazzling hues of eloquence,
> And Sophist-Wit ...

Seward was especially critical of Johnson for his dismissal of the sonnet as a serious literary form, defending it as 'a highly valuable species of verse', and it must have given her a sense of triumph that she could use the form politically to demolish his claim to literary authority. More positively, she turned her sonnet 'To Mr Henry Cary, on the Publication of his Sonnets' into a tribute to Milton:

> Our greater Milton, hath, by many a lay
> Form'd on that arduous model, fully shown
> That English verse may happily display
> Those strict energic measures, which alone
> Deserve the name of Sonnet, and convey
> A grandeur, grace and spirit, all their own.[30]

The sestet of this sonnet is an implied challenge to Johnson's arch and condescending comments about Milton, and the glib unsuitability of the sonnet for the English tongue. These poems bring into the open the partially concealed literary politics of the time, when the sonnet became a litmus test for the two schools or traditions that respectively define the antagonistic cultural circles of the eighteenth century: the French-influenced neo-classical and the 'sentimental'. Seward wrests the sonnet form from an antiquarian veneration of Petrarchanism, opening it up as a vehicle for subjects designed to comment on contemporary literature and to express emotions like indignation and anger. The 'sonnet on the sonnet', like the poem addressed to Henry Cary, was to become a Romantic theme, evidenced by Burns's 'A Sonnet Upon Sonnets' and Keats's 'If by dull rhymes our English must be chained'.

Seward also had intense relationships with women, particularly Honora Sneyd, who had been adopted into Anna's family and came to be an emotional replacement for a beloved younger sister who had died young. Their troubled relationship survived estrangement and Seward's hostility when Sneyd married, descending into profound grief when Sneyd died. Two contrasting works show the depth of the rift between the two and also incidentally Seward's willingness to use the sonnet to reveal strong feelings that are created in her by actual events. Sonnet IV, written in 1770, 'To Honora Sneyd, Whose Health Was Always Best in Winter', greets the 'youthful, gay, capricious Spring' with the appreciation of new bird-calls, and cowslips flinging 'Rich perfumes o'er the fields' and driving away thoughts of the sleet, rain and frost of 'Dim winter's naked hedge and plashy field' – feelings driven by the enthusiasm of close, female affection, 'For thy dear sake'. However, just two years later, Sneyd is upbraided for her 'Scorning remembrance of our vanish'd joys', for her refusal to give again 'love-warm looks' and instead showing only 'cold respect' and passing by 'with averted eyes, Feigning thou see'st me not …' This time winter is a state of despair:

> I could not learn my struggling heart to tear
> From thy loved form, that thro' my memory strays;
> Nor in the pale horizon of Despair
> Endure the wintry and the darken'd days.   (11–14)

Later still comes a bitter Sonnet, 'Farewell, false Friend! – our scenes of kindness close!', recriminating 'a broken vow'. In other sonnets, Seward follows the lines developed by Warton and Gray, of using the form to contemplate nature while expressing also a mood:

> The cloudy moonshine in the shadowy glade,
> Romantic Nature to th'enthusiast Child
> Grew dearer far than when serene she smil'd,
> In uncontrasted loveliness array'd   (Sonnet VII)

Even the humble poppy could stimulate emotional states:

> … Thus, lulling grief and pain,
> Kind dreams oblivious from thy juice proceed,
> Thou flimsy, shewy, melancholy weed.   (Sonnet LXXI)

Two other women, Charlotte Smith and Mary Robinson, extended the range of the sonnet in ways that properly take them into the next chapter, though a few words on each are relevant here to link them to the literary line outlined in this chapter. Both vehemently opposed Johnson's demeaning attitude to the sonnet, and both looked back to Milton as their inspiration. If there is one volume that almost single-handedly brought the sonnet to the attention of those who later became the most elevated Romantic poets, it is Charlotte Smith's *Elegiac Sonnets*, first published in May 1784. It is the first such collection to become a best-seller in the author's lifetime, going through nine editions by 1800, each augmented by new poems. Their celebrity displeased Anna Seward, who condemned Smith's poems as 'pretty', suggesting they were plagiarized, and concluded 'It makes me sick.'[31] Wordsworth, on the other hand, who was not the easiest poet to please, praised the 'true feeling for rural nature, at a time when nature was not much regarded by English Poets', and described Smith as 'a lady to whom English verse is under greater obligations than are likely to be either acknowledged or remembered'.[32] However, Smith's 'Preface to the First and Second Editions' shows her also smarting from Johnson's condescension: 'I am told, and I read it as the opinion of very good judges, that the legitimate Sonnet is ill calculated for our language.'[33] She describes her own sonnets as 'no improper vehicle for a single Sentiment', some written 'on the Italian model' others 'less regular'. Like Seward, however, Smith does not disguise an autobiographical motive: 'Some very melancholy moments have been beguiled, by expressing in verse the sensations those moments brought', and her words link up her approach with the popular 'graveyard poetry' written by, among others, Warton. Sonnet 32, 'To Melancholy', embraces the feeling: 'Oh Melancholy! – such thy magic power', since her words 'soothe the pensive visionary mind!' The therapeutic 'melancholy moments' spring not from literary conventions but her own bitter experiences, and given the facts of her life she can surely be forgiven for them. Her childhood abruptly ended at the age of fifteen when she was married against her will to a feckless Richard Smith, whom she never loved and who squandered her entire dowry. Even his own father, who liked and protected Charlotte, was so appalled at his son's financial wastefulness that he attempted to bypass him and leave all his fortune to the grandchildren, only to write such a complex will that it ironically meandered through chancery at the snail's pace of 'Jarndyce and Jarndyce' in *Bleak House* and was not resolved until after Charlotte's death. She showed almost culpable loyalty by accompanying her husband into debtors' prison and later to a deserted part of France, to avoid his repeat imprisonment. She finally said 'enough is enough' and separated 'amicably', going on to provide for their family alone and without money, except what she could earn from her writing, even as she became more ill and gout-ridden. 'Family' referred at one stage to no fewer than ten children and three grandchildren, and it would have been larger without the tragic deaths of two in childbirth and four who predeceased her at various ages. Rather than succumbing under the weight of circumstances, Smith turned melancholy into poetry, thus quite consciously providing an outlet for her feelings in sonnets. She extended Warton's use of the sonnet into an even deeper linking of an occasion observed in nature to the emotional circumstances of her own life, making the sonnets into what T. S. Eliot was later to describe in his essay on *Hamlet* as an 'objective correlative' for feelings.

Another woman whose poetry deserves to be revalued is Mary Robinson, though her use of the sonnet was very different from Smith's. In the lengthy series *Sappho and Phaon* (1796) she revived the sonnet *sequence* as a dramatized, fictional narrative, and flamboyantly feminized her otherwise Petrarchan poems by presenting the story from the point of view of a sexually frank and frustrated Sappho rebuffed by her aloof, disdainful and fickle male love object, Phaon. From Milton she took the practice of ending sonnets fluidly with a quatrain rather than a couplet. The vehicle of Greek mythology is consistent with the practice of the Della Cruscans and anticipates poems by Keats and his friend, Charles Reynolds; and by choosing Sappho as persona she opens the way for an overtly feminine voice. The work paves the way for the later, powerful sonnet sequences by writers such as Elizabeth Barrett Browning and Adrienne Rich.

If Charlotte Smith inspired Wordsworth, Coleridge's muse was William Lisle Bowles, whose *Fourteen Sonnets Written Chiefly on Picturesque Spots during a Journey* was first published in 1789, the same year as the fifth edition of Smith's *Elegiac Sonnets*, and almost certainly was influenced by them. Like Smith's collections, the number of sonnets swelled considerably over the years as his poems were reprinted following Coleridge and Southey's praise. Bowles's immediate stimulus was the experience of being jilted by two fiancées, but his response was more Romantic than Petrarchan, since in poetry he found a soothing emotional connection to nature that distracted him from his amatory grief, rather than dwelling on feelings of unrequited love. He strives to express in verse his real feelings rather than relying on Petrarchan conventions. Descriptions of scenery and buildings, rivers and ruins are foregrounded, to the extent that the sequence becomes like a travelogue, encompassing sights from Scotland and the north of England, Oxford and Dover, and abroad from Ostend and the Rhine. Bowles later described his youthful combination of emotion and landscape in the third person:

> They can be considered in no other light than as exhibiting occasional reflections, which naturally arose in his mind, chiefly during various excursions, undertaking to relieve, at the time, depression of spirits. They were, therefore, in general, suggested by the scenes before them; and wherever such scenes appeared to harmonise with this disposition at the moment, the sentiments were involuntarily prompted.[34]

While Smith uses the sonnet to enact and sometimes allay present anguish, finding some aesthetic way to externalize it, Bowles, even when writing initially as an anguished young man, adopts the stance of one looking back in time to former distress. Retrospection becomes as much a strategy to measure time and to lament lost youth, as to trace an unhappy love affair. That influence may come from Shakespeare rather than Petrarch or the Milton whose 'unconquerable mind, and genius high' he had saluted in 'In Youth', in defiance of Johnson. However, while Shakespeare often uses the ravages of time as a premise and ends on a note of hope, Bowles reverses the order,

starting with contented appreciation of a scene and gradually working
toward a couplet expressing emotional loss:

> Soothed by the scene, thus on tired Nature's breast
> A stillness slowly steals, and kindred rest;
> While sea-sounds lull her, as she sinks to sleep,
> Like melodies that mourn upon the lyre.
>   ['At Tynemouth Priory, After a Tempestuous Voyage'][35]
> And many a softened image of the past
> Sadly combine, and bid remembrance keep,
> To soothe me with fair scenes, and fancies rude,
> When I pursue my path in solitude.
>   ['On Leaving a Village in Scotland'][36]

One of Bowles's sonnets is called 'Associations', and the Hartleian word
sums up his treatment of the way scenery stimulates, creates, or re-creates
past emotion. Linked by an omnipresent sense of elegy, Bowles feels that
'fourteen lines seemed best adapted to unity of sentiment'. His titles tell
their story: 'Influence of Time on Grief', 'Bereavement', 'In Memoriam',
'Woodspring Abbey', 'Art and Nature: The Bridge between Clifton and
Leigh Woods' and 'On a Beautiful Landscape'. Feelings drive the poems, but
they are firmly located in a place and time, locating the 'elegiac sonnet' in
picturesque landscape.

By the time Robert Burns came to write in 1795–6, he could in an unforced
way begin a sonnet by saying 'I call no Goddess to inspire my strains / A
fabled Muse may suit a Bard that feigns', and instead turn his poem into one
that celebrates living friendship.[37] In doing so, he builds upon the increasing inventiveness of the writers canvassed in this chapter, who maintained
the continuity of the sonnet in England and opened up its range of subjects
even while adhering to one of its formal models. Sociability and solitude,
scenery and emotions, contemporary politics and public events, discursive
meditation and passionate emotion: all could by this time augment love and
praise as worthy topics. Autobiographical reflection could replace feigned
and fictional situations, so that an unashamed 'I' need not be equated with
a *persona*. Johnson's dismissal of the sonnet had been overturned and his
low estimate of Milton's sonnets was definitively replaced by a Wordsworth
who claimed to find inspiration in poems that addressed a nation's politics.[38] Bowles and Smith had paved the way for Wordsworth to see the
miniature poems as tailor-made for revealing 'spots of time'. Coleridge had
raised Shakespeare's Sonnets from obscurity to the top of a poetic pantheon,
while Hazlitt could triumphantly redeem Milton by claiming Johnson's
strictures were made under the influence of a 'rage for French models', and

use Milton's sonnets to reverse the low estimation of Milton's sonnets.[39] Having been kept on life support for 150 years by a small, dedicated coterie, the sonnet form was once again truly alive.

Notes

1 Mark Raymond, 'The Romantic Sonnet Revival: Opening the Sonnet's Crypt', *Literature Compass* 4:3 (2007), 721–36 (p. 721).

2 John Milton, *Milton's Sonnets: The Texts with an Introduction and Commentary*, ed. E. A. J. Honigmann (London: Macmillan, 1966), p. 41. Quotations, and much information, are taken from this edition. See also John Milton, *Milton: The Complete Shorter Poems*, ed. John Carey (London: Longman, 1997).

3 William McCarthy, 'The Continuity of Milton's Sonnets', *Publications of the Modern Language Association* 92 (1977), 96–109 (p. 96).

4 Anna K. Nardo, *Milton's Sonnets and the Ideal Community* (Lincoln, NE: University of Nebraska Press, 1979).

5 Kurt Schlueter, 'Milton's Heroical Sonnets', *Studies in English Literature 1500–1900* 35 (1995), 123–36 (pp. 124, 135).

6 Translations by Carey, from Milton, *The Complete Shorter Poems*.

7 Carey's translation.

8 David Norbrook, *Writing the English Republic: Poetry, Rhetoric and Politics 1627–1660* (Cambridge: Cambridge University Press, 1999), pp. 182–6.

9 Schlueter, 'Milton's Heroical Sonnets', p. 135.

10 Phillis Levin, 'Introduction', in *The Penguin Book of the Sonnet: 500 Years of a Classic Tradition in English* (New York: Penguin, 2001), p. lxiii.

11 See Lucy Newlyn, Paradise Lost *and the Romantic Reader* (Oxford: Oxford University Press, 1993), though the sonnets are barely mentioned.

12 Edward, earl of Clarendon, *The Life of Edward, Earl of Clarendon … Written by Himself*, 3 vols. (new edn, 1827), Vol. 1, pp. 36–7.

13 Paul Hartle, 'Cotton, Charles (1630–1687)', *The Oxford Dictionary of National Biography* (Oxford: Oxford University Press, 2004), available online at www.oxforddnb.com/view/article/6410?docPos=1.

14 Charles Cotton, Sonnet 3, in Levin, *The Penguin Book of the Sonnet*, p. 83.

15 John Dryden, *Discourses on Satire and Epic Poetry* (London: Cassell, 1888), p. 67.

16 Samuel Johnson, 'John Milton', in *Lives of the Poets*, in Mona Wilson, ed., *Johnson: Poetry and Prose* (London: Rupert Hart-Davis, 1970), p. 834.

17 See Thomas P. Roche, Jr, *Petrarch in English* (London: Penguin, 2005); and George Watson, *The English Petrarchans: A Critical Bibliography of the 'Canzoniere'* (London: Warburg Institute, 1967).

18 Philip Ayres, 'If love it be not', in Roche, *Petrarch in English*, p. 165.

19 See Arthur Sherbo, *The Birth of Shakespeare Studies: Commentators from Rowe (1709) to Boswell-Malone (1821)* (East Lansing: Colleagues Press, 1986).

20 William Wordsworth, 'Preface to the Second Edition of *Lyrical Ballads* (1800)', in *William Wordsworth: Selected Poems and Prefaces*, ed. Jack Stillinger (Boston: Houghton Mifflin Press, 1965), p. 446.

21 Paula R. Feldman and Daniel Robinson, eds., *A Century of Sonnets: The Romantic-Era Revival 1750–1850* (Oxford: Oxford University Press, 1999), p. 4.

22 *Ibid.*, pp. 25–6.

23 *Ibid.*, pp. 27–9, where Southey's words are also quoted.

24 *Ibid.*, p. 48.

25 Coleridge, 'Preface' to *Sonnets from Various Authors* (1796), quoted by James C. McKusick, 'Nature', in Michael Ferber (ed.), *A Companion to European Romanticism* (Oxford: Blackwell, 2005), pp. 413–32 (p. 422).

26 Quotations are from Dodsley's *A Collection of Poems by Several Hands* (1775 edn), reprinted in the *English Poetry Database*, available online at http://dev.hil.unb.ca/Texts/EPD/UNB/index.html.

27 Thomas Gray, 'Sonnet on the Death of Mr Richard West', in David Nichol Smith, ed., *The Oxford Book of Eighteenth Century Verse* (Oxford: Clarendon Press, 1926), p. 371.

28 Wordsworth, 'Preface to the Second Edition of *Lyrical Ballads*', pp. 450–1.

29 Quoted from Paula R. Feldman, ed., *British Women Poets of the Romantic Era: An Anthology* (Baltimore: Johns Hopkins University Press, 2000), p. 659.

30 Anna Seward, *The Poetical Works of Anna Seward* ..., 3 vols. (Edinburgh and London, 1810), Vol. III, Sonnet LXIV, p. 186. Subsequent reference is to this edition.

31 Anna Seward, *Letters of Anna Seward*, 6 vols. (London: 1811), Vol. I, pp. 162–3, quoted in Feldman, *British Women Poets of the Romantic Era*, p. 673.

32 William Wordsworth, *Poetical Works*, 8 vols., ed. W. Knight (London, 1896), Vol. VII, p. 351,

33 Charlotte Smith, *Elegiac Sonnets* [1789] (Oxford: Woodstock, 1992).

34 From Bowles's 'Memoir', in Preface to William Lisle Bowles, *The Poetical Works of William Lisle Bowles*, 9th edn (Edinburgh: Ballantyne, 1855), p. 23.

35 Sonnet III. Written at Tinemouth, Northumberland, after a Tempestuous Voyage', *Sonnets, Written Chiefly on Picturesque Spots, During a Tour*, 2nd ed (Bath: R. Cruttwell, 1789) p. 12.

36 'Sonnet VIII. On leaving a Village in Scotland', *ibid.*, p. 18.

37 Robert Burns, 'Sonnet to Robert Graham, Esq. of Fintry On Receiving a Favour, 19th August 1789', in *Poems and Songs of Robert Burns*, ed. James Barke (London and Glasgow: Collins, 1955), p. 291.

38 See Jennifer Ann Wagner, *A Moment's Monument: Revisionary Poetics and the Nineteenth-Century English Sonnet* (Madison, WI: Fairleigh Dickinson University Press, 1996).

39 William Hazlitt, 'On Milton's Sonnets', in *Table Talk: Essays on Men and Manners*, 2 vols. (London: Henry Colburn and Co., 1822), Vol. II, Essay 2.

10

MICHAEL O'NEILL

The Romantic sonnet

'Scorn not the Sonnet; Critic, you have frowned, / Mindless of its just honours'.[1] So Wordsworth opened a poem composed around 1802, and first
published in 1827. It suggests the form's relative lack of prestige at the beginning of the nineteenth century, but also a new awareness of what the sonnet
could achieve. Chastening the bumptious critic, Wordsworth embarks on a
roll-call of poets who were mindful of the sonnet's possibilities: Shakespeare,
Petrarch, Tasso, Camões, Dante, Spenser and Milton, effectively the major
poets since the Renaissance. Formally Wordsworth establishes continuity
among these poets and himself by a rhyme scheme that pays homage to both
Petrarchan and Shakespearean schemes. The poem consists of three quatrains and a couplet, recalling the English poet's staple pattern, but the octave rhymes are *abbaacca*, a modifying echo of the Italian form. Moreover,
Wordsworth enjambs the eighth line, refusing to allow the octave to remain
a self-sufficient unit, as though the links between sonnet-writing poets over-
rode cultural divisions between them.

   In the poem, Wordsworth seeks to re-establish the sonnet's canonical
prestige. The gathering syntax of the last five lines enacts the form's surprising but indisputable capacity for grandeur in Milton: 'in his hand', the poem
concludes, 'The Thing became a Trumpet, whence he blew / Soul-animating
strains – alas, too few!' These lines embody in their concentrations of phrase
and rhythm the power to which they pay tribute. Sonnets are not merely
epic poets' pastimes: they distil their authors' creative essence. The critic
is comprehensively driven from the field, as 'The Thing', at once colloquial
and a mocking form of understatement, 'became', and becomes, 'a Trumpet'.
For Wordsworth, the sonnet is a form that requires us to reassess the poets'
achievements, to see them in a new, more personal light. '[W]ith this Key /
Shakespeare unlocked his heart' showcases the Romantic sense of the sonnet as a paradigm of the expressive. It articulates, too, the view that the sonnet form is a 'Key', a means of escaping from a prison, presumably that of
an inability to communicate personal feelings. That Milton was able to blow

'Soul-animating strains' reveals, conversely, that the sonnet is equally valuable for what it offers the reader. If it unlocks the poet's heart, it animates the reader's soul.

Wordsworth's poem closes with an elegiac regret that Milton wrote 'too few' sonnets. But after Milton the form had fallen on stony ground. If the sonnet returns like a lost planet to the generic heaven of Romantic forms, a harbinger and shaper of its fortunes was Charlotte Smith's volume of *Elegiac Sonnets* (1784). Smith's revival of the sonnet bequeaths to subsequent writers, both male and female, a sophisticated poetic instrument, one that permits the exploration of what it is to express feeling in a poem. Fascinated with the extremes of emotion, her work is characteristic of the literature of sensibility. It exhibits a conviction that the self contains depths and mysteries beyond the reach of reason, and affirms a gendered if muted individualism that can be read as a challenge to the regulatory control of dominant systems of power. Certainly it catalyzes a resurgence of interest in the sonnet for writers of the Romantic era.

Behind Smith's work lies the example of Thomas Gray's 'Sonnet on the Death of Mr Richard West', a great and isolated example of the sonnet in the pre-Romantic period. A poem on the subject of suppressed passion, as Stuart Curran notes, its theme resonates in Mary Robinson's sonnet sequence *Sappho and Phaon* (1796).[2] Competing with Smith's work as claimants for initiating the Romantic sonnet revival are the topographical, elegiac musings of William Bowles and Thomas Warton, a mode picked up by Coleridge, who emerges, in this as in other genres, as a poet who opened doors for other poets. Crucially, the example of Coleridge's *Sonnets on Eminent Characters* also allowed Milton's long-dormant influence to flower again in Wordsworth's sonnets, by making the sonnet a vehicle for matters of public and political moment.

The sonnet's status as an imaginative space, a formally potent solution to the quest for 'home', enjoys particular privilege in Wordsworth's works. As with all the sonneteers of the period, such a poetics is also a politics: Wordsworth holds in tension an individualist but humane politics with a commitment to an ideal of national solidarity. Second-generation Romantics, Shelley and Keats endorse the sonnet's newly rediscovered confidence to engage in quest and questioning, reflecting their ex-aristocratic and upwardly mobile social positions respectively. Their sonnets tackle a range of themes including private feeling: would-be creations of gossipy or exalted community; sublime, prophetic reflections on the role of the poet and poetry, politics, history and existential metaphysics. At the most suggestive formal extreme, the sonnets of John Clare are organized in ways that give priority to the accidental and chanced-upon, and spurn syntaxes of co-ordinated order in favour of a poetics close to the improvisatory. Ecological spaces loved and lost find consoling and desolate mirroring in sonnets that imitate the ragged, casual felicity of a mouse's or a squirrel's nest. What follows is for convenience divided into subdivisions, but overlap between the categories is frequent.

Charlotte Smith, Mary Robinson and sensibility

Charlotte Smith's poems make private distress public in ways that are far reaching; serving as a vehicle for the expression of 'sentiment', they exhibit a stylish candour and poetic self-consciousness, as the first poem in the sequence shows:

> The partial Muse, has from my earliest hours
>> Smil'd on the rugged path I'm doomed to tread,
> And still with sportive hand has snatch'd wild flowers,
>> To weave fantastic garlands for my head:
> But far, far happier is the lot of those
>> Who never learn'd her dear delusive art;
> Which, while it decks the head with many a rose,
>> Reserves the thorn, to fester in the heart.
> For still she bids soft Pity's melting eye
>> Stream o'er the hills she knows not to remove,
> Points every pang, and deepens every sigh
>> Of mourning friendship, or unhappy love.
> Ah! then, how dear the Muse's favours cost,
> *If those paint sorrow best – who feel it most!*[3]

A Shakespearean sonnet of three quatrains and a couplet, the poem travels toward the last line's allusion, pointed out by Smith's own note: 'The well-sung woes shall soothe my pensive ghost; / He best can paint them, who shall feel them most. *Pope's Eloisa to Abelard, 366th line*'.[4] What in Pope is close to a boast becomes in Smith a wry hypothesis, as her 'If' converts the earlier assertion into something more self-inspecting. The poem explores the idea that the 'Muse's favours' exact a 'dear' price. Such is the case, if the reader concedes the point on which the exclamatory sadness underlying the final couplet insists – that the ability to '*paint sorrow*' requires the poet to experience sorrow with greater acuteness than others do.

The 'partial Muse' has shown partiality to the poet, having 'Smil'd on the rugged path I'm doomed to tread'. But the smile flatters to deceive, since in the first use of 'dear' in the poem Smith refers to the greater happiness 'of those / Who never learn'd her dear delusive art'. The alliterative phrase 'dear delusive' implies the poet's mixed feelings. The Muse's 'art' may be much prized but it is also deceptive, and the sonnet discovers this futility in the act of its own formal realization. If it 'decks the head with many a rose', it, too, 'Reserves the thorn, to fester in the heart'. The imagery of rose and thorn seems blandly familiar. But it takes on new force when one realizes that the poem itself is decking the head (in that it is earning critical admiration for its author, or in that it is appealing to the reader's critical intelligence), yet reserving a thorn to fester in the heart (in that it provokes us to recognize the curious folly of admiring a production that entraps the poet in an emotionally vicious if creatively virtuous cycle of sorrow and composition). The third quatrain disconcertingly enacts our own consciously aestheticizing response; 'soft Pity's melting eye' is that of the reader who, conniving with the poet, turns the poet's suffering into a landscape, a suggestion conveyed by 'hills'. 'Hills', not 'ills': one momentarily suspects a typographical error, but Smith's word choice makes us see sorrow as objectively immovable.

Poetry, or the Muse, savours this relish of pain; it 'Points every pang, and deepens every sigh / Of mourning friendship, or unhappy love'. Smith's point is that sensibility thrives on artifice, as her sonnet thrives on its pointings and deepenings of feeling. It implies both a kinship and a friction between the pangs and sighs of human experience, and the artful resources of poetry. Wearing their feelings on their sleeve, Smith's sonnets cast shrewd glances at their own becomings and their readers' responses. The author creates a suffering, sombre persona, yet this persona proves hard to separate from what we sense is the author's experiental self.

A comparable effect occurs in Mary Robinson's *Sappho and Phaon*, whose forty-four sonnets chart the development and tragic outcome of Sappho's unrequited love for Phaon. The sequence is a reassertion of female imaginative power. Sappho, as Robinson reminds us in her note 'To The Reader', 'was the unrivalled poetess of her time'.[5] Robinson herself, the famous, much painted beauty and former mistress of the Prince Regent, lived in the public eye, and she plays with our impulse to read biographically by reminding us in her 'Preface' (which includes an explanation of the 'disrepute into which sonnets are fallen') of the capacity of 'the *legitimate sonnet*' to provide 'a series of sketches ... forming in the whole a complete and connected story'.[6] By 'legitimate sonnet' Robinson means a sonnet that follows the Petrarchan form, and she enters into a dialogue, across the centuries and gender-barriers, with the disillusioned wisdom that shadows the Italian poet's *Canzoniere*. Her 'Sonnet Introductory' claims that 'FAVOUR'D by Heav'n are those, ordain'd to taste / The bliss supreme that kindles fancy's fire; / Whose magic fingers sweep the muses' lyre / In varying cadence, eloquently chaste!' There are scarcely bidden ironies here, pointed up by 'eloquently chaste'.[7] The phrase 'fancy's fire', here applied to poetic inspiration, reminds us, after reading the sequence, of the way in which 'fancy' has been associated with Sappho's feelings, as when she hopes through her death 'To calm rebellious Fancy's fev'rish dream' (XLIII). And 'bliss supreme' has the air of a primarily erotic state.

But such ironies, insisting on the interplay between experience and poetry, cannot wholly undercut the elevated status accorded to poetry in this and other poems in the sequence. Robinson may inveigh against 'Reason' as 'A visionary theme! – a gorgeous shade!' (XI), but the very shrewdness of her interplay with Petrarch and Sappho suggests a mind that retains control in the midst of dramatizing 'the soul's rebellious passions' (XI). *Sappho and Phaon* deploys its rhetorical skills, its command of anaphora and antithesis, with an impassioned poise that bears out the declaration that marks the *volta* of its 'Sonnet Introductory': 'For thou, blest POESY!, with godlike pow'rs / To calm the miseries of man wert giv'n'. That Robinson could not simply enforce the truth-claims of this statement makes it no less important for the dramatic dynamics of her work than do comparable assertions in Keats, from *Sleep and Poetry* through to *The Fall of Hyperion*.

Warton, Bowles, Coleridge and the loco-descriptive sonnet

Thomas Warton's 'To the River Lodon', published in 1777, uses the sonnet to express the poet's sense of connections and differences between past and present selves, and to do so in relation to a particular landscape:

> Ah! what a weary race my feet have run,
>   Since first I trod thy banks with alders crown'd,
>   And thought my way was all through fairy ground
>   Beneath thy azure sky, and golden sun:
> Where first my muse to lisp her notes begun!
>   While pensive memory traces back the round,
>   Which fills the varied interval between;
>   Much pleasure, more of sorrow, marks the scene.[8]

The writing ingeniously places the idea of melancholy fatigue in our minds in the first line's mention of the 'weary race', before it sets it aside in ensuing lines that relive a time when the poet 'thought my way was all through fairy ground'. The real and the imagined marry in that rhyme between 'fairy ground' and the 'banks with alders crown'd; the subdued metaphor in 'crown'd' hints at the poet's act of imaginative coronation, of investing the scene with significance both in the past and in the present. As the poet re-enters his former condition, an excitement shows itself in the expressive run-on from lines 4 to 5, repeating the idea of an 'origin' in line 2 ('Since first') but with more metapoetic reference to the time and place 'Where first my muse to lisp her notes begun'. Immediately, as so often in the Romantic sonneteering of which Warton's poem is a forerunner, a dialectical process comes into play, and 'pensive memory' offsets the initial exultation of line 5. Warton consoles himself at the close with the thought that his 'days' are not 'with the Muse's laurel unbestowed'. But even there the double negative suggests the need to keep at arm's length a fear of failure.

William Bowles, in the sonnets that Coleridge found inspirational, would return to and build on Warton's formula – one part memory, one part topography, one part reflection – in works such as, and especially, 'To the River Itchin'. This sonnet interrogates the poet's feelings in a way that suggests the question has greater weight than the answer:

> Itchin, when I behold thy banks again,
> Thy crumbling margin, and thy silver breast
> On which the self-same tints still seem to rest,
> Why feels my heart the shivering sense of pain?[9]

The circling syntax and suggestive detail (the river's '*crumbling* margin') locate us simultaneously in an ongoing present and as though we viewed time's passage in the blink of an eye.

When Coleridge produces his own variation on Bowles's sonnet in his 1796 poem 'To the River Otter', he is less interested than his mentor in the discovery of 'solace', to use Bowles's word, and more intent on a keener apprehension of memory's workings. The result is a poem that ushers in a full-blown Romantic poetry of loss and recompense. Bowles conveys his attachment to the river through the reference to its 'self-same tints'; Coleridge seems less decorously and more immediately immersed in his experience of the coexistence of past and present, the interpenetration of 'happy' and 'mournful hours', as he thinks back to when 'I skimm'd the smooth thin stone along thy breast, / Numbering its light leaps!' Hurrying across the river's physical surface leads immediately, as David Fairer notes sensitively, into the sense of memory's depth: 'so deep imprest / Sink the sweet scenes of childhood'.[10]

It is not just that Coleridge's skimming monosyllables mime the stone's passage or that the subsequently 'imprest' 'scenes' 'Sink', in an eloquent stress-shift, as though the stone fell below the water's surface into the underworld of memory; it is also that the detailed recollection persuades by its sharp images and rhythms. True to Coleridge's view of 1796 that the sonneteer ought to 'consult his own convenience' regarding 'metre' and 'rhymes', and trust 'whatever the chastity of his ear may prefer, whatever the rapid expression of his feelings will permit',[11] 'To the River Otter' employs a subtly irregular rhyme scheme that carries over rhymes from the first quatrain to the second and from the second to the third and, indeed, into the penultimate line. The result is to embody the startlingly 'bright transparence' with which the invoked 'Visions of childhood' materialize themselves in his adult memory. Cunning sound patterns, evidenced in the last line's 'Ah! that once more I were a careless child!', redeem the poem from sentimental self-pity, as they make neighbours of apparent opposites: the exclamatory '*Ah*' begins the weaving of a web of cognate sounds that catches the longing for past joy in '*were*', the recognition of loss and its desired reversal in 'once *more*' and the pivotal admission of present '*care*' in the wish to be '*care*less'. The poem's desire to recover a 'careless' state ties itself intricately to a complex adult consciousness only too aware of 'Lone manhood's cares'. Played against the visionary political hopes of the 1794 sonnet co-written with Samuel Favell on 'Pantisocracy', which opens with the injunction, 'No more the visionary Soul shall dwell / On Joys, that were!', the poem suggests how the latter's utopian politics involve too absolute a rejection of the past.

'The Sonnet', Coleridge wrote in the 1790s, 'is a small poem, in which some lonely feeling is developed'.[12] Coleridge runs with no crowd, such a comment avers, despite the community that the sonnet's processes of exchange create. In 'Work without Hope', Coleridge would eloquently exploit this nuanced capacity for disjunction. This later poem appears to aim at a unified effect, yet it thrives on the sonnet's impulse to turn, to alter direction, to concede inevitable division. Mays has shown how the poem's '14-line form' was originally the opening of a more extended notebook account of how, 'I speak in figures, inward thoughts and woes / Interpreting by Shapes and Outward Shews'.[13] The published 1828 poem is daringly simplified, a reversed sonnet, written in couplets that hold the idea of harmony before us, and mock it. Harmony ought to exist between the poet and the 'Nature' in which 'All ... seems at work', even the 'Slugs' who 'leave their lair', but it does not. He is 'the sole unbusy Thing', who watches the processes of life. Yet even as the poet says that he does not 'build, nor sing', he builds a sonnet; he sings of his incapacity to sing. The sonnet pursues what Morton D. Paley calls the poet's 'strategy of recuperation' as Coleridge 'makes his sense of loss a source of lyric expression'.[14] Negation is a kind of positive in this space where the Romantic imagination finds inspiration in the dungeon of writer's block. Coleridge's description of his lips – 'unbrighten'd, wreathless Brow' – seems to possess in the act of conceding dispossession. In part, this is because the poem's music, its control of poetic technique, means that we involuntarily concede to Coleridge all that is implied in his 'turn' at the start of the reversed octave, 'Yet well I ken the banks, where Amaranths blow, / Have traced the fount whence streams of Nectar flow. / Bloom, O ye Amaranths! bloom for whom ye may – / For Me ye bloom not!' Paley notes finely how the initial stress on 'Bloom' 'only makes the poet's renunciation more poignant'.¹⁵ And, one might add, more authoritative. This valediction to the blooming, never-fading flowers of poetic immortality is uttered by a poet who persuades us that such a farewell intimates a closer knowledge of 'banks, where Amaranths blow' than is possessed by those for whom they cheerfully 'bloom'. Coleridge packs a life into a sonnet, moving toward a close that successfully evokes failure, as though failure were itself a vocation, a discovery of some deep-riven chasm at the heart of things:

> And would you learn the Spells, that drowse my Soul?
> WORK without Hope draws nectar in a sieve;
> And HOPE without an Object cannot live.

That a life, a poetic career, even an era can reduce itself to 'Spells' that mimic Augustan elegance while possessing depths of suggestion shows how complexly productive a form the sonnet could be for the Romantics. Despite its overt sense, the poem lends 'HOPE without an Object' its despairing magnanimity. The sonnet itself is the 'sieve' through which poetic 'nectar' has been drawn.

Politics: Coleridge, Southey, Wordsworth, Hunt

To return from this late poem's stoical conquest of self-pity to Coleridge's earlier sonnets is to be reminded how his uses of the form sustain dialogue with one another. In his earlier work, Coleridge puts centre-stage the double consciousness involved not only in being an adult aware of having been a child, but also in being a poet seeking to understand history. In his *Sonnets on Eminent Characters*, major documents of his turbulent involvement in the revolutionary and counter-revolutionary politics of the 1790s, Coleridge compresses biographies of leading political figures, while expanding their significance under the pressure of the poet's admiration or rage. The 1794 attack on Pitt demonstrates considerable political courage, and daringly infuses the sonnet with the kind of hyperbolical conceit found in Donne's 'Batter my heart'.¹⁶ Whereas Donne shocks by twining sexual with sacred idioms, taking the sonnet back to its erotic origins with a daring never matched by Petrarch, Coleridge mingles religion with politics, crucifying Pitt's political perfidy on the cross of New Testament imagery. Pitt is one who:

> kiss'd his country with Iscariot mouth
> (Ah! foul apostate from his Father's fame!)
> Then fix'd her on the cross of deep distress,
> And at safe distance marks the thirsty lance
> Pierce her big side!

To adapt Keats on Shakespeare's Sonnets, the wording is full of packed suggestions thrown out 'in the intensity of working out conceits'.[17] Thus, Pitt is at once Judas and, half blasphemously, a Christ fallen away from his Father's mission. Indeed, the active verbs – 'kiss'd', 'fix'd' and 'marks' – grant Pitt a knowing involvement in his cunning betrayals and attempts at self-distancing. The sonnet form, placing a premium on saying a great deal in a short space, wins from Coleridge's political voice an urgency that fails, if it fails, only through excess of force. Coleridge's allusive dexterity shows in his 'Sonnet: To Burke', where he adapts, as Mays points out, one of Milton's most personal sonnets, 'Methought I saw my late espoused Saint', to his own political ends: for Milton's 'Saint', Coleridge's dream-vision supplies 'the sainted form of FREEDOM', lamenting Burke's falling-off and longing to 'clasp [him] with a Mother's joy!'[18]

Between Coleridge's sonnets and Wordsworth's 'Sonnets Dedicated to Liberty' in his *Poems, in Two Volumes* (1807), however, a further instance of the public Romantic sonnet deserves attention: Robert Southey's anti-slavery sequence, later entitled *Poems Concerning the Slave-Trade*, first published in 1797.[19] Varying in their rhyme schemes, the poems can seem merely righteous, but can also polemicize effectively. An example is the sixth and final poem, opening 'High in the air expos'd the Slave is hung'.[20] The cruelty-saturated historic present passes swiftly into a injunction against an imagined audience, emphasized by the rhyme – 'hither gaze O ye / Who tore this Man from Peace and Liberty!' – and rhetorical sarcasm at the expense of fellow travellers with the slave traders, namely 'ye who weigh with scrupulous care / The right and prudent'. Southey's imperatives grab the latter by their lapels, haul them across the gulf between the octave's presentation of slavery's horror and the sestet's response to it, and confront them at the close with Macbeth at his most conscience-stricken and imaginatively roused, his blank verse made to fit Southey's rhymes. Just as Macbeth fears the consequences of his act, so the tortured Slave 'Before the Eternal, "thunder-tongued shall plead" / Against the deep damnation of your deed'. Southey's thunderously reworked allusion aligns the killing of Duncan with the cruelty shown to the slave both by his owners and traders, and by those who support the slave trade; they, too, have become the deed's creatures.

Southey's sequence shows how the Romantic sonnet had become a means of working on and communicating political feeling, not merely a means of expressing inward feeling. Indeed, poetry that dwelt on personal feeling, especially in its more lachrymose, sensibility-deriving modes, was brilliantly caricatured by Coleridge in his parodic 'Sonnets Attempted in the Manner of "Contemporary Writers"'. In the first he mocks pseudo-Petrarchan and Della Cruscan egotism ('Most of MYSELF I thought'); in the second he ruthlessly guys the simpering idiom of 'meek *Simplicity*', associated with sonnets of sensibility, and its Della Cruscan offshoot; and in the third he sends up contemporary bombast, his own among others, in an amusing telling of 'This is the House that Jack Built'. Charles Lloyd and Charles Lamb, fellow contributors to a pamphlet of sonnets, may have been affronted, along with Robert Southey.[21] But Coleridge, the Ezra Pound of his day, was clearing the poetic ground, allowing others to make it new.

In Wordsworth's hands, the Romantic sonnet fuses inwardness and public concern. Indeed, the intersection of the self and a wider world is at the core of poems such as 'With Ships the sea was sprinkled far and nigh', in which the poet explores processes of imaginative identification with power. Baudelaire in 'À une passante' ('To a Woman Passing-By', 1861) would seize on a chance encounter with a woman passing by as an emblem of the poet's search for fragmentary epiphanies amidst the chaos of modern city life. His sonnet is a swirl of broken phrases and contrasts, sudden metaphors and leaping impassioned conjectures. The unknown woman revives the poet's hopes, only almost certainly to dash them, leaving him with radiant, crazed insight into contingency's mockery of meaning: 'O toi que j'eusse aimée, ô toi qui le savais!' ('O you whom I could have loved, O you who knew it!').[22] Wordsworth, writing half a century earlier, does not make his plucking out of a particular vessel from a sea of crowded ships matter for cruel awareness of conditional fulfilment and actual loss. But his strategy shows how the sonnet thrives on an identification between the lover's and the poet's desires. Imaginative pursuit of special meaning assumes in the poem's sestet a willed, erotic charge; Wordsworth breathes new life into the conventional gendering of a ship as female: 'This Ship was nought to me, nor I to her, / Yet I pursued her with a Lover's look'. And as the woman in Baudelaire yields no information about her destination, so Wordsworth's ship declines to answer the questions 'she' provokes: 'When will she turn, and whither?'. The ship is the more prized for refusing to 'brook' any 'tarrying'.

Lighthearted in its way, the poem suggests the paradoxical capacity of the sonnet – a form, associated with confinement – to speak eloquently of the imagination's search for the infinite. Wordsworth writes with acute consciousness of this aspect of the sonnet in 'Nuns fret not at their Convent's narrow room', contending that 'the prison, unto which we doom / Ourselves, no prison is', an expressive run-on across the octave's 'prison' doubling his point. This sonnet may seem to sell Wordsworth's dealings with the sonnet short when it suggests that a major attraction of the form is the comfort it gives those 'Who have felt the weight of too much liberty'. And yet the political resonance of 'liberty' is important, there. The poems are 'Dedicated to Liberty', but the liberty to which they dedicate themselves is a far cry from the French revolutionary slogan that attracted the young Wordsworth. The liberty Wordsworth has in mind is at an absolute – and Miltonic – remove from licence. In the sestet of 'Milton! thou should'st be living at this hour', Wordsworth praises his mentor in terms that Shelley would later pick up with ironic resonance in *Adonais*:

> Thy soul was like a Star and dwelt apart:
> Thou hadst a voice whose sound was like the sea;
> Pure as the naked heavens, majestic, free,
> So didst thou travel on life's common way,
> In cheerful godliness; and yet thy heart
> The lowliest duties on itself did lay.   (9–14)

Wordsworth's very rhyming bears witness to an impulse to hold Milton 'apart', yet see him as praiseworthy for having travelled on 'life's common way'. The word 'apart' is held at a distance from the 'heart' of the penultimate line, in which Milton, for all his stellar singleness, is willing to embrace all the obligations exacted by 'life's common way'. The active phrasing of the final sentence has Milton as an agent, laying upon himself 'The lowliest duties'. If the effect is of a diminuendo, even anticlimax, after the image of the poet's starlike soul, 'majestic, free', then such is the poem's pointed wish.

Joseph Phelan has pointed out how Wordsworth's sonnets end up 'articulating a new and in many ways radically altered version of masculinity, one which includes not just self-restraint and fortitude in adversity, but also domesticity, seclusion and passivity', and how the poet finds in the formal demands of the sonnet a form of 'submission to authority' in which traces of the '"Victorian" Wordsworth' are revealed.[23] Yet, as Phelan also notes, a poem such as 'I grieved for Buonaparte', one of the first sonnets Wordsworth wrote after Dorothy read him Milton's sonnets in 1802, is not simply counter-revolutionary. It was the independence of Milton's sonnets that had impressed him, and here, Wordsworth's highly individual voice serves as a guide to the vigilance he enjoins. The poem charts a movement away from grief for the spectacle of Bonaparte, succumbing to personal ambition when he allowed himself to be declared First Consul of France, toward imagining the education necessary for 'The Governor who must be wise and good' (6). Such a 'Governor' needs to 'temper with the sternness of the brain / Thoughts motherly, and meek as womanhood' (7–8). The gender stereotypes may seem commonplace; but the poem's rebuke of an undisciplined idea of masculinity is powerful, delivered through a sestet that builds in short-phrased sentences to a conclusion that earns the 'rights' it claims: 'these are the degrees / By which true Sway doth mount; this is the stalk / True Power doth grow on; and her rights are these' (12–14). The circling back to 'these' mimics the sonnet's returning rhymes, making it a place where 'True Power' can be embodied. Plain speaking coexists with metapoetic ingenuity. The rhyme scheme is itself a 'stalk' on which the virtues embodied in 'the *talk* / Man holds with week-day man in the hourly *walk* / Of the mind's business' (10–12; emphases mine) is able to 'grow'. And like 'true Sway' the sonnet develops by 'degrees', through incremental assertions that avoid over-insistence.

Dwelling, quest: Wordsworth, Hunt, Byron, Shelley and Keats

Wordsworth's sonnets, as John Kerrigan has argued, can seem to communicate an almost Heideggerean commitment to 'dwelling'.[24] 'The immortal Mind craves objects that endure', Wordsworth concludes in 'These words were uttered in a pensive mood', and the 'objects that endure' include, and are figured by, the very form of the sonnet. For Wordsworth, 'the Sonnet's scanty plot of ground'[25] repeatedly affirms the possibility of 'short solace': provisional stays against the fears of ruination, literal and metaphorical, which mark his work.[26] 'Composed after a Journey across the Hamilton Hills, Yorkshire' enacts a movement of feeling vital to Wordsworthian and British Romanticism; it speaks of wishing to get somewhere, 'the wished-for place', regrets being 'too late' to do so, and affirms a natural beauty that did 'recompence us well', where the sustained *a* rhyme restores a sense of purpose, before conceding the final insubstantiality of all that 'the eye / Delighted in'. '[T]hey are of the sky', Wordsworth summarizes, 'And from our earthly memory fade away'. Desire, in chastising itself, spurs itself on.

The sonnet's primary function, for Wordsworth, is its embodiment of the longing to dwell, transcendentally or immanently. The beauty of 'Composed upon Westminster Bridge' derives from the way that it reconciles opposites and allows them to share in one another's life in the poem. When Wordsworth writes, 'This City now doth like a garment wear / The beauty of the morning' (4–5), he sees the 'City' invested in 'The beauty of the morning', and he insists on a specificity of occurrence to which the sonnet, with its ability to monumentalize the moment, is suited. The poem marries confinement and freedom: 'The river glideth at his own sweet will' (12): that hallmark line is so because of its delighted attention to a being beyond Wordsworth's own, yet one that is in harmony with, and knowable only by, an attuned subjectivity.

For Leigh Hunt, the form's potential for shaped reworkings of experience through reanimating diction becomes the perfect medium to express those 'double pleasures' that Nicholas Roe has located at the centre of his

imaginative being.[27] As Roe intimates, Hunt's 'hybrid, virtuously "impure"'
poetry allows for the collocation of 'mirth and melancholy' in the sonnets
related to his experience of imprisonment for having supposedly libelled the
Prince Regent.[28] In 'Written during the Author's Imprisonment, November
1814', Hunt first evokes the return of winter, then turns on his depiction of
the season's disagreeable weather, to ask, 'And do I love thee less, to paint
thee so?'[29] The answer is at once a resolute 'No', and an affecting tribute to
the mind's power to represent experience in poetry, where the sense of 'represent' is strong: 'This the season is of beauty still, / Doubled at heart; of
smoke, with whirling glee / Uptumbling ever from the blaze below'. 'Doubled
at heart' injects a self-referring energy into the verse, and is in turn released
from self-absorption by the participles that follow with their evocation of an
incessant process caught but not tamed in the sonnet. The conclusion, 'And
home remembered most – and oh, loved hill, / The second and the last, away
from thee!', moves beyond that evocation of process to hint at the quiet
heartbreak of exile from sources of affection and love: 'home'; 'loved hill';
and – finally, a touching tripling at the close of the poem's already 'Doubled'
activity – 'thee', a significant other, whose otherness and significance assert
themselves through Hunt's restraint. Hunt writes of the domesticated scenery of Hampstead in a way that claims for his descriptions and feelings the
authority of the Petrarchan form. The quotidian is 'doubled' by the poetry
into the newly astonishing.

The Wordsworthian notion of the sonnet as a place where freedom might
be purchased with a concentration of power resonates in the period. Byron,
in his most Wordsworthian phase, produced in his 'Sonnet on Chillon' a
magnificently *ne plus ultra* variation on the theme of being bounded in a
nutshell, yet counting oneself king of infinite space. The organ notes of the
opening blare forth the poem's theme: 'Eternal spirit of the chainless mind! /
Brightest in dungeons, Liberty, thou art, / For there thy habitation is the
heart – / The heart which love of thee alone can bind!'[30] With its shimmering
stress-shift in the second line and its use of a rhyme involving 'bind' to celebrate the 'chainless mind', the opening of this (mainly) 'legitimate sonnet'
cocks a snook at what in the Dedication to *Don Juan* Byron calls the 'legitimately vile' character of the victors at Waterloo, who were in the process
of restoring 'legitimate rule' throughout Europe.[31] The sonnet uses its form
to give overtly libertarian force to Wordsworth's assertion that 'the prison,
unto which we doom / Ourselves, no prison is'.[32] It pivots on the paradox
that opposites meet, so that powerlessness, when coupled to a 'chainless
mind', has a potency that transcends worldly power.

Shelley's sonnets, too, seek to speak truth to power. His early address 'To
Wordsworth' deplores the senior poet's falling-off, as the younger poet saw it,

from his early political radicalism, betraying his Miltonic star. 'Ozymandias' allows the tyrant's pedestalled boast, 'Look on my Works, ye Mighty, and despair!' to undo itself, exposed as an empty vaunt by 'The lone and level sands' that 'stretch far away' in the last line.[33] Those sands show time levelling the pretensions of tyranny, bringing low one who described himself, and had himself described, as 'King of Kings'. The poem's intricate rhyme scheme may betoken an impulse to complicate, without blurring the force of the poem's thrust through the arrogant armour of earthly rule. We are alerted to art's complex role in relation to power. Only because of the artistic skill of a 'sculptor' is posterity in a position to discern Ozymandias' 'sneer of cold command', and only through the ability of art to subvert its manifest purpose (which must have been the exaltation of power) is a later age alerted to the cunning with which the sculptor did 'those passions read'. At the same time, time will erode, the poem suggests, the traces not only of tyranny but also of art.

Impressively absent from the poem is any tagged-on gloss. The poem works through a series of perspectives: the 'I' of the poem vanishes after introducing the 'traveller from an antique land'; the legend on the base of the ruined statue echoes emptily in the void of the final lines. Elsewhere, the Shelleyan sonnet is equally resistant to the merely moralizing. In 'Ye hasten to the grave! What seek ye there', Shelley again runs rhymes across any supposed bipartite division to evoke the tragic pathos of 'restless thoughts' proceeding from the 'vainly curious mind which wouldest guess / Whence thou didst come and whither thou must go'.[34] For all the assertions of vanity, however, the poem cannot prevent itself from an imagined speeding to the brink of where 'restless thoughts' may lead, a final questioning gaze into 'the dark abyss of – how little we know', as Shelley phrases it in his essay 'On Life'.[35] 'England in 1819' catalogues the topsy-turvy ills and horrors of things as they are, a demonstration of out-of-jointness that finds a formal parallel in the poem's reversal of octave and sestet. It, too, refuses to resolve the poem's tensions, qualifying with ironic intelligence its impatient wish to imagine a utopian resurrection. Despite the full stop in Shelley's fair copy after line 6, the poem is effectively a single sentence, a virtuoso listing of 'graves' followed by the hope that, out of these graves, 'a glorious Phantom may / Burst, to illumine our tempestuous day'. Much hinges, as many critics have noted, on the behaviour, there, of 'may', thrust into prominence by virtue of its function as a rhyme and teetering between hope and caution. As it teeters, it invites the reader to inspect closely the suggestions of insubstantiality in 'Phantom' and the fact that the Phantom will 'illumine' rather than transform 'our tempestuous day'.

Shelley's instinct here, at one with the sonnet's fascination with lack of simplistic commitment, is to turn a searchlight on his own hopes as well as on England's woes.[36] Bringing the Romantic period's handling of the sonnet to a sophisticated pitch, 'Ode to the West Wind' keeps its quality of compactness and restraint, but extends its scope and reach.[37] Section scatters ashes and sparks to section: when, at the close, Shelley invokes 'the incantation of this verse' (65), the echoic reversal of the opening, in which 'the leaves dead / Are driven, like ghosts from an enchanter fleeing' (2–3), confirms the sense we have of the poet having risen, phoenix-like, from the ashes of the fourth section's self-abasement. Through the use of hurtling enjambment and the resources of the ode, along with *terza rima* rhyming (pulled into finality, but only just, by each section's concluding couplet), the poem releases tremendous energy from the sonnet. Shelley's technical precursor, as in so much of what he wrote, is Coleridge – here the Coleridge of 'France: An Ode' – a poem whose twenty-one-line stanzas are, in effect, each a sonnet and a half. In both cases, the atom of the sonnet is subjected to a power that unleashes great rhetorical force; in both cases, it is less the political message of the poem that counts than the poet's dramatization of his poetic role.

Keats, like Shelley, makes the sonnet an arena for the exploration of discovery. But whereas Shelley drives toward conclusions that unsettle their accommodating structures, as in the closing question of 'Ode to the West Wind', Keatsian quest delights in discovery. 'On First Looking into Chapman's Homer' is a Petrarchan sonnet in which Keats falls in love with and enacts his own capacity for imaginative possession. From the sense of restless travelling in 'realms of gold', the sonnet depicts, in its sestet, an arrival that is at the same time an awareness of illimitable possibility. Two similes comparing the poet to 'some watcher of the skies' and 'stout Cortez' locate this complex of feelings.[38] At once anchored and ardent, the comparisons detain the poet in the act of search, even as he catches himself in the posture of looking forward eagerly. The poem's finish, 'Silent, upon a peak in Darien', warrants Hunt's praise in *Lord Byron and his Contemporaries* (1828) for its 'energetic ... calmness', as Miriam Allott has noted, and bespeaks Keats's trust in the sonnet to provide brief, richly imaginative landing stages.[39]

Comparable effects of what might be called stationed vision occur in two other literary sonnets by Keats. One is 'To Homer', which succeeds not only in communicating a 'structure of paradoxes',[40] but in seeming with joyful stoicism to inhabit, even to recommend, the value of such a structure, as it asserts, 'Aye, on the shores of darkness there is light, / And precipices show untrodden green'. This sestet of a Shakespearean sonnet, the form that Keats imbued with a new resonance, might describe, in miniature, how his sonnets seek and find a value in the positing of contrasts, a value apparent here in the undemonstrative strength of the two uses of 'is' and the grace-extending surprise of 'show'. The second poem, 'As Hermes once took to his feathers light', about a dream of circling in 'sad hell' with Paolo and Francesca, exults in the dark transgressions of eros, dream and imagination. If its final couplet rhyme – 'Pale were the lips I kissed, and fair the form / I floated with, about that melancholy storm' – implies that poetic 'form' must accommodate an experiential 'storm', it commits itself uncompromisingly to an imagined state.[41]

As with Coleridge and Shelley, Keats experimented with the sonnet, experiments that would form the basis of the stanza form he employs in his Odes. His 'If by dull rhymes our English must be chained' is among the most directly self-reflexive treatments of the form in the Romantic period. The poem sustains the parallel between the sonnet's apparent confinement and the pursuit of liberty that is key to the Romantic poetics of the sonnet. But Keats differs from Wordsworth and Byron by expressing overt discontent with the sonnet's traditional rhyme schemes, searching for 'Sandals more interwoven and complete / To fit the naked foot of Poesy', and expressing through his new, 'interwoven' scheme a longing for a poetry that will at least be 'bound with garlands of her own'. That last line may imply that the sonnet embodies the capacity of the imagination to create autonomous worlds, but the Keatsian sonnet is remarkable for its openness to the existential.

This openness does not exactly take the form, though at times it has something of the spirit, of John Clare's rhymed lines bundled into sonnet form, each line phrased with delight in creaturely detail. Clare's '[The Mouse's Nest]' captures an intent interest in the natural world and an alertness to chance: 'I found a ball of grass among the hay / And proged it as I passed and went away', it begins, the age-old, often courtly pentameter given new energy by the down-to-earth dialect of 'proged' (prodded).[42] The transient going 'away' triggers off a vivid re-viewing, rewarded by the 'odd and ... grotesque' sight of 'an old mouse ... / With all her young ones hanging at her teats'. No moral is drawn, no view offered at the close, merely the sense of life's physical continuance as 'broad old cesspools glittered in the sun'. Clare's groundbreaking achievement in such poems is to evoke, but not fetter, a 'somthing' that 'stirred'. He does so in a sonnet form that, shaped into seven couplets, implies, not an orb, or an urn, or a statue, but potentially endless pathways and energies. Clare may have 'fancied somthing stirred'. In his sonnet, however, the self is subdued to the natural element it works in.[43]

In Keats, by contrast, one finds a capacity to rehearse with a brave, spacious calm the ultimate poetic geography of self and world: the relationship between the speaking 'I', with its hopes and anxieties, and its gaze toward 'the shore / Of the wide world' on which it stands alone.[44] Keats echoes there the opening of Shakespeare's Sonnet 107, with its reference to 'the prophetic soul / Of the wide world, dreaming on things to come'.[45] But he offers not so much a Shakespearean 'topsy-turvy reversal of micro- and macrocosmic' as a single-sentenced series of orchestrated chords in which the full implications of mortality – both its terrors and its conferring of significance – unroll themselves.[46] The poem itself has the glamour and aura that it fears it must leave behind. If it is, in the end, like many of the finest Romantic sonnets, a quietly fierce witness to the imaginative power of the 'sole self',[47] it reminds us that the Romantic sonnet combines its intricate formal precisions with a pressing desire to feel on its pulses the 'mighty workings', to borrow a phrase from another Keatsian sonnet ('Great spirits now on earth are sojourning'), of the 'wide world'.[48]

Notes

1 William Wordsworth, *The Major Works*, ed. Stephen Gill (Oxford: Oxford University Press, 2008). Further reference is to this edition.

2 Stuart Curran, *Poetic Form and British Romanticism* (New York: Oxford University Press, 1986), p. 30.

3 Quoted from Michael O'Neill and Charles Mahoney, eds., *Romantic Poetry: An Annotated Anthology* (Malden, MA: Blackwell, 2007) p. 11.

4 *Ibid.*, p. 12n. For Smith's appeal, see Sarah M. Zimmerman, *Romanticism, Lyricism and History* (Albany: SUNY Press, 1999) p. 4ff.

5 Mary Robinson, *Selected Poems*, ed. Judith Pascoe (Peterborough, ON: Broadview, 2000), p. 150.

6 *Ibid.*, pp. 145, 144.

7 For an account of the way in which the sequence 'represents with fine poetic exactitude a confusion of heart and mind', see Jerome McGann, *The Poetics of Sensibility: A Revolution in Literary Style* (Oxford: Oxford University Press, 1996), p. 110.

8 Thomas Warton, 'To the River Lodon', in David Fairer and Christine Gerrard, eds., *Eighteenth-Century Poetry: An Annotated Anthology* (Oxford: Blackwell, 1999). On landscape, see David Fairer, *Organising Poetry: The Coleridge Circle, 1790–1798* (Oxford: Oxford University Press, 2009), pp. 108–11.

9 William Bowles, 'To the River Itchin', in Jonathan and Jessica Wordsworth, eds., *The Penguin Book of Romantic Poetry* (London: Penguin, 2005).

10 Fairer, *Organising Poetry*, p. 199.

11 Samuel Taylor Coleridge, *The Collected Works of Samuel Taylor Coleridge*, ed. Kathleen Coburn, 16 vols. (Princeton: Princeton University Press, 1971–2001), Vol. XVI: *Poetical Works I: Poems (Reading Text)*, ed. J. C. C. Mays (2001), Part II, pp. 1206, 1235. Coleridge is quoted from this edition.

12 *Ibid.*, p. 1205.

13 *Ibid.*, p. 1031.

14 Morton D. Paley, *Coleridge's Later Poetry* (Oxford: Clarendon Press, 1999), p. 77.

15 *Ibid.*, p. 75.

16 Curran, *Poetic Form*, pp. 167–68.

17 John Keats, *The Letters of John Keats*, ed. Hyder E. Rollins, 2 vols. (Cambridge, MA: Harvard University Press, 1958), Vol. I, p. 188.

18 Coleridge, *Collected Works*, Vol. XVI: *Poetical Works* I, Part I, p. 156.

19 See Curran, *Poetic Form*, p. 35.

20 Quoted from Robert Southey, *Poems 1797*, introd. Jonathan Wordsworth (Oxford: Woodstock, 1989) p. 38.

21 Samuel Taylor Coleridge, *Samuel Taylor Coleridge: The Complete Poems*, ed. William Keach (Harmondsworth: Penguin, 1997), p. 495.

22 Charles Baudelaire, *The Complete Verse*, introd. and trans. Francis Scarfe (London: Penguin, 1961) p. 221).

23 Joseph Phelan, *The Nineteenth-Century Sonnet* (Basingstoke: Palgrave Macmillan, 2005), pp. 16–17.

24 John Kerrigan, 'Wordsworth and the Sonnet: Building, Dwelling, Thinking', *Essays in Criticism* 35 (1985), 45–75.

25 Wordsworth, 'Nuns fret not', Penguin Book of Romantic Poetry, eds. Wordsworth and Wordsworth, p. 433 line 11.

26 Kerrigan, 'Wordsworth and the Sonnet', pp. 50–1.

27 Nicholas Roe, *Fiery Heart: The First Life of Leigh Hunt* (London: Pimlico, 2005), p. 5.

28 *Ibid.*, pp. 7, 5.

29 Quoted from Wordsworth and Wordsworth, *The Penguin Book of Romantic Poetry* p. 435.

30 Quoted from *ibid* p. 435.

31 Line 98, quoted from O'Neill and Mahoney, *Romantic Poetry* p. 261.

32 Wordsworth, 'Nuns fret not', lines 8–9.

33 Percy Bysshe Shelley, 'Ozymandias', in *Percy Bysshe Shelley: The Major Works*, ed. Zachary Leader and Michael O'Neill (Oxford: Oxford University Press, 2003).

34 Lines 6–7, in Leader and O'Neill, (eds) *Percy Bysshe Shelly: The Major Works*, p. 474.

35 *Ibid.*, p. 636.

36 See Susan J. Wolfson, 'Poetic Form and Political Reform: *The Mask of Anarchy* and "England in 1819"', in Donald H. Reiman and Neil Fraistat, eds., *Shelley's Poetry and Prose* (New York: Norton, 2002), p. 735; and Curran, *Poetic Form*, p. 55.

37 In Leader and O'Neill, (eds) *Percy Bysshe Shelly*: The Major Works, p. 347.

38 Quoted from John Keats, *The Poems of John Keats*, ed. Miriam Allott (London: Longman, 1970) p. 521. Further reference is to this edition.

39 *Ibid.*, p. 62n.

40 Curran, *Poetic Form*, p. 53.

41 Cf. Susan J. Wolfson, 'What Good is Formalist Criticism? Or: *Forms* and *Storms* and the Critical Register of Romantic Poetry', *Studies in Romanticism* 37 (1998), 77–94.

42 Quoted from Eric Robinson and David Powell, eds., *John Clare* (Oxford: Oxford University Press, 1984) p. 263.

43 Clare's sonnet is also discussed by Jeff Hilson in Chapter 1.

44 Keats, 'When I have fears that I may cease to be', in *Poems* p. 296.

45 See *ibid.*, p. 297n.

46 Helen Vendler, *The Art of Shakespeare's Sonnets* (Cambridge, MA: Harvard University Press, 1997), p. 456.

47 Keats, 'Ode to a Nightingale', line 72, in *Poems*, p. 523.

48 Keats, 'Great spirits now on earth are sojourning', in *Poems*, p. 68.

11

MATTHEW CAMPBELL

The Victorian sonnet

Toward the end of the reign of Queen Victoria, Oscar Wilde's literary detective story 'The Portrait of Mr W. H.' sketched the 'onlie begetter' of Shakespeare's Sonnets, a young actor speculatively called 'Willie Hughes'. Wilde's narrator said that Hughes was 'not merely a most delicate instrument for the presentation of [Shakespeare's] art, but the visible incarnation of his idea of beauty'.[1] First published in 1889 and extensively revised before his death in 1900, the story is a late Victorian reply to the censure of the Sonnets at the beginning of Victoria's reign, in particular to Henry Hallam's notorious comment, 'it is impossible not to wish that Shakespeare had never written them'.[2] Hallam's objection to the 'weakness and folly in all excessive and misplaced emotion' was an allusion to the unsayable, the love that dare not speak its name. Yet Hallam's son Arthur Henry Hallam might also have been one of those 'young men of poetical tempers' whom the older Hallam said shared a tendency 'to exaggerate the beauties of these remarkable productions'.[3] Certainly Hallam's friend Alfred Tennyson's view 'in his weaker moments' (according to Benjamin Jowett), that Shakespeare was 'greater in his sonnets than in his plays', caused a slight loss of nerve in Tennyson's biographer, his son Hallam Tennyson.[4] Reprinting Jowett's memoir, the younger Tennyson excised the gloss suggesting his father had ever 'expressed ... a sort of sympathy with Hellenism'.

By the mid nineteenth century, Hellenism could mean a broadly aestheticist attraction to Greek culture, but the Victorians also understood 'Greek love' to be a heightened sense of male friendship. The term was coined by J. A. Symonds, and for his acquaintances Wilde and Walter Pater, finding Hellenism in the Sonnets enabled them to read there what Wilde called 'the soul, as well as the language, of neo-Platonism', which meant something physical as well as ideal. In Wilde's hands, this would become the classic late Victorian theory of the sensual emerging from the material of art. Alluding to Pater, he states,

I saw that the love Shakespeare bore him [W. H.] was as the love of a musician
for some delicate instrument on which he delights to play, as a sculptor's love
for some rare and exquisite material that suggests a new form of plastic beauty,
a new mode of plastic expression. For all Art has its medium, its material, be
it that of rhythmical words, or of pleasurable colour, or of sweet and subtly-
divided sound; and, as one of the most fascinating critics of our day has pointed
out, it is to the qualities inherent in each material, and special to it, that we owe
the sensuous element in Art, and with all that in Art is essentially artistic.[5]

The ideal impresses itself by means of sensual pleasure, and what appears to be
an abstracted aesthetic idealism presents itself through sensation and appetite.
Wilde's rehabilitation of the Sonnets, then, involved rethinking the formal *and*
moral relation between sensuous and ideal, fleshly and abstract in art itself, a
debate that preoccupied the Victorian poetry of love and marriage for similar
reasons. For the Victorian sonnet writers in particular, however, it was the restoration of narrative and character to lyric form that enabled this pull between
sensual and ideal to be worked out in a new way, through the sequence.

While the dramatic monologue might have been the great poetic innovation of the period, the exhuming of Renaissance models also allowed
Victorian sonnet writing to become more narrative and more dramatic.
From its loss of fashion after Milton and through its revival in the hands of
Charlotte Smith and William Wordsworth, the English sonnet had been conceived as an occasional form, something that could be ordered into volumes,
but not necessarily into a dramatic series. Wordsworth's view, as expressed
in a letter of 1833 to the sonnet anthologist Alexander Dyce, emphasized
its individual formal integrity, explaining that the sonnet should 'consist of
three parts, like the three propositions of the syllogism'.[6] But rather than
allow this to suggest too clearly a notion of formal closure, he then went
on to develop 'the image of an orbicular body, – a sphere – or a dew-drop'.
From Wordsworth's beautiful conception of sonnet form as an ephemeral
globe, promising a mingling while retaining a formal coherence, there was a
renewal of the idea of individual sonnets mingling from one into the other,
as if the dew were being allowed to drop. Henry Hallam characterized
Shakespeare's Sonnets as a single poem:

> But though each sonnet has generally its proper unity, the sense, I do not mean
> the grammatical construction, will sometimes be found to spread from one to
> another, independently of that repetition of the leading idea, like variations
> of an air, which a series of them frequently exhibits, and on account of which
> they have latterly been reckoned by some rather an integral poem than a col-
> lection of sonnets.[7]

So when the Italian-speaking Dante Gabriel Rossetti sought in 1872 to rescue his 'Nuptial Sleep' from accusations of fleshliness, he needed to point

to its dramatic status within the *House of Life* as a 'sonnet-stanza' or in, Italian, a room.[8] Preparing a longer edition of the poem in 1881, Rossetti claimed back from his friend, the sonnet anthologizer T. Hall Caine, the coinage that poets and critics have held to since: *The House of Life* was subtitled *A Sonnet-Sequence*.[9]

The relation between sequence and 'sonnet-stanza' is of course a difficult one. Not all Victorian sonnets found homes as part of a series, and not all series imply a thematic or narrative connectedness. The 103 sonnets collected in *The House of Life* were written over a thirty-three-year period, and their numerous orderings and reorderings served theme as much as plot. For each of the other major sequences – Elizabeth Barrett Browning's *Sonnets from the Portuguese*, George Meredith's *Modern Love*, Christina Rossetti's *Monna Innominata* and *Later Life* – there were occasional sonnets of no less distinction, most notably the nineteen-year-old Christina's sonnets of isolation and imagined death, or the 'terrible sonnets' of the desolation of faith written in 1885 by Gerard Manley Hopkins. Recent critics of Victorian sonnets reflect this problem of whether the sonnet is a dew-drop or a series when they debate its subject matter. Working from the sonnet revival led by Wordsworth, Jennifer Ann Wagner takes a phrase from Dante Rossetti's 'Proem', or sonnet on the sonnet, from the 1881 *House of Life* for her title, *A Moment's Monument*. She emphasizes the sonnet's lyric temporality, saying that her sonnet history is 'told through the perception of form, which I take to be not simply a "site" but rather a "situation", a time, a place, and a problem – a problem concerning the poet himself, and concerning that time and place – that is to be solved in the poem'.[10] For Wagner, the individual sonnet form ultimately shapes the problem of its content. While the post-Romantic sonnet seeks to solve contingent problems, it is best thought of as much as a process as a premeditated and concluded engagement with a chosen subject. The Wordsworthian dew-drop holds itself suspended, not releasing itself or breaking.

By contrast, Joseph Phelan opens up the varying contents of Victorian sonnets, finding them much more directly engaged with the social and the historical. Wordsworth himself had not shied away from difficult content and the closure of an argument forcefully made and concluded in syllogistic sonnet-shape, as in his *Ecclesiastical Sonnets* (1822), or *Sonnets upon the Punishment of Death* (1839). He was aware that in its syllogistic construction, the form was suitable for public argument, and Phelan describes sonnets as serving political and devotional as well as autobiographical and amatory ends. Its importance in British cultural history is not to be underestimated: 'It begins the nineteenth century as the bearer of what Raymond Williams calls "emergent" cultural values, those of Victorianism, carries these values through to dominance, and then becomes the site of both of these values in their "residual" form and of the new "emergent" values of aestheticism, decadence and proto-modernism.'[11] Tied to the moment in a fourteen-line frame (which admittedly expanded considerably in the hands of a Meredith or a Hopkins), the single Victorian sonnet was also connected with its various afterlives. These afterlives might be the next in a series or a revealed plot. They might also be the response that would come from lover, reader or society. Like Shakespeare's before them, Victorian sonnets were frequently conceived as drama, or even in dialogue. As the history of the criticism of Shakespeare's Sonnets might tell us, an argument that seems to be about aesthetic form entails matters of social and personal value.

Tennyson and the Brownings

The two most significant poets of the Victorian period were not noted sonneteers. But the poetry of Alfred Tennyson or Robert Browning is nevertheless implicated in a Victorian sonnet history. Toward the end of his life, Browning published this fourteen-line lyric, seemingly about the moment of its conception:

Now.[12]

> Out of your whole life give but a moment!
> All of your life that has gone before,
> All to come after it, – so you ignore
> So you make perfect the present, – condense,
> In a rapture of rage, for perfection's endowment,
> Thought and feeling and soul and sense –
> Merged in a moment which gives me at last
> You around me for once, you beneath me, above me –
> Me – sure that despite of time future, time past, –
> This tick of our life-time's one moment you love me!
> How long such suspension may linger? Ah, Sweet –
> The moment eternal – just that and no more –
> When ecstasy's utmost we clutch at the core,
> While cheeks burn, arms open, eyes shut and lips meet!

Whether this poem is a sonnet is a moot point. The rhyme scheme is highly irregular, breaking expected quatrain or octave forms. While there is a turn in the argument, it occurs at the eleventh line, thus allowing the poem to close with the quatrain that provides an answer to a question. Yet it has Victorian sonnet sense. That is, the poem works around one idea, the giving

and receiving of assent and the consequent transfiguring power of the promise in a sacramental moment out of time. It resolves itself in the physical
confirmation of assent, the kiss.

For all that it appears to celebrate a very specific moment, though, this
sonnet is insecure in the selfhood it asks us to imagine. Who is the 'you'
addressed at the beginning of the poem? At first it appears to be the impersonal pronoun, representing all possible readers who might receive the counsel of the poem. The 'Now' of the title is either its subject matter, or a direct
address to its imagined audience, gathering itself up as an imperative picked
up in the first line: 'Now. Out of your whole life give but a moment!' But
the 'you' gradually emerges as a loved one who envelops the poet from the
past. The communion occurs 'at last', 'for once', and thus the great turning
of the pronouns from 'you' to 'me': 'You around me for once, you beneath
me, above me – / Me – sure that despite of time future, time past, – / This tick
of our life-time's one moment you love me!' Before its erotic transfiguration
of the momentary through the physical in the packed stresses of the last line,
the poem celebrates a moment of reciprocity. This is not 'Me – sure that …
I love you' but 'Me – sure that … you love me'. It is the Browning moment
of absolute adequacy, 'The moment eternal – just that and no more – '.[13] An
earlier Browning character had spoken from a failed marriage of his wife's
inadequacy: 'Just this / Or that in you disgusts me; here you miss / Or there
exceed the mark' ('My Last Duchess', 37–9). If 'Now' revises that misogyn-
ist moment, it still casts us back into the sacramental drama of the Victorian
love poem, as remembered here by one of the partners in one of Victorian
literature's most celebrated marriages.

A biographical reading suggests that 'Now' commemorates the poet's dead
wife and is thus inflected by elegy. The poem celebrates an eternalizing vow
that is recreated as consolation. It takes us back to the middle of the century, to Browning's own poetry of marriage and relations of power between
men and women, and it is primarily in dialogue with the sequence of courtship, assent and marriage told through Elizabeth Barrett Browning's *Sonnets
from the Portuguese*, in which Robert Browning himself had provided one
model of an ideal partner giving assent. But also published in 1850 was perhaps the dominant model for lyric sequence in the Victorian age, Tennyson's
In Memoriam, an elegy that ended in an epithalamium, where the result of
the poet's sister's marriage vow was that 'out of twain / her sweet "I will"
has made you one' ('Epilogue', 55–6). While composed entirely in tetrameter quatrains, the stanza of Tennyson's *In Memoriam* is closely related to
the quatrain of the Italian sonnet. As a sequence commemorating a male
friendship it is also indebted to Shakespeare's Sonnets. And it brought to
Victorian poetry a lyricism that, for all its great personal grief, still sought

the dramatic: Tennyson insisted that '"I" is not always the author speaking of himself, but the voice of the human race speaking through him.'[14] With a narrative structured around three Christmases, from loss to marriage (albeit not the poet's own) and thus suggesting a psychic pattern from grief to consolation, it looked like conventional elegy or even theodicy. Its influence on the sonnet sequence was to wed great local particularity of the moment to the significant narrative ambitions of the lyric sequence. Offering elegiac form, the example of *In Memoriam* was picked up by the amatory sonnet sequence, returning it, as it were, to its early modern sources.

Such sequences contrast the seeming finality of the moment and the larger ambitions for the closure of plot. These manifest themselves in a number of narrative ways, most frequently the desired and often achieved closing of lover and loved one in the act and figure of the kiss. But the sequence can tend to the opposite, the falling out of love or even the death of the loved one. The elegiac pressure of Tennyson along with the disappointments and amatory failures of the older Shakespeare offered conflicting models for Victorian poetry of love and marriage that veered between the eternalizing of the moment ('Now') to the facts of divorce ('My Last Duchess'). Elizabeth Barrett Browning's is one of the first of these love sequences, and she tells a love story that completes itself, resulting in marriage and domestic security. If hers is the first significant marker in an ongoing innovation of form and content, it is also a rare example of a sonnet ending rendered happy.

For all that they presented themselves as fictionalized, supposed translations from an unnamed Portuguese poet, we cannot avoid reading Barrett Browning's sonnets as only one half of their story. That is, we follow the feelings of one lover seeking both assent and equality in the affair which she undertakes. It so happens that we have Robert's half as well, and this might be read through the dramatic monologues of *Men and Women*, published in 1855, and picked up also in Elizabeth's 1856 narrative poem, *Aurora Leigh*, a drama of creativity and personal compromise. These poems are in conversation, at the very least, with one another, and frequently celebrate shared moments. If the first kiss of 'Now' is a memory from the two poets' clandestine courtship of 1845–6, then Elizabeth's version, in Sonnet XXXVIII, treats it playfully:

> First time he kissed me, he but only kissed
> The fingers of this hand wherewith I write;
> And ever since, it grew more clean and white,
> Slow to world-greetings, quick with its 'Oh, list',
> When the angels speak. A ring of amethyst
> I could not wear here, plainer to my sight,
> Than that first kiss. The second passed in height

The first, and sought the forehead, and half missed,
Half falling on the hair. O beyond meed!
That was the chrism of love, which love's own crown,
With sanctifying sweetness, did precede.
The third upon my lips was folded down
In perfect, purple state; since when, indeed,
I have been proud and said, 'My love, my own.'[15]

As a recollection of moments from a love affair this is at once fond and self-deprecating, wistfully removed from the actual experience. The present tense of the sonnet is actually about looking at the hands of the writer, holding a pen and wearing a ring. It conveys the conceit of being in some way physically marked by kisses. Its little slapstick moment, of an uncertain lover's awkwardness in kissing hair rather than brow, allows comic rhymes – kissed, list, amethyst, missed – as well as the little topple over the turn after the eighth line. The narrative business is gathered up in the half-line – 'Half falling on the hair' – and is then ecstatically recollected: 'O beyond meed!' The marking by chrism (as in baptism), and then the 'purple state' of the kiss on the lips, allow the fully engaged writer to proclaim, in absolute reciprocity, 'My love, my own.'

That reciprocal moment, celebrated by Elizabeth in the 1840s and remembered by Robert forty years later, was not won without difficulty. Sonnet XII, like *Aurora Leigh* later, takes seriously the matter of promise and compromise.

When our two souls stand up erect and strong,
Face to face, silent, drawing nigh and nigher,
Until the lengthening wings break into fire
At either curvèd point, – what bitter wrong
Can the earth do to us, that we should not long
Be here contented? Think. In mounting higher,
The angels would press on us and aspire
To drop some golden orb of perfect song
Into our deep, dear silence. Let us stay
Rather on earth, Belovèd, – where the unfit
Contrarious moods of men recoil away
And isolate pure spirits, and permit
A place to stand and love in for a day,
With darkness and the death-hour rounding it.

Elizabeth takes for text the thirteenth chapter of St Paul's first letter to the Corinthians, a reading long associated with the Anglican marriage service. But Paul's meeting 'face to face' is a meeting that confers the knowledge of the afterlife.[16] This sonnet envisages a moment of equality between man and woman, two souls erect and strong. They are also souls who will remain resolutely on earth: for Robert's adequacy, read Elizabeth's 'contented'. And for his rhetorical 'Now', we get her suggestion that the reader 'Think'. In a wonderful reversal of the expected description of physical love transcending the bodily in angelic ecstasy, Elizabeth opts for the earthly, fearing the contamination of silence by the angels' 'golden orb of perfect song'. Whether Elizabeth knew of Wordsworth's orbicular body or dew-drop, she seems to repudiate this orb. The turn that follows the caesura after 'silence' in the ninth line brings the poem back to an earth of division and isolation. But the two standing mortal souls will take their day's love because it tells of their momentary equality.

Of course, this is a drama of one marriage and, through the fictionalized sequence, of other possible marriages. Just to glance at Robert's evocation of the same text after his wife's death, indeed an evocation of Elizabeth's evocation of it, can show that 'Contrarious moods of men' might also be lurking in the politics of human relations. In *The Ring and the Book*, woken up by her tyrant husband Guido Franceschini after her escape with the priest Caponsacchi, the usually pacific Pompilia is described turning on Guido thus:

> She started up, stood erect, face to face
> With the husband: back he fell, was buttressed there
> By the window all a-flame with morning-red,
> He the black figure, the opprobrious blur
> Against all peace and joy and light and life.
> 'Away from between me and hell!'–she cried:
> 'Hell for me, no embracing any more!
> I am God's, I love God, God – whose knees I clasp,
> Whose utterly most just award I take,
> But bear no more love-making devils: hence!'[17]

Alluding to Elizabeth's poem of reciprocity in marriage, this tells of its opposite, exchanging 'love-making devils' for angels, dramatizing the full 'recoil' of 'Contrarious moods of men' as full-blown marital hatred.

Elizabeth's difficulty is that the compromises attendant on the promises of marriage may result in the loss of identity, and that the exchange of vows might involve other, more mundane exchanges. Robert's 'Two in the Campagna' famously asked,

> I would that you were all to me,
>   You that are just so much, no more.
> Nor yours, nor mine, nor slave nor free!
>   Where does the fault lie? What the core
> O' the wound since wound must be?

The paradoxes of commitment, freedom and the adequacy of perfection ('just so much, no more') are played through again. They are followed up, though, by anxious questions about division – of gender and of soul. The other party in this conversation, the one who doesn't supply answers in Robert's monologue, is still circumspect in answer to these questions, as in the opening question of *Sonnets from the Portuguese*'s Sonnet xxxv, 'If I leave all for thee, wilt thou exchange / And be all to me?' For every giving, there seems to be a consequent return, or indeed an 'exchange'. This seems monetary as much as emotional, the wife's surrender of worldly goods to the husband and the wonder whether he will surrender in his turn. The loss of one home-life is felt keenly, and the commercial metaphors sound through the sonnet: when Barrett Browning refers to 'a new range / Of walls and floors', it seems to suggest the commercial business of shopping for a new home consequent on the wrench of leaving family.[18] Elizabeth mixes emotions and registers in this sonnet, running seemingly small domestic matters into larger issues of power and partnership in marriage. The conquering of the power of love – and the implicit giving up of the self – will be matched by the conquering of the grief of the loss of family. This is a difficult 'exchange', and the answer is a sort of testing of the sonnet answer. The sonnet's structure is marked strongly around the problem it needs to solve at the turn in the ninth line on the phrase 'That's hardest'. Neither the poet-wife nor the syllogistic Italianate sonnet structure seem to resolve this weighing-up of love and its necessary losses: 'as all things prove'. So she ends only with the embrace of consolation, the poet figuring herself female (as 'thy dove') and tearful, if not quite humbled by an imminent loss of selfhood in union.

Christina Rossetti

Sonnets from the Portuguese ends in a garden, the familial home exchanged for wedded bliss. Subsequent sequences kept up for decades the conversation that the Brownings had between themselves. In 1881 Christina Rossetti specifically stated that Barrett Browning was in her sights when composing her *Monna Innominata* or 'unnamed lady' sequence. Rossetti imagines the female object of the lyric sequence speaking back to the idealizing male lover, 'sharing her lover's poetic aptitude'.[19] Ideally, 'the barrier between them [male poet and female poet] might be one held sacred by both, yet not such as to render mutual love incompatible with mutual honour'. But the difficulty with Barrett Browning's treatment was her felicity, for had she 'only been unhappy instead of happy, her circumstances would have invited her to bequeath to us, in lieu of the "Portuguese Sonnets", an inimitable "donna innominata" [unnamed woman] drawn not from fancy but from feeling, and worthy to occupy a niche beside Beatrice and Laura'. Rossetti later protested that this was not a criticism of her forebear, rather a wish that she had left off the dramatic fiction of a translated sequence and given voice to a figure as memorable as Dante's Beatrice or Petrarch's Laura. As suggested above, what we now know of the autobiographical content of Barrett Browning's sequence perhaps renders the objection a little less just. However, Rossetti's dialogue with the newer English love-sonnet sequences, adding to them the renascent interest in the Italian rather than the Shakespearan model, suggests something of the considerable power of Barrett Browning's example over the poetry of the second half of the nineteenth century and beyond. For one thing, Rossetti sees that the matter of the woman poet's 'poetic aptitude' set against 'mutual honour' is shared between them.

As I have suggested, this is not marked entirely in fourteen-line forms. Coventry Patmore's *Angel in the House* (1854–63) also described a successful love affair and marriage in a lyric sequence, albeit from the idealizing husband's point of view. The lyric and monologue conversation between poems by the Brownings tested ideas about equality in marriage. Rossetti enters that conversation much like Thomas Hardy, in his *Poems of 1912–1913* many years later, whose sequence is as much an elegy for the Victorian marriage poem as for his estranged wife. Rossetti adheres to the sonnet form, but her contribution is to test the 'poetic aptitude' of its traditional object to speak as lover in her own right, not someone translated, idealized, or even a ghost. *Monna Innominata* was subtitled *A Sonnet of Sonnets*, that is a sequence of fourteen lyrics. The 'barrier', or Browningesque 'fault' or 'wound' occurs when the anonymous loved one realizes that the art of her lover is outstripping hers, no matter that the quality of feeling was initially hers. In the fourth sonnet, Rossetti takes up again ideas of exchange and adequacy from the Brownings, adding in the unsettling question of cost and measurement:

> I loved you first: but afterwards your love
> Outsoaring mine, sang such a loftier song
> As drowned the friendly cooings of my dove.
> Which owes the other most? my love was long,
> And yours one moment seemed to wax more strong;
> I loved and guessed at you, you construed me
> And loved me for what might or might not be –
> Nay, weights and measures do us both a wrong.   (1–8)

That friendly cooing dove, and the question of who owes the most, rephrases Barrett Browning's question of what will be left of one self when it gives up all to the other. The question of return is paramount, but just how much, and who gives or receives the most? The two lovers calculate in different ways: 'I loved and guessed at you, you construed me'. This is not equal: to

construe is so much more an act of deliberate interpretation than her trust-
ing guess. '[W]eights and measures do us both a wrong', Rossetti's speaker
can say at the end of the octave, and the sestet allows her to move to something more consoling:

> For verily love knows not 'mine' or 'thine';
>> With separate 'I' and 'thou' free love has done,
>>> For one is both and both are one in love:
> Rich love knows nought of 'thine that is not mine';
>> Both have the strength and both the length thereof,
> Both of us, of the love which makes us one.   (9–14)

The sense of what it is with which 'free love has done' in the tenth line
moves two ways. Primarily, free love has done with or is no longer interested
in ideas of I and thou, since 'both' become 'one' in love. But selfhood can
also be done with, as in finished, forgotten about, or even done in by, seeming unions. The word 'both' nevertheless resists sublimation in this sonnet,
retaining its sense of two-ness through a fivefold repetition. This persists in
the last line, testing the separateness of 'Both of us' even when union is the
predominant sense of the lyric, 'the love which makes us one'.

As a *Sonnet of Sonnets*, *Monna Innominata* turns at its ninth lyric, and
that replays the Victorian love compromise as loss of the female self in the
triumph of the power of the artist lover and the male in the larger gender
relations of sonnet sequence and sonnet history.

> Thinking of you, and all that was, and all
>> That might have been and now can never be,
>>> I feel your honoured excellence, and see
> Myself unworthy of the happier call:
> For woe is me who walk so apt to fall,
>> So apt to shrink afraid, so apt to flee,
>>> Apt to lie down and die (ah, woe is me!)
> Faithless and hopeless turning to the wall.
> And yet not hopeless quite nor faithless quite,
> Because not loveless; love may toil all night,
>> But take at morning; wrestle till the break
>>> Of day, but then wield power with God and man: –
>> So take I heart of grace as best I can,
> Ready to spend and be spent for your sake.

This is a logical pursuing of the abasements of courtly love poetry into the
ghastly idea that the self can gain emotional consolation for its weakness in
its usefulness as a unit of exchange. Seeking humility, it finds humiliation.
The Browning echoes, 'all … all', resolve through the octave's rhymes in the
awful 'turning to the wall'. The word 'apt', so important in Rossetti's notion

of shared 'poetic aptitude' between poets, is picked up as a misconstruing of adequacy. That is, one version of an aptitude, 'what can I do well?' is rephrased as a failing, 'what is my weakness?' A train of association brings it from 'so apt to fall' to 'so apt to shrink' to 'so apt to flee' to 'Apt to lie down'. The words that follow are like an automaton of language completing the phrase, 'Apt to lie down *and die*', barely redeemed by the glimmer of self-awareness in the parenthetical cliché that follows: '(ah, woe is me!)'. The sestet suggests that it is enough not to be 'loveless'. But the spending here is more the expense of spirit, and the rest of the sequence imagines the waste of shame. It ends its fourteenth lyric with the *donna innominata* elderly, alone and in the 'silence of love that cannot sing again'.

Meredith and Dante Gabriel Rossetti

Between these two examples of a debate carried out in the pages of Victorian sonnet sequences by women, there is of course a tradition written by men with which these poems enter into dialogue. The destructive emotional narratives we can construe from Meredith's *Modern Love* or Dante Gabriel Rossetti's *House of Life* provide in one sense material for Christina's later critique of the form. In Section XVIII of *Modern Love*, Meredith, for instance, asks again, in 1862, Robert Browning's question of 1855:

> Yet it was plain she struggled, and that salt
> Of righteous feeling made her pitiful.
> Poor twisting worm, so queenly beautiful!
> Where came the cleft between us? whose the fault?

As a sequence founded in the experience of adultery (by the poet's wife), and the impossibility of legal divorce, it tells of a marriage sundered, briefly put back together again, and then concluded only with the wife's suicide. The 'cleft' or the 'fault' – what it is that causes the falling out of love – results in an exacerbation of the feelings of self-abasement inherent in the sonnet sequence, and tested so much by Rossetti twenty years later. The answer in this lyric is of the loss of knowledge of the self not in the union of marriage but in the aftermath of separation:

> I do not know myself without thee more:
> In this unholy battle I grow base:
> If the same soul be under the same face,
> Speak, and a taste of that old time restore![20]

The restoration of lost time is dependent on the continuity of selfhood across that time, and the suspicion as here that neither lover nor loved one is 'the same soul ... under the same face'.

The sense of change, as opposed to the eternalizing sacramental moment of marriage, is told through Meredith's sequence. Its sixteen-line lyrics might not strictly be sonnets, and the dominant four-quatrain structure looks like the turning on itself of the *abba* stanza of *In Memoriam*. But the contrasting narrative sense of the lyrics is given by a structure that employs the orbicular, distended argumentative shapes of the post-Romantic sonnet. These lyrics can thus allow poet and characters to think about temporality in ways that other Victorian sonnets do, even when, as in Section XII, running time backwards.

> Not solely that the Future she destroys,
> And the fair life which in the distance lies
> For all men, beckoning out from dim rich skies:
> Nor that the passing hour's supporting joys
> Have lost the keen-edged flavour, which begat
> Distinction in old times, and still should breed
> Sweet Memory, and Hope, – earth's modest seed,
> And heaven's high-prompting: Not that the world is flat
> Since that soft-luring creature I embraced,
> Among the children of Illusion went:
> Methinks with all this loss I were content,
> If the mad Past, on which my foot is based,
> Were firm, or might be blotted: but the whole
> Of life is mixed: the mocking Past will stay:
> And if I drink oblivion of a day,
> So shorten I the stature of my soul.

The poem starts in the future, goes back through the present and ends with the past. Mixing 'the mad Past' and 'the mocking Past' results in a wilful daily forgetting that will shorten the future, matched by a hint at the new temporal concerns of the post-Darwinian nineteenth century. The flatness of the world is an illusion no more substantial than the shared past of the married couple. The speaker emerges as a character located in his mid Victorian period, voicing an overpowering agnosticism in the light of a new knowledge about marriage and nature.

As Stephen Regan has pointed out, such effects can be novelistic, a richness of detail that is as much the stock-in-trade of realist fiction as it is of lyric observation. When this works, the effects can be exquisite, combining the clarity of good prose with the affective and symbolist suggestiveness of the English lyric after Keats and Tennyson, as in Section XLVII:

> We saw the swallows gathering in the sky,
> And in the osier-isle we heard them noise.
> We had not to look back on summer joys,

Or forward to a summer of bright dye:
But in the largeness of the evening earth
Our spirits grew as we went side by side.
The hour became her husband and my bride.
Love that had robbed us so, thus blessed our dearth!
The pilgrims of the year waxed very loud
In multitudinous chatterings, as the flood
Full brown came from the West, and like pale blood
Expanded to the upper crimson cloud.
Love that had robbed us of immortal things,
This little moment mercifully gave,
Where I have seen across the twilight wave
The swan sail with her young beneath her wings.

Regan calls this sonnet a 'brief interlude', and reminds us that it 'precedes, and perhaps even precipitates' the narrative closure of the sequence, the wife's suicide.[21] It is responsive both to its moment and to the momentary, which is part of the sonnet sequence. Yet it also shares in the psychological concerns of motive and plot of the Victorian novel. The turn, shifted to the tenth line, is not logical or even emotional: rather the portent of the 'flood' coming in from the West suggests what will break over this poem, no longer a dew-drop but a gathering catastrophe, a species of prophetic irony more at home in tragedy than lyric poetry.

This sense of a sequence attuned to the breaking of relationships rather than their unions, all the while mixing generic expectations, is also apparent in Dante Gabriel Rossetti's *House of Life*. As with Meredith and Barrett Browning before him, the sequence connects with the remarkable biography of its poet, even if in his case they remember various relationships. Seven years after the death of his first wife, Elizabeth Siddal, a number of the sonnets were exhumed from her coffin, into which the grief-stricken and guilt-ridden Rossetti had thrown them. But Rossetti's narrative is less distinct than Meredith's, and has the sense of a sustained poetic experiment determined by Renaissance visual as much as poetic forms. In terms that would prefigure the arguments of Pater and Wilde, Rossetti insisted that, whatever the personal conditions behind some of the sonnets, they also served an idealizing function: 'Surely there is nothing in any one of these subjects so limitedly personal as to present an obstacle to any reader who cares for writing that has an abstract side at all.'[22]

Rossetti admitted that 'A Day of Love' began in 'a meeting between lovers who have much to remember'.[23] Written for publication in the emerging sequence in 1870, it was eventually to find a place as the sixteenth sonnet in the 1881 reordering of the sequence into two parts (one tells of a failed love affair or affairs, the other addresses more abstract concerns of time and mutability). This sonnet bears deliberate echoes of the Renaissance lyric, imagining presence and absence, remembering and forgetting, in terms that wear their learning with some ostentation.

> Those envied places which do know her well,
>   And are so scornful of this lonely place,
>   Even now for once are emptied of her grace:
>   Nowhere but here she is: and while Love's spell
> From his predominant presence doth compel
>   All alien hours, an outworn populace,
>   The hours of Love fill full the echoing space
> With sweet confederate music favourable.
>
> Now many memories make solicitous
>   The delicate love-lines of her mouth, till, lit
>   With quivering fire, the words take wing from it;
> As here between our kisses we sit thus
>   Speaking of things remembered, and so sit
> Speechless while things forgotten call to us.

Presence, as in present tense and in the present place, is what this sonnet abstracts; that is, it constructs a conceit of physical and mental presence that nevertheless imagines absence and forgetting elsewhere. As the sonnet is in two places and times, while seeming to tell of one, its lovers perhaps should be in another.

As is typical with Rossetti, the dalliance with the archaic and the recreation of a stylized mode of art can draw attention to themselves, even to the suggestion of a deliberate ineptitude. Those multisyllabic abstractions, 'predominant presence ... outworn populace ... sweet confederate music favourable' seem irresistible to a poet who relishes a strenuous tussle with scansion. 'Favourable' must be allowed to half-rhyme with compel, but the temptation to force a full rhyme can lead to the comic effect of doggerel. The sestet works even more strange effects at end-line, as if over-decorating the right-hand side of the page with echo: the *c* rhyme in 'solicitous' gains a two-syllable rhyme with 'sit thus' and a near-full-elided repetition with 'to us'. But 'solicitous' is heard in the *d* rhymes and cross-rhymes as well: 'delicate ... till, lit ... it ... sit thus ... so sit'. These near-anagrammatic effects may be the callings of things forgotten, something not receiving either expression or meaning in the poem. They may just be sonic decoration. Either way, Rossetti makes the reader attend to something not entirely contained within the formal structure of the poem. Formally, it is a recreation of one of the conversations that takes place within and between Victorian sonnet lyricism. Thematically, it also hints at something illicit in the form: a conversation with an unnamed loved one, or *innominata*, who really ought to be with someone else.

Rossetti is at his most successful when he crosses the 'limitedly personal' with an urge to abstraction that links his sonnets with various sonnet and aestheticist moments. In the notorious attack on Rossetti's poems as exemplary of the 'fleshly school of poetry', Robert Buchanan had stated, 'Mr Rossetti is never dramatic, never impersonal – always attitudinizing, posturing, and describing his own exquisite emotions.'[24] Whatever the distress this review caused Rossetti, the sense of something transgressively overpersonal serves to strengthen its opposite, an abstracting or idealizing dramatic structure. The result is the play of a Victorian historicizing impulse set against a present-tense subjectivity. The sonnet form must do both, to be sounded through a history of its practitioners and the lives and losses of its current writer. 'Life-in-Love' is not about life at all, but ends with the body of the loved one. It fixes on the physical, while drawn to an image of the corpse.

> Not in thy body is thy life at all,
>   But in this lady's lips and hands and eyes;
>   Through these she yields thee life that vivifies
> What else were sorrow's servant and death's thrall.
> Look on thyself without her, and recall
>   The waste remembrance and forlorn surmise
>   That lived but in a dead-drawn breath of sighs
> O'er vanished hours and hours eventual.
>
> Even so much life hath the poor tress of hair
>   Which, stored apart, is all love hath to show
>   For heart-beats and for fire-heats long ago;
> Even so much life endures unknown, even where,
>   'Mid change the changeless night environeth,
>   Lies all that golden hair undimmed in death.

It is impossible not to see Siddal's abundant undecayed hair here, as reported to Rossetti after the rescue of his poetry from her coffin. There is a ghoulish playing through of unbelieved notions of resurrection and a rounding on the word 'life'. It is the title of the sequence, *The House of Life*, and is hammered together with the word 'love' in the odd hyphenated title of the sonnet. 'Life-in-Love': that is, our life in love with each other? Or Life-in-Love, life is only life in love? Or does it mean to be in love with life? Whichever way, 'Life' is 'Not in thy body', but in that of the loved one, and 'she yields thee life that vivifies'. That odd near-tautology, 'life that vivifies', suggests a sort of Frankensteinian electric charge, as if connected to the lover by jump leads. Jerome McGann tells us that this sonnet is filled with Dantean echoes, to *La vita nuova* and particularly to Dante's wife.[25] The Rossetti sonnet does seem typically to have two lovers in mind, but it is the wife, not Beatrice, who is in the grave. The octave ends with time heading where it inevitably will, 'hours eventual', the multisyllable half-rhyming word 'eventual' forestalling 'recall' or memory. There will be neither time nor memory in the grave: ''Mid change the changeless night environeth'. Only the great head of pre-Raphaelite hair persists as both art object and bodily remain.

The occasional sonnet

If the Victorian period is the second great age of the English sonnet sequence, it may be that it is ultimately remembered most for the single or occasional sonnets of Christina Rossetti and Gerard Manley Hopkins. While their work is intimately connected with the dialogue implicit in the sonnet sequence, that sense of dialogue frequently serves as a formal marker of the irony that can be heard in the terrifying instrument of isolation the sonnet can become in their hands. This is writing from celibate lives inhabiting forms primarily associated with married, or indeed adulterous, love. Of course, for Hopkins, the sonnet could be a political or devotional form, and is thought of most distinctively as the medium through which he conveyed his remarkable engagement with the natural world. 'Harry Ploughman' and 'Tom's Garland' are poems about work and society. 'The Windhover' or 'As Kingfishers catch fire' are poems celebrating the active principle that Hopkins called 'instress' of a world created and informed by a beneficent God. And while Rossetti's early sonnets of rejection and the choice of a single life ('After Death', 'Life Hidden', 'Remember') seem to close themselves in celibacy as a sort of death, they are also remarkable for a virtuoso riddling and semantic play that are always in dialogue with notions of oblivion and isolation.

In later life, and toward the later life of the Victorian age, these poets extracted the sonnet from its incessant coupling, and found loneliness and the hauntings of selfhood and the ultimate tautology of self-expression. Rossetti's 'The Thread of Life' was a three-sonnet series, which contemplated cutting that thread. The second sonnet abruptly begins with the thought that 'Thus am I mine own prison' and concludes:

> I am not what I have nor what I do;
> But what I was I am, I am even I.

The riddle of being at the end is an echo of God speaking to Moses from the burning bush, 'I AM THAT I AM.'[26] It strips out both possession and activity, and leaves the self asserting only itself. There is no room here for the negotiations of the Brownings or the adventures of Meredith or Christina's brother. The next in the series begins, 'Therefore myself is the one only thing / I hold to use or waste, to keep or give'.

Indebted as he was to Christina Rossetti's example as a devotional poet, and convert as he was from Rossetti's Anglo-Catholicism to Roman Catholicism, Hopkins found himself in similar moments of anxiety. 'I wake and feel the fell of dark, not day' is in one way about the taste of the self – as if indigestion conveys only the return of the self upon the self – and the attendant insomnia is a ghastly premonition of hell:

> I wake and feel the fell of dark, not day.
> What hours, O what black hoürs we have spent
> This night! what sights you, heart, saw; ways you went!
> And more must, in yet longer light's delay.
> With witness I speak this. But where I say
> Hours I mean years, mean life. And my lament
> Is cries countless, cries like dead letters sent
> To dearest him that lives alas! away.
>
> I am gall, I am heartburn. God's most deep decree
> Bitter would have me taste: my taste was me;
> Bones built in me, flesh filled, blood brimmed the curse.
> Selfyeast of spirit a dull dough sours. I see
> The lost are like this, and their scourge to be
> As I am mine, their sweating selves; but worse.[27]

The 'dead letters' are the unanswered prayers of the lonely, and also the unread poems of a poet who, regardless of his own inveterate letter writing, shared his poetry with only a tiny circle of friends. Sympathy at the end is with the lost. They may be 'worse' than the poet, but there is still the isolation inherent in the verb to be itself: 'their scourge to be / As I am mine, their sweating selves'. The only intellectual or bodily issue appears to be the perspiration of a sleepless night.

Hopkins could find the evidence of a benignly created world through the contemplation of individual identity as a confirmation of faith and an assertion that the 'inscape' or uniqueness of all things could be perceived and revealed through instress. Like Wilde after him, Hopkins had been in Walter Pater's circle in Oxford. But the result was less the Neoplatonic idealism of Pater and Wilde and rather the strenuous aestheticism influenced by the scholastic philosophy of Thomas Aquinas and Duns Scotus: their Aristotelean insistence on the quiddity of things, and the ethical duty of individual and artist to engage with the variety and diversity of the created, and thus material, world. Hopkins's poetry strives to be made out of the same stuff as the vigorous manifold of his perceptions, and to convey that experience he extended to the sonnet an elaborate prosody of sprung rhythm, outriders and codas. These innovations were on the one hand prefigurations of the modernism that welcomed his poetry when it was eventually published in 1918; on the other hand, they were like flying buttresses holding up the Gothic and Renaissance inheritance of the English sonnet.

That Nature is a Heraclitean Fire and of the comfort of the Resurrection

Cloud-puffball, torn tufts, tossed pillows flaunt forth, then chevy on an air-
built thoroughfare: heaven-roysterers, in gay-gangs they throng; they glitter in
                                                                    marches.
Down roughcast, down dazzling whitewash, wherever an elm arches,
Shivelights and shadowtackle in long lashes lace, lance, and pair.
Delightfully the bright wind boisterous ropes, wrestles, beats earth bare
Of yestertempest's creases; in pool and rut peel parches
Squandering ooze to squeezed dough, crust, dust; stanches, starches
Squadroned masks and manmarks treadmire toil there
Footfretted in it. Million-fuelèd, nature's bonfire burns on.
But quench her bonniest, dearest to her, her clearest-selvèd spark
Man, how fast his firedint, his mark on mind, is gone!
Both are in an unfathomable, all is in an enormous dark
Drowned. O pity and indignation! Manshape, that shone
Sheer off, disseveral, a star, death blots black out; nor mark
                    Is any of him at all so stark
But vastness blurs and time beats level. Enough! the Resurrection,
A heart's-clarion! Away grief's gasping, joyless days, dejection.
                    Across my foundering deck shone
A beacon, an eternal beam. Flesh fade, and mortal trash
Fall to the residuary worm; world's wildfire, leave but ash:
                    In a flash, at a trumpet crash,
I am all at once what Christ is, since he was what I am, and
This Jack, joke, poor potsherd, patch, matchwood, immortal diamond,
                    Is immortal diamond.

'Every word in the poem has the complex suggestiveness of a whole sentence in prose', as Norman Mackenzie has said of Hopkins's other great innovative sonnet of his Dublin period, 'Spelt from Sibyl's Leaves'.[28] Not content only with that, this great poem on the flux of a world of, at one and the same time, evidence of seemingly infinite variety, and of fixed and solid identities, extends itself beyond the bounds of the sonnet. Hopkins sent it to his friend and eventual editor, Robert Bridges, and said that it was written in 'sprung rhythm, with many outriders and hurried feet; sonnet with two codas'.[29] There actually seem to be three codas, but they are all bound back up into the main body of the sonnet by rhyme. One rhyme sound in particular sounds through sonnet and coda, from 'Million-fuelèd, nature's bonfire burns on'. Thus 'gone ... shone ... Resurrection ... dejection ... shone', and then the very slight half-rhyming modulation once the verb 'to be' appears – 'I am and' – and its resolving double-rhyme, 'immortal diamond / Is immortal diamond'. The tautologies and repetitions are added to by the pun many readers have seen hidden in that diamond, the 'I am' that nestles within the symbol for unrepeatable selfhood. The sonnet itself is inimitable, and when modern readers eventually got to see Hopkins's poetry it seemed to show an experimentation that scarcely seemed Victorian. The 'onlie begetter' of this sonnet was a celibate Jesuit priest. But the Victorian sonnet, like that of Shakespeare and his contemporaries before it, remained engaged with the flux both in self and world, and the ethics of a struggle with change and time.

Notes

1 Oscar Wilde, 'The Portrait of Mr W. H.' (1921 version), in *The Artist As Critic*, ed. Richard Ellmann (New York: Random House, 1969), p. 187.

2 Henry Hallam, *Introduction to the Literature of Europe in the Sixteenth and Seventeenth Centuries*, 4 vols. (London: Murray, 1837–9), Vol. III, p. 504.

3 *Ibid.*, p. 501.

4 Quoted in Alfred, Lord Tennyson, *The Poems of Tennyson*, ed. Christopher Ricks, 3 vols. (London: Longman, 1987), Vol. II, p. 313.

5 Wilde, 'Portrait', p. 182.

6 William and Dorothy Wordsworth, *Letters of William and Dorothy Wordsworth*, 2nd edn, 8 vols., Vol. V: *The Later Years, Part II: 1829–1834*, ed. Alan Hill (Oxford: Clarendon, 1967), pp. 603–5.

7 Hallam, *Introduction*, p. 501.

8 Dante Gabriel Rossetti, 'The Stealthy School of Criticism', *Athenaeum* (December 1871), in *The Complete Writings and Pictures of Dante Gabriel Rossetti: A Hypermedia Archive*, ed. Jerome McGann (Ann Arbor: University of Michigan, 2000), available online at www.rossettiarchive.org.

9 See the account of settling on a subtitle for the revised sequence in Dante Gabriel Rossetti, *The House of Life: A Sonnet-Sequence*, ed. Roger C. Lewis (Cambridge: Boydell and Brewer, 2007), pp. 27–8.

10 Jennifer Ann Wagner, *A Moment's Monument: Revisionary Poetics and the Nineteenth-Century English Sonnet* (Madison, WI: Farleigh Dickinson University Press, 1996), p. 22.

11 Joseph Phelan, *The Nineteenth-Century Sonnet* (Basingstoke: Palgrave Macmillan, 2005), p. 8.

12 'Now', *The Poetical Works of Robert Browning* (Oxford: Clarendon, 1983), XV: *Parleyings* and *Asolando*, ed by Stefan Hawlin and Michael Meredith (2009), p. 323.

13 On Browning and adequacy, see my discussion of Pompilia's 'adequate protest' in *Rhythm and Will in Victorian Poetry* (Cambridge: Cambridge University Press, 1999), pp. 120–3.

14 Tennyson, *Poems*, Vol. II, p. 312.

15 Elizabeth Barrett Browning, *A Variorum Edition of Sonnets from the Portuguese*, ed. Miroslava Wein Dow (New York: Whitston, 1980). Future reference is to this edition.

16 1 Corinthians 13:11–12 (King James Version): 'When I was a child, I spake as a child, I understood as a child, I thought as a child: but when I became a man, I put away childish things. For now we see through a glass, darkly; but then face to face: now I know in part; but then shall I know even as also I am known.'

17 Robert Browning, *The Ring and the Book*, ed. Richard Altick (London: Penguin, 1971), VI, lines 1523–32.

18 *OED* does not record 'range' to mean 'a set of goods manufactured or for sale', definition 12b, until 1884.

19 Christina Rossetti, *Poems and Prose*, ed. Simon Humphries (Oxford: Oxford University Press, 2008), p. 227. Future reference is to this edition.

20 George Meredith, *Poems*, ed. Phyllis Bartlett, 2 vols. (New Haven: Yale University Press, 1978).

21 Stephen Regan, 'The Victorian Sonnet, from George Meredith to Gerard Manley Hopkins', *Yearbook of English Studies* 36:2 (2006), 17–34 (pp. 23, 26).

22 Rossetti, *The House of Life*, p. 70.

23 Rossetti, 'The Stealthy School of Criticism'.

24 Robert Buchanan, 'The Fleshly School of Poetry' (1871), p. 339, repr. in Rossetti, *Archive*.

25 Rossetti, *Archive*, gloss to 'Life-in-Love'.

26 Exodus 3:14.

27 Gerard Manley Hopkins, *Gerard Manley Hopkins: The Major Works*, ed. Catherine Phillips (Oxford: Oxford University Press, 2002). Future reference is to this edition.

28 Norman MacKenzie, 'Hopkins, Yeats and Dublin', in Joseph Ronley, ed., *Myth and Reality in Irish Literature* (Waterloo, ON: Wilfrid Laurier University Press, 1977), p. 83.

29 Hopkins, *The Major Works*, p. 385.

12

PETER HOWARTH

The modern sonnet

If the modernists had got their way, this book would have ended right here. To its late Victorian and Georgian enthusiasts, the sonnet epitomized compact lyric perfection, its critical high-water mark probably being Crosland's assertion in *The English Sonnet* (1917) that 'when great poetry is being produced, great sonnets are being produced'.[1] But to the modernists, the sonnet represented the worst of the previous generation; its formal pattern was complicit with production-line thinking, and its polish with the genteel unreality in which an industrialized culture had wished to preserve its art. 'The sonnet is the *devil*', snarled Pound, because it was the modern West's first mass-produced, 'habitual' form, the lyric blueprint for 'anything not needing a new tune perforce for every new poem'.[2] 'Perish all sonnets!', wrote Wallace Stevens to his fiancée, after reading Stedman's *Victorian Anthology*. 'Sonnets have their place ... but they can also be found tremendously out of place: in real life where things are quick, unaccountable, responsive.'[3] Though Eliot's 'Reflections on *Vers Libre*' (1917) reassured traditionalists that 'formal rhymed verse will certainly not lose its place' with the coming of free verse, he added darkly, 'as for the sonnet I am not so sure'.[4] And for the surrealists, the sonnet was the refuge of poets who could no longer feel poetry's unconscious, electric charge, as Breton complained in 1933:

> All these 'sonnets' that still get written, this senile horror of spontaneity, all this rationalistic refinement, these stiff-lipped supervisors, all this incapacity for love, leave me convinced that escape is impossible from this ancient house of correction ... Correct, correct yourself, be corrected, polish, tell off, find fault, never plunge blindly into the subjective treasury purely for the temptation to fling here and there on the sand a handful of frothy seaweed and emeralds.[5]

It isn't clear how the sonnet can be both 'senile' and 'rationalistic', but this tirade sums up how the sonnet form had, in a short space of time, become everything poetry wasn't. Although Mallarmé's sonnet 'Salut' may have given Breton his 'froth' metaphor for poetry, the sonnet's closed order now signified every *ancien régime*, the discipline of the prison and the calculations of economics. Its 'correct' form was the superego's idea of poetry in which relentless criticism in the name of order stifled the unconcious's creative, unpredictable and irresponsibly plentiful power. Or as Williams remarked most bluntly of all, 'to me the sonnet form is thoroughly banal because it is a word in itself whose meaning is definitely fascistic'.[6]

Far from withering away, of course, the sonnet flourished in the twentieth century, but not because its best poets carried on regardless. The sonnet became more innovative in form and more diverse in content than in any previous age because of the climate that its modernist opponents created, and the new relationship their anti-sonnet forms negotiated between poetry and the social order. And the fact that Eliot, Stevens and even Williams ended up returning to sonnets of sorts suggests their discomfort was less with the form itself than with what it had come to stand for, the peculiar compact sealed by the sonnet's *fin de siècle* admirers between cultural elevation and formal rigidification. For despite the remarkable inventiveness of the nineteenth-century sonnet in both sequence and style, much late-nineteenth-century criticism still held that the true sonnet must be decasyllabic, must clearly divide octave from sestet with certain permissible rhyme variations, could express only a single thought and should chart the unfolding stages of that thought exactly according to the divisions of quatrain and tercet. For some, this was not enough: Crosland supplies twenty-one 'fixed, established, stable and unassailable' prohibitions, including rhymes ending in -ly, couplets, prosaism, cant, Americanism and too many lines beginning with 'And'.[7] Ironically, these formal prescriptions slashed through the sonnet canon as radically as the modernists ever would. Tomlinson's *The Sonnet* (1874) and Pattison's introduction to *The Sonnets of John Milton* (1883) doubt whether Wordsworth and Shakespeare's sonnets are sonnets at all. But the absurdity of dismissing so many actual sonnets to find a Platonic ideal is testimony to the extreme cultural pressure that the idea of a single, correct form represented. It had become the microcosm of the civilizing work culture was supposed to perform on the grandest scale, showing how the most intimate feelings of the modern buffered, detached and expressive self really could be disciplined into a freely chosen self-limitation. 'Where law is arbitrary', argued Pattison, 'the only authority that can bind is the consent of those who live under it', so Milton's sonnets become 'not deference to authority' but a training in self-discipline for author and reader.[8] Its difficulty made it token of cultural aspiration, while what de Vere called its 'bracing discipline' also appealed to the post-Evangelical, imperial ideology of masculine power achieved through voluntary self-restraint. As Quiller-Couch claimed: 'The

Sonnet is no arbitrary or haphazard invention ... every rule has its reason; and ... (in a phrase which I may be allowed to repeat) it is the men big enough to break the rules who accept and observe them most cheerfully.'[9] The sonnets of the war poets in general, and the double sonnet of Owen's 'Dulce et Decorum Est' in particular, would gain terrible plangency from their suspicion that the codes of nobility and 'the highest' that their form connotes are complicit with the heroic culture whose ugly result they are recording.

Modernism's demand for an organic, intimate relation between the poet's form and her content, on the other hand, anticipated the wider cultural shift later in the twentieth century from a social good based on respectability, discipline and restraint to a social good impossible without the expressive and authentic. Harriet Monroe, the editor of *Poetry* who had done so much to publicize the new verse forms, thought 'the free verse movement has been essentially a plea for a personal rhythm, for the poet's independence in working out his most expressive form and using it without prejudice'.[10] Though Eliot and Pound feared such independence in the mass, their attempts to find a new tradition of organic social order reappraise the poetry of the past according to the expressive standards that the new poetry had made its *raison d'être*: 'To create a form is not merely to invent a shape, a rhyme or rhythm. It is also the realization of the whole appropriate content of this rhyme or rhythm. The sonnet of Shakespeare is not merely such and such a pattern, but a precise way of thinking and feeling.'[11] Judging the sonnet by the standards of free verse means there is no simple way to turn the clock back by using an old form. Shakespeare's sonnet, Eliot believed, belonged to a vanished social order that today's poet cannot share: 'Only in a closely-knit and homogeneous society, where many men are at work on the same problems, such a society as those which produced the Greek chorus, the Elizabethan lyric, and the Troubadour *canzone*, will the development of such forms ever be carried to perfection.'[12]

Eliot was half right. For a wider culture made suspicious of established authority and self-sacrifice by the First World War, where informal directness was becoming the mark of honesty and public-spiritedness, the formal pattern of the sonnet really would never sound the same again. But it had not sounded the same since Baudelaire wrote sonnets about modern Paris, sonnets whose ironic poise Eliot himself had thoroughly absorbed. Eliot's scepticism about the possibility of the modern sonnet, in fact, depends on believing that poetry should epitomize the social relations of its society and its age, as if there were one society and one age to be expressed. But poetic forms may inherit new significances as they move through cultures; they may also mediate between societies or within cultures, and older forms may acquire new possibilities by the arrival of new ones. As the introduction of television gave radio a new role, rather than eradicating it, the new poetics that Eliot did so much to inculcate were, in fact, instrumental in reviving the sonnet they despised.

The old-fashioned sonnet

When free and fragmented verse became the accepted face of 'the modern', the sonnet acquired a new aura of antiquity, the worn-out remnant of an older society that could never now be naturally the form of the present. This is how it appears in *The Waste Land*, where the jerky quatrains of the empty-hearted sex in 'Trams and dusty trees' become a metrically aborted sestet with the postcard title 'On Margate Sands'. Although the writer claims 'I can connect / Nothing with nothing', the fragmented lines still preserve the rhyme scheme of the Petrarchan sestet, as if the ghostly frame of the sonnet is the remnant of a now lost habit of mind, which ironically haunts the seduction in the canoe and the nervous breakdown that follows. But this sense of mismatch between a worn-out form and modern content was useful for poets writing about feelings that really were being engulfed by the past. Edna St Vincent Millay's more successful sonnets of bohemian bed-hopping in Greenwich Village, for instance, sound modern by allowing the adored but silent woman of so many male sonnets to be politely ruthless with her suitor now:

> I shall forget you presently, my dear,
> So make the most of this, your little day,
> Your little month, your little half a year,
> Ere I forget, or die, or move away,
> And we are done forever; by and by
> I shall forget you, as I said, but now,
> If you entreat me with your loveliest lie
> I will protest you with my favourite vow.[13]

The 'as I said' is a nice touch, as if her attention were so fleeting that it has drifted off during the writing of the poem. But that 'favourite' vow is not merely a nasty way of telling a lover he or she is one of many, or more subtle kind of seduction, drawing from Shakespeare's Sonnet 138, to the effect that 'I am telling you I will lie to you because I want you not to believe me'. Millay's even pace, unruffled diction and perfectly metrical closures are so out of kilter with her free-love ethos of being 'faithless' to any particular person 'save to love's self alone' (Sonnet 3) that they suggest how endless novelty has become just as predictable as any vow of fidelity. The well-worn form is essential to her sonnets' cool, melancholy and self-protective air of knowing every move of the affair well in advance.

By running the sonnet form against a brutal present, on the other hand, the war poets could draw attention to the distance between the high ideals represented by Rupert Brooke's infamous sonnet 'The Soldier' and the mess they were actually in. In Sassoon's 'Dreamers', the soldiers are supposed to long for 'some flaming, fatal climax', but in the sestet they actually dream of 'things they did with balls and bats … and going to the office by the train'. 'Trench-Duty' uses a sonnet of mostly heroic couplets to express the panicky, unheroic thoughts of a real officer struggling awake to find one of his men might have killed himself. As well as ironizing noble ideals, the sonnet could also a tacitly signify an erotic devotion to the men; as Sassoon's sonnet 'Banishment' claims, 'love drove me to rebel'. Owen's 'Anthem for Doomed Youth' is a sonnet, because the actual anthem is being sung by the 'wailing shells'. Pounded into the mud, the soldiers' only memorial among the living will be the looks and unspoken emotions of boys and girls back home. By using the sonnet form, however, Owen quietly aligns his own protesting feelings with these quiet, longing looks that the nation prefers not to recognize. Ivor Gurney's 'Strange Hells' is also about emotions for which no public form is available, and it buckles the metrical and argumentative patterns of the sonnet to say so. In an unusual 5.5.4 pattern, the first stanza slides between grammatical subjects and sentence topics as it is drawn into this inner hell:

> There are strange hells within the minds war made
> Not so often, not so humiliatingly afraid
> As one would have expected – the racket and fear guns made
> One hell the Gloucester soldiers they quite put out:
> Their first bombardment, when in combined black shout
>
> Of fury, guns aligned, they ducked lower their heads

We can't tell whether the 'they' in the fourth line are the guns or the soldiers, and the confusion is exactly the mental experience of saturation bombardment the poem is talking about, the memory running over stanza boundaries and metrical restraints alike. This uncontainable hell persists for all ex-soldiers, whatever their civilian lives:

> Some civic routine one never learns.
> The heart burns – but has to keep out of face how heart burns.

Twisting the romantic cliché, the 'heart burns' because it is scorched, not because it is in love – and the penumbra around 'heartburn' suggests a stomach sick with fear, and the emotions of 'jealous enmity' (OED) toward that civic routine.

The discovered sonnet

As Gurney's example suggests, though, modern sonnet writers were not limited to ironizing an old-fashioned form with unexpectedly modern content. They also made the form itself far more flexible in rhyme, rhythm, diction and spacing, and they were freed to do this because of modernism's attack on the idea of 'correct' form itself. The *moral* shock of open forms was that they claimed the same intensity of feeling and self-chosen law as the sonnet, without having any prior ideal to live up to. But in making their forms rather than being made by them, modernist poetics also gave those writing sonnets in the wreckage of that idealistic tradition the chance to save the form from the twentieth century's gut reaction against overt authority, and all the hierarchies of ideal-over-real, mind-over-body or government-over-governed that set form now connoted. Rather than being an *a-priori* list of requirements to which the poet's skill must bend, the modern sonnet became a genre, a set of expectations that the poet might conform to, rebel against or simply sidle along with for as long as necessary. To survive in an anti-authoritarian age, the sonnet had to incorporate a sense of process and the possibility of being otherwise into its accomplishment, rather than already knowing the solution from the start. Robert Frost's remark that 'the sonnet is the strictest form I have behaved in, and that mainly by pretending it wasn't a sonnet' sums up this turn, by making the genteel cultural discipline of his upbringing into school rules that the adult knows not to be all that serious, and that the poet realizes he mustn't think about in order to avoid frightening off his creativity.[14]

In his early poem 'Mowing', for instance, Frost discarded the quatrain–tercet pattern and its rhymes for a fourteen-line meditation on the way poetry and mowing are both kinds of self-distraction. Although this is a poem about 'labor', there is an odd passivity to the mower; it is the scythe's 'earnest love' that 'laid the swale in rows', rather than his hard work, and it is the abstract 'labor' that dreams of facts, not the labourer. The rhythm and whispering of mowing are self-sustaining, leaving 'the hay to make' and the mower's mind to listen only in its wake. That sense of belated creativity is also present in the unpredictable rhymes, in which every line will turn out to have a partner – and 'Mowing' to be a more-or-less sonnet – only after it's been finished; nothing in the form predestines it to turn out that way. Despite the hard work that goes into making both of them, then, the poem suggests hay and poems are both things that make themselves as well as being made: the poem's 'most precious quality will remain its having run itself and carried away the poet with it', thought Frost, for it remains fresh only by having 'a meaning that once unfolded by surprise as it went'.[15]

Writers who have the end in mind at the beginning 'have it all fixed up to set like a trap to close with', but 'it should not be that way at all', for even the intricacies of a sonnet must be discovered en route. In 'The Constant Symbol', Frost imagines Shakespeare writing the first line of Sonnet 29 and wondering what should come next:

> He may proceed in blank verse. Two lines more, however, and he has let himself in for rhyme, three more and he has set himself a stanza. Up to this point his discipline has been the self-discipline whereof it is written in so great praise. The harsher discipline from without is now well begun. He who knows not both knows neither. His worldly commitments are now three or four deep.[16]

Discovering yourself to be writing a sonnet is also discovering what people will expect of you for writing it: form becomes an extended negotiation between self and society that, even for Shakespeare, was tricky:

> As a matter of fact, he gets through in twelve lines and doesn't quite know what to do with the last two.
> Things like that and worse are the reason the sonnet is so suspect a form and has driven so many to free verse and even to the novel. Many a quatrain is salvaged from a sonnet that went agley.

This sense of the sonnet's necessary precariousness is perhaps why so few of Frost's sonnets repeat their rhyme schemes, and it's essential to 'Acquainted with the Night', which begins untraditionally in *terza rima* stanzas. Wandering the lonely streets in the rain, Frost's speaker is mortified by the city's failure to give his misery any meaning: the cry of another was not meant 'to call me back or say good-bye', and the town clocks 'proclaimed the time was neither wrong nor right'. But then the *terza rima* – Dante's form for a voyage into the eternal because it endlessly generates the next stanza from its middle line – simply stops, and the poem becomes a sonnet by bathetically returning to its first line. Its achieved form is the result of not being able to go anywhere else, in other words, rather like the speaker himself. And the collapse from an epic to a sonnet also suggests how much its grandiose melancholy may have been all along covertly in love with failure, as the coy word 'acquainted' is so often a polite cover-up for a real passion. 'Design' also plays games with form and intention. At first, it seems like an hysterical reaction to a natural coincidence of coming on a white spider eating a white moth on a flower that isn't normally white. Frost was no purveyor of country lore, though, and the final couplet sends the poem swerving away somewhere else:

> What but design of darkness to appall? –
> If design govern in a thing so small.

The last line seems to recognize how implausible it is that 'darkness' has conspired to 'appall' (i.e. whiten) us alongside all these deathly whitenesses. But on the other hand, if no design governs at this level, as the modern sceptical reader wants to say, when does it start, since we are also so small in the scale of the universe, or of evolution? And design *is* definitely governing in this small poem, because it is an almost perfectly Petrarchan sonnet that manages the difficult feat of repeated rhymes in English (*abbaabba*). But its very skill then provokes the teasing, Frostian question of how much the demands of that rhyme and form locked the poet into writing what the poem says about design in general: if it surprised its author in the making, at what level of formal complexity was it, or evil, or good, 'designed'?

'Design' also demonstrates Frost's reinvention of the sonnet as an argumentative, self-testing form, unlike the genteel sonnet's pursuit of frictionless, lyric exaltation. He adopted the easy-going tone, story-telling and naturalistic language of his immediate New England predecessor, Edwin Arlington Robinson, because he also wanted to make sonnets that sounded like a real person talking. Unlike Robinson, though, he also experimented a great deal with the sonnet's form, running sentences across the nominal boundaries of quatrains and tercets, or making novel rhyme patterns that pull against the syntax, because this push-and-pull of talk against the sonnet's form was a scaled-up version of the 'strained relation' Frost liked between speech and metre, and the strained relations he also thought made good art itself.[17] 'Form exists when one principle is locked in its opposite' in 'the clash of two goods', he wrote, and poetry *is* that dynamic opposition: 'Poetry is play. Even King Lear is called "a play", isn't it? I'd even rather have you think of it as a sport. For instance, like football – than as some kind of academic solemnity.'[18] Perhaps this is why Frost discusses Shakespeare's writing like a sports commentator watching a player set up a shot, and why he thought to write free verse was as pointless an exercise as 'to play tennis with the net down'.[19] In 'The Silken Tent', Frost's beautiful sonnet about a woman's 'ease' and upright 'sureness' being created by her countless 'silken ties of love and thought' to others, those 'loosely bound' ties are a playful allusion to the tugs of the sonnet's rhymes and rhythms as the poem's single sentence glides through all fourteen lines:

> And only by one's going slightly taut
> In the capriciousness of summer air
> Is of the slightest bondage made aware.   (12–14)

Placing the unassuming 'of' in a metrically stressed position in the final line is the only sign of tension between metre and speaking voice, as the line draws the slightest attention to its bondages. But Frost's tent metaphor is not just about poetry's ability to reconcile freedom and commitment, like love should. For if one admiring tie goes slack, another goes taut: all the woman's ties are actually pulling against each other, not just the tent. And if Frost's biographers are right to think that, over its gestation, this sonnet came to be about Kay Morrison – the secretary who kept several admirers, including Frost, on the go – then Frost's sense of form as live competition becomes even more palpable.

Although Frost hints that modernists were failed sonnet writers, his anti-Platonic intuition that abstract form lives by being *performed* in concrete instantiations was also the motive for more radical experiments in the sonnet by E. E. Cummings and, despite himself, an older Wallace Stevens. Stevens's 'Autumn Refrain', 'The Dwarf' and 'The Poem that Took the Place of a Mountain' are all maybe-sonnets: they don't rhyme or split into sestets and octave, and the latter two are both seven separate couplets amid a number of other multiple-couplet poems whose length is not particularly significant. But, as with most of Stevens, they are poems about the make-believe necessary for art to happen. 'Autumn Refrain', for instance, describes the stillness of everything gone: light, the world, summer and a Keatsian nightingale. Yet a 'skreaking and skrittering residuum' remains to grate against the poet's imaginary hearing of that nightingale, perhaps the sound of the poet's pen itself writing. By the last line, 'the stillness is all in the key of that desolate sound'. The felt, unheard stillness has become attuned to the residuum and/or the imagined sound of the nightingale, as if poetry itself has a *musical* relationship with its own absence. Belated and autumnal, modern poetry happens anew through the withdrawal of poetry, just as the sonnet's form is present in a new way through not being obviously there in the older sense. Feeling its presence engages the sceptical, imaginative faith that Stevens thought it was art's role to encourage in an age of religious disillusionment and compensatory political dogmatism.

Cummings's sonnets, on the other hand, stretch the boundaries of the form beyond anything Frost or Stevens, or anyone, had ever tried. The 'Sonnets-Realities' section of *Tulips and Chimneys* (1923) opens with an attack on 'the Cambridge ladies who live in furnished souls', and one assumes those rented, upholstered spiritual apartments have their formal equivalent in the genteel cosiness of the sonnet form in which the poem is couched. But Cummings wanted to refurnish the form, not to abandon it, and the first thing he did was to knock out any sense of Cambridge's satisfied closure by abandoning octaves, sestets, full metres, predictable rhymes and any formal pressure to begin at the beginning, or come to rest at the end of a line. The second was to make the sonnet as ungenteel as possible:

O It's Nice To Get Up In,the slipshod mucous kiss
of her riant belly's fooling bore
– When The Sun Begins To(with a phrasing crease
of hot subliminal lips,as if a score
of youngest angels suddenly should stretch neat necks
just to see how always squirms
the skilful mystery of Hell)me suddenly
grips in chuckles of supreme sex.
In The Good Old Summer Time
My gorgeous bullet in tickling intuitive flight
aches,just,simply,into,her. Thirsty
stirring. (Must be summer. Hush. Worms.)
But It's Nicer To Lie In Bed
        –eh? I'm
not. Again. Hush. God. Please hold. Tight

Cummings's sonnets begin and end in the middle of things. Subject and object switch places, co-ordinating phrases are overwritten by lines from other thoughts (here a song) running concurrently through the mind, and the syntactical hierarchies of main and subordinate clauses are suspended, all to make a myriad of contrary feelings take place simultaneously and intersubjectively. The only requirement is that the experience should be of breathless, overwhelming intensity, refusing the separations of the oppressive techno-rational 'normality' he despised. This is more than a de-idealization of strict form in the name of sexual honesty, however. Cummings's explicit sonnets are really reinventions of the mutability sonnet, here rhyming 'worms' with 'squirms' to suggest corpses as well as copulation, while the connotations of 'fooling bore' suggest the vagina is a hard-to-find waterhole *and* a rifle shooting at him – not to mention his boredom and dissatisfaction with the prostitutes about whom these sonnets were written. A note on modern art from around this time says: 'The highest form of Composition is the Squirm, it is made of Creeping, Stretching, Gliding, Shrinking, Gripping. As emphasis tends towards angularities, the composition Wags, Hops, Bounds, Fiddles, Sprints, Fumbles, Trembles and Struts.'[20] In Cummings's hands, the sonnet itself squirms, stretching and shrinking its lines, hopping over line endings with rhymes on unstressed words ('suddenly', 'I'm') and fiercely gripping others with those erased spaces and panting commas. Squirming, of course, is what small children do a lot of, and the squirm was, for Cummings, the supreme achievement of children's art and its power to fuse doing and depicting. It's also what adults do in sex, crossing the bodily limits from which the grown-up self, its laws and its embarrassments have been made. Both content and form of these modernist sonnets blend the infantile, the erotic and the morbid, and the wilful naiveté and refusal to 'develop' that so grated on his critics are essential to their outlook. After Cummings found some personal happiness later in life, though, his later sonnets lose some of that greedy intensity, becoming collations of drifting phrases whose out-of-order connections are gentler intimations of love's power to resist death's closure and the sequence of time. In the seventy poems of *W*, he anticipates the postmodern hyper-sonnet by spacing sonnets every seven poems and then finishing with a sequence of seven; just as the proportions of the sonnet invisibly structure the whole order of the volume, so love, it's hinted, will turn out to have been the principle all along, whether the poet knew it at the time or not.

The politics of the sonnet

But by making form something to be discovered en route, rather than anxiously aspired to, modernism also unwittingly created a new cultural politics of the sonnet. For one virtue of the cultural prestige of a strict sonnet form had been to act as a means of public recognition for poets whose race, gender or class had otherwise debarred them from attention. The sonnet's role as the gold standard of civilized self-discipline made achieving it, for a late-nineteenth-century African American writer like Paul Lawrence Dunbar, effectively a claim for public equality. For the modernist sensibilities of some Harlem Renaissance writers, on the other hand, the stiff, unreal vocabulary and rhythm of Dunbar's sonnets were aping a hidebound white gentility, not a sign of universal culture. 'The mountain standing in the way of any true Negro art in America', to Langston Hughes, was 'this urge within the race towards whiteness, the desire to pour racial individuality into the mold of American standardization'.[21] Standardization meant the contented, respectable folk of the aspiring middle class, whereas the unruly, gin-sipping lives of the 'common folk' will 'furnish a wealth of colorful, distinctive material for any artist because they still hold their own individuality in the face of American standardizations'.[22] Effectively a manifesto for his own blues poetry, Hughes's folk poetics were a challenge to the bourgeois poetics of his rival, the formalist Countee Cullen, whose most famous sonnet, 'Yet do I marvel', smoothly claims that God must doubtless have reasons to justify the torments of Tantalus or Sisyphus, but that his own faith cannot understand God's will 'to make a poet black, and bid him sing'. But Cullen complains about being set up by the Almighty for a life of unceasing failure in a perfectly metrical sonnet ending in three deft couplets; for the new poetics of culturally self-defining authenticity, this anguish felt rather too urbanely expressed.

Cullen, however, thought Hughes's poems had fallen into the same racial trap that Dunbar's dialect poems had:

> 'The selections in this book seem one-sided to me. They tend to hurl this poet into the gaping pit that lies before all Negro writers, in the confines of which they become racial artists instead of artists pure and simple. There is too much emphasis here on strictly Negro themes.'[23]

Both were accusing each other of pandering to a white audience, in effect. For Hughes or his promoter Alain Locke, the poet's job was to create a new sense of pride on the model of Romantic nationhood, by uniting the individual artist and the unconscious poetry of the folk, which explains the unblinking switches between 'individuality' and the 'common' in Hughes's article, and his fear that difference in class taste within the black community indicated allegiances other than race. For integrationists like Cullen, on the other hand, cultivating the folk or primitive was still acting up to a white audience's prejudices, whereas the black artist should seek respect as a human being through the continuity of his work with the western cultural tradition; given the situation of black poverty in white America, he wrote in 1928, 'Negroes should be concerned with making good impressions.'[24]

For a younger generation of African American poets, however, making the sonnet more idiomatic also meant renegotiating these terms of cultural approval: trying to see whether the sonnet, and its implied audiences, would fit them, rather than the other way round. Gwendolyn Brooks was the first to make the sonnet *sound* like it was written by an African American poet, rather than just saying so, but her sequence *Gay Chaps at the Bar* expresses her reservations about it by making complex triangulation between the form and two other themes: the uniform equality promised by the inclusion of black sailors in the US Navy, contrasted with real pervading racism (they were usually not allowed to fight, though they were in just as much danger), and the remorseless readjustment of ideals in love, patriotism and faith that the women left behind to wait experience. All three are twisted together in the second sonnet of the sequence, which begins 'each body has its art, its precious prescribed / Pose', and ends:

> And even in death, a body, like no other
> On any hill or plain or crawling cot
> Or gentle for the lilyless hasty pall
> (Having twisted, gagged, and then sweet-ceased to bother),
> Shows the old personal art, the look. Shows what
> It showed at baseball. What it showed in school.

Zora Neale Hurston had identified posture as one of the 'characteristics of Negro expression', the 'whole body panging and posing' in the unscripted public art that was black social life.[25] Here the pose is still a provocation, but to grief: because it was made by twisting in agony, because the dead were so recently at school themselves, and because wrapped in a pall, the pose is now the property of both black and white. So far, so multiracial, but the mid-line stop before the final sentence is a beautifully timed pose itself, asserting the speaker's independence from *having* to fulfil the form, and a catch in the throat that the sonnet, too, is a living pose 'showed in school' and now also *rigor mortis*. Many of the poems that follow keep that discreet analogy going between the pulls of speech against the sonnet form and the discovery that pre-war commitments (to purity, lovers, God or the 'fixed … instructions' of race) may now be outdated shells, while Brooks's skilful consonant-only rhymes keep the feeling of bonds coming apart but not yet finished. These fears culminate in the final sonnet about commitment to America itself. 'Still we wear our uniforms', it begins, but wonders how long we can 'salute the flag, thrill heavily, rejoice / For death of men who too saluted, sang':

> For even if we come out standing up
> How shall we smile, congratulate: and how
> Settle in chairs? Listen, listen. The step
> Of iron feet again. And again   wild.

The ambiguity of whether the 'step of iron feet' is the Allied forces or the Axis threat suggests that all American soldiers may find themselves in conflict with their own nation, as African American civilians had long felt they were. But as the iron feet of the sonnet, they also express Brooks's issue with the form: is using it falling in rhythmically with an abstract promise of equality such as the military offer, or committing oneself to the ranks of the dead?

Robert Hayden's stirring unrhymed sonnet to Frederick Douglass takes a more positive stance, however, by running the rising accents of black oratory over all its line endings to tell how Douglass's sense of universal liberty came *through* the culturally restricted, white-dominated forms he experienced:

> this man, this Douglass, this former slave, this Negro
> beaten to his knees, exiled, visioning a world
> where none is lonely, none hunted, alien,
> this man, superb in love and logic, this man
> shall be remembered.

The syllabic links between 'Negro' and 'knees', or 'none', 'lonely' and 'alien' suggest how closely Douglass's sense of liberty and identity came from his bondage, which neatly heads off problems with Douglass's later politics – supporting the imperial US annexation of Dominica in the interests of a greater black nationhood, for instance – while quietly acknowledging that the sonnet form itself is also a limit to what Douglass will mean. We will only really remember him, it begins, when freedom 'belongs at last to all, when it is truly instinct', or, in other words, when the sonnet itself has disappeared.

The sonnets in Louis Zukofsky's "*A*"-7 and "*A*"-9, on the other hand, seek political freedom through formidable technical obstacles. The first part of "*A*"-9 runs excerpts from Marx (on the divorce of labour from value) across the internal and external rhyme schemes of Cavalcanti's *canzone* 'Donna mi prega' (a touchstone for Ezra Pound), while ensuring the distribution of the letters 'r' and 'n' according to the mathematical ratios of the conic section. The second re-runs some of the same words and rhymes in the transforming light of extracts from Spinoza (on thinking God's thoughts), making the sonnet form a construction device where sound and sense, chance and design or intended and unintended meanings are kept constantly interdependent. The patient work required to assemble and to read them was for Zukofsky one way to restore poetry to the unalienated craft tradition he admired; they are labours of love, forms whose intricate delight in both work and family he felt were sorely lacking in cynical, industrialized America, not to mention the fascism that his erstwhile mentor Pound had espoused.

But perhaps the most persistent politician of the sonnet was Hayden's one-time tutor, W. H. Auden. In Auden's hands, the sonnet became potted psychobiography, in profiles of artists and thinkers (Rimbaud, Housman, Luther and Nietzsche), vocations ('The Composer', 'The Traveller', 'The Quest'), a cultural mindset ('Macao', 'Hongkong') and, in *Journey to a War*, the fall of man himself; almost anything but the task he had early on employed it for, lyrical seduction. 'If Art were magic' he later wrote, 'then love lyrics would be love charms which made the Cruel Fair one give one her latch key. In that case a magnum of champagne would be more artistic than a sonnet.'[26] There is more here than Auden's opposition to the crudely instrumentalist uses of art as persuasion or propaganda. As the keyword 'magic' suggests, Yeats is in the back of his mind, and Auden's mature ethos of poetic form was largely worked out as a response to the power of Yeats's style, and the political irresponsibility he felt it entailed. Both Auden and Yeats were committed to reinventing the political sonnet, but they divided sharply on what it could do to its readers.

For Yeats, form in poetry was a continuation of his belief in magic, and the poet is the 'successor' of the magician: 'All sounds, all colours, all forms, either because of their pre-ordained energies or because of long association, evoke indefinable and yet precise emotions, or, as I prefer to think, call down among us certain disembodied powers, whose footsteps over our hearts we call emotions.'[27] Traditional forms do not merely refer to or comment on a past, in other words, but move modern minds onto the eternally present plane of the spiritual world, shaping our small feelings now into the patterns laid down by the great myths that structure historical events far more than any individual actor knows. For a nation whose past had so many wrongs that remained unrighted, poems could be interventions, as well as commentary. But until the great crises of the Easter Rising and the First World War, Yeats did not call down the Italian or English aristocrats of the sonnet. 'Precisely because of its centrality to English literature', argues Helen Vendler, 'the sonnet compelled from Yeats both his literary allegiance and his nationalist disobedience'.[28] Only as Yeats began to identify himself with an Anglo-Irish heritage opposed to monocultural Catholic nationalism did his imagination really seize on the half-alien form, and in 'Leda and the Swan' he made his famous sonnet about the hybrid birth of new civilizations through a disturbing fusion of violence and desire. Using a mixture of English octave and Italian sestet, Yeats alters the older tradition of Leda's gradual seduction by Zeus into the 'sudden blow' of rape, perhaps registering his shock at the killings of the Easter Rising and the massacres he feared in Bolshevik Russia. But the language refuses entirely to separate the god's will from his victim's:

> And how can body, laid in that white rush
> But feel the strange heart beating where it lies?
> A shudder in the loins engenders there
> The broken wall, the burning roof and tower
> And Agamemnon dead.

'White rush' could refer to the swan's violent snatch, or Leda's reclining in the cushion of his feathers, as if she were both attacked and enticed. And it is deliberately ambiguous whose 'strange heart' she is feeling, or whose loins 'shudder' in both horror and desire, as the line itself shudders with a skipped stress on 'in'. That mixture of attack and unexpected intimacy would repeat itself in the Trojan war between rivals for beautiful Helen, and then in the family vengeance that kills Agamemnon after the war; and Yeats was horribly acute to sense it coming in the future civil war in Ireland, too, with its cycle of revenge attacks between those in charge of the new Irish state and their former resistance comrades. Yet to ask 'did she put on his knowledge with his power' is odd, since it assumes Leda had power to 'put on' at all. Can one put on a pregnancy? But it makes more sense if Leda is a figure for the poet-magician Yeats himself, who can 'put on' the borrowed symbolic forms of the spirit world, like a robe or a mask, and know himself an instrument of their design. Being 'caught up', of course, means both being snatched and being utterly absorbed, and the horrifying events Leda might be intimating seem to be coming to the poet in a continual present, like a film. The 'and's of 'the burning roof and tower / And Agamemnon dead' are followed by those daring half-lines of complete silence, as if Yeats himself were stunned by his own vision of coming desolation. But such empty-mouthed astonishment is, at the same time, a confirmation of the poem's own performative power, astounding the one through whom it is being made. Yeats's vision of violence is, in both senses of the word, a ravishing one.

For Auden, on the other hand, Yeats was enticing his own nation toward such violence by writing poems that are thrilled as well as appalled by seeing it coming. Yeats's fusion of form and power wanted to make poetry the doorway to a world where poems, our emotions on reading them and the activity of the spirits in creating the events of history all merge. But however attractive Auden thought a world recreated by poetry would be, magic has no space in it for choice and consent, and with it, freedom and democracy: 'Art … is not Magic, i.e. a means by which the artist communicates or arouses his feelings in others, but a mirror in which they may become conscious of what their own feelings really are: its proper effect, in fact, is disenchanting.'[29] That disenchantment should be the means of transforming closed communities into open ones, by making our response to art one of painful recognition, rather than one that encourages the fantasies of identification with a hero or a community that dictators rely on. Rather than seduce, then, Auden's first task for the sonnet was disenchanting, by uncovering the blind spots, weaknesses and unforeseen consequences that really make up the life of a person or a place. In 'Luther', for instance, the great reformer unwittingly accelerates the decline of real Christianity by insisting that 'the Just shall live by Faith', and condemning all social action as justification by works:

> And men and women of the world were glad
> Who'd never cared or trembled in their lives.

By separating faith from all worldly activity, Luther unwittingly enabled people to carry on as usual, privatizing faith into mere Sunday belief. While this Shakespearean couplet looks at first like an ironic counterpart to Luther's anguish in the previous three quatrains, its rhymes actually show it is a separate part of an Italian sestet, as if to show that worldly indifference is actually a *consequence* of Luther's efforts at interiorizing faith.

In the sonnets of *Journey to a War*, his metaphysical counterpart to Isherwood's limpid account of their actual travels in China, Auden writes directly about disenchantment in the more sociological sense, describing mankind's uneven progress to recognition that democratic freedom depends on law ungrounded by *any* prior order, unlike racist or totalitarian ideologies. Sonnet XXV asserts baldly that 'Nothing is given: we must find our law', and Auden's snapshot content, surprise adjectives, unpredictable rhymes and formal deviations in these sonnets are all to confirm how much the form is being remade, rather than inherited. But any order was at odds with the chaos in China that Auden was witnessing at the time, and Sonnet XVI, about the unreal calm of a command tent away from the front, also has poetry in the back of its mind when it criticizes monuments that simplify a war or the 'flags on a map' that deny 'living men in terror of their lives'. The silences as the sestet's lines grow shorter reflect the poet's sense of the inadequacy of his own representations, and Auden's lurking guilt about being a detached observer:

> But ideas can be true although men die,
> And we can watch a thousand faces
> Made active by one lie:
> And maps can really point to places
> Where life is evil now:
> Nanking; Dachau.

But they also speak of the poet's power to bring that failure to attention, and this is the oddity of Auden's sonnets in a nutshell. To seduction and magic, they oppose an aesthetic of disenchantment, 'a bringing to consciousness, by naming them, of emotions and their hidden relationships', stressing artifice to make readers alert to their own motives for being interested.[30] But they also want to dazzle by the sheer verve of their analysis, as if disenchantment were enchantment by other means. 'The Quest', Auden's most sustained experiment with the sonnet form, comes nearest to recognizing this. Sonnet XII has an unusual 3.3.3.5 pattern:

> Incredulous, he stared at the amused
> Official writing down his name among
> Those whose request to suffer was refused.
> The pen ceased scratching: though he came too late
> To join the martyrs, there was still a place
> Among the tempters for a caustic tongue

The gap where we expect the final line of a quatrain is the blankness of the would-be martyr finding that the life and death he had anticipated won't now happen. Instead, the *b*-rhyme on 'among' connects unpredictably to the tempters' 'caustic tongue' and his aim 'to test resolution of the young', because the disenchanter's own 'informal style' and 'worldly smile' are actually a reaction to his own frustrated idealism. If this is a self-portrait, its cruelty only confirms the emotional wellsprings of its passion to disenchant the disenchanter. Sonnet x addresses Yeats even more explicitly, describing a tower where 'Lost Love in abstract speculation burns / And exiled Will to politics returns', which is a brilliant summary of the compensations politics and magic supply in *The Tower*. But the sestet's warning applies to Auden too:

> Here great magicians, caught in their own spell,
> Long for a natural climate as they sigh
> 'Beware of Magic' to the passer by.

Conclusion

Auden's acute discomfort at his own role is perhaps emblematic of the change modernism brought to the sonnet. When form is thought of not as an ideal, but a concentration of the 'mental outlook' of its age, then form becomes not just the internal organization of the art, but a mediator of the ever-shifting social relations between the artist and the public.[31] Making the sonnet's form more optional and democratizing its diction does not, therefore, mean that the modern sonnet becomes, simply, more 'free'. It might better be said that the modern sonnet had to become more responsive to be felt as art, and more responsible. Indeed, I have avoided analyzing twentieth-century sonnets in the terms of artistic freedom and formal limitation, not because that binary doesn't motivate some great modern examples – Patrick Kavanagh's chafing 'Inniskeen Road: July Evening' or Claude McKay's 'superhuman' restraint in 'The White House', for instance – but because the option of free verse so altered where that limit was sensed. Free or fragmented verse did not abandon the act of voluntary self-discipline for which the nineteenth century praised the sonnet, it presupposed it. Indeed, one might say that free verse is the purest internalization of sonnet discipline, so pure it leaves no external trace, allowing Imagist poetics to take over the sonnet's status as *the* condensed lyric form, as well as its difficulty and remoteness. But if early modernists scorned the sonnet because it represented their own disavowed reformist urges, they also gave it a new sense of social dependence. Able to shape any poem according to its inner logic rather than agreed pattern, free-verse writers encountered new limits in the generic expectations of 'poetry', the frameworks of cultural authority that their poems wanted to evade. For sonnets and fragments alike, a successful form would now have to be preternaturally sensitive to the changing ways its audiences would hear it.

Notes

The text of each sonnet quoted is taken from its author's *Collected Poems* unless otherwise indicated.

1 T. W. H. Crosland, *The English Sonnet* (London: Secker, 1917), p. 21.

2 Ezra Pound, *ABC of Reading* [1951] (London: Faber and Faber, 1979), p. 157.

3 Wallace Stevens, *Letters of Wallace Stevens*, ed. Holly Stevens (London: Faber and Faber, 1966), p. 42.

4 T. S. Eliot, *Selected Prose of T. S. Eliot*, ed. Frank Kermode (London: Faber and Faber, 1975), p. 36.

5 André Breton, 'The Automatic Message' [1933], in *The Automatic Message; The Magnetic Fields; The Immaculate Conception*, trans. Antony Melville (London: Atlas, 1997), pp. 11–12.

6 William Carlos Williams, 'The Tortuous Straightness of Chas Henri Ford', in *Selected Essays* (New York: Random House, 1954), pp. 235–6 (p. 236).

7 Crosland, *The English Sonnet*, pp. 56, 88–97. For Petrarchan standards, see [C. W. Russell], 'Critical History of the Sonnet', *Dublin Review* 27:54 (October 1876), 400–30 (p. 404).

8 John Milton, *The Sonnets of John Milton*, ed. Mark Pattison (London: Kegan, Paul, Trench, 1883), pp. 20, 46, 27. For disciplinary sonnet form, see Gillian C. Huang-Tiller, *The Power of the Meta-Genre: Cultural, Sexual, and Racial Politics of the American Modernist Sonnet*, unpublished Ph.D. thesis (University of Notre Dame, 2000), pp. 93ff.

9 Aubrey de Vere, 'Memoir', in *Sonnets* (London: Basil Montague Pickering, 1875), p. xiii; Arthur T. Quiller-Couch, ed., *English Sonnets* (London: Chapman and Hall, 1897), p. xx.

10 Harriet Monroe, *Poets and Their Art*, rev. edn (New York: Macmillan, 1932), pp. 321–2.

11 T. S. Eliot, 'The Possibility of a Poetic Drama', in *The Sacred Wood* (London: Methuen, 1920), pp. 54–63 (p. 63).

12 T. S. Eliot, 'Reflections on *Vers Libre*', in *Selected Prose*, p. 36.

13 Edna St Vincent Millay, Sonnet 11, lines 1–8, in *Collected Sonnets of Edna St Vincent Millay* (New York: Harper and Brothers, 1941).

14 Robert Frost, *The Letters of Robert Frost to Louis Untermeyer* (New York: Holt, Rinehart and Winston, 1963), p. 381.

15 Robert Frost, *The Collected Poems, Prose and Plays of Robert Frost*, ed. Richard Poirier and Mark Richardson (New York: Library of America, 1995), p. 778.

16 *Ibid.*, p. 789.

17 *Ibid.*, p. 680.

18 Robert Frost, *Collected Prose*, ed. Mark Richardson (Cambridge, MA: Belknap, 2007), p. 314; Selden Rodman, *Tongues of Fallen Angels* (New York: New Directions, 1974), p. 43.

19 Frost, *Collected Poems*, p. 735.

20 Quoted in Richard S. Kennedy, *Dreams in the Mirror: A Biography of E. E. Cummings* (New York: Liveright, 1980), p. 180.

21 Cary D. Wintz, ed., *The Harlem Renaissance 1920–1940*, 7 vols. (New York: Garland, 1996), Vol. II: *The Politics and Aesthetics of 'New Negro' Literature*, p. 166.

22 *Ibid.*, p. 167.

23 *Ibid.*, Vol. IV: *The Critics and the Harlem Renaissance*, p. 145.

24 Countee Cullen, 'The Dark Tower', *Opportunity* (March 1928), p. 90.

25 Zora Neale Hurston, 'Characteristics of Negro Expression', in Nancy Cunard, ed., *Negro* (New York: Negro Universities Press, 1934), p. 39.

26 W. H. Auden, 'Squares and Oblongs', in *The Complete Works of W. H. Auden: Prose*, ed. Edward Mendelson, 3 vols. (London: Faber and Faber, 2002), Vol. II: *1939–1948*, p. 346.

27 W. B. Yeats, 'The Symbolism of Poetry', in *Yeats's Poetry, Drama and Prose*, ed. James Pethica (New York: Norton, 2000), p. 272.

28 Helen Vendler, *Our Secret Discipline: Yeats and Lyric Form* (Oxford: Oxford University Press, 2007), p. 147.

29 Auden, 'The Poet of the Encirclement', in *Prose*, Vol. II, p. 198.

30 Auden, 'Squares and Oblongs', in *ibid.*, p. 345.

31 T. S. Eliot, 'The Music of Poetry', in *On Poetry and Poets* (London: Faber and Faber, 1961), p. 37.

13

STEPHEN BURT

The contemporary sonnet

There are more kinds of beetles than kinds of sonnets, more beetles on earth than sonnets by living authors, but sometimes it seems a close call. Poets writing in English over the last half-century have produced extravagantly traditional sonnets about beauty and about cruelty; sixteen-line sonnets modelled on George Meredith's *Modern Love*; sonnets in blank verse; sonnets on love erotic, parental and filial; a political sonnet in Miltonic pastiche; a sonnet composed entirely of clichés; a sonnet history of Glasgow; sonnets spoken by Bruce Wayne as Batman; 'sonnets' without words presented as conceptual art; sonnets called 'Sonnet' in demotic, unrhymed free verse; sonnets on Japanese-American subjects with haiku for the final couplet; sonnets that tell historical stories for children; a widely lauded literary novel in tetrameter sonnets modelled on Alexander Pushkin's *Eugene Onegin*; sonnets in Newfoundland dialect; a crown of fifteen sonnets about e-Bay; and a sonnet in which each line ends on a different letter but all the lines rhyme with 'oh'.[1] Not only have poets kept on writing sonnets; readers, and publishers, have continued to seek them, to set them apart in collections of their own, from the useful, comprehensive website www.sonnets.org (now twelve years old), to all-sonnet journals such as *14*, to *The Making of a Sonnet: A Norton Anthology*, by the American poet Edward Hirsch and the Irish poet Eavan Boland. Many of the poems Boland and Hirsch include – and many of those described above – would not, a hundred years ago, have been called sonnets at all; some might not have been called poems.[2]

Questions about what counts as a sonnet, about how we should use the term, are now centuries old; a strong sense that such questions have no stable answers, that they can never be resolved, distinguishes the late twentieth and the early twenty-first centuries, and affects how their strongest and strangest sonnets sound. A list of contemporary sonnets would be its own book (though a list of critical writings on the contemporary sonnet in general might be surprisingly short). This chapter does not attempt such a list; it looks instead at what some writers have done to make the sonnet especially contemporary, and especially memorable, since the mid-point of the twentieth century. Five characteristics distinguish the most original recent uses of sonnet form. Firstly, there is *formal play*, even gamesmanship; the sonnet gets stretched to its limits, broken up and reinvented, so as to show how we make the very orders we seem to find. Secondly, there is *a sense of history*: because we recognize the sonnet as a form from the past, a form with its own past, a poet who adopts it says that she cannot begin anew, that she acknowledges some sort of past in her poem. Contemporary sonnets, just because we recognize them as sonnets, work against modern hopes that an artist, or a family, or a society, can leave the past entirely behind. The form thus lets some poets acknowledge historical guilt; it lets others point out the distance between their own backgrounds, their own brands of English, and the white, privileged, European or male backgrounds that the most famous earlier writers of sonnets had.

Sonnets may also present, alongside or against their sense of cumulative history, a *commitment to dailiness*, to impressions without an overarching order, each in its separate frame, as in a notebook or calendar, or in the unforced, ongoing social exchanges implied by fluent light verse. As each sonnet records an occasion or a day, a set of sonnets can take its own larger shape: verse journal or diary, fragmentary narrative, post-Petrarchan lyric sequence. (Contemporary sonnets can thus return – though not all their authors seem equally aware of it – to the calendrical or diaristic modes described, earlier in this book, by Catherine Bates.) As a *unit in series*, or within its fourteen (or so) lines, the contemporary sonnet can thus register the opposition that Roland Greene finds in lyric sequences generally, setting narrative (one thing after another, connected by causal change) as against ritual (recurring) time.[3] It can therfore *register the tension* that Nick Halpern finds in recent American poems between prophetic, authoritative language, which gives direction and shape from outside and above, and 'the everyday', the uninflated language of conversation and of diaries: 'the everyday wants to trap the prophetic poet in time', in history or else in minute-by-minute ephemera.[4] These five tendencies (formal play, a sense of history, a commitment to dailiness, use within sequences, and tension between vatic ambition and ordinary experience) do not compete but coexist, and speak to one another, in the strongest sonnets of our time.

When does that time – when does 'contemporary poetry' – begin? After the end of modernism (whenever that is)? Of hostility to modernism (which continues to this day)? At some hinge in global political history, such as 1945 or 1968? It might begin, as far as the sonnet goes, with the best-known opponent of sonnets in the early twentieth century. William Carlos Williams reconsidered his stance against the sonnet as early as 1938, calling it a 'dialogue unit upon which all dramatic writing is founded'.[5] Later he published unrhymed sonnets himself. His *Three Sonnets* (1942) use none of the formal resources of sonnets past; their unrhymed free verse (of eleven, twelve and thirteen lines) portrays a 'mudbank / crowded, sparkling / with diamonds big as fists', another landscape where mountains form a 'broken line', and an ambivalent scene of married love: 'In the one woman, / I find all the rest'. Each poem represents a traditional *subject* for sonnets (either erotic or locodescriptive), a subject that Williams's American 'line' could renew. His 'Sonnet in Search of an Author' (1962) works self-consciously with and against sonnet form:

> Nude bodies like peeled logs
> sometimes give off a sweetest
> odor, man and woman
>
> under the trees in full excess
> matching the cushion of
> aromatic pine-drift fallen
> threaded with trailing woodbine
> a sonnet might be made of it
>
> Might be made of it! odor of excess
> odor of pine needles, odor of
> peeled logs, odor of no odor
> other than trailing woodbine that
>
> has no odor, odor of a nude woman
> sometimes, odor of a man.

With 'Sonnet in Search of an Author' the sonnet becomes contemporary inasmuch as it no longer represents something inimical to the modern, the new, the natural or the genuine. Here are fourteen lines, octave and sestet, differentiated in tone, in pace and in rhetoric; here, too, is a final 'couplet', in which 'woman' matches 'man'. 'Threaded' with green renewal, the peeled logs are at once a stack of parallels (like lines in a poem) and a symbol for sexual discovery. Another poet might make a (proper, regular, traditional, stifling) sonnet from such an erotic scene; Williams will make his own, rough-hewn, American sonnet instead.[6]

To some poets now, Williams's fourteen lines might not count as a sonnet; to others, they might seem markedly traditional, compared to what the sonnet later became. Ted Berrigan composed *The Sonnets* in 1962–3.[6] None of these sonnets uses regular rhyme; most avoid consistent scenes, stories or prose sense. Some have more, or fewer, than fourteen lines, so that only their presence in that sequence connects them securely to sonnet-ness as an idea. The sonnets' fast pace and their many references to Berrigan's friends suggest attention to the bustle of New York City (where Berrigan had just moved), and to the poetry of Frank O'Hara (whom Berrigan admired). The sonnets also emulate O'Hara in their praise for spontaneity, their sometime self-satire, their attempts at urban pastoral:

> The blue day! In the air winds dance
> Now our own children are strangled down in the bubbling quadrangle
> To thicken! He felt his head
> Returning past the houses he passed
> 'Goodbye, Bernie!' 'Goodbye, Carol!' 'Goodbye, Marge!'[7]

Like their distant Renaissance precursors, Berrigan's sonnets aspire to an intimate, cumulative, but not quite narrative, record of the poet's inner tumult, of what we call private life. Some of the sonnets (including the first and last) bring up Berrigan's infatuation with Christine Murphy ('Chris'), whom he met when he taught her in eighth grade in Tulsa: she is for him something like Petrarch's Laura, though (unlike Petrarch) he can try to reach her by phone – the last line of the final sonnet reads: 'It is 5:15am Dear Chris, hello' (p. 76).

Yet despite their apparent intimacy, *The Sonnets* make it hard to assign all their features to one consistent speaker's emotions: the poems incorporate chance operations, quote other writers at length and share lines with one another – two of them use just the same lines, in different orders. Berrigan recorded the start of *The Sonnets* in a journal entry from 1962: 'Wrote (?) (Made) five sonnets tonight, by taking one line from each of a group of poems, at random, going from first to last poem then back again until 12 lines, then making the final couplet from any 2 poems, in the group, one line at random from each. Wrote by ear, and automatically, very interesting results.'[8] These 'interesting results' may just sound like a mess:

> Squawking a gala occasion, forgetting, and
> 'Hawakaaaaaaaaa!' Once I went scouting
> As stars are, like nightmares, a crucifix.
> Why can't I read French? I don't know why can't you?
> Rather the matter of growth
> My babies parade waving their innocent flags
> Huddled on the structured steps
> Flinging currents into pouring streams
> The 'jeunes filles' so rare.   (p. 31)

These lines make more prose sense in context (some refer to Berrigan's trans-lations of Rimbaud), but not much more. Such scrambled, unmelodic, diffuse language has made *The Sonnets* less than amenable to anthologists for the same reasons that make it so attractive to certain poets and critics: they require us to think of *The Sonnets* as a single project, not only as a set of discrete poems, and they require us to view its parts sometimes as personal lyric, sometimes in terms appropriate for conceptual art. The British poet and critic Tony Lopez finds elsewhere in Berrigan 'echoes of the sonnet's argumentative structure', 'with turns away from the character "Berrigan" and from "I" to "you", but ... no scheme of rhyme ... and no snapping into place of dialectic synthesis'.[9] Instead, 'the wish to project a coherent "self" onto the text remains a function of ... expectations'.[10] The sonnets were for Berrigan, in a sense that Eliot never quite intended, both 'expression of personality' and 'escape from personality': they brought to the sonnet the anti-individualist, anti-humanist or proceduralist techniques that would, by the end of the 1960s, become frequent in music and in gallery art.[11]

In Williams's late sonnets the form ceased to be anti-modern; with Berrigan the form became postmodern, in the sense of that vexed word explained by Linda Hutcheon: it 'acknowledges the human urge to make order, while pointing out that the orders we create are just human constructs, not natural or given'.[12] The sonnet itself is such a constructed order, as the debates about its boundaries show. For writers attracted to an avant-garde, Berrigan's volume remains the most important contemporary use of sonnet form, the one that stands farthest apart from what came before. The avant-garde sonnet persists in America in the disarmingly personal sonnets of Bernadette Mayer ('My hand is like a muffin just baked in the electrocuting / toaster ... This is my new form of sonnet / This is the closing of it / Please don't stop loving me right this moment'), and in sequences by Lyn Hejinian, whose end-stopped, ametrical lines suggest a collage, or a dream: 'Then the sparrow went to sleep in a lumber castle / And so we come to chapter LIX, in which I learn that I have failed / Can you believe this shit?'[13] Postmodern sonnets emerged in Australia in the 101 fourteen-line poems of John Tranter's *Crying in Early Infancy* (1977), whose evasions of prose sense become less playful than aggressive: saying 'goodbye to the glue / that used to hold everything together', 'goodbye / to the countryside of honorable rifles', the poet rejects the complacencies that (in his view) exacerbated the war in Vietnam, while mimicking, or parodying, warmongers' temperament.[14] For more avant-garde sonnets, with special attention to Britain, we may look to *The Reality Street Book of Sonnets* (2008), whose editor, Jeff Hilson, includes blank-verse sequences (such as Lopez's) that defy prose sense; concrete poems and typographical experiments; awkwardly jocular rhymed sonnets (such as Edwin Denby's); and works that, as Hilson cheerfully admits, 'are not sonnets at all'.[15] Contemporary avant-garde (or 'post-avant', as some of them have it) writers often present their projects as reactive – they resist closure, undermine confidence, prevent the suspension of disbelief; sonnet form, sonnet tradition, sonnets' weight of historical examples give such writers rules to break, and expectations to react against.

Berrigan's poems were, by almost any definition, experimental, open to inconclusive or failed results. But 'all poetry is experimental poetry', as Wallace Stevens wrote; some of the strongest contemporary sonnets have little truck with avant-garde goals.[16] Translators have kept bringing Renaissance sonnets into English, with Elizabeth Jennings's version of Michelangelo winning particular attention. Poets who learned from Robert Frost, from Patrick Kavanagh, from Auden and from Yeats, have renovated the form in subtler ways. William Meredith in 'The Illiterate' reflected his speaker's limited verbal resources by using only *rime riche*:

> Touching your goodness, I am like a man
> Who turns a letter over in his hand
> And you might think that this was because the hand
> Was unfamiliar but, truth is, the man
> Has never had a letter from anyone.[17]

James Merrill often used the sonnet as a flexible stanza in longer poems, analogous to *ottava rima* in Yeats: Merrill's quatorzains retain the sonnet's progress from octave to sestet, from thesis to antithesis, or from three quatrains to a couplet. 'The Broken Home' (1966) sets the failed marriage of Merrill's parents against Merrill's own adult life as a childless gay man. The first of its seven sonnets uses a trimeter norm and a 4.4.3.3 division: the poet comes home to his apartment, lights a candle and prays, or mock-prays, 'Tell me, tongue of fire, / That you and I are as real, / At least, as the people upstairs.'[18] The second sonnet remembers the poet's father (who helped to found the finance giant Merrill Lynch) in snappy, almost sarcastic pentameter quatrains. The seventh and last sonnet concludes:

> The real house became a boarding school.
> Under the ballroom ceiling's allegory
> Someone at last may actually be allowed
> To learn something; or, from my window, cool
> With the unstiflement of the entire story,
> Watch a red setter stretch and sink in cloud.   (p. 200)

The sonnet in 'The Broken Home' becomes simultaneously a stanza form and a freestanding poem, as the 'red setter' – one of Merrill's many puns – is both the sun and the family dog.

Because he alluded so much to the literary past, and because he wrote of lives marked by inherited wealth, Merrill was sometimes called, pejoratively, conservative. Such designations rest on oversimple analogies between political and artistic 'conservatisms', and in Merrill's case they were simply mistaken: as M. K. Blasing writes, Merrill's 'rhetoric of forms, in their exaggerated artificiality, decorum and anachronism ... questions the historical and metaphysical authority of conventions'.[19] Other recent writers, however, do consider sonnets as a means of resistance to cultural change, as assertions of fealty to older standards: the American poet William Baer, for example, has edited both *150 Contemporary Sonnets* (2005) and *The Conservative Poets* (2006). In the sixteen-line Meredithian sonnets of Adam Kirsch's *Invasions* (2008), formal regularity becomes a bulwark against 'pure self-assertion', though Kirsch sees ironies in such claims too: his maker of sonnets, like the shoppers in his sonnet 'Outlet Mall in Western Massachusetts', 'do compulsively what must be done / To make ourselves forget' the chaos outside, 'The hoarse owl, and the forest closing in'.[20] In his poems as in his criticism, Kirsch works in the tradition of Yvor Winters, both anti-modernist and anti-Romantic, for whom 'the poem is good in so far as it makes a defensible rational statement': such a stance is – in our time as in Winters's – provocative and atypical.[21]

For poets quite distant in style and affect from Merrill (and even more distant from Winters or from Kirsch), the sonnet can nonetheless provide a sign of security, a link to prior poetry, a version of home. John Ashbery (not known for his sonnets) concludes one fourteen-line poem with 'this is our home'.[22] The rhymed sonnet, claims Tony Barnstone (who has published books of them), 'gives the writer certainty about the world ... Sonnet-mariners know they will arrive in port after a voyage of fourteen lines.'[23] Rita Dove in *Mother Love* (1995), a book composed largely of sonnets, calls the form 'a talisman against disintegration', a 'charmed structure', a 'beautiful bubble', even or especially where 'chaos is lurking outside the gate'.[24] That book concerns the myth of Demeter and Persephone: Dove's 'I' is sometimes an errant daughter, more often a bereft mother, making of sonnets irregular refuges, spaces in which a growing daughter cannot take shelter, because she cannot be found. Printed as a sestet, but rhymed in Shakespearean fashion (*efe fgg*), the last lines of Dove's sonnet 'Protection' ask:

> Is there such
> a thing as a warning? The Hawaiian
> mulberry is turning to ash
> and the snail has lost its home.
> Are you really all over with? How done
> is gone? (p. 11)

Writing a poem in which fall turns to winter, plants shrivel and hair 'comes out / in clusters', Dove plays on the African American proverb 'Every closed eye ain't sleep and every goodbye ain't gone': into the missing syllables of that final line Persephone might fit, if she ever comes home.

Dove integrates (I use the word advisedly) a European-derived form with African American speech. Such integrations mark the contemporary African American sonnet. Cultural nationalists in the 1960s and 1970s, including the later Gwendolyn Brooks, avoided the form. Black poets of the 1980s and afterwards, however, take cues from the earlier Brooks, and from Robert Hayden, by stretching the form to incorporate Black speech and Black music, making it feel like home. Elizabeth Alexander describes Brooks's sonnets as ways to organize 'interior space', demonstrations that 'any space can be sanctified'; we find in the sonnets of Marilyn Nelson (who has collaborated with Alexander on a book-length sonnet sequence), and of Gary Copeland Lilley, interior spaces marked as African American, celebrated for their complexity and defended against race-based oversimplification.[25] Alexander's 'House Party Sonnet '66' and Dove's 'Golden Oldie' (from *Mother Love*) even quote the same song, 'Where Did Our Love Go?' by The Supremes.[26] Copeland Lilley's unrhymed sonnet 'Cicada' observes refugees from Hurricane Katrina, relocated to the mountains of North Carolina, temporarily happy in their temporary home:

> God snatched
> this old man and woman from everything
> but each other, and blessed them to have just that.
> A peep of red flowers in the woodchips
> and weeds by the door of their motel room.
> Miles down the road, a disembodied drone,
> a 'dozer, a dreadhead at the controls.[27]

We may remember that 'stanza' means 'room', and that a motel has many rooms in a fixed order, through which people come and go; we may notice the encouraging 'peep' of flora amid weeds (the motel cannot afford elaborate groundskeepers). We may notice the 'dreadhead' (an operator with dreadlocks, likely African American) controlling the bulldozer, moving earth where it should go, as the African American poet operates the equipment of phrase and line; and we may see the sonnet itself as a refuge, a vexed but 'blessed' shelter, showing domestic affection in rough times.

Other Black poets still view the sonnet with suspicion, as a form made by privileged white folks, an ill-fitting mask. Terrance Hayes's 'Sonnet' consists of one line, 'We cut the watermelon into smiles", printed fourteen times: Hayes plays on racist stereotypes that associate rural Black Americans with watermelon, and with fixed grins, and on the assumption that all sonnets say, or mean, the same thing.[28] If the sonnet no longer seems at odds with modernism, it remains marked, and not only for Black

Americans, by its white, European, metropolitan, standardizing (Tuscan Italian, standard English) origins: some poets have therefore re-marked the form by loading it with non-white, non-European or non-metropolitan words and sounds. Though not itself a sonnet sequence (components vary from ten- to twenty-odd lines), *Lotería Cards and Fortune Poems* (1999), by the Mexican American poet Juan Felipe Herrera, draws amply on the turns and returns of sonnet form. Each of the poems responds to a woodcut of a traditional *lotería* (Mexican tarot) image: many incorporate Spanish, or street slang. The fourteen-line 'El Dios' presents God as a homeless man in a basketball shirt, introducing himself ('Hey corazonsito / I am back from the races') in the octave and asking for help, for 'change', in the sestet.[29] Sonnets by A. K. Ramanujan, and more recently by Vivek Narayanan, flaunt the cadences of Indian English: Narayanan's sequence *Invocation* promises (with a nod to Rilke) that his poems may 'spring from anachronistic torsos / into common air', and that they may 'do honour to our race / of hungry-eyed passengers on longing trains'.[30] The final, hypermetrical line suggests at once the crowded journeys that western travellers associate with modern India, and the one-after-another succession of equal units in the sonnet sequence.

The most celebrated contemporary sonnets in non-standard English, the set of sonnets most concerned to raise, and to overturn, the idea that the sonnet 'belongs' only to one location or class, came from England: they are the sixteen-line sonnets of Tony Harrison, collected in *The School of Eloquence* (1976–87), the work that made Harrison's name. Many of those sonnets remember, with overt if also defensive pride, Harrison's origins in working-class Leeds; they praise and mourn his father and his mother, and they present the accents of his youth. Eclectic (though always political) in its final, seventy-six-poem version, 'the sequence was more blatantly and single-mindedly a thesis about political and linguistic oppression', as Blake Morrison writes, in its earlier, shorter form.[31] The introductory sonnet, 'On Not Being Milton', likens Harrison's poetry to documents circulated by British revolutionaries, 'read and committed to the flames' (i.e. burned after reading): 'these sixteen lines that go back to my roots' bring into their pentameter quatrains and couplets the destructive, democratic accents that governors hoped to keep down, or keep out:

> The stutter of the scold out of the branks
> of condescension, class and counter-class
> thickens with glottals to a lumpen mass
> of Ludding morphemes closing up their ranks.

Flouting stereotypes of working-class English as a 'restricted code', Harrison's sequence deploys a strikingly wide variety of English (and Latin, and even

Cornish) words. 'Branks' are metal or wooden bridles for human beings, used especially to punish gossipy women ('scolds'): 'Ludding' means doing as Luddites did, breaking capitalists' machines. Harrison manages here as throughout the sequence to decry class injustice, to show his roots and to call attention phonically to the gap in opportunity (as one of his titles has it) that separates 'Them & [uz]'.[32]

Seamus Heaney's sequence *Clearances* (1987) commemorates his mother, and incorporates her diction – unlettered, and sometimes notably Irish – into its supposedly English form:

> I governed my tongue
> In front of her, a genuinely well-
> Adjusted adequate betrayal
> Of what I knew better. I'd *naw* and *aye*
> And decently relapse into the wrong
> Grammar which kept us allied and at bay.[33]

Here Heaney's project resembles Harrison's: both place non-standard English and its speakers in positions of respect within a metropolitan form, creating (as Meg Tyler writes) 'a voice from both inside and outside the tribe'.[34] Yet Heaney's many other sonnets have other acoustic and architectonic goals. When he moved from the North to the Republic of Ireland, from the outward angst of *North* (1975) to the renewed, careful confidence of *Field Work* (1979), he marked the shift with his rightly celebrated *Glanmore Sonnets*, poems of love for his wife and family, and for their rural cottage: the 'deliberately middle-voiced Wordsworthian sequence' laid grounds for the fluent pentameters of many later poems.[35] *District and Circle* (2006) includes twenty-one sonnets, some tender, some vaunting, some wary: 'The Nod' remembers the tense coexistence of Catholic and Protestant in the towns of Heaney's youth:

> Saturday evenings too the local B-Men,
> Unbuttoned but on duty, thronged the town,
> Neighbors with guns, parading up and down,
> Some nodding at my father almost past him
> As if deliberately they'd aimed and missed him
> Or couldn't seem to place him, not just then.[36]

'B-Men' are B-Specials, the sometimes brutal police auxiliaries who helped enforce Protestant rule in the Ulster of Heaney's youth. The octave, about a butcher's shop, rhymes *abbaabba*; the unusual rhymes in this *effgge* sestet, with their congruent 'm's and 'n's and their disyllabic 'past him … missed him', suggest the side-by-side life of Catholic and Protestant, dominated and dominant, in the same 'place', always similar, never the same.

'The Nod' places the child Seamus Heaney in political, public history; in family history; and in the history of the sonnet form. The sonnet can stand in 2010 (far more than it could in 1610 or 1810) for fixed or for inherited form in general, for history or for literary history, since it is by far the best-known fixed form, one of few still in common (and classroom) use. As other parts of pre-modernist literary history recede, the sonnet becomes important as a sign that contemporary poetry *has* a history, one that includes several centuries and nations. No wonder, then, that the form attracts poets who want to write history, and to write, in effect, historiography: to consider how writers (poets among them) record and interpret successions of public events. Harrison is one such poet; Geoffrey Hill is another. The thirteen sonnets of Hill's *An Apology for the Revival of Christian Architecture in England* (1979) consider the beauty, the sacrifices and the cruelty in English, and in British imperial history, from records of the Raj to the 'quaint mazes' of formal gardens and estates:

> And, after all, it is to them we return.
> Their triumph is to rise and be our hosts:
> Lords of unquiet or of quiet sojourn,
> those muddy-hued and midge-tormented ghosts.[37]

Here and in earlier sequences (such as 'Funeral Music' (1969), about fifteenth-century martyrs) Hill's work can seem to resist the label 'contemporary', as it resists the tenor of its own time: it asks, as Stephen James writes, 'to what extent an author's work, in gesturing towards an ideal, perfected realm, [can] partake of the ... authority it apprehends'.[38] That authority – at once political, religious, moral and aesthetic – remains in Hill's sonnets forever desirable, and forever in dispute. Nor is Hill alone in these aims. Peter Scupham's verse style is Horatian rather than Alexandrian, concerned as much with fluency and lightness as with intricacy and learning, but Scupham (born, like Hill, in England in 1931) has also made the contrasts in sonnet form stand for the half-buried, half-acknowledged contradictions in England's ideas of itself. Scupham's crown of sonnets, *The Hinterland* (1977), honours the war dead as it alludes to *Macbeth*: 'A silence runs beneath these silences / Where the shut churches founder in the green', 'Where honour and dishonour share the rolls / And night plays rook about the stiffening elms'.[39]

American sonnets can record American history. David Wojahn's *Mystery Train* (1990) comprises a sonnet history of rock and roll, from Buddy Holly and the young James Brown to Altamont and to Graceland. In one poem, William Carlos Williams watches Elvis on the Ed Sullivan show: Wojahn casts that poem in Williams's late tripartite line – 'The tube, / like the sonnet, / is a fascist form.'⁴⁰ To resist Elvis on TV ('this pomped-up kid'), to reject the sonnet as a frame for contemporary popular experience, is for Wojahn to remain stuck amidst the limited alternatives of modernism and anti-modernism – alternatives that the contemporary sonnet rejects.

Other American sonnets address world history in tones close to despair. Robert Lowell wrote hundreds of unrhymed sonnets between 1967 and 1973, organizing, revising and rearranging them into five books, and then into the brief sequences in *Selected Poems* (1976). In these sonnets' stacked, corrosive lines, with their isolated images and their jarring transitions, public history and private life are juxtaposed over and over, and neither can serve as reliable guide. One of the strongest sequences, *1930s*, remembers the poet's adolescence: in one poem, a bonfire reminds Lowell of autos-da-fé in late medieval Europe, 'burdened with its nobles, serfs and Faith'.⁴¹ At the end of the sonnet a lobster husk's 'two burnt-out, pinhead, black and popping eyes' watch over the 'ash-heap' of history, from which we learn nothing. Lowell's sonnets on public events – 'Two Walls', for example, about the assassination of Martin Luther King, Jr – reach similar epistemological and moral dead ends:

> Somewhere a white wall faces a white wall,
> one wakes the other, the other wakes the first,
> each burning with the other's borrowed splendor –
> the walls, awake are forced to go on talking,
> their color looks much alike, two shadings of white,
> each living in the shadow of the other. (p. 226)

The lines – like the white liberals for whom Lowell speaks – must 'go on talking', animated by 'guilt, doubt, and ironic self-recrimination', in restless futility.⁴²

Lowell's late sonnets arose from his practice, in 1967–8, of writing (or at least beginning) one sonnet per day; Berrigan's sonnets resembled journals, too. The contemporary sonnet lends itself to such dailiness, to diary form, to what historiographers call 'chronicle' (one thing, one day or one year after another). Sonnets come one by one, in same-sized units, like days, or years: the use of the sonnet for versified diaries, to chronicle events even as they happen, is not a contemporary invention (it is one way to read Astrophil's misadventures), but it remains a resource. Randall Jarrell, Lowell's contemporary and friend (and best early critic), wrote in his only mature sonnet, 'Well Water' (1965), about the rare moments in which we welcome 'the dailiness of life'.⁴³ Even a sonnet of transcendental and explicitly religious ecstasy (as Jarrell's is not) can emphasize the unremarkable recurrences, the hours and weeks of ordinary schedules, from which their epiphanies start. Donald Revell's religious sonnets draw both on traditions of sonnets as akin to prayer (for example in Gerard Manley Hopkins) and on the form's history as occasional verse. 'All days take instruction from accident', he writes, and only when 'emptiness / Rises and falls according to no pattern' can he say that 'Jesus Christ is the next thing.'[44] Elizabeth Bishop's 'Sonnet', the last poem she wrote and one of her shortest, uses its broken-open nonce form to celebrate an escape from the everyday: it ends

> Freed – the broken
> thermometer's mercury
> running away;
> and the rainbow bird
> from the narrow bevel
> of the empty mirror
> flying wherever
> it feels like, gay![45]

Reversing octave and sestet, launching the second and final sentence in line 7, and adopting two- and three-beat lines (half a pentameter), 'Sonnet' imagines the 'spirit' of the poet, of the sonnet, liberated at last from the body, from matter, from the face in the mirror, from daily responsibility and from the one-day-after-another sequences to which other sonnets (but not this one) belong. Yet the 'mirror' effects in the rhyme scheme (which ties the reversed 'octave' to the initial sestet) and the chemistry behind the metaphor (mercury droplets evaporate as they 'run away') suggest some irony in Bishop's promise of escape, her promise that we, too, might be 'Freed'.

The persistence of the sonnet not only as an isolated lyric form but as a unit for long works implies (as Greene put it) 'that the Western lyric sequence from Petrarch to the present day is a single form' (another critic might say 'genre' or 'subgenre'), 'with a more or less constant set of principles'.[46] John Berryman's *Sonnets to Chris* (composed 1947; published 1967 as *Berryman's Sonnets*) record his extramarital affair; they are the closest a modern poet has come to the sonnet sequence as practised by Sidney – indeed, so close as to constitute pastiche (he even retranslates Petrarch: 'And I begin now to despair of port').[47] The sequence now looks like a rehearsal for his more original *Dream Songs* (1963–9), whose eighteen-line units do not replicate sonnet form. Other American poets after Berryman created other fixed non-sonnet forms for book-length lyric sequences: John Ashbery (four unrhymed pentameter quatrains) for *Shadow Train* (1981), John Hollander (thirteen lines of thirteen syllables each) for *Powers of Thirteen* (1984), Dave Smith (thirteen lines of usually unrhymed pentameter) in *Fate's Kite* (1995), Yusef Komunyakaa (four irregular quatrains) for *Talking Dirty to the Gods* (2000). The popularity of the lyric sequence (in sonnets or in other repeated forms) like the popularity of the journal, the diary, the chronicle as a model for recent poems reflect the diminished credibility in the wide-ranging explanatory models (sacred or secular, mimetic or hermetic) on which other sorts of book-length poems, from *Paradise Lost* to Pound's *Cantos*, must rest. With its strict Petrarchan schemes (each octave rhymes *abbaabba*) and its semantic difficulty, Karen Volkman's sonnet sequence *Nomina* (2008) returns to the source, as it were, of the lyric sequence, while admitting that even that source is by no means natural. Volkman reacts to vicissitude by stressing the artificiality of any repeated form: 'music will need walls to defend itself'.[48]

Because the most famous Renaissance sonnets are love poems, the fate of the sonnet in recent decades has seemed to some observers bound up with the fate of the love poem as a genre. Adrienne Rich's sequence *21 Love Poems* (1975), widely noted and admired on publication for its lesbian content, could not exist without its Petrarchan and anti-Petrarchan precedents, though most of its components are not sonnets. Marilyn Hacker's book-length sonnet sequence *Love, Death and the Changing of the Seasons* (1986) pursued the rise and fall of a love affair, the texture and pace of a year in determinedly contemporary, casual language that made its lesbian contexts unmistakable. Her *Regent's Park Sonnets* acknowledge Berryman's precedent: 'One master, aged as I am, thirty-two, / all summer sonneted adulterous / love.'[49] Praising sequences by Hacker, Rafael Campo and Henri Cole, David Caplan has argued that 'gay and lesbian poets have dominated the art of the love sonnet' since 1980.[50] Because they react to centuries of disparagement (and sometimes to the crises around HIV), these poets can find in 'love's knowledge, its salvations that approach misery … a new discovery, not a cliché' (p. 85). Like Hacker, and like the (heterosexual) Tony Barnstone of *Sad Jazz* (2005), Campo makes love sonnets that combine strict rhyme with colloquial, 'unmarked' American English (p. 70); they represent a healthy continuity, rather than a remarkable discovery, in the history of the form.

Such continuity implies not an isolated master, but a community of teachers and learners, professional or amateur, who carry on the traditions of practice, the habits of listening, associated with rhymed and metred poetry in general, and in particular with the sonnet form. No wonder, then, that a handful (at least) of contemporary sonnets compare the form to amateur piano performance, or to piano practice: consider Louis MacNeice's famous 'Sunday Morning' ('Down the road someone is practicing scales'), Donald Justice's 'Mrs. Snow', Marilyn Nelson's 'Chopin', Carol Ann Duffy's 'Prayer' ('Grade I piano scales / console the lodger') or Greg Williamson's 'Music' (in which 'your real life' resembles 'the walking twelve-bar blues').[51] Earlier centuries found the sonnet a congenial form for amateurs; these newer poems remind us that the practice of sonnet writing, like the practice of scales and teaching pieces on the piano, can be at once a repeated, ritual action; part of a story (in which the student improves); and a domestic, relatively familiar art that poets must nonetheless work to learn.

The very familiarity of the sonnet has also made it a useful vehicle for light verse in Britain (as in the many sonnets of Sophie Hannah), and for comic poets in America who play with, or make fun of, sonnet form. Billy Collins's 'Sonnet', well known in the USA, begins 'All we need is four-teen lines, well, thirteen now' and ends 'where Laura will tell Petrarch to put down his pen … and come at last to bed'.[52] Carol Rumens used the sonnet for *Letters Back*, ten poems spoken to or by Sylvia Plath, in a stroppy, speedy cadence strongly reminiscent of Auden's 'Letter to Lord Byron': 'Take up your quill. Don't bother me again', says Rumens's Plath; 'I'm dead. Just try to get the scansion right. / And don't come on all tra-gic. Keep it light.'[53] This 'Plath', and this poet, ask whether the division between 'light verse' and serious writing does less than justice to women's experience, shaped as it has been (especially during Plath's lifetime) by tacit obligations, by politesse.

Anglophone sonneteers of the past fifty years look back at earlier English uses for the form, but they also notice modernist examples from other lan-guages. The Scottish poet Don Paterson has recently made an English 'version' (not, he insists, a translation) of Rainer Maria Rilke's *Sonnets to Orpheus* (1922): Rilke's '*Sonnets* themselves', writes Paterson, 'constitute a kind of meta-essay on the sonnet form'.[54] Paterson's effort – determinedly conversa-tional in its diction, inevitably vatic in stance – becomes a kind of meta-essay on the sonnet after the Romantics and the moderns, joining 'Well Water' and Bishop's 'Sonnet' in its ambivalence toward escape from the everyday. As Rilke himself sought permanence in transience, another world only in and through our own, so Paterson seeks a high style within the colloquial, a ver-sion of contemporary language that does justice to the venerable form, and to the high claims about poetic power that we find in earlier eras, and that we do not find in (for example) late Lowell. Paterson's *Orpheus* declaims:

> Song is being. Easy for a god.
> But when are *we*? When will the Earth and stars
>
> be squandered on us, on *our* living? Youth –
> don't fool yourself that love unlocks this art;
> for though love's voice might force your lips apart
>
> you must forget those sudden songs. They'll end.
> True singing is another kind of breath.
> A breath of nothing. A sigh in a god. A wind.   (p. 5)

The sonnet, *Orpheus* says, cannot become (and in fact never was) a form suited only for poems about erotic love; it must be 'a breath of nothing', both colloquial (fit for expressions such as 'don't fool yourself') and theophanic, in order to give the contemporary poet the 'True singing' he still seeks. 'The world can no more keep its form', another of Paterson's Rilkean sonnets begins, 'than a cloud can in the sky; / yet all perfected things fall home / to their antiquity' (p. 21). Embedding a ballad quatrain within his sonnet, Paterson suggests that only an imperfect, altered colloquial sonnet can stay with us, that only un-'perfected' forms can remain in *our* sky. These sorts of adaptations owe much to Auden, who had also read his Rilke, though their status as 'versions', their vision of modernist sonnets as material that must itself be adapted and brought down to earth, mark Paterson's *Orpheus* as a product of no period but ours.

Because we may still recognize it, or its traces, even when poets have bent it far out of shape, the contemporary sonnet may well show how much of any pattern, any form (and not only in poetry) is not what we discover, but what we create, or impose. Poets who start where modernism ends (whether or not we dub them postmodernists) are, as Lynn Keller has written, especially likely to 'illustrate the opacity of experience and to highlight the artificiality and autonomy of linguistic or artistic structures'.[55] Such illustrations – whether playful or frustrated – pervade the many sonnets of Paul Muldoon. Consider the atypically laconic, but typically virtuosic, sonnet 'The Ox':

> They had driven for three hours non-stop
> that April afternoon
> to see the Burren's orchids
> in bloom.
>
> Milltown Malbay. They parked
> in front of a butcher's shop.
> 'A month too early. I might have known.'
> 'Let's find a room.'
>
> They reversed away from the window.
> To the right hung
> one ox-tail,
>
> to the left one ox-tongue.
> 'What's the matter? What's got into you?'
> 'Absolutely nothing at all.'[56]

It is an anti-love sonnet, a piece of anti-Petrarchism, a frustrated idyll or ideal, with a rhyme scheme ripe for second thoughts: *abcd cabd efg feg*, despite the stretch of 'window'–'into you' and the interference of the vowel rhyme 'afternoon'–'bloom'. The famous wildflowers of County Clare (which grow well in dry, inhospitable rock) are not to be seen – it is 'too early' for them, and perhaps too late for these lovers, who might not even want to 'find a room': the sonnet can barely find room for its descriptions amid the clutter made by the little they say. We assemble the terse, frustrated utterances to 'create' a sonnet shape, putting ourselves in the place, as it were, of the writer, just as he and his girlfriend (who might be about to split up) put themselves in the place of the slaughtered ox: is it mind or body, writer or reader, that gives to this sonnet its 'tongue'?

Using the analogy of computers' 'fuzzy logic', Andrew Osborn has described Muldoon's 'fuzzy rhyme', where neither vowel nor consonants need match: the sonnets, Osborn explains, are Muldoon's 'most powerful artillery' in his 'formally expansionist' but philosophically relativist campaign.[57] One sonnet chosen at random from Muldoon's *Meeting the British* (1987), 'The Marriage of Strongbow and Aoife', rhymes *aabb ccdd edd acb*; the next, 'The Wishbone', consists entirely of off-rhymed couplets ('Guelph'–'grave', 'myself'–'enough'); the next, 'Profumo', rhymes *abcd ecfb ebd bfa*.[58] In such poems uncertainty about what counts as a sonnet joins up with uncertainty about what counts as a rhyme, and with uncertainty about whether and where we make the patterns – in political life, in family life, in romantic life – that we believe we find. Not by coincidence, all three sonnets concern pairs of people (mother and son, father and son, a couple about to divorce) who cannot get along. 'None will, / I trust, look for a pattern in this crazy quilt / where all is random, "all so trivial"' (p. 117) – so Muldoon warns in the diary-like sonnet sequence *The Prince of the Quotidian* (1994). Yet he writes such lines knowing we seek patterns nevertheless.

The contemporary sonnet at its best manifests gamesmanship or formal reinvention, accompanied by a sense of its own artifice; a sense of the past, of cumulative history; a sense of daily or periodic recurrence; mixed feelings about the vatic impulse that promises an escape from such recurrence; and a sense of its place in some larger sequential structure, either a tradition of sonnet writing or a sequence that the poet herself has made. We have found most of these five qualities in the durable sonnets of recent decades, from Berrigan and Lowell to Dove and Muldoon; we can find them all in the sonnets of James K. Baxter. With his large opus of poetry and stage plays, his far-left political stance, his idiosyncratic Catholic faith, his tumultuous private life (marked by alcoholism) and his sympathy with the counterculture, Baxter was the most accomplished, most controversial poet in New Zealand, and one of its most famous artists of any sort, even before 1968: in that year he moved to the village called Jerusalem (in Maori, Hiruharama) in order to set up a commune. *Jerusalem Sonnets* (1969) records his first attempt to make a life there, his prophetic vocation, his self-doubt and the practical difficulties of his fluctuating household. *Autumn Testament* describes his flight to Wellington and his second try at Jerusalem, cut short by his death in 1972.

'The Jerusalem poems are', as M. P. Jackson and Elizabeth Caffin say, 'a spiritual diary', with the 'intimacy of personal communication' set against 'characteristic ... self-dramatization' (we might think here of Petrarch again).[59] Baxter's tonal range is vast – it includes self-loathing, heroic ambition, religious humility, lust, bemusement, broad humour and cries of acute pain; vast, too, are the speeds and textures he can accomplish with unrhymed pentameter couplets (he is a particular master of triple rhythms within a generally iambic line), and the internal divisions he creates. *Autumn Testament* 12 may introduce the whole:

> The wish to climb a ladder to the loft
> Of God dies hard in us. The angels Jacob saw
>
> Were not himself. Bramble is what grows best
> Out of this man-scarred earth, and I don't chop it back
>
> Till the fruit have ripened. Yesterday I picked one
> And it was better in my mouth,
>
> And all the ladder-climbing game is rubbish
> Like semen tugged away for no good purpose
>
> Between the blanket and the bed. I heard once
> A priest rehearse the cause of his vocation,
>
> 'To love God, to serve man'. The ladder-rungs did not lessen
> An ounce of his damnation by loneliness,
>
> And Satan whistles to me, 'You! You again,
> Old dog! Have you come to drop more dung at Jerusalem?'[60]

Sacred and abject, holy and shaming, sainthood and daily obligation, Maori and *pakeha* (New Zealanders of European descent), ambition and self-abnegation, the line as a unit with its own integrity and the sentence that cuts across the line, the sonnet as self-sufficient poem and the sonnet as page in a diary: these are binaries that Baxter's sonnets raise, and in each case they settle on neither side. The sonnet itself, with its lineated series, its aspiration to higher things, is like Jacob's ladder (Genesis 28:12–13), and its vertical succession, its figure for individual ambition, plays against the bramble that Baxter chops back, whose tangles hug the earth. Though Baxter's sonnets do not seek regular rhyme schemes, they make copious, varied use of terminal consonance: 'rubbish'–'purpose', 'once'–'loneliness', 'vocation'–'lessen'–'again'. Baxter also divides the sonnet in unusual proportions, 6.6.2 – firstly Jacob's

unclimbable ladder to heaven, then, secondly, the priest's 'damnation by loneliness'. Rather than find, after two wrong paths, the right one, Baxter concludes with a hostile interlocutor: Satan asks (as Baxter asks himself) whether
sonnet writing is worth anything, whether it is merely the waste product of his
ambition, or whether (like 'dung') it might make something grow.

Ultimately the sonnet is what each poet makes it: each inventive writer of
sonnets finds new potentialities in the old form, and each influential writer
(though not all inventive writers become influential) leaves the same form
altered for others to use. We can say as much of the sonnet in general, and
of sonnets within national or stylistic traditions: American; Canadian; Irish;
avant-garde; demotic free verse; conversational-formalist (like Rumens or
Barnstone); high-style formalist (like Scupham or Kirsch); sceptical, riddling
and boundary-testing (like Muldoon); or neo-Romantic and serious (like
Rilke). The New Zealand poet Michele Leggott, in her sonnet sequence *as
far as I can see*, incorporates autobiography, dailiness and religious feeling,
as does Baxter, yet the two antipodeans sound nothing alike. Leggott draws
on the American avant-garde (and on the late-Romantic New Zealand poet
Robin Hyde) for her meditations on eros and agape, and on motherhood.
Her sonnet 'a nautilus' begins 'I put the children to bed'; in its last seven
lines, those children

> stir as the house gears down they call out
>
> as I pass I call back I am there when they stagger about
>
> to gulp water and pee   they lock the doors I left open
>
> and skim up ladders in their sleep   I need them
>
> they prevent my disappearance from the world
>
> they bring me back howling overacting for my blurred
>
> attention the cradle boat drawn out on the falling tide[61]

Working in a tradition created by men, one whose most famous examples
are, still, largely male (and whose most famous New Zealand example,
Baxter, could be aggressively, self-accusingly masculine), against a tradition of sequences with 'parts ... more independent than parts usually are',
Leggott exalts the oceanic, the already attached, the interdependent and
the maternal.[62] She uses, for *volta*, her own return indoors; for rhythm, a
loose hexameter base, with its faint Homeric or 'Greek' associations; for
a conclusion, the 'little boat' of the child's bed. That boat in turn sends us
back to Petrarchan tradition ('My galley charged with forgetfulness') and to
Leggott's title. The bed, the boat, the family and the sonnet all resemble the
nautilus, a sea creature that (like the sonnet) can cross the ocean, and whose

small chambers (like stanzas, like poems in a sequence) give the living animal its set of adequate homes.

Notes

1 Beauty and cruelty: Anthony Hecht, *Collected Earlier Poems* (New York: Knopf, 1990), pp. 71, 150; sixteen-line sonnets: Tony Harrison, *Collected Poems* (New York: Penguin, 2007); blank verse: Robert Lowell, *Notebook 1967–68* (New York: Farrar, Straus and Giroux, 1969); erotic love: Marilyn Hacker, *Love, Death and the Changing of the Seasons* (New York: Norton, 1995); parental love: Forrest Gander, *Torn Awake* (New York: New Directions, 2001); filial love: Seamus Heaney, *Opened Ground* (New York: Farrar, Straus and Giroux, 1998), pp. 282–90; Miltonic pastiche: Richard Wilbur, *Collected Poems 1943–2004* (New York: Harcourt, 2005), p. 221; clichés: Paul Muldoon, *Poems 1968–1998* (New York: Farrar, Straus and Giroux, 2001), p. 409; Glasgow: Edwin Morgan, *Collected Poems* (Manchester: Carcanet, 1990), p. 289; Batman: Chad Parmenter, 'Four Poems', *Diagram* 5:6 (2004), available online at www.newmichiganpress.com/5_6/parmenter.html; conceptual art: Jeff Hilson, ed., *The Reality Street Book of Sonnets* (Hastings: Reality Street, 2008); free verse: Gerald Stern, *American Sonnets* (New York: Norton, 2002); haiku 'couplets': J. D. McClatchy, *Mercury Dressing* (New York: Knopf, 2009), pp. 23, 30; history for children: Elizabeth Alexander and Marilyn Nelson, *Miss Crandall's School for Young Ladies and Little Misses of Color* (Honesdale: Wordsong, 2007); literary novel: Vikram Seth, *The Golden Gate* (New York: Vintage, 1991); Newfoundland dialect: Mary Dalton, *Merrybegot* (Montreal: Vehicule, 2005), pp. 59, 66, 68; e-Bay: Denise Duhamel, *Ka-Ching!* (Pittsburgh: University of Pittsburgh Press, 2009), p. 13; rhyming with 'oh': George Starbuck, *The Works* (Tuscaloosa: University of Alabama Press, 2003), p. 60.
2 Eavan Boland and Edward Hirsch, eds., *The Making of a Sonnet: A Norton Anthology* (New York: Norton, 2008).
3 Roland Greene, *Post-Petrarchism: Origins and Innovations of the Western Lyric Sequence* (Princeton: Princeton University Press, 1991).
4 Nick Halpern, *Everyday and Prophetic* (Madison: University of Wisconsin Press, 2003), p. 22.
5 William Carlos Williams, 'Merrill Moore's Sonnets, Present Total, Steadily Mounting, 50,000' (1938), in *Something to Say: William Carlos Williams on Younger American Poets* (New York: New Directions, 1985), pp. 91–2.
6 William Carlos Williams, *Collected Poems*, 2 vols., Vol II (1939–62), ed. Christopher MacGowan (New York: New Directions, 1988), pp. 73–4, 429–30.
7 Ted Berrigan, *Collected Poems*, ed. Alice Notley, Anselm Berrigan and Edmund Berrigan (Berkeley: University of California Press, 2005), p. 46.
8 *Ibid.*, p. 668.
9 Tony Lopez, *Meaning Performance* (Cambridge: Salt, 2006), p. 48.
10 *Ibid.*, p. 51.
11 T. S. Eliot, 'Tradition and the Individual Talent' (1919), in *Selected Prose of… .* ed. Frank Kermode (London: Faber and Faber, 1975), p. 43.
12 Linda Hutcheon, *A Poetics of Postmodernism* (New York: Routledge, 1988), pp. 41–2.

13 Bernadette Mayer, *Sonnets* (New York: Tender Buttons, 1989) p. 22; Lyn Hejinian, in Hilson, *Reality Street*, p. 83.
14 John Tranter, *Urban Myths* (Cambridge: Salt, 2006), p. 81.
15 Hilson, *Reality Street*, p. 17.
16 Wallace Stevens, *Collected Poetry and Prose*, ed. Frank Kermode and Joan Richardson (New York: Library of America, 1997), p. 918.
17 William Meredith, *The Open Sea* (New York: Knopf, 1958), p. 10.
18 James Merrill, *Collected Poems*, ed. J. D. McClatchy and Stephen Yenser (New York: Knopf, 2001), p. 197.
19 M. K. Blasing, *Politics and Form in Postmodern Poetry* (Cambridge: Cambridge University Press, 1995), p. 157.
20 Adam Kirsch, *Invasions* (Chicago: Ivan R. Dee, 2008), p. 6.
21 Yvor Winters, *In Defense of Reason* (Denver: Alan Swallow, 1947), p. 11.
22 Phillis Levin, ed., *The Penguin Book of the Sonnet: 500 Years of a Classic Tradition in English* (New York: Penguin, 2001), p. 248.
23 Tony Barnstone, 'A Manifesto on the Contemporary Sonnet', *Cortland Review* (December 2006), available online at www.cortlandreview.com/features/06/december/barnstone_e.html.
24 Rita Dove, *Mother Love* (New York: Norton, 1995), p. xi.
25 Elizabeth Alexander, *The Black Interior* (St Paul, MN: Graywolf, 2004), p. 16.
26 Dove, *Mother Love*, p. 19; Elizabeth Alexander, *The Venus Hottentot* (Charlottesville: University of Virginia Press, 1990), p. 19.
27 Gary Copeland Lilley, *Alpha Zulu* (Keene, NY: Ausable, 2008), p. 28.
28 Terrance Hayes, *Hip Logic* (New York: Penguin, 2002), p. 13.
29 J. F. Herrera, *Lotería Cards and Fortune Poems* (San Francisco: City Lights, 1999), p. 44.
30 A. K. Ramanujan, *The Oxford India Ramanujan* (New Delhi: Oxford University Press, 2004), p. 228; Vivek Narayanan, *Universal Beach* (Mumbai: Harbour Line, 2006), p. 69.
31 Blake Morrison, 'The Filial Art', in Neil Astley, ed., *Tony Harrison* (Newcastle-upon-Tyne: Bloodaxe, 1991), p. 56.
32 Harrison, *Collected Poems*, p. 122.
33 Heaney, *Opened Ground*, p. 286.
34 Meg Tyler, *A Singing Contest: Conventions of Sound in the Poetry of Seamus Heaney* (New York: Routledge, 2005), p. 83; for the comparison to Harrison, see also Neil Corcoran, *The Poetry of Seamus Heaney*, rev. edn (London: Faber and Faber, 1998), p. 160.
35 Helen Vendler, *Seamus Heaney* (Cambridge, MA: Harvard University Press, 1998), p. 66.
36 Seamus Heaney, *District and Circle* (New York: Farrar, Straus and Giroux, 2006), p. 34.
37 Geoffrey Hill, *New and Collected Poems 1952–1992* (Boston: Houghton Mifflin, 1994), p. 140.
38 Stephen James, *Shades of Authority: The Poetry of Lowell, Hill and Heaney* (Liverpool: Liverpool University Press, 2007), p. 70.
39 Peter Scupham, *Collected Poems* (Manchester: Carcanet, 2002), p. 107.
40 David Wojahn, *Mystery Train* (Pittsburgh: University of Pittsburgh Press, 1990), p. 27.

41 Robert Lowell, *Selected Poems*, ed. Frank Bidart (New York: Farrar, Straus and Giroux, 2006), p. 277.

42 Vereen Bell, *Robert Lowell: Nihilist as Hero* (Cambridge, MA: Harvard University Press, 1983), p. 183.

43 Randall Jarrell, *Complete Poems* (New York: Farrar, Straus and Giroux, 1969), p. 300.

44 Donald Revell, *Pennyweight Windows: New and Selected Poems* (Farmington, ME: Alice James, 2005), pp. 168, 190.

45 Elizabeth Bishop, *Complete Poems 1927–1979* (New York: Farrar, Straus and Giroux, 1983), p. 192.

46 Greene, *Post-Petrarchism*, p. 4.

47 Levin, *The Penguin Book of the Sonnet*, p. 221.

48 Karen Volkman, *Nomina* (Rochester, NY: Boa, 2008), p. 35.

49 Marilyn Hacker, *Selected Poems* (New York: Norton, 1990), p. 90.

50 David Caplan, *Questions of Possibility: Contemporary Poetry and Poetic Form* (New York: Oxford University Press, 2005), p. 62.

51 Louis MacNeice, in Levin, *The Penguin Book of the Sonnet*, pp. 244; Donald Justice, in *ibid.*, p. 214; Marilyn Nelson, in *ibid.*, p. 297; Carol Ann Duffy, in *ibid.*, p. 322; Greg Williamson, in *A Most Marvelous Piece of Luck* (Ewell: Waywiser, 2008), p. 61.

52 Boland and Hirsch, *The Making of a Sonnet*, p. 73.

53 Carol Rumens, *Hex* (Newcastle-upon-Tyne: Bloodaxe, 2002), p. 74.

54 Don Paterson, *Orpheus* (London: Faber and Faber, 2006), p. 62.

55 Lynn Keller, *Re-Making It New* (Cambridge: Cambridge University Press, 1987), p. 10.

56 Paul Muldoon, *New Selected Poems* (London: Faber and Faber, 1995), p. 106.

57 Andrew Osborn, 'Skirmishes on the Border: The Evolution of Paul Muldoon's Fuzzy Rhyme', *Contemporary Literature* 41:2 (2000), 323–58 (p. 328).

58 Muldoon, *New Selected Poems*, pp. 148, 109, 110.

59 M. P. Jackson and E. Caffin, 'Poetry', in *The Oxford History of New Zealand Literature in English* (Oxford: Oxford University Press, 1991), p. 416.

60 James K. Baxter, *Collected Poems*, ed. J. E. Weir (Oxford: Oxford University Press, 1982), p. 546.

61 Michele Leggott, *As Far as I Can See* (Auckland: Auckland University Press, 1999), p. 16.

62 John Berryman, *The Freedom of the Poet* (New York: Farrar, Straus and Giroux, 1976), p. 330.

FURTHER READING

Adames, John, 'The Frontiers of the Psyche and the Limits of Form in Auden's "Quest" Sonnets', *Modern Language Review* 92 (1997), 573–80.

Alexander, Gavin, *Writing after Sidney: The Literary Response to Sir Philip Sidney, 1586–1640*, Oxford: Clarendon Press, 2006.

Bates, Catherine, *The Rhetoric of Courtship in Elizabethan Language and Literature*, Cambridge: Cambridge University Press, 1992.

    Masculinity, Gender and Identity in the English Renaissance Lyric, Cambridge: Cambridge University Press, 2007.

Beyers, Steven, *A History of Free Verse*, Fayetteville: University of Arkansas Press, 2001.

Blasing, M. K., *Politics and Form in Postmodern Poetry*, Cambridge: Cambridge University Press, 1995.

Boland, Eavan and Edward Hirsch (eds.), *The Making of a Sonnet: A Norton Anthology*, New York: Norton, 2008.

Campbell, Matthew, *Rhythm and Will in Victorian Poetry*, Cambridge: Cambridge University Press, 1999.

Caplan, David, *Questions of Possibility: Contemporary Poetry and Poetic Form*, New York: Oxford University Press, 2005.

Coles, Kimberly Anne, *Religion, Reform, and Women's Writing in Early Modern England*, Cambridge: Cambridge University Press, 2008.

Colie, Rosalie, *The Resources of Kind*, Berkeley: University of California Press, 1973.

Cousins, A. D., *Shakespeare's Sonnets and Narrative Poems*, Harlow: Longman, 2000.

Cunnar, Eugene R. and Jeffrey Johnson (eds.), *Discovering and Recovering the Seventeenth Century Religious Lyric*, Pittsburgh: Dusquesne University Press, 2001.

Curran, Stuart, *Poetic Form and British Romanticism*, New York: Oxford University Press, 1986.

Distiller, Natasha, *Desire and Gender in the Sonnet Tradition*, Basingstoke: Palgrave, 2008.

Dubrow, Heather, *Echoes of Desire: English Petrarchism and Its Counterdiscourses*, Ithaca, NY: Cornell University Press, 1995.

    The Challenges of Orpheus: Lyric Poetry and Early Modern England, Baltimore: Johns Hopkins University Press, 2008.

Enterline, Lynn, *The Rhetoric of the Body from Ovid to Shakespeare*, Cambridge: Cambridge University Press, 2000.

Fairer, David, *Organising Poetry: The Coleridge Circle, 1790–1798*, Oxford: Oxford University Press, 2009.

Feldman, Paula R. and Daniel Robinson (eds.), *A Century of Sonnets: The Romantic-Era Revival 1750–1850*, New York and Oxford: Oxford University Press, 1999.

Ferry, Anne, *The 'Inward' Language: Sonnets of Wyatt, Sidney, Shakespeare, Donne*, Chicago: University of Chicago Press, 1983.

Fineman, Joel, *Shakespeare's Perjured Eye: The Invention of Poetic Subjectivity in the Sonnets*, Berkeley: University of California Press, 1986.

Freccero, J., 'The Fig Tree and the Laurel: Petrarch's Poetics', in P. Parker and D. Quint (eds.), *Literary Theory/Renaissance Texts*, Baltimore: Johns Hopkins University Press, 1986, pp. 20–32.

Gallagher, Catherine, 'Embracing the Absolute: The Politics of the Female Subject in Seventeenth-Century England', *Genders* 1 (1988), 24–9.

Gottlieb, Sidney, 'Milton's "On the Late Massacre in Piemont" and Eisenstein's *Potemkin*', *Milton Quarterly* 19:2 (1985), 38–42.

Greene, Roland, *Post-Petrarchism: Origins and Innovations of the Western Lyric Sequence*, Princeton: Princeton University Press, 1991.

Greer, Germaine, Jeslyn Medoff, Melinda Sansone and Susan Hastings (eds.), *Kissing the Rod: An Anthology of Seventeenth-Century Women's Verse*, New York: Farrar, Straus and Giroux, 1988.

Haber, J., *Desire and Dramatic Form in Early Modern England*, Cambridge: Cambridge University Press, 2009.

Halpern, Nick, *Everyday and Prophetic*, Madison: University of Wisconsin Press, 2003.

Hanke, Michael and Michael R. G. Spiller (eds.), *Ten Shakespeare Sonnets: Critical Essays*, Trier: Wissenschaftlicher Verlag, 2006.

Haselkorn, A. M. and B. S. Travitsky (eds.), *The Renaissance Englishwoman in Print: Counterbalancing the Canon*, Amherst: University of Massachusetts Press, 1990.

Heale, Elizabeth, '"Desiring Women Writing": Female Voices and Courtly "Balets" in Some Early Tudor Manuscript Albums', in Victoria E. Burke and Jonathan Gibson (eds.), *Early Modern Women's Manuscript Writing*, Aldershot: Ashgate, 2004, pp. 9–31.

Henderson, Diana E., *Passion Made Public: Elizabethan Lyric, Gender, and Performance*, Ithaca, NY: Cornell University Press, 1995.
  'Female Power and the Devaluation of Renaissance Love Lyrics', in Yopie Prins and Maeera Shreiber (eds.), *Dwelling in Possibility: Women Poets and Critics on Poetry*, Ithaca, NY: Cornell University Press, 1997, pp. 38–59.

Hilson, Jeff (ed.), *The Reality Street Book of Sonnets*, Hastings: Reality Street, 2008.

Holmes, Olivia, *Assembling the Lyric Self: Authorship from Troubadour Song to Italian Poetry Book*, Minneapolis: University of Minnesota Press, 2000.

Homans, M., *Women Writers and Poetic Identity*, Princeton: Princeton University Press, 1980.

Houston, Natalie M., 'Reading the Victorian Souvenir: Sonnets and Photographs of the Crimean War', *Yale Journal of Criticism* 14 (2001), 353–83.

Hsiao, Irene, 'Early William Carlos Williams: "Bad Keats"?', *Cambridge Quarterly* 37 (2008), 195–223.

Huang-Tiller, Gillian C., *The Power of the Meta-Genre: Cultural, Sexual, and Racial Politics of the American Modernist Sonnet*, unpublished Ph.D. thesis, University of Notre Dame, 2000.

Johnson, Anthony L., 'Formal Messages in Keats's Sonnets', in Allan C. Christensen, Lilla Maria Crisafulli Jones, Giuseppe Galigani and Anthony L. Johnson (eds.), *The Challenge of Keats: Bicentenary Essays 1795–1995*, Amsterdam and Atlanta, GA: Rodopi, 2000.

Kennedy, William J., *Authorizing Petrarch*, Ithaca, NY: Cornell University Press, 1994.

    The Site of Petrarchism: Early Modern National Sentiment in Italy, France, and England, Baltimore: Johns Hopkins University Press, 2003.

Kerrigan, John, 'Wordsworth and the Sonnet: Building, Dwelling, Thinking', *Essays in Criticism* 35 (1985), 45–75.

Kerrigan, William, and Gordon Braden, *The Idea of the Renaissance*, Baltimore: Johns Hopkins University Press, 1989.

Kleinhenz, Christopher, *The Early Italian Sonnet: The First Century (1220–1321)*, Lecce: Milella, 1986.

Knight, G. Wilson, *The Mutual Flame*, London: Methuen, 1955.

Kuenz, Jane, 'Modernism, Mass Culture and the Harlem Renaissance: The Case of Countee Cullen', *Modernism/Modernity* 14 (2007), 507–15.

Leishman, J. B., *Themes and Variations in Shakespeare's Sonnets*, New York: Harper and Row, 1961.

Levin, Phillis (ed.), *The Penguin Book of the Sonnet: 500 Years of a Classic Tradition in English*, New York: Penguin, 2001.

Lewalski, Barbara, *Protestant Poetics and the Seventeenth-Century Religious Lyric*, Princeton: Princeton University Press, 1979.

McGann, Jerome, *The Poetics of Sensibility: A Revolution in Literary Style*, Oxford: Oxford University Press, 1996.

Marotti, Arthur F., *Manuscript, Print and the English Renaissance Lyric*, Ithaca, NY: Cornell University Press, 1995.

Martz, Louis L., *The Poetry of Meditation*, New Haven: Yale University Press, 1954.

Mazzotta, Giuseppe, *The Worlds of Petrarch*, Durham, NC: Duke University Press, 1992.

Mortimer, Anthony, *Petrarch's* Canzoniere *in the English Renaissance*, Rome: Minerva Italica, 1975.

Nardo, Anna K., *Milton's Sonnets and the Ideal Community*, Lincoln, NE: University of Nebraska Press, 1979.

Nelson, Lowry, Jr, *Poetic Configurations: Essays in Literary History and Criticism*, University Park: Pennsylvania State University Press, 1992.

Oppenheimer, Paul, *The Birth of the Modern Mind: Self, Consciousness, and the Invention of the Sonnet*, New York: Oxford University Press, 1989.

Parker, Tom, *Proportional Form in the Sonnets of the Sidney Circle*, Oxford: Clarendon Press, 1998.

Phelan, Joseph, *The Nineteenth-Century Sonnet*, Basingstoke: Palgrave Macmillan, 2005.

Prins, Yopie, *Victorian Sappho*, Princeton: Princeton University Press, 1999.

Regan, Stephen, 'The Victorian Sonnet, from George Meredith to Gerard Manley Hopkins', *Yearbook of English Studies* 36:2 (2006), 17–34.

Robinson, Daniel, 'Reviving the Sonnet: Women Romantic Poets and the Sonnet Claim', *European Romantic Review* 6 (1995), 98–127.

Roche, Thomas, *Petrarch and the English Sonnet Sequences*, New York: AMS Press, 1989.

Roche, Thomas P., Jr, *Petrarch in English*, London: Penguin, 2005.

Sedgwick, Eve Kosofsky, *Between Men: English Literature and Male Homosocial Desire*, New York: Columbia University Press, 1985.

Seth, V., *The Golden Gate*, New York: Vintage Books, 1986.

Shell, Alison, *Catholicism, Controversy and the English Literary Imagination, 1558–1660*, Cambridge: Cambridge University Press, 1999.

Sitter, John (ed.), *The Cambridge Companion to Eighteenth-Century Poetry*, Cambridge: Cambridge University Press, 2001.

Spiller, Michael R. G., *The Development of the Sonnet: An Introduction*, London: Routledge, 1992.

Steinberg, Justin, *Accounting for Dante: Urban Readers and Writers in Late Medieval Italy*, Notre Dame: University of Notre Dame Press, 2007.

Travitsky, Betty (ed.), *The Paradise of Women: Writings by Englishwomen in the Renaissance*, New York: Columbia University Press, 1989.

Vendler, Helen, *The Art of Shakespeare's Sonnets*, Cambridge, MA: Harvard University Press, 1997.

Vickers, N. J., 'Diana Described: Scattered Woman and Scattered Rhyme', *Critical Inquiry* 8 (1981), 265–79.

'The Body Re-membered: Petrarchan Lyric and the Strategies of Description', in J. D. Lyons and S. G. Nichols, Jr (eds.), *Mimesis: From Mirror to Method, Augustine to Descartes*, Hanover: University Press of New England, 1982.

Wagner, Jennifer Ann, *A Moment's Monument: Revisionary Poetics and the Nineteenth-Century English Sonnet*, Madison, WI: Fairleigh Dickinson University Press, 1996.

Wall, W., *The Imprint of Gender: Authorship and Publication in the English Renaissance*, Ithaca, NY: Cornell University Press, 1993.

Wilson, Katharina M. (ed.), *Women Writers of the Renaissance and Reformation*, Athens, GA: University of Georgia Press, 1987.

Woudhuysen, Henry, *Sir Philip Sidney and the Circulation of Manuscripts 1580–1640*, Oxford: Clarendon Press, 1996.

Wroth, Mary, *The Poems of Lady Mary Wroth*, ed. Josephine A. Roberts, Baton Rouge: Louisiana State University Press, 1983.

INDEX

Cambridge Companions to ...

AUTHORS

TOPICS

Printed in Great Britain
by Amazon